COVERING IOWA

COVERING IOWA

The History of the Des Moines Register and Tribune Company 1849–1985

William B. Friedricks

Iowa State University Press / Ames

WILLIAM B. FRIEDRICKS, who received his Ph.D. from the University of Southern California, is associate professor of history at Simpson College in Indianola, Iowa. He is also the author of *Henry E. Huntington and the Creation of Southern California.*

Iowa State University Press
2121 South State Avenue
Ames, Iowa 50014

Orders:	1-800-862-6657
Office:	1-515-292-0140
Fax:	1-515-292-3348
Web site:	www.isupress.edu

♾ Printed on acid-free paper in the United States of America

1st edition, 2000

Library of Congress Cataloging-in Publication Data

Friedricks, William B.
Covering Iowa : the history of the Des Moines Register and Tribune Company, 1849–1985/William B. Friedricks.
p. cm.
Includes index.
ISBN 0-8138-2620-9
1. Des Moines Register and Tribune Company—History. 2. American newspapers—Iowa—Des Moines—History. 3. Journalism—Iowa—Des Moines—History. 4. Des Moines Register—History. 5. Tribune Company—History. I. Title.
PN4899.D485 D47 2000
071' .7758—dc21 99-052461

The last digit is the print number: 9 8 7 6 5 4 3 2 1

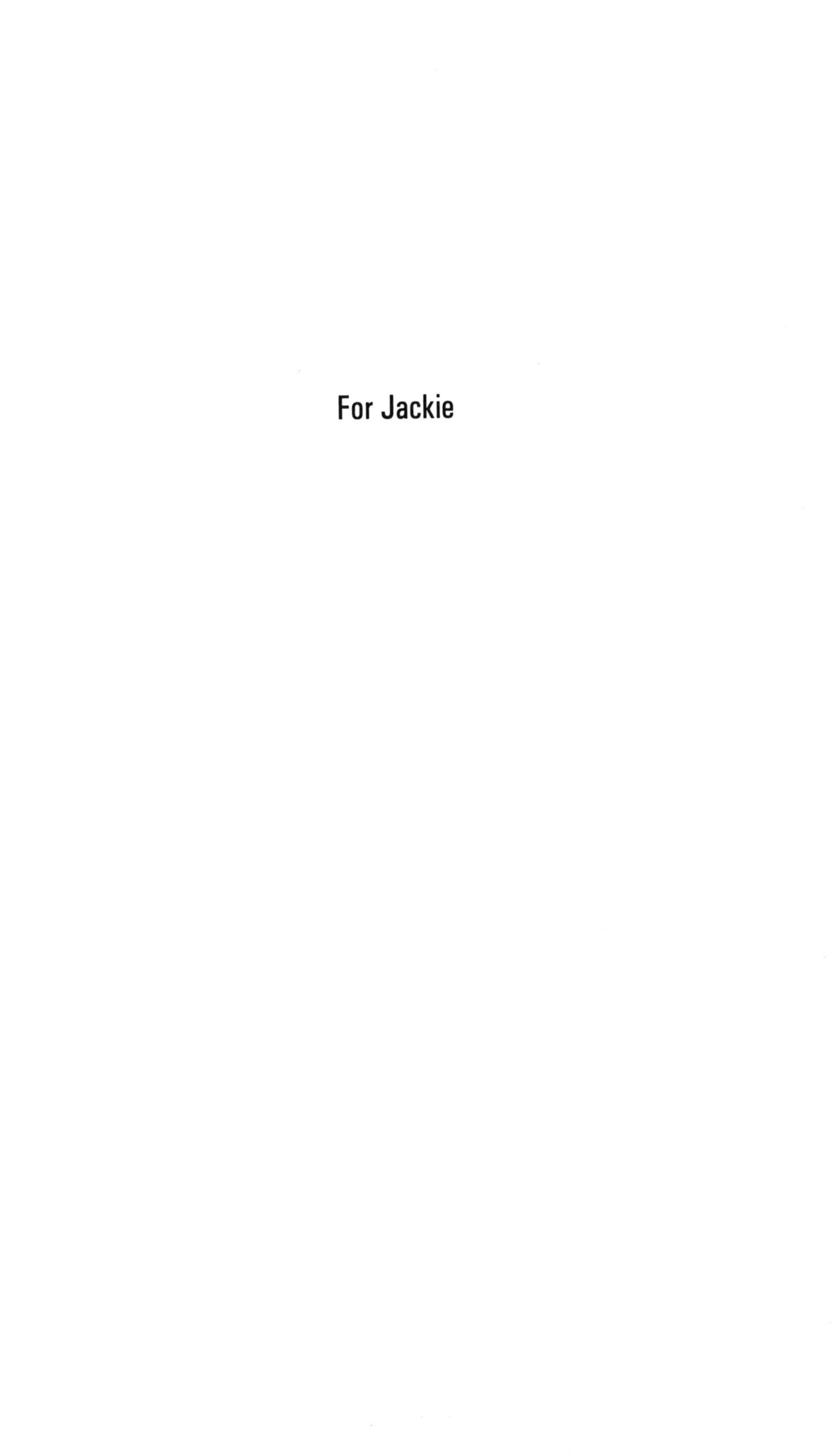

For Jackie

CONTENTS

ACKNOWLEDGMENTS

This book could never have been written without the assistance of many people. First I would like to thank David Kruidenier. He introduced me to this project, submitted himself to countless questions, and gave me complete access to his papers and photographs. Several others also opened their private papers to me. They included David and Jeanetta Housh, J. Robert Hudson, Shawn Kalkstein, Glenn Roberts, and Harry Watts.

I again benefited from my friendship with Ed Perkins. He read the entire manuscript and helped clarify my thinking about the Register and Tribune Company. Herb Strentz and Marvin Bergman each reviewed portions of my work and offered valuable suggestions.

Other individuals contributed in a variety of ways. Jim Alcott, author of a book on Cowles Media, graciously shared information with me. Pat Dawson and Inga Hoifeldt guided me through the John and Gardner Cowles Jr. Papers at Drake University. Phyllis Mumford was of great help with the Kruidenier material. Billie Noah, whom I have never met, happily provided timely information over the phone. Local historian John Zeller offered insights into Des Moines and central Iowa.

I also was lucky to work with a number of fine library staffs. Special thanks go to Kristi Ellingson at Simpson College, Mark Stumme at Drake University, and Ruth Bartles, Leslie Gardner, Ellen Sulser, and Vern Tyler, all at the State Historical Society of Iowa library in Des Moines.

Simpson College granted me a sabbatical leave, which gave me uninterrupted time to devote to this research. During the sabbatical, I was fortunate enough to receive a sesquicentennial grant from the State Historical Society of Iowa. It resulted in "The Newspaper that Captured a State: A History of the Des Moines Register, 1849–1985," *Annals of Iowa* 54 (Fall 1995): 303–37. Portions of chapter 1 are based on this article, and I would like to thank the State Historical Society of Iowa for permission to reprint this material.

Four people at Simpson deserve special mention. Michael Adams was kind enough to reproduce many of the photographs. Nancy St. Clair, our acting academic dean, enthusiastically backed my research and picked up the costs of some additional photographs. Linda Sinclair helped me prepare the final manuscript for submission. Owen Duncan, a good friend and colleague in the history department, encouraged me and endured my many monologues about the Register and Tribune.

At Iowa State University Press, Judi Brown and Anne Bolen were wonderful editors. Judi showed immediate interest in the manuscript and pushed the project rapidly forward. Anne oversaw the process of bringing the book into print with diligence and grace. Constructive criticism from the anonymous readers for the press made this a better book.

I owe the greatest debt to my family. As always, my parents were a steadfast source of support. My children, Sarah and Emily, literally grew up with this book. They constantly reminded me of the many joys in life beyond research and writing. Finally, my wife, Jackie, patiently put up with me. For her love, tolerance, and good humor, I dedicate this book to her.

COVERING IOWA

YOU AREN'T UP ON YOUR TIP TOES ARE YOU?
WELL, NOT JUST THIS MINUTE BUT I TRY TO BE MOST OF THE TIME.
GOSH I REMEMBER WHEN HE WASN'T KNEE HIGH TO A GRASSHOPPER
DESMOINES REGISTER.
100,000 CIRCULATION DAILY
UNCLE JOHN IOWA
OLD SUBSCRIBERS
MA DESMOINES
J.N. DING

CHAPTER 1

Iowa's Newspaper

Ding Darling's front-page *Register* cartoon entitled "My How He Has Grown," January 8, 1926, celebrating the morning paper's attainment of 100,000 circulation. *Reprinted with permission from the Ding Darling Collection, Special Collections Department, University of Iowa Libraries, Iowa City.*

At its circulation peak in the mid-20th century, the Register and Tribune Company (R&T) distributed at least one of its dailies, the morning *Des Moines Register* or the evening *Des Moines Tribune,* to nearly half of all Iowa homes, while its Sunday *Register* was read by two-thirds of the state's households. This unprecedented statewide reach declined from that point, but by the 1970s, the Sunday *Register*'s circulation was still over 450,000, or more than double the population of Des Moines. With this comprehensive circulation, a strategy of publishing a quality news and editorial product, and a policy of covering of the entire state the way most newspapers covered local events, the company more than fulfilled the *Register's* motto: it published "the Newspaper[s] Iowa Depends Upon."[1]

Although recent scholarship has not overlooked the importance of newspapers, in general, these studies have focused on the prominent, nationally recognized papers such as the *New York Times,* the *Washington Post,* or the *Los Angeles Times.* While some respected regional dailies have been examined, a history of the *Des Moines Register* is noticeably absent.[2] Because the *Register,* perhaps more than any other paper in the United States, reached into all areas of its state, a history of the Register and Tribune Company is intimately intertwined with the history of Iowa. Its newspapers' expansive circulation and distribution made it unique: lacking the population base of a big-city daily, the R&T's strategy was to look beyond the confines of the metropolitan area to create statewide newspapers. Such wide reach and influence led one former employee to characterize the *Register* as "the conscience of Iowa."[3]

In the early decades of the 20th century, the *Register* moved toward statewide news coverage and circulation, and by the 1960s, the *Saturday Review* reported: "The Des Moines *Register* has, with the exception of the *Christian Science Monitor,* the highest percentage of circulation-outside-the-city-of-publication—i.e., throughout Iowa—of any paper in the country."[4] Longtime *Register* reporter, editor, and columnist Jim Flansburg explained: "Iowa was the paper's beat ... and it fostered a community spirit. ... As a result of the *Register's* news report and editorial pages and their influence on other papers and broadcast media, Iowans in every corner of the state knew what other Iowans were up to."[5]

In fact, from the late 19th century up to 1985, when the R&T was broken up and the *Des Moines Register* was sold to the Gannett chain, company owners and managers made a concerted effort to cultivate a special relationship with the entire state of Iowa. This association was suggested as early as 1870, when the paper boasted: "The *Register* is emphatically an Iowa paper, a champion of Iowa interests, and an advocate of the Iowa people. ... No other paper in the Union has ever made its own state a specialty like the *Register* has in Iowa."[6] With the Clarkson family's purchase of the paper later that year, attempts were soon made to produce a paper worthy of such a grandiose vision. The Clarksons increased the *Register's* agricultural coverage and its reporting of news from around the state. Gardner Cowles bought the *Register* in 1903, and with his editor, Harvey Ingham, the two men dramatically extended the Iowa scope of the company. They created a state news department to coordinate statewide reporting, added a full-time farm editor, and, whenever possible, started stressing the Iowa angle to national or international stories.

When Cowles' sons, John and Gardner (Mike), took over management of the paper in the 1920s, they continued to focus on all-Iowa coverage. With more and more farm policy coming out of the nation's capital, the brothers decided to establish a Washington Bureau to cover the Iowa perspective on the workings of the federal government. Later, in the early 1940s, Mike Cowles, who had been impressed with the results of scientific polling techniques used by both George Gallup and the federal government, created the nation's first statewide poll to be owned and operated by a newspaper. Run weekly, the Iowa Poll told readers what fellow Iowans thought about a variety of issues. None of the competition had such a feature, and it proved to be a draw for an increase in both readers and advertisers.

Later editors and managers built on these traditions. In the 1960s, for instance, the R&T set up news bureaus in key cities across Iowa. These bureaus were founded to improve the paper's local coverage of the state's other major population centers. The following decade, the company's dedication to remaining a statewide institution was reaffirmed at a management retreat. Emblematic of this commitment to its all-Iowa strategy was the 1973 establishment and continued sponsorship of the Register's Annual Great Bicycle Ride Across Iowa (RAGBRAI). This popular, weeklong trek takes thousands of bicyclists from around the country on a ride across the state. The route varies from year to year but generally starts at one edge of the state, often passes through Des Moines in the middle, and reaches the other edge at the end.

Over the years, however, the *Register* did much more than merely describe and reflect the Iowa experience; it actually shaped and molded it. Because it was read throughout the state, the paper provided a shared experience for Iowans and a forum for the exchange of ideas. The *Register* sought to appeal to all Iowans, and in so doing, it became a unifying force within the state. In an age when tensions between farmers and businessmen, politicians and professionals, rural and city people, and even men and women were increasing, the paper provided a common meeting ground for all Iowans. It held the attention of the state's various constituents by providing special sections to appeal to certain groups—for example, offering detailed coverage of agriculture; campaigning for programs of statewide interest, such as the construction and maintenance of good roads; or identifying the views of Iowans on important issues through the Iowa Poll. As a result of such efforts, the *Register* brought citizens of the state together and in many ways helped define what it meant to be an Iowan.

Likewise, the vast statewide circulation provided a large audience for the paper's editorial opinions. Reaching into all 99 counties of Iowa, the *Register*'s ability to educate, guide, and lead the opinion of an entire state was unmatched.

Under the Cowles family, the *Register* was often ahead of its time editorially, and it guided Iowa's public opinion toward a more progressive position than many of its midwestern neighbors. From the editorial leadership of Harvey Ingham up through Jim Gannon, the *Register* had a liberalizing impact on the state. It pushed Iowans away from conservative isolationism and toward an internationalist position. Over the years, for example, it supported the League of Nations, the United Nations, and the Marshall Plan. When many in the region accepted the anticommunist position, the *Register* denounced McCarthyism, spoke out against the hard-line rhetoric, and supported better relations with the Soviet Union. It consistently championed women's rights and civil rights. By the 1970s, the *Register* remained in the forefront of progressive causes when, for example, it came out in favor of the Equal Rights Amendment and supported a woman's right to abortion.

While the R&T's story illuminates much about Iowa, it is also an important window into the nation's newspaper industry. The company sometimes acted as a pioneer in the newspaper business, while at other times it mirrored ongoing transformations. The *Register* was on the cutting edge of American journalism in its distribution, utilization of photographs, branching into radio ownership, using airplanes, and creating a statewide opinion poll. In other ways—such as the move from partisanship to independence, the creation of a syndicate to sell columns and cartoons, the expansion into other communications media, or in finally being taken over by a larger newspaper company—the *Register* reflected a fairly common pattern in the field.

For much of its history, the R&T enjoyed growth and rising earnings when its owners, managers, and editors strengthened their core business by employing innovative techniques or adopting new technologies and market forces remained relatively stable. Developing technologies often provided new opportunities and competitive advantages in the distribution, production, and news-gathering capabilities of the newspaper. Following World War II, however, the social environment was radically transformed, markets changed, and company profit margins dropped sharply. By the 1960s, technological advancements outpaced the independent firm's managerial ability to deal with the drastic changes. To reverse the R&T's stagnant performance, a new strategy of acquisition was tried in the 1970s, but inexperience at managing a diversified media concern led the company to become overextended. Minority stockholders became disgruntled, and the family firm was ultimately broken up.[7]

From Mid-19th Century to Late 20th Century

The R&T's roots date back to the mid-19th century, when small, highly partisan weeklies sprang up on the frontier. Important advances in technology—such as the telegraph and Linotype machines, for instance—and rapid industrialization vastly changed American newspapers. By the 1860s, the telegraph reached Des Moines and drastically improved the *Register*'s news-gathering capability. With more reliable access to the outside world via the telegraph, the Clarksons increased the *Register*'s national and international coverage. Meanwhile, although the paper's ties to the Republican Party remained strong throughout the century, the commercialization of the marketplace was making advertising much more important. Responding to this new environment, the Clarksons put in the bigger and faster printing presses available by the 1880s, and they doubled the paper's size. That allowed more space for additional advertising and an expansion of features and non-political stories designed to broaden the newspaper's appeal.

When Cowles took over the paper in the early 20th century, he adeptly responded to market forces. Because the *Register* was one of several small newspapers in Des Moines, potential circulation in the city was limited. Like many other publishers at the time, he began buying up his local competition (in 1908 he acquired the city's evening *Tribune,* for instance), but he considered the entire state of Iowa as a largely untapped newspaper market. Using the railroad, the best available transportation technology, Cowles began distributing his paper throughout Iowa. His editor, meanwhile, followed the trend in the industry by moving the paper away from its partisan past toward a more independent editorial stance.

Although trains succeeded in spreading the *Register* across the state, Cowles kept looking for better ways to distribute the paper and became a major supporter of the Iowa Good Roads Movement. Better roads and using trucks soon proved a more efficient means of distribution, and by World War I, the *Register* was easily the largest daily in Iowa. When John and Mike Cowles took over the management responsibilities at the R&T, they continued in their father's tradition of applying the latest technology, and the strategy paid off. As others in the industry were doing, the Cowles brothers took the paper into the radio business. They also employed George Gallup, then a doctoral student, to do some of the first scientific readership surveys for the *Register.* The surveys showed that the highest readership in the newspaper went to stories that were accompanied by pictures. Meanwhile, a photographer at the R&T developed a special, high-speed shutter camera that made sequence pictures feasible. And to shuttle photographers and reporters to all corners of Iowa, the company became one of the first newspapers in the nation to purchase its own airplane. Gallup's studies, therefore, told management what readers wanted; the innovative camera made new types of photographic essays possible; and the airplane allowed the paper to rush photographers and reporters to and from breaking stories. Taken together, these factors led Mike Cowles to increase the use of photographs, particularly in a special Sunday section of the paper. Circulation of the Sunday *Register* shot up, and Cowles soon took the idea of photojournalism to new heights by launching *Look* magazine in 1937.

That was not the only expansion, however. Following the creation of *Look,* Mike and John Cowles had visions of building their own diversified media firm, and over the next few years, the family purchased all the newspapers in Minneapolis. Meanwhile, plans to establish a communications group around the flagship *Register* proceeded, with the acquisition of several additional radio stations and a move into television. These ventures were not as profitable as had been hoped and required large capital outlays. It eventually became clear that the R&T could not muster the expertise needed for success in broadcasting. In the mid-1950s, therefore, the radio-and-television subsidiary was spun off as an independent company, and the firm returned all its energies to publishing newspapers.

With Mike and John focusing on *Look* and the *Minneapolis Star and Tribune,* respectively, the R&T was largely administered by Luther Hill and Ken MacDonald. The post–World War II years were a time of both growth and change in the industry. While the R&T's circulation peaked during this period, rapid societal change would soon hurt the firm's performance. By the company's centennial in 1949, it was clear that the reliance on new technologies and creative techniques gave the R&T an advantage over rival papers in the state. The firm's combined morning and evening circulation of 380,000 was larger than any other newspaper in an American city the size of Des Moines.[8]

Up to midcentury, the R&T's success took place in a relatively stable market and social environment. While it had monopolized the newspaper market in Des Moines since the late 1920s, a large part of the company's earnings depended on selling papers to the state's many rural residents. In addition, because it provided the best national and statewide news coverage in Iowa, the morning *Register* was bought by urban residents throughout the state, often in addition to their local daily.

Beginning in the 1950s and accelerating during the 1960s, two trends upset the company's markets. First of all, changes in the American lifestyle hurt the newspaper industry. The growing prevalence of two-income families left less leisure time to read a second newspaper. Instead, people spent more of their free time in front of the television. Compounding this problem for the *Register,* the other Iowa dailies increased their efforts to build circulation and advertising. Now pressed for time, many families chose to take only one newspaper, and they often decided in favor of their local daily instead of the *Register.* Worse still, population shifts also proved detrimental to the R&T. The migration from farm to city increased in the postwar years, and by the mid-1950s, urban Iowans outnumbered the state's rural residents for the first time. This meant that the R&T lost readers in agrarian markets it had long dominated to urban areas where competition was mounting. Even though the company still published a fine newspaper and continued to garner Pulitzer Prizes, these trends cut into circulation figures that began steadily declining in the early 1950s.

Struggling with these transformations, management discussed moving away from its all-Iowa strategy. Costs could be significantly reduced by paring down its extensive distribution system and dropping readers in distant counties. Instead, the company could concentrate on readers within a more reasonable radius of Des Moines. Although this option made good business sense, it was never seriously considered. John and Mike Cowles as well as most top managers saw the entire state as the R&T franchise, and they were unwilling to break from that proud tradition.

Swift changes in technology were also pressuring R&T managers. In the 1960s, advances in newspaper production, such as photocomposition and computerization, were proceeding rapidly to increase efficiency and cut costs. Introducing the new machinery, however, was expensive and required significant reconfiguring of work space. Here again, management labored to keep up with the pace of change. Like many larger newspapers in the industry, conversion was slow.

After 10 years of poor financial performance, David Kruidenier, the paper's chief executive and a grandson of Gardner Cowles, decided on a strategy of acquisition to revitalize the firm. During this decade of the 1970s, the media industry was in the process of consolidation, and the R&T hoped the addition of radio, television, and other newspapers could return the company to growing profitability. Kruidenier had an acquisition plan drawn up and hired a new management team—including Michael Gartner, former page one editor of the *Wall Street Journal,* and attorney Gary Gerlach, a specialist in communications law. With Gartner and Gerlach on board, media properties were aggressively pursued. By 1981, the R&T was a large multimedia company: it owned several weekly newspapers, two dailies (besides the *Register* and *Tribune*), two television stations, and several radio stations.

Although expansion appeared logical, it did not prove the salvation Kruidenier and his team had hoped. Once again, operating enterprises outside the company's core area of business failed to deliver the projected benefits. The newly acquired units were not as profitable as anticipated, and the acquisitions were financed through borrowing. Unexpected rising interest rates made servicing the debt a huge burden. In an effort to turn company fortunes around, Kruidenier and cousin John Cowles Jr., who had taken over the reins of the Minneapolis Star and Tribune Company, discussed merging the family's properties in Des Moines with those in Minneapolis. Plans were scrapped in 1982, however, when the cousins could not agree on the details. Later that year, the R&T, like many other newspaper companies of the period, opted to cut costs by stopping production of its evening offering, the *Tribune*. Meanwhile, a concerned minority stockholder, Shawn Kalkstein, had begun writing a series of letters to R&T shareholders critical of company management.[9]

Although the merger was called off in 1982, its possibility worried then R&T president Gartner and company general counsel Gerlach. Each was concerned about maintaining local control of the paper, and if the two Cowles' properties were combined, Gartner's and Gerlach's jobs were not necessarily secure. In the wake of the failed merger and in an effort to restore profitability, strategic planning at the R&T took on a new urgency. More and more Cowles family shareholders worried about the company's future, but there was no consensus about potential solutions. Kalkstein's critical letters suggested selling the company as one possibility, while Kruidenier apparently still thought the solution might be to merge with Minneapolis. Yet, in the midst of these troubles, the R&T was still publishing an award-winning newspaper. In April 1984, *Time* magazine ranked the *Register* among the nation's top ten newspapers, and the following year, the paper won its 13th Pulitzer Prize.

Several months after the *Register* received national recognition from *Time,* Gartner and Gerlach put together a deal to buy the R&T. The Dow Jones Corporation would purchase half the R&T stock, and a local group, headed by Gartner and Gerlach, would buy the remaining portion. Although the offer was rejected, key Cowles family shareholders came to believe that selling the struggling company was a sound idea. Kruidenier felt he had no choice but to put the firm up for sale. By summer 1985, the company was broken up and sold. The R&T joined several other prominent, once independent midwestern papers as a target of large media companies. Gannett purchased the *Register* and the company's Iowa weeklies for $165 million. When all the firm's assets were sold, the R&T shareholders were huge beneficiaries; stock that had traded internally for between $15 and $30 per share was sold for nearly $280 per sharc.[10]

Gannett's purchase of the *Register* ended three generations of Cowles family ownership and altered the relationship of the paper to the state. One prominent shareholder saw the sale as serving the interest of the owners at the expense of the readers. He argued that while stockholders made a huge profit, the community lost an independent, locally owned newspaper with the mission of setting an agenda for the state.[11] Journalism professor Jean Folkerts articulated this idea of loss for local communities: "As outsiders came in to run family ... papers, the lament was of a loss of individuality—of midwestern local values giving way to the values of a national or international media conglomerate." And in fact, some longtime readers saw the *Register* under Gannett as being "less aggressive and less innovative editorially."[12]

Although Gannett chief executive Al Neuharth promised local managerial autonomy and retained Charlie Edwards, a great-grandson of Gardner Cowles, as publisher, the *Register* soon became a very different newspaper. Edwards explained that for Gannett, "all you do is deliver a number."[13] He was referring to the chain's bottom-line strategy. Cutting costs and reducing its statewide franchise became the key elements in meeting the parent company's high profit expectations. In fact, based on financial statements, Gannett's *Register* was highly successful. By 1989, the paper's earnings had quadrupled. The following year, the *Register* changed its mission statement, moving away from the statewide strategy to declaring central Iowa its primary market. It closed down many of its Iowa news bureaus, drastically cut back its circulation area, and focused its attention on local coverage of Des Moines. By the mid-1990s, 75 percent of the *Register* readers resided in central Iowa.[14]

After heading up the operation for nearly 12 years, Edwards had had enough, and he resigned in 1996. With this move, the last vestige of the Cowles connection to the paper was severed. Barbara Henry, who had 22 years of experience with several Gannett papers, took over the R&T helm. The company's strong financial performance continued, and by 1997, the *Register* was a "bonanza," with "pre-tax profits probably far exceeding 20 percent."[15]

Chronicling a Newspaper and a State

The following study examines the *Register*'s rise from a small, 19th-century weekly to its heyday in the mid-20th century and its eventual decline and sale. Throughout its history, the *Register* played an important role in the history of both Iowa and American journalism. Often a leader in the newspaper industry, the R&T with its goal of broad distribution and news coverage created a unique statewide audience. For decades, the Clarksons and, to a greater extent, the Cowleses rode this strategy to financial success. Although several metropolitan dailies had larger total circulations, no other newspaper reached into every corner of its home state the way the *Register* did. The *Register* was read by all demographic groups in all Iowa counties. Its news and opinion were sought out by the state's movers and shakers, while its Iowa Poll told readers what Iowans thought about important issues. According to Flansburg, the R&T led people of the state "to see themselves, first, as Iowans."[16]

By focusing on the Iowa angle in its news stories, the *Register* made national and international news palatable to its audience. In so doing, the paper projected an internationalist and cosmopolitan air that rejected the provincial insularity so often associated with residents of the Midwest. That the paper should educate its readers made sense to John Cowles, who once defined a good newspaper as "a university on your doorstep."[17] And so it was with the *Register*: its news product was superior to most others available because it explained Iowa and the world at large to its readers. Because it was read throughout the state, the paper served as a meeting ground for all Iowans. David Kruidenier saw the *Register*'s importance from this perspective: "More than any institution, other than state government, it [the *Des Moines Register*] tied the state together."[18]

But rapid societal and technological changes of the post–World War II period created difficulties for the firm's all-Iowa strategy. Unwilling to cut back on this tradition and unable to maintain healthy profits amid the cultural transformations, the R&T and its subsidiaries were ultimately sold. Gannett bought the *Register* and, over the next 10 years, modified the paper. The statewide mission was dropped in favor of a greater Des Moines concentration, and the *Register*'s costly distribution to many outlying counties was abandoned. Redesigned, refocused, and reinvented, the *Register* once again became very profitable, but it was no longer the newspaper of all Iowans.

CHAPTER 2

Frontier Newspapers in Des Moines

1849–1870

Barlow Granger, editor of Des Moines' first newspaper, the *Iowa Star. Courtesy of the State Historical Society of Iowa, Des Moines.*

The *Register*'s origins date back to a 19th-century America that, in the words of historian Robert Wiebe, amounted to "a collection of island communities."[1] Prior to the coming of the railroad and a connection to the developing national transportation network, many American towns and villages were relatively isolated. Society tended to be segmented and localized, with people relying on their small communities for most everything. Local weekly newspapers provided the news and tried, whenever possible, to provide information of the outside world. These isolated villages, in fact, shared "a common interest in news of national and state affairs, most notably of debates and decisions in state capitals and in Washington." Newspapers, therefore, even in small towns, generally attempted to cover these events and served "mainly as sources of political information."[2] Such was certainly the case in frontier Iowa.

In the first decades of the 19th century, settlers moved into the Midwest, and the creation of towns was usually followed by the establishment of small newspapers. These early papers were almost always founded for promotional and political purposes. The same process repeated itself time and again as Americans pushed into Iowa. Present-day Iowa was opened to settlers in 1833 following the federal government's acquisition of eastern Iowa—the Black Hawk Purchase—the previous year. Iowa's first paper was soon thereafter established in Dubuque, an old lead mining center, by John King, who set up the Democratic, booster-oriented *Du Buque Visitor* in 1836. At that point, the region had recently been designated part of the Wisconsin Territory.[3]

Two years later, President Martin Van Buren signed a bill creating the Iowa Territory. But the central portion of Iowa was not acquired from the Sauk and Meskwaki tribes until 1842. Once this land was opened, pioneers headed farther west, scrambling across the rich prairie soil, and over the next few years settlements were concentrated along the Mississippi River in eastern Iowa and in the east-central Cedar River Valley and the central Des Moines River Valley. In the midst of this growth, Iowa became a state in 1846. And as its communities expanded, 16 newspapers, including the *Iowa Star* in Fort Des Moines, were founded between 1847 and 1849.[4]

At the time that these Iowa newspapers were established, American journalism was undergoing revolutionary changes. During the 1830s, the newspaper industry experienced tremendous growth, notes historian Michael Schudson: "In 1830 the country had 650 weeklies and 65 dailies. The average circulation of a daily was 1,200, so the total daily circulation was roughly 78,000. By 1840 there were 1,141 weeklies and 138 dailies. The dailies averaged 2,200 in circulation for an estimated total circulation of 300,000."[5] In addition, new technology was being introduced. By the early 1830s, steam-powered printing presses increased the output of older hand-operated presses tenfold. Such an advance made it possible to print a newspaper that could be sold for one cent, compared to the standard six-cent price. Lower prices made it possible to create a paper for the masses. The so-called penny press originated in large urban areas along the eastern seaboard. New York had the first successful penny presses. Led by Benjamin Day's sensationalist *New York Sun* in 1833, the strategy was imitated two years later by James Gordon Bennett's innovative *New York Herald*. Bennett broadened the scope of coverage to encompass international and national events as well as local news, societal events, and sports. From New York, the penny press spread south to cities such as Philadelphia and Baltimore.[6]

Although important to the world of journalism, these innovations hardly touched Iowa or the frontier Midwest. As late as 1850, Iowa, Minnesota, and territories that were to become the states of Nebraska, Kansas, and North and South Dakota lacked daily newspapers. The area's first publications were modest weeklies and small operations; often one man served as his own reporter, editor, printer, and business manager. In fact, in some isolated frontier Iowa towns, newspapers were published in handwritten form. Usually these early papers were tied to and subsidized by a political party. A paper's partisanship sometimes led to political rivals beginning papers to voice competing views. Such papers featured favorable stories about one political party, carried mostly local news (often slipping into promotional boosterism), and included literary pieces. National news, when it could be gleaned from telegrams or lifted from out-of-town papers, also appeared.[7]

While the journalistic revolution did not have an immediate impact upon Iowa newspapers, the changes in the world of politics did. Because the state's papers were largely political organs, their fortunes usually tracked the relative success of their sponsoring parties. From the late 1830s through the 1840s, Iowa was decidedly Democratic, and it is not surprising that the first newspapers in both the state and in Des Moines were tied to that party. By the Civil War, however, the new Republican Party was moving toward preeminence, and in Des Moines, the newspaper of that persuasion, the *Iowa State Register,* grew to be the city's most important. Within the party, the paper had become a leading voice of the state's Radical Republicans.[8]

First Paper in Des Moines

Des Moines' first paper, the *Iowa Star,* was a fairly typical frontier weekly. It was founded in 1849 as a Democratic journal by attorney and land agent Barlow Granger (who at one time had worked in a New York print shop with Horace Greeley) in partnership with others including fellow land agent, Judge Curtis Bates. With a Washington hand press that Bates had obtained in Iowa City for $150, Granger set up shop in an old army barrack building located near what is today the intersection of Second and Vine streets in downtown Des Moines.[9] The premier issue came out on July 26, 1849. Granger promised that the *Star* would be "decidedly democratic, not to be circumscribed or governed by dictations of any party, clique, or influenced in any way by the mere prejudice of party sectarianism." Later in that same issue, he revealed the self-serving boosterism that remained throughout his short tenure at the paper. Iowa was, he noted, "in the heart of the most attractive country in the world" and had "within itself all the resources necessary to sustain a dense agricultural and commercial population."[10]

The intended weekly publication schedule was hampered by the difficulties of frontier living, and the second issue did not come out until a month later. Thereafter, the seven-column *Star* came out on a fairly regular schedule. The bulk of the paper's stories focused on issues of the Democratic Party or on transportation needs of central Iowa (specifically the question of the navigation on the Des Moines River and the acquisition of a railroad connection). In February 1850, for example, Granger wrote: "Our hope for the future growth and prosperity of the town [Des Moines] and the development of the wealth and prosperity of central Iowa all depend on the success of this road [a railroad built through central Iowa]."[11] But funding was a constant problem. Although Granger believed the paper's prospects were good, partner Bates was having financial setbacks and was thus unable to supply the necessary capital to provide a cushion of support. Because Bates did "not want the paper to stop [publication]," he suggested that Granger add a young partner who was a "good democrat."[12] Unfortunately, no one suitable was found.

By early 1850, Granger was having more financial trouble. During the winter, he was forced to put buckets of hot coals under the ink to keep it from freezing. Granger shortened the January 7 issue, explaining that freezing weather had driven him to shut down the press; he noted that these interruptions were the "trials incident to carrying on business in a new country."[13] Besides problems with the weather, by the beginning of 1850, the *Iowa Star* faced competition from a rival Whig newspaper, the *Fort Des Moines Gazette,* started with the promise of a $350 capital contribution by the Whig Party. Initially, Granger thought the second newspaper spoke well of the town: "It tells well for the prosperity of this town—only three years old—that two papers can be established with even a hope of being sustained."[14] But by February, the many difficulties proved too much for Granger, who was ready to give up the fight and turn his attention to the practice of law. In his editorial farewell, he thanked his readers for "their kind indulgences and just appreciation of the many difficulties we have had to encounter. Notwithstanding the frequent freezings up of our press and types, causing delays in the issue and our own editorial neglect, caused by the many difficulties that surrounded us, subscribers continued to 'take the paper,'—nay more, they have cheered us on with their kind words and generous sympathies."[15]

With Granger gone and no worthy buyer on the horizon, Bates assumed control of the Democratic weekly. Initially, he found a junior partner, Luther Johnson, to serve as editor. Soon, however, Johnson left the paper, and Bates reluctantly took editorial control. Within the year, Bates obtained the editorial services of A. Y. Hull.[16] Whether under Johnson, Bates, or Hull, the editorial stance of the paper remained much the same. The *Star* constantly railed against the Whigs, suggesting they were nothing but federalists.

Editorials continued to promote the virtues of Iowa by comparing the state's rich agricultural land to the gold in California. The editors mused from time to time about Manifest Destiny, suggesting, for example, that Cuba would inevitably be annexed by the United States.[17] The paper was always strapped financially and in fact was not published between February 3 and April 28, 1853.[18] The *Star* remained unprofitable, and Bates, who had supported the paper through his law practice, decided to give it up in January 1854. Now the Democratic nominee for governor, he sold the paper to S. W. Hill & Company, and his associate editor Daniel O. Finch took over editorial duties. But the new owners could not turn the paper around. Seven months later, in August 1854, the last issue of the *Star* appeared.[19]

Mid-1850s Competition

In early 1855, the Democratic paper was re-established as the *Iowa Statesman* by new owner Will Tomlinson. Two years later, in February 1857, it was bought by the managing editor, Will Porter, who renamed it the *Iowa State Journal.*[20] Porter sold the *Journal* to a 22-year-old Harvard graduate, Stilson Hutchins, and a New York native, George Todd. Hutchins, a fervent Democrat, found the Republican dominance of the capital too much to bear, and he sold his interest in the paper to his partner, Todd, in 1862.[21]

Meanwhile, the city's Whigs were struggling to keep their paper going. Following the demise of the *Fort Des Moines Gazette* in 1851—the monetary support from the party never materialized—another Whig paper, also called the *Iowa State Journal,* which had started just one month after the *Gazette,* failed in 1852. Not until February 1856 did the city's rival political party, now the Republican Party, obtain an organ, when editor Thomas Sypherd and banker A. J. Stephens established the Free-Soil Republican *Iowa Citizen.*[22] After being purchased and owned by Des Moines businessman and hotelier James C. Savery for a short time, the paper was bought by John Teesdale, the recently elected state printer, in December 1857.

Born in England, Teesdale came to America as a child in 1818. He apprenticed in a print shop and eventually became editor of the *Wheeling Gazette* in Virginia (soon to be West Virginia). Moving west, he held several editorships in Ohio before purchasing the *Akron Beacon.* In 1856, he moved to Iowa City and bought the *Iowa City Republican.* When the capital was transferred to Des Moines, Teesdale was encouraged by Governor James W. Grimes and businessman Samuel Kirkwood to move to the new capital city, acquire a newspaper, and support Kirkwood in the 1859 gubernatorial campaign. Teesdale took the advice, moved to Des Moines, and purchased the *Citizen.*[23] Here he became a powerful voice within the state's Republican Party. Known for his radical antislavery views, he took the Free-Soil Republicanism stance of the newspaper quite seriously. Teesdale was one of several men operating the Des Moines stop on the Underground Railroad, which assisted escaped slaves making their way northward to freedom in Canada. In this capacity, Teesdale had the opportunity to interview abolitionist John Brown.

In December 1858, Brown and his band had attacked two northwestern Missouri plantations, freeing 11 slaves and killing one of their owners. Brown's group then escorted the rescued slaves across Iowa, with the notion of ultimately getting them to freedom in Canada. When the group arrived in Des Moines, Teesdale paid their ferry passage across the Des Moines River. Brown continued to escort the escaped slaves east, and with the aid of several other prominent Iowa Republicans, they made it to Chicago and later to Canada.[24] Later that year, the zealot Brown, attempting to start a slave rebellion, led a small band of whites and blacks in an attack at a federal armory in Harpers Ferry, Virginia. After Brown was easily defeated and captured, Teesdale wrote: "He [Brown] has rendered his name immortal. His boldness and frankness command admiration even of his enemies; while his prisoners all testify with one voice to his kindness and forbearance to them."[25]

By the end of the 1850s, it was clear that Des Moines, whose population was approaching 4,000, could support two papers, one Republican and one Democratic in orientation. While these papers were changing hands over the decade, important changes were also occurring in the city. The town of Fort Des Moines was officially chartered in September 1852 and incorporated the following January. But for several years prior to its chartering, the community had been working to have the state capital moved from Iowa City to Fort Des Moines. In 1855, the Iowa General Assembly passed a law calling for the moving of the capital to Fort Des Moines; to mollify Iowa City, it was named as the permanent site for the state university. In 1857, the new capital was renamed Des Moines and a new state constitution was passed, marking the ascendancy of the Republicans as the party in power.[26]

Iowa State Register

In January 1860, Teesdale changed the name of his paper to the *Iowa State Register.* The new moniker, taken from a defunct Black Hawk County newspaper, seemed fitting to Teesdale for "a journal at the capital of the State."

But more grandiose than the renaming, Teesdale (somewhat prophetically) proclaimed the *Register* the "Official Paper of the State."[27] It was issued as an afternoon daily throughout the Iowa legislative session, January through April, then as a weekly for the remainder of the year. Although still a small, four-page, five-column paper, it focused on state and national politics, with little attention devoted to local events.[28] In 1861, Teesdale was appointed postmaster of Des Moines and sold the paper to Frank W. Palmer.[29]

Palmer, who was raised in Jamestown, New York, learned the newspaper business at the *Jamestown Journal,* which he eventually owned. He was active in the Whig and later the Republican parties and served two terms in the New York State Assembly. In 1858, Palmer moved to Dubuque, Iowa, where he became editor and part owner of the *Dubuque Times.* Following his election as State Printer of Iowa in 1860, he moved to the capital city and bought the *Register.*[30] Once at the paper, he proved to be an able publisher and editor, expanding the four-page *Register* to include more local news. Beginning on January 12, 1862, Palmer instituted two more changes: he moved the *Register* from an afternoon to a morning paper, and it became the city's only regularly issued daily. While it improved qualitatively, the paper remained unabashedly abolitionist and Republican in orientation. Frank Mills, a printer who would soon purchase the paper from Palmer, positively appraised the editor as "a radical of radicals" who had "acquired quite a reputation for his paper."[31] Palmer's Radical Republican views were clear, for instance, in the paper's coverage of a speech delivered by Methodist minister William F. Cowles (coincidentally, the father of Gardner Cowles, another future owner of the paper). The *Register* described the clergyman as an "independent, honest, and fearless speaker ... [who] truthfully characterized human bondage as the cause of this Rebellion [the Civil War] and its extinction was regarded as the only true specific for the disease which threatens the life of the Government."[32]

As the defeat of the Confederacy neared, Palmer and the *Register* took up the cause of black rights and suffrage in earnest. A state referendum on black suffrage had failed badly in 1857, but the Civil War had solidified the Republicans' dominance in Iowa. The party's strong position now made the enfranchisement of blacks much more likely. In February 1865, the paper noted that the issue of black rights would soon be dealt with in the political arena and wrote: "The War has upset many a silly and barbarous notion and there is no telling how far traitorous aristocrats who have been accustomed to teach that the Ethiopian race are scarcely better than apes, may have their nerves shocked by revolutions in social and political franchises."[33] More directly, Palmer became the first Iowa editor to come out for enfranchising black war veterans, and he continued to muse about the movement toward black suffrage.[34]

Besides being a leading voice for enfranchising blacks, Palmer had ensured the paper's continued growth and success by hiring a number of talented young men, including future owners and political figures Richard and James Clarkson. But by December 1866, the strain of simultaneously serving as the paper's editor and publisher, in addition to acting as state printer, had taken its toll, and Palmer sold the *Register* to Frank and Jacob Mills. Frank Mills, a longtime, prominent Des Moines printer, together with his brother promised to maintain the paper's current course: "Having purchased the interest of Mr. Palmer in this journal it is proper for us to state that the paper will be published in the future as it has been in the past in the interest of the Radical Republican Party and in pursuit of an independent, straight forward course."[35] According to the deal, Palmer stayed on as editor for a year when he left to campaign successfully for a seat in the U.S. Congress in 1868.[36]

New Ownership

The new publisher, Frank Mills, was born and raised in Indiana. He attended Wabash College and learned the printing trade apprenticing at his brother Jacob's newspaper, the *Greenburg Repository.* Mills moved to Des Moines in 1856 and set up a shoe and boot shop. He soon returned to printing, however, when a younger brother, Noah, followed him to the capital city and established a small job-printing business. The two joined together in a partnership, Mills and Company, which received a real business boost when Frank was elected state binder in 1857. Growth continued with federal government contracts during the Civil War, and even though Noah was killed in the conflict, Frank continued to prosper. By 1866, he was looking to widen his operations, and he and older brother Jacob teamed up to purchase the *Register.*[37]

In March 1866, several months prior to Mills' purchase of the paper, the Republican-controlled Iowa legislature passed five constitutional amendments "striking the word 'white' not only from the suffrage clause but also from those covering state census enumerations, senate apportionment, house apportionment, and militia service."[38] Two years later, after the legislature approved the proposed changes a required second time, they were ready to be put before the people in November 1868. This time, voters approved the amendments, and along with Minnesota, which had passed a similar measure, Iowa had the distinction of being one of only two states to grant suffrage to African-Americans by popular referendum before passage of the

15th Amendment. As the Mills brothers had promised, their Republican paper continued to support the cause. Following the successful vote, a *Register* headline exclaimed that in Iowa, "Color No Longer The King of the Ballot!" Several days later it wrote: "To the colored people of Iowa and Minnesota, at least, the 3d day of November [election day] will henceforth be what the Fourth of July is to all Americans. Of that day they achieved their independence, arrived at their manhood, [and] acquired full citizenship."[39]

In the midst of the campaign for black suffrage, Frank Mills was busy trying to run the paper while also managing an expanding printing business. When he and his brother acquired the *Register,* the popular city editor of several years, J. M. Dixon, was forced to resign because of blindness. Initially unsuccessful in finding a satisfactory replacement, Mills eventually looked to James Clarkson, who was setting type in the composing room. The proprietor had known of Clarkson's father as an Indiana newspaper editor, and when the young man showed promise, Mills decided to advance him first to full-time reporter, then night editor, and finally city editor. The choice proved a good one, and the sparkling writing of the 27-year-old Clarkson soon landed him a job as editor in chief in 1869.[40]

Under the Mills' ownership, the *Register* expanded its horizons beyond the scope of Des Moines. The brothers worked at improving the paper's coverage of the state. They acquired correspondents from various areas in Iowa and started a series of reports from around the state on a county-by-county basis. Although they devoted time and resources to improving the *Register,* the Millses were first and foremost printers, and the paper never became their main endeavor. Frank Mills described the firm's busy printing operation:

> We were publishing the Daily and Weekly Register, the Iowa Homestead, the Western Jurist, the Iowa School Journal, two country weekly newspapers, an Annotated series of Iowa Supreme Court Reports, besides the regular series of Reports, also the Federal Supreme Court Reporter with a list of near a hundred volumes of general and local law books, including the Code of Iowa, in addition to our large business in job and book printing and our county supply business, besides the state printing of which [the] latter however we were relieved after 1872, until re-elected [to State Printer] some six years later.[41]

By 1868, this booming business had outgrown the brothers' facility at 46 Court Avenue, and they moved the enterprise, along with the newspaper, which had been located in the Exchange Block at Third and Walnut streets, into their new four-story building on Fourth Street between Walnut Street and Court Avenue.[42]

City Growth

While Teesdale, Palmer, and then Frank and Jacob Mills increased the *Register*'s influence, the city of Des Moines was undergoing change. Growth continued in the capital city; by 1870, its population topped 12,000, while Iowa reached nearly 1.2 million. Besides becoming more densely populated, Des Moines began to shed its isolated, "island community" tinge. In 1862, the telegraph finally reached the city. Originally established in the eastern Iowa cities of Burlington and Bloomington (Muscatine), telegraph lines stretched westward across the state as far as Cedar Rapids by 1860. Omaha and Council Bluffs were also soon reached, but the lines had been built through northern Missouri rather than Des Moines and central Iowa. This lack of a telegraph connection led one Des Moines editor to complain that "news from the east was brought to Des Moines by stage from the west (Council Bluffs)." In early 1862, telegraph lines finally reached Des Moines, and on January 14, the *Register* carried its first telegraph news column featuring dispatches from the Civil War.[43]

Now, via the telegraph, Des Moines had convenient and reliable access to news of the outside world. The news dispatches were put together by the New York Associated Press (NYAP), which sold the reports. Prior to this time, editors largely relied on newspaper exchange as their major form of news gathering outside their locale.[44] The telegraph, however, offered news more immediately and more consistently. The change was not lost on *Register* editor Palmer, who gleefully explained:

> Ever since Adam was an infant, the City of Des Moines, or the site where it is located, has been cut off from the exterior world. We have no Railroads. We have no telegraph. We have been excluded from the activities of commerce. Situated midway between the two great rivers of the continent, without anything but coaches and stage roads to connect us with the rest of mankind, our condition has not been the most pleasant in the world.
>
> Today our situation is immensely improved. We have the privilege of reading the latest dispatches in our own paper. The lightning and telegraph company have at length made us even with the Mississippi cities.[45]

But unlike many mid-19th century cities where the telegraph and railroad arrived simultaneously, Des Moines did not obtain a railroad connection until 1866. That August, the Des Moines Valley Railroad from Keokuk (a town on the Mississippi River in the southeastern corner of the state) reached the capital. More important, however, was the 1867 arrival of the Chicago, Rock Island & Pacific Railroad: Des Moines was directly hooked into the national rail network, and it was now becoming not only the political, but also rapidly the commercial, center of the state.[46]

Associated Press Affiliation

The same year the Rock Island arrived in Des Moines, the Millses' *Register* and 12 additional Iowa newspapers joined 17 others from Illinois and Nebraska in creating the Northwestern Associated Press. This organization embraced all of Illinois (except Chicago), all of Iowa, and the eastern portion of Nebraska. Prior to the Northwestern's founding, these small dailies had received their telegraphic news through individual contracts or agreements with the Western Associated Press (WAP), which was formed in 1865 and consisted of big-city dailies largely in the Ohio River Valley. The creation of the Northwestern AP gave the small papers some leverage in negotiating their contract and fees with the WAP. At the same time, its organization simplified the latter's dealings with the many dailies.[47]

As Richard Schwarzlose noted in *The Nation's Newsbrokers,* "The post-Civil War growth of state and regional Associated Press organizations sprang from newspapers' desire to protect themselves from local competition by monopolizing the nation's only stable and relatively complete news report, a report sustained and protected by its exclusive transmission over the circuits of the Western Union monopoly and by its exclusive news exchange contract with Reuters News Company in London."[48] Following an arrangement between the New York AP and the WAP in January 1867, each organization shared all its news with the other. Meanwhile, the WAP obtained complete control over its individual clients, such as the Northwestern AP, for example. The WAP thus determined how much news the member papers received and at what cost. For access to eastern and international news, the WAP paid the telegraph company, Western Union, $60,000 per year for a daily report of 6,000 words and a 2,000-word regional report from within its own territory.[49]

Under these agreements, the amount of news distributed over the wires increased dramatically; while WAP members and clients received approximately 750,000 words in 1866, they were sent about 3 million in 1868 and over 7 million by 1882. Meanwhile the cost of receiving telegraphic reports was falling from approximately 3.5 cents a word in 1866 to .075 cents a word in 1880.[50] While the vast expansion of such news improved the caliber of the *Register*'s international, national, and midwestern coverage, the owners used this new addition to sell their product. An 1867 advertisement in the *Iowa State Register* proclaimed, "New Special Arrangements have recently been perfected with the New York Associated Press and the North-Western Associated Press by which Special Agents in New York and Chicago in connection with Agents of the Atlantic cable in London will furnish the latest telegraphic news! To the hour of going to press, [dispatches] from all parts of the world, together with full and reliable market reports of the East and West [will be received]."[51]

Meanwhile, over the course of the 1860s, the *Register*'s rival Democratic *Iowa State Journal,* now linked to the state's weaker political party, went through several changes. Late in 1862, it had been merged with another paper, the *Commonwealth,* and the new entity became the *Times.* The end of that year, however, the paper was again sold and renamed the *Iowa Statesman.* After several changes of ownership, it suspended publication in November 1870, when Joseph Snow, one of the proprietors, died. But the city's Democrats were not without a paper for long; by the end of that year, the evening *Statesman* was succeeded by the *Iowa State Leader.*[52]

Two Decades of Publishing

During the first 21 years of journalism in Des Moines, many small, party-affiliated newspapers opened amid high hopes, only to change hands or cease publication altogether. As 1870 came to a close, the capital city's newspaper industry had stabilized, with two highly partisan papers dividing up the news market: the *Iowa State Register* was by this time the leading paper in the city and influential in Republican circles; its competition, the *Iowa State Leader* (a descendant of Barlow Granger's *Iowa Star*) was new to the field but offered Democrats a more favorable forum.

The end of 1870 also opened a new period at the *Register.* Late that year, Editor Clarkson, along with his brother and father, purchased the paper from the Mills brothers. Under their ownership, the paper's power reached new heights: the *Register* became the organ of a small clique of politicians and businessmen who dominated the Iowa GOP, and it rose to greater prominence throughout the state.

CHAPTER 3

"Ret," the Regency, and the *Register*

The Clarksons, clockwise from top, Coker, Richard, and James. *Courtesy of the State Historical Society of Iowa, Des Moines.*

The Clarkson family's purchase of the *Register* in 1870 ushered in a new era in Iowa journalism. During the family's 32 years of control, Coker Clarkson and sons Richard and James made it the voice of the state's Republican Party and the most influential Iowa newspaper. James, known as "Ret," a nickname he acquired because he scrawled the editorial abbreviation for "return" across copy he wanted to proofread personally, served as editor and used the paper to further the agenda of his wing of the party. In so doing, he advanced his own position in GOP ranks. Because of the editorial power he wielded, Ret became a leading figure in the circle of politicians and businessmen called the Des Moines Regency, a group that dominated the state's Republican Party for the last third of the 19th century.

In Ret's words, the *Register* was dedicated to maintaining "in power the great party of real Republicanism which saved the nation from destruction by war, returned it to peace, and is fast advancing it to unexampled prosperity."[1] Under Clarkson control, the paper was utilized to meet challenges to the preeminence of the Republican Party. Because the GOP controlled politics in Iowa, changes to the status quo threatened its position and needed to be co-opted or quashed altogether. Such problems were already manifest in 1870. Most menacing was the growing dissatisfaction among the state's large agricultural constituency. In an age when their autonomy seemed to be slipping away, farmers were organizing to protect their interests. These efforts encompassed the Grange movement, the short-lived Anti-Monopoly Party (and the issue of railroad regulation), the Iowa Farmers' Alliance, and the Populists. Less threatening but still of concern were reformers calling for temperance legislation. In addition, there was the controversial issue of women's suffrage. Any of these movements had the potential to alter the political landscape, and Ret and the *Register* worked to avoid any disruptions.

While fighting political battles from their newspaper's pages, the Clarksons also improved and modernized the *Register.* Much like other publishers of the period, they broadened the scope of their coverage to include many areas besides politics. One of their most successful new additions was Coker Clarkson's column "Farm, Orchard and Garden." Unlike most, however, they decided to widen their reporting net beyond the confines of their city of publication (Des Moines) and chose to include a growing number of stories from across the entire state. Finally, although many in the industry were moving toward a less partisan stance, the *Register* remained committed to advancing the fortunes of the Republican Party up to the time Richard Clarkson finally sold the paper in 1902.

Clarksons' Journalistic Heritage

The Clarksons' connection to journalism and Republican politics began long before their arrival in Des Moines. In 1838, Coker, then age 17, left his Indiana family farm to learn the printing trade. He apprenticed at the Lawrenceburg (Indiana) *Western Statesman* and by the early 1840s had become its owner. Soon thereafter, he purchased his hometown paper in Brookville and renamed it *The Indiana American.* A successful editor and publisher, Coker continued farming on the side and, much like his peers in the newspaper industry, he was devoted to politics. Coker had, for example, earlier served as a regional campaign manager for Henry Clay and helped nominate William Henry Harrison for president in 1840.[2]

Coker's interest in both journalism and politics filtered down to his two young sons. Years later, Ret liked to recall that he first learned to set type at his father's Brookville paper when he was 10. He also remembered his introduction to politics: "I really began in politics when I was 10 years old, going in the year 1852 at that age, with my father, to Lexington, Ky., to visit Henry Clay, where I saw a slave auction and encountered the cruelties of slavery, with the result of my leaving the Whig Party then joining the Abolitionists, and I have belonged to the band ever since."[3]

Coker sold the paper in 1853. Two years later, he moved his family west to Grundy County, Iowa. Here he wrote about farming, conducted agricultural experiments on his Melrose Farm, worked with the area's Underground Railroad, and remained active in Whig and then Republican politics. Richard and Ret, however, did not share their father's interest in farming, and they left the family acreage, taking up jobs as printers at the *Iowa State Register* in 1866.[4] Both advanced at the paper, but Ret's writing showed more promise, and he rose rapidly. He became the paper's local editor while also serving as the Des Moines correspondent for the *Chicago Tribune.*[5] The young editor's interest in politics soon became known. In a lengthy story for the *Tribune,* Ret discussed the leading contenders for the Iowa U.S. Senate seat that would be selected by the state legislature in January 1870. After describing the virtues of all running, he gave a slight edge to Iowa Supreme Court Justice George G. Wright over Congressman William B. Allison.[6]

Although the younger Clarkson's story indicated his penchant for politics, it was revealing in other ways as well. This Senate campaign was largely a battle between two factions within the Republican Party vying to dominate the GOP machinery rather than ideology. On the one hand, there was the group surrounding the seated Iowa senator, James Harlan. Judge Wright was the candidate of this wing. This group was opposed by a clique headed by General Grenville M. Dodge, a prominent businessman and chief engineer of the Union Pacific Railroad; his candidate was four-term Congressman William Allison. Although Clarkson's article gave a meager nod to Wright, who in fact went on to win the election, the editor took a relatively neutral stand. That, however, was soon to change.

Meanwhile the Mills brothers, publishers of the *Register,* had noticed Ret's journalistic promise. In an effort to keep him, they had promoted him to editor in chief in 1869, and then the following year they offered him a one-third interest in the paper. On his father's advice, Ret turned down the overture but countered with another proposal: the Clarkson family would purchase the *Register* outright. The Mills brothers, preoccupied with their expanding commercial printing business, agreed, and the deal was consummated in mid-November 1870. The Clarksons' premiere issue came out on December 6. Each family partner owned a third of the company, and responsibilities were divided so that Ret handled the editorial side, Richard managed the business side, and Coker headed up the agricultural news department.[7]

Two weeks after the change of ownership was announced, the *Register*'s editorial page carried a long piece describing the Clarksons' conception of their new paper: "[The *Register*'s] location at the political, railroad, commercial, and geographic center of the State, gives it the pre-eminent advantage over its competitors, and [at] every opportunity thus presented it will intelligently and industriously improve. ... Hereafter and heretofore, the first and most prominent feature of THE REGISTER will be Iowa and Iowa interests. ..." After promising to do all it could to "conserve and promote" the state's agricultural interests and its farmers, the article pledged that the paper "in politics, of course, it will be Iowa Republican, which is Radical and progressive."[8]

Much like other editors early in the 19th century, Ret easily combined his vocation of journalism with his avocation of politics. Soon after he and his family bought the *Register*, Ret became chairman of Iowa's central Republican committee. Communications professor Gerald Baldasty has examined this close connection between the press and political parties: "Editors did much more than edit newspapers. They were extensively involved in politics outside of their newspaper offices. They served as central committee members, public speakers, and organizers of meeting and conventions." Baldasty noted that editors "were the party strategists who created coalitions, chose party tickets, and guided campaigns. Parties were not ... dictated by newspapers; rather newspapers had been integrated into the party apparatus."[9] Such was the case with the Clarksons' *Register*.

After the family acquired the *Register*, they moved the company out of the Mills' building back to its former address on the Exchange Block on the corner of Third and Walnut streets.[10] During the Clarksons' first year of publishing the paper, Ret moved away from his middling position in the party and drifted toward the Dodge group. The process began during the gubernatorial campaign of 1871. Because U.S. senators were selected by state legislatures, the 1872 senatorial elections depended heavily on the outcomes of the state legislative races the preceding year. The Dodge faction, stung by Allison's defeat in 1870, redoubled its efforts to win a senate seat at the next opportunity. That meant working to elect a governor who was amenable to their senatorial candidate. Cyrus Clay Carpenter, a Fort Dodge surveyor and Civil War–era colleague of Dodge, seemed to fit the bill. Although Ret privately supported Carpenter for governor, neither he nor the *Register* offered public support. Covertly, using the pseudonym "Mum," Clarkson explained to Carpenter in April 1871: "I do not want to be known in this matter, but what stones I can throw in your yard, *will be there.*"[11] Carpenter won the Republican nomination, and because of that party's dominance in the state, it assured his victory in the fall elections.

Dodge and his cronies realized that Clarkson was a rising editorial power "who must be won" over to their side. Their wooing apparently began in 1871. That year, on the suggestion of Congressman Frank Palmer, a Dodge friend and former *Register* owner, the office of Des Moines postmaster was given to Ret Clarkson. Distribution of such patronage positions was a common way of lining up political allies, and the postmastership provided Ret with a handsome income of $4,000 annually.[12]

Clearly leaning toward the Dodge camp, Clarkson was still unwilling to offend the Harlan wing of the party. Likewise, because Coker was a good friend and ardent supporter of Harlan, Ret may not have wanted to upset his father and business partner. All of this changed in the midst of the 1871 Senate race, where the leading contenders were the incumbent Harlan and ex-Congressman Allison. Coker supported Harlan; Ret and Richard were for Allison. For most of the campaign the *Register* remained generally neutral. In October, for example, the editor noted: "We hold with two-thirds of the Republican papers of the state which advocate no particular person's cause in this contest. ... We have the fullest faith that either Allison, Harlan or [Congressman James F.] Wilson would make a Senator of whom the State would be faithfully and honoringly served."[13]

By the late fall, however, neither Coker nor his sons could bear remaining neutral in the election. Rather than see his paper support Allison, Coker sold his one-third interest in the business to his sons, but he stayed on as agricultural editor. Various interpretations of the terms of the sale have been put forward, but the most likely explanation is that Ret and Richard paid for Coker's share of the paper with a loan from banker B. F. Allen.[14] No longer held back by his father, Ret and the *Register* came out for Allison on December 13 and soon after began attacking Harlan. Allison was elected to the U.S. Senate by the Iowa Legislature in January 1872, and he held that post for more than a quarter century.[15]

Allison's victory was Ret Clarkson's as well. Evidence of Ret's win first came in the form of a political plum for his brother and business associate, Richard, who was elected state printer soon after the election.[16] More specifically, though, the victory marked Ret's ascendancy as a guiding force in the state's Republican Party. The Dodge faction acknowledged the connection between Allison's triumph and Ret's rise. Frank Palmer wrote Dodge: "The fight for Allison and Ret was made splendidly."[17] Furthermore, the election represented a shift in power within Iowa's Republican ranks and opened a 30-year era in which the Des Moines Regency controlled the party. Ret was a leading voice in this group, and his *Register* became the acknowledged organ of that body. According to historian Robert Cook, members of the Regency were "essentially pragmatic, business-orientated Republicans whose allegiance to consensus politics rendered them intensely suspicious of moralistic ideologues. ... Under their control it was unlikely that the party would ever be ruled for long by the heart rather than the head."[18]

Editorial Positions

Such pragmatism was also visible on the *Register*'s editorial pages. Ret used the paper to fight off many challenges to the Regency's control. Although certainly used as a partisan political organ, the *Register*'s editorial positions generally did what journalism historian David Paul Nord sees as conflict avoidance: "As self-proclaimed custodians of the whole public's interest, newspapers not surprisingly abhorred conflict in the community. ... Conflict subverted the newspapers' social world and they opposed it. In their efforts to do business with the *whole* public, or large segments of it, newspapers sought broad consensus."[19]

Grange Movement

On the eve of the Clarkson era, discontent was brewing among Iowa's large farm population. Beginning in the late 1860s, farmers regularly complained about economic conditions. While crop prices were falling, marketing costs associated with farming, such as shipping rates and elevator storage, were rising. In response, many joined a nascent organization in the rural Midwest—the Patrons of Husbandry, more popularly known as the Grange. Begun as a benign social organization, the Grange soon branched out into the economic and political arena. The first Iowa Grange was established in 1868, and by the early 1870s, the state boasted the largest Granger membership in the country.[20]

Initially, the *Register* endorsed the Grange, and Coker became a member. In January 1871, he described the organization as a society "designed to protect by mutuality of understanding the business of agriculturalists and to promote among them a greater and freer sociality of intercourse and acquaintance."[21] With the onset of the depression of the 1870s, however, the Grange became more active, moving into the economic realm with such ventures as cooperative elevators or packing plants. This activism did not sit well with the Clarkson family, and Coker told the Grangers to "move cautiously in any enterprise not strictly a part of farming."[22] These cooperatives were established to provide farmers with a way to battle with the outside companies—"monopolies" was the Grange's term—that were charging farmers high prices for equipment, grain storage, and transportation. Of all these monopolies, the railroads seemed the most unfair.

In January 1873, the Grange organization called upon the Iowa legislature to pass a law setting maximum passenger and freight rates in the state. When the bill did not pass, Ret lamented the failure, noting that "this question will meantime never be at rest in Iowa, nor the people satisfied, till our State Legislature attempts such control."[23] Ret's reading of the political climate proved correct. Unhappy with the General Assembly's inaction, a group within the Grange sought to enact railroad regulation through the creation of the Anti-Monopoly Party. This entry into politics represented a threat to the Regency, and the *Register* attacked the move. From his column "Farm, Orchard and Garden," Coker tried to redirect the Grange away from the third-party movement. Although he agreed that it was time to "war upon the railroads," he encouraged them to stay within the ranks of the Republican Party: "The most serious consequence to the Patrons if they plunge into separate political action will be the alienation of both the Republican and Democratic Parties."[24]

The Anti-Monopoly Party held its state convention in August 1873 to select candidates for the upcoming elections. The *Register* claimed that the convention was a "mere farce" because it was held during harvest season and few farmers attended. Furthermore, the paper charged that the party had been captured by Democrats.[25] When state elections were held in October, the Republicans and the Anti-Monopoly/Democrats evenly split the Iowa General Assembly, each winning 50 seats. This outcome pushed Ret, who had earlier come out for railroad regulation, to take up the call with greater urgency. To derail the antimonopoly movement and assuage the public's belief that the Regency was beholden to business, he wrote a *Register* editorial arguing that the Republicans needed to enact a regulatory law or "the Republican party in Iowa may be written of as dead."[26]

Republicans took up the issue of railroad regulation as their own, and in early 1874, the General Assembly passed the Iowa Granger Law. Iowa was not alone in passing such legislation. Other midwestern states with strong coalitions of small businessmen and farmers—including Illinois, Minnesota, and Wisconsin—enacted or were in the process of enacting similar legislation. In general, these laws created commissions with the authority to set rates railroads could charge within the various states.

With the passage of the Granger Law, the Iowa GOP successfully coopted the antimonopolists' major issue and blunted the movement's threat. The measure set maximum freight and passenger rates that could be charged by railroads within Iowa.[27] The railroads' response was predictable; they raised interstate fees and challenged the law in the courts. But when crop prices did not rise and the depression that had commenced in 1873 showed no signs of abating, many in Iowa began to believe the Granger Law needed to be revised. With public opinion moving against the legislation and two-thirds of the Iowa Legislature believing reform was necessary, the Regency began to have second thoughts about the law. According to historian Robert Cook, "Deregulation came to be seen as a major panacea for the depression."[28] Ret reversed his position, and the *Register* led the Regency's charge to rid the state of the Granger Law. In January 1876, the paper referred to "the railroad question" as the most pressing issue facing the General Assembly. Later that month, Ret's editorials called for "amending the present law or ... any different legislation that will better secure the interests of all the people."[29]

During the debate over the Granger Law, the U.S. Supreme Court weighed in on the issue. In its famous *Munn v. Illinois* decision in 1877, the Court upheld the states' authority to regulate companies such as railroads that operated in the public interest.[30] A year later, the railroad question was still being discussed in Iowa, and the *Register* was directing the debate. The paper argued that although the law had effectively controlled the railroads, it had slowed rail construction and investment in the state. Ret wrote: "We all know the State never prospered so much as in the days when the rapidly increasing railroad system of the State changed our wide prairies, almost like magic, into farms, towns, and cities." But the editor, who had been leaning toward federal railroad regulation since 1876, did not call for total repeal. Rather, he supported replacing the legislation with a regulatory commission appointed by the governor.[31] In March 1878, the Grange Law was repealed and, as the *Register* had wanted, supervision of Iowa's railroads was placed in the hands of a weak, governor-appointed, and usually railroad-friendly board of commissioners.

Agricultural Unrest

Although the Regency succeeded in quieting the antimonopoly movement for the moment, its dominance was almost constantly endangered by agricultural unrest over the next 20 years. As its mouthpiece, the *Register* fought to keep Iowa's farmers in the Republican fold. In the late 1870s, the GOP had another brief scare with the creation of the Greenback Party. Formed in 1876, this party stressed the need for expanding the money supply by reissuing previously retired Civil War currency—greenbacks. The goal was to raise prices and make mortgage debts easier to pay off. In the midst of the 1870s depression when prices were falling, this idea appealed to many Iowa farmers. In 1878, the Greenback-Democrat fusion ticket succeeded in winning two of the state's nine congressional seats, electing General James B.

Weaver and Edward Gillette. Over the next two years, the *Register* editor pounded away at the two Greenbackers, frequently referring to Gillette as "our congressional idiot."[32] The 1880 elections signaled a Republican recovery and a fading of the Greenback movement. That year, the GOP won all Iowa's congressional seats, and Weaver, the Greenbackers' presidential candidate, received only 10 percent of the vote in his home state. By the early 1880s, the Regency and the Republicans did not appear to face any serious opposition. Their confidence was expressed in a speech by Republican orator and future Iowa senator Jonathan P. Dolliver in 1885: "Iowa will go Democratic when Hell goes Methodist."[33]

Even as Republicans were celebrating victory, persistent agrarian problems led to a growing radicalism on the prairie. With prices for their crops tumbling and concerns growing that railroads and other giant corporations were controlling the economy, farmers continued to seek answers through organization. By early 1881, Iowa had two distinct farmers' organizations. One, the Iowa State Farmers' Alliance, was an independent group founded in Des Moines. Coker Clarkson, one of the original members, was elected secretary of the association. Soon thereafter, an Iowa branch of the National Farmers' Alliance (NFA) was organized. Both groups basically sought the same goals—to unite farmers, protect their interests, and regulate railroads—and the two ultimately merged, forming the NFA-affiliated Iowa Farmers' Alliance (IFA).[34]

The *Register*'s response to these groups was to say that Iowa farmers had great potential to influence public policy but had not learned to exercise that power: "The intelligent, prosperous farmer is always too busy to pay attention to such things, and so the poorer class of farmers are utilized by the professional politicians made to serve their purpose."[35] The solution, the paper went on to argue, was for Iowa farmers to work for reforms through the local Republican Party. Leaders of the IFA and its national organization tended to agree, for neither espoused the creation of a third party. In fact, the IFA did not appear to be much to fear: after the consolidated organization was established, it was relatively inactive until 1886.

Yet the *Register* stayed on top of agricultural issues and appeared to be the farmers' friend. Its agricultural editor used his column to battle one of the major enemies of Iowa farmers in the 1880s: barbed wire manufacturer Washburn and Moen. To fight the company, Coker and several key figures of the Iowa Farmers' Alliance organized the Farmers' Protective Association (FPA) in April 1881. In the eyes of rural Iowans, Washburn and Moen unfairly controlled the price of barbed wire. Coker, who had attacked the monopolistic practices of the company two years earlier, took up the issue in earnest after the creation of the FPA. In "Farm, Orchard and Garden," he explained that after the firm had acquired the patent rights to barbed wire, it set up a licensing arrangement with "some 40 establishments in the United States to manufacture it [barbed wire], for which they pay a royalty to Washburn & Moen of $.75 for every 100 pounds of wire barbed, and they obligate the licensees not to sell a pound of wire except at the price established by Washburn & Moen." He pledged that the *Register* would not be still until "a free and unrestricted sale of wire by the manufacturers" was attained.[36]

The FPA took direct action against Washburn and Moen by chartering its own company to manufacture barbed wire. By joining the organization for $1.00, farmers could purchase barbed wire at 7.25 cents a pound, compared to the Washburn ring's price of 9 cents a pound. From its operation called the "free factory" in Des Moines, the FPA put out 12,000 pounds of barbed wire a day, and by 1885, it was advertising its product for 6 cents a pound.[37] This cheaper wire on the market—coupled with pressure from the *Register* and smaller papers such as the *Iowa Homestead,* the *Iowa Farmer,* and the *Winterset Madisonian and Chronicle*—pushed Washburn and Moen to lower its price equal to that charged by the free factory.[38]

Meanwhile, after briefly stabilizing in the early 1880s, agricultural prices began falling again. This led to a resurgence of the Greenback-Democratic union (fusionists) and stepped up Alliance activity. As historian Jeffrey Ostler notes, "In 1885, the president of the Iowa State Agricultural Society testified before a congressional committee that most Iowa farmers believed that a corporate lobby had been behind the repeal of the Granger Law in 1878 and that the railroad commission had since neglected the legitimate interests of producers."[39] Fusionists hoped to win elections based on this discontent; IFA leaders hoped it would result in the election of a General Assembly in 1887 that would revise the railroad legislation. During the campaign, the *Register* reminded voters that the next legislature they were electing would select two U.S. senators and implored them to maintain "the [Republican] party of order, loyalty, temperance, and honest government" in power.[40] Although the Republicans held on, the Regency had little to rejoice about since most elected to state legislature were committed to reform.

Try as they might, Ret and his Regency allies could not reverse the popular mandate for revising railroad regulation. One bill, embracing the views of the IFA, called for electing commissioners and establishing maximum rates. The *Register* countered with a proposal for maintaining the appointed commission with the authority to deal with specific charges of unfair rates.[41] Ret's idea was soon the essence of a bill sponsored by first-term representative and future U.S. Senator Albert B. Cummins. But when the IFA refused to support the more conservative Cummins bill, others interested in reform moved to their position, and the Railroad Commissioner Law was enacted. The measure was a defeat for the Regency. In conjunction with supplemental legislation, the law established maximum rates that lowered freight rates and stipulated an elected railroad commission.[42]

Populism

Oddly enough, the IFA and the *Register*, enemies in the fight over the railroad act, ended up as allies in the 1890s. Together, they effectively stemmed the possibility of a successful third party in Iowa. Such parties had grown out of farmers alliances in neighboring states. The push for a third party in Iowa did not come from the IFA, which, because of its past successes in attaining reforms, chose to stick with its nonpartisan approach. Rather, it came from the Southern Alliance, a national farmers' organization competing with the NFA and former Greenback leader James Weaver. After setting up an Iowa branch of the Southern Alliance in 1891, organizers moved to create a political party. The Iowa People's Party (Populists) was founded in June 1891. In response, the IFA leadership stepped up its attacks on the Southern Alliance and its entry into politics, while the *Register* began singing the praises of the IFA. The paper stressed the important differences between the two agricultural organizations. The IFA, the *Register* noted, had enjoyed real legislative successes and consisted of "real farmers," but the Southern Alliance was "merely a stool pigeon trap baited with demagogues."[43]

The Populists fared poorly in the state elections of 1891. Their gubernatorial candidate received only 3 percent of the vote. On the brighter side, they won two seats—one in each house—in the Iowa Legislature. From that point on, the Regency did not see the Populists as much of a threat. By June 1892, the *Register* wrote that it no longer planned to devote serious attention to the party, explaining that it would not "take issue with any of the things done or said" by the People's Party.[44] Instead of focusing on the Populists, the paper returned to familiar ground: battling the Democrats. Republican leaders and the *Register* had read the political climate correctly, and their strategy paid off handsomely in the elections that November. The Republicans recaptured the governorship, held a majority in both legislative houses, and won eight of nine congressional races. Meanwhile, the Populist candidate for president, Iowan James Weaver, received only 4.7 percent of the popular vote in Iowa.[45] Following the trouncing of Populism and the big Republican victory in 1896, the *Register* gleefully exclaimed: "This is a state without the blight of Populism. It is a business man's state."[46]

The *Register* might have added that Iowa was also a state without a forceful farmers' organization. Even as a serious Populist challenge failed to develop, the IFA began to collapse. Membership had been decreasing since 1891 and, by 1894, the IFA failed to hold its annual convention. As the organization folded, its leaders were incorporated into either the Democratic or Republican parties.[47]

Prohibition

Just as the *Register* acted pragmatically in handling farm matters, so too did it deal with the volatile topics of prohibition and women's suffrage. According to historian Samuel Hays, prohibition was the most important issue in late-19th-century Iowa.[48] In 1855, the state legislature had passed a law prohibiting the sale and manufacture of intoxicating liquor, but subsequent revisions—such as an 1858 clause exempting beer and wine—had weakened the measure considerably. The various versions of the law reflected the division among temperance reformers: some demanded outright prohibition, while others called for regulation and alcohol in moderation. By the mid-1870s, Iowa had essentially adopted local option, and city officials were empowered to determine whether liquor would be allowed within their municipalities. This situation pushed prohibition advocates to redouble their efforts to rid the state of the evils of alcohol.[49]

Early on, the Clarksons' *Register* supported prohibition, and it continued to so do until the early 1890s, when GOP leaders concluded that the party was being hurt by its outright antialcohol position. Activities of prohibition crusaders received frequent coverage. Women temperance workers, for example, were repeatedly praised for their battle against alcohol. Lengthy stories portrayed their protest marches or "pray ins," groups of women praying either inside or outside saloons, as heroic. Often too, the *Register* linked drinking to "stunning" social costs resulting from alcohol-related litigation, criminal activity, and indigents.[50]

By 1877, Republican leaders were being pressured by the State Temperance Alliance to advocate prohibition, and the *Register* supported such an endorsement. But like the paper's stand on farm issues, its position was motivated by pragmatism and politics. For example, even while calling for prohibition, the *Register* approved of the establishment of a distillery in Des Moines that would employ 100 men year-round, purchase local corn, and then ship all the alcohol it produced out of the state. It concluded: "This enterprise, if it becomes a substantial reality will be a great addition to this section of the state."[51] Although not wanting morality to get in the way of good business, Ret realized that prohibition seemed to be the will of the majority, and it was better to keep the movement within Republican ranks than to fight a third party. This position became clear in the paper's coverage of a temperance rally. It summarized one speaker's position by writing: "His speech was a strong ... appeal to the people—the temperance people especially— ... not to organize a new political party, but to refuse to support at the polls the candidates of whatever political party, who favor the liquor traffic."[52]

In 1880, the Republican legislature passed a resolution to put a constitutional prohibition amendment before the people in a special election. Two years later, Iowa voters followed the advice of a *Register* headline announcing that "the saloon must go" and passed the amendment. After the amendment was struck down on a technicality by the State Supreme Court, the Republican majority in the General Assembly fulfilled their 1883 campaign pledge by enacting a strict prohibition law the following year. Proud of the statute, the *Register* boasted: "The great work of the session—the greatest and bravest work of any Legislative session in the history of the state—was the enactment of the prohibitory law. This work, and the faithful, magnificent way in which it was done, is enough of itself to make this Assembly historic."[53] Such lofty praise notwithstanding, enforcement proved impossible and violations were ubiquitous.

During the next 10 years, the more radical prohibitionists pushed for stricter enforcement and closing the various loopholes in the legislation. Opponents, meanwhile, lobbied for replacing the law with local option. In the late 1880s, Republican platforms "committed their party to the defense of prohibition,"[54] and by the early 1890s, party chiefs began to worry that such support had helped Democrats make big gains in the General Assembly. The *Register* stepped up its coverage of antiprohibition Republicans. In March 1892, such a group held a conference in Des Moines, where they pledged to "use every influence to induce the Republican party to discontinue the policy of prohibition as a party measure."[55] Leaders of the GOP began backing away from absolute prohibition in 1893. At a meeting in March, the Republican State Central Committee concluded that the ardent antiliquor wing was willing to compromise "in order to save the life of the party in the state."[56] Later that year, the platform announced that "prohibition was no test of Republicanism" and suggested that the liquor law might need revision.[57]

When the General Assembly convened in 1894, the *Register* reminded Republicans to honor the platform and solve the problematic liquor issue. At the same time, the paper continued reporting the growing antiprohibition sentiment within the ranks of the GOP and the need to hold the party together. In March, an editorial explained: "It is a serious thing to amend the prohibitory law, but not to do so is still more serious. The Republican party is confronted with one of the gravest of all political duties, but must not, it cannot fail to keep ... the terms of the platform upon which [it] appealed to the people for votes last fall."[58] The compromise legislation that ultimately resulted was the Mulct Law. Although it failed to repeal prohibition, it exempted saloons from state liquor laws if they paid a licensing fee. In essence, the new law granted local option.[59]

The *Register* applauded the party for fulfilling its pledge, but with faint praise noted that the "law is not unsatisfactory and ought to be given fair trial."[60] In fact, while the compromise measure pleased no one, it successfully put the tricky issue of prohibition to rest for the GOP. As historian Ballard Campbell explained, "Republicans split between men who fought to retain prohibition as a universal code of behavior, and men who were willing to relax liquor regulations for the greater good of their party. The result was that Republicans tried to have the best of both worlds by retaining prohibition as a general ethical norm while permitting deviations from it as local option dictated."[61]

Women's Suffrage

As with temperance, the *Register*'s position on women's rights and suffrage was dictated by practical politics. By the time the Clarksons obtained the paper, the question of women's suffrage in Iowa had divided the GOP. After extending the vote to black men, some Republicans wished to do the same for women. However, in an era "when female suffrage was regarded as ridiculous by most Northerners," party leaders were cautious.[62] Nevertheless, the early 1870s were critical years for Iowa suffragists. In 1870, the General Assembly approved a women's suffrage amendment. Before being put to the voters, the proposed amendment was required to get a second approval by the next legislature.[63]

The divisive nature of the "woman question," as it was called, was reflected in Ret's *Register* in the months leading up to the vote on the amendment in the 1872 General Assembly. Diana Pounds found that of the 86 *Register* news stories about women's rights and suffrage from October 1871 to January 1872, 41 percent opposed expanding women's rights or granting suffrage, 35 percent supported the women's cause, and the remaining 24 percent were neutral. Meanwhile, the 12 *Register* editorials on women's issues during the same period carried a similar mixed message—four favored suffrage and women's rights, three opposed them, and five were noncommittal.[64]

When the 1872 Iowa Legislature failed to pass the amendment, the immediate issue of women's suffrage faded away for the rest of the 19th century. Although no longer a real political danger, women's rights continued to be a hotly debated topic, and the *Register*'s persistent indecision on the matter appeared to mirror a divided society. The paper was occasionally progressive on women's rights. For example, it praised a woman who went to Oberlin Theological Seminary and became a Methodist minister. It commended a speaker who said that every "girl and boy should be put to a trade or profession." And it reprinted a *Chicago Tribune* article extolling the idea of female physicians and breaking down gender barriers in the professions: "Every calling should be thrown open to every human being and those who are qualified to fill them."[65]

At the same time, however, the *Register* could look like a bastion of conservatism. On women's reading habits, the paper suggested females were not interested in weighty matters: "But of journals serious and frivolous they [women] prefer the latter, and their choice is for a daily paper which prints jaunty leaders, and for a weekly paper which is crammed with gossip, personality and scandal."[66] The *Register,* in fact, took its own statement to heart. Like many other papers of the 1870s and 1880s, it worked to attract more female readers by adding a regular column, "The World of Womankind," that dealt with such topics as cooking, decorating, and fashion.[67]

In addition to offering a *Register* women's section, articles appeared that encouraged women to remain in the traditional sphere. The paper approved of a speaker who "exalted marriage as the ideal status for women," and it provided guidance to young women with stories such as "How to Become a Belle." In reprinting a humorous piece from the *Philadelphia Progress,* it suggested a female's proper role: "The girly girl is the truest girl. She is what she is and not a sham or pretense. The slangy girl has a hard job of it not to forget character. The boy girl and the rapid girl are likewise wearers of masks. The girly girl never bothers with women's rights and women's wrongs. She is a girl and proud of it." And at other times, the *Register* celebrated women for using traditional means to effect positive change. It quoted a piece from the *Sioux City Journal*: "The women of Iowa have won their first distinctive victory in a popular election. They had no ballots of their own to cast, but through their influence, the [Prohibition] Amendment passed."[68]

Improvements

Besides championing Republican causes from its pages, the Clarksons improved, enlarged, and modernized the paper. When the family took control, the *Register* was a four-page Republican morning daily with a circulation of approximately 2,000.[69] Typically, the paper provided a heavy dose of state and national political news, some international coverage, editorials and letters to the editor, reprinted stories from other newspapers, and reporting on local events. Advertising, largely from local merchants, generally filled approximately 40 percent of the paper.[70] During this period, newspapers across the country relied slightly more on subscription sales than advertising income for their total revenues. In 1879, for instance, subscriptions accounted for 56 percent of American newspaper revenue while advertising made up the remaining 44 percent.[71]

By the late 1870s, Ret started making subtle changes in his paper's content. Like other newspapers throughout the nation, the *Register* carried a growing number of nonpolitical stories. In an effort to appeal to a broader spectrum of readers, the paper began to feature regular departments. This trend had actually already started in 1871, when the Clarksons initiated Coker's weekly column "Farm, Orchard and Garden," designed to reach the region's many farmers. Later in the decade, other standard features included the women's section, book reviews, church news, the criminal calendar, courthouse news, and a gossip column.[72]

A larger readership produced greater revenues, but it was equally important for advertising dollars. Because "advertisers wanted to reach consumers, and circulation determined advertising rates ... newspapers worked hard to produce news that would attract large numbers of readers."[73] Advertising was becoming more important for newspaper revenue. By 1889, advertising and subscription sales accounted for nearly equal shares of American newspaper revenue, but 10 years later, advertising dollars made up 54.5 percent of total revenue while subscriptions had fallen to 45.5 percent.[74] Because Des Moines, with a population of 22,000 in 1880, was relatively small and because the *Register* was competing with the Democratic *Leader* for readers, the Clarksons chose to expand their coverage—in hopes of expanding circulation—beyond the confines of the city. In a section originally known as "Iowa Intelligence," the paper reported on events around the entire state. As with other small newspapers, the *Register* relied on local correspondents—who could usually be obtained cheaply or at no cost at all—to supply this news. The *Register* was relatively unique, however, in its move toward broader statewide coverage.[75] For example, in the 1870s and 1880s, it reported on such issues as gold mining in the northern Iowa county of Winnebago, the reduction of the Davenport police force in eastern Iowa, and a suicide in Cedar Rapids in east-central Iowa.[76]

The Clarksons explained their goals and strategies in 1885: "From this time on, the *Register* will be made a ... paper of the enterprising and intelligent citizens of every city and town and farm neighborhood in the state. We shall strive to be still more an Iowa paper, putting our own state first in all our efforts and bending our strength in every good way."[77] While giving greater attention to events beyond the capital city, the owners increased their effort to distribute the paper throughout the state. By mid-decade, the *Register* was available from news dealers in seventy locales in Iowa. Vendors sold the paper in towns as far away from Des Moines as Avoca, 80 miles to the west; Spencer, 170 miles to the northwest; Algona, 120 miles to the north; Waterloo, 100 miles to the northeast; Iowa City, 110 miles to the east; Ottumwa, 80 miles to the southeast; Leon, 70 miles to the south; and Red Oak, 110 miles to the southwest.[78]

The many improvements the Clarksons made at the *Register* attracted readers. From 1870 to 1890, the paper's daily circulation more than tripled, rising from approximately 2,000 to 7,157.[79] Advertising dramatically increased, and although local advertisements still dominated the paper, an increasing number came from big businesses selling brand-name products nationally. Rising circulation and advertising revenues translated into profits. In 1883, the *Muscatine Journal* reported that the *Register* "is to-day the the best paying newspaper office in the State, yielding a net income to the [Clarkson] brothers of $25,000 a year."[80] Other newspapers throughout the state were singing the paper's praises. In December 1884, for example, the *Algona Republican* wrote:

> The new press and type for the State Register are at last en route from the east and ... the long contemplated [changes] in the form and dress of the paper will positively be made January 1st. Under the new regime, the Register will be eight pages and a facsimile in form and type of the Chicago Tribune minion and agate. The change is rendered absolutely necessary because of the Register's growing advertising patronage much of which has been obliged to be refused lately. Another improvement will be a direct wire from the Chicago Tribune office into the Register building over which the cream of the former's special telegraphic news will be received and will appear simultaneously. In a word the Register will step from the garb of a big country paper into that of a metropolitan journal. It might not be inappropriate to add that the Register is, as it ever was, the leading Iowa newspaper.[81]

As reported, the *Register* expanded from a four to an eight-page paper beginning in 1885. Newspapers of such size were already common in larger cities by the 1870s. The push for growth came from the increase in advertising volume. In doubling its size and increasing its advertising space, the

Register was merely following a decade-old trend in the industry. It was part of a movement Gerald Baldasty identified as commercialization of the news. By the late 19th century, many once partisan newspapers were moving toward an independent stance. The declining interest in party politics and the increasing costs associated with publishing were beginning to make such a move advisable. Meanwhile, with the development of a national market, businesses grew larger and, seeking customers for their products, they turned to advertisements. As advertisers began to replace political parties as the chief financial supporters of newspapers, publishers and editors altered their content to entertain and capture as large an audience as possible. To avoid offending potential readers, many newspapers adopted a neutral political position.[82]

Although the majority of newspapers did not drop their political affiliation during this period, a trend was apparent. Historian Michael McGerr estimated that in the mid-19th century, 95 percent of American newspapers were partisan. In fact, leaving the party fold could be costly. In the 1872 election, for example, several Republican papers, including the *New York Tribune* and the *Cincinnati Commercial,* broke from their party's ranks and supported the Liberal Republican-Democratic presidential candidate, editor Horace Greeley. Such a move proved damaging in terms of losses in readership and advertising dollars. Following their candidate's defeat, these papers soon returned to mainstream Republicanism. Nevertheless, by 1890, more and more newspapers were moving toward an independent position; by that date, papers that identified themselves as partisan had declined to 66 percent of the total.[83] The *Register,* however, was not among those leaving the ranks of political parties. While conceding the growing commercialization of the industry with a greater variety of features and carrying more advertising, it remained committed to the GOP throughout the Clarksons' ownership. In 1886, Ret explained his paper's political connections: "We give to the Republican party all the power we have, and take nothing from it."[84]

The *Register*'s close ties to the party and Ret Clarkson's prominence as its editor led to his rise in the Republican hierarchy. After holding several local and state positions within the party, Ret began to think about opportunities beyond the horizons of Des Moines. He sold his portion of the newspaper to brother Richard in 1888 and moved to the East Coast. In 1889, he was appointed first assistant postmaster general by President Benjamin Harrison. From 1890 to 1892, he was chairman of the National Republican Executive Committee. He later accepted the political appointment of surveyor of customs for the port of New York.

Time to Sell

Meanwhile, the newspaper market in Des Moines became more crowded. The 1880s saw the number of dailies in the city increase from two to five. In addition to the morning *Register* and *Leader* (which changed from an evening to morning paper in 1888), two evening papers entered the field: the *Des Moines Capital* in 1881 and the *Des Moines News* in 1886. Another daily, the short-lived *Hawkeye Blade,* was published from 1883 to 1885 before being absorbed by the *Leader.* This increased competition hurt the *Register*'s market share in Des Moines and cut into advertising revenue. With Ret in New York, Richard, who was the paper's business manager, took over the editorial duties as well. Unfortunately, Richard's writing lacked flair, and he did not possess the public relations acumen of his brother. These factors, combined with Richard's declining health, hampered his attempts to battle the rival newspapers. By 1902, in fact, the *Register* had not only been dislodged as the state's largest daily; it was now the smallest in the capital city. After unsuccessfully battling the competition for a decade, Richard was ready to sell.[85]

Although Ret was no longer financially interested in the *Register,* he handled its sale. In disposing of the paper, he was guided by both business and political factors. As he explained to Jonathan Dolliver, U.S. senator from Iowa, in 1901, "Richard has placed it [the *Register*] in my hands for sale, induced thereto by his failing health and advancing years. After Richard's interest is served to its best advantage, I would like next to consider ... the interests of yourself, Senator Allison, Speaker [of the House David] Henderson, and all the old time friends." He then went on to name the man he hoped would purchase the paper: "In desiring to guide the old paper into the hands of men friendly to my old friends ... I would first prefer George Roberts."[86]

Roberts had been the editor and publisher of the Republican *Fort Dodge Messenger* and served as state printer for six years. After writing several prominent articles on the money question during the 1896 campaign, he was named director of the United States Mint and moved to Washington, D.C. When the *Register* came up for sale, Roberts, who apparently had always dreamed of owning the influential paper, was interested.[87] Negotiations dragged out, however, because Roberts would not meet Richard Clarkson's asking price of between $175,000 and $200,000. In the meantime, other political factions made overtures to buy the paper, but Ret convinced his brother that Roberts was the best buyer. The price was eventually lowered to $125,000, and political allies such as Allison and Dolliver helped Roberts raise the cash needed for the purchase.[88]

After various negotiations, Roberts and Samuel Strauss, owner of the *Des Moines Leader*—which had moved from being a Democratic to an independent paper in 1896—decided to end the ruinous competition between the papers and consolidate the two properties. When the deal was finally worked out in June 1902, the two jointly purchased the *Register* for $125,000 and merged it with the *Leader.* Roberts paid Richard Clarkson $25,000 in cash, and the remaining $100,000 was paid in notes and bonds of the new company. Roberts and Strauss each held 50 percent of the paper—now the *Register and Leader*—but as the agreement stated, the former had absolute control of the "policies and preferences of the company," and the paper was to be "Republican in politics." Strauss became the business manager.[89]

On June 29, 1902, the paper's low-key headline "Register and the Leader are One" announced the merger but did not capture the importance of the event. At one level, the consolidation of the two rival papers indicated the closing of a partisan battle that had been running for nearly 30 years. More important, however, it marked the passing of the Clarkson era. During the last three decades of the 19th century, the Clarksons made the *Register* the voice of the Regency and the Republican Party. While using the paper for political ends, they also broadened the scope of its coverage, doubled its size, and expanded its circulation base outside of Des Moines.

The sale of the *Register* appropriately coincided with the decline of the Regency's domination of state politics. Although Republicans continued to control the statehouse and the Iowa delegation in Congress for another 30 years, the progressive wing of the party assumed power. Ret, of course, found the shift in the Iowa GOP deplorable, but worse still was his reaction to what soon occurred at the paper. Eighteen months after Richard Clarkson sold out to Roberts and Strauss, the *Register* changed hands again, and by late 1903 the new owners were ardent advocates of progressive Republicans. A voice of pragmatic conservatism for more than three decades, the paper had been converted into a vehicle of reform.

CHAPTER 4

The Cowles Years Begin

1903–1924

In the last decades of the 19th century, the Clarkson family had created the foundation for the modern *Register*; they guided it toward statewide coverage and made it the most powerful newspaper in Iowa. After George Roberts' brief ownership, banker Gardner Cowles acquired a controlling interest in 1903 and began a family dynasty that lasted for the next eight decades. Once at the *Register*, Cowles and editor Harvey Ingham found themselves publishing

Gardner Cowles and sons, from left to right, John, Russell, Gardner Sr., and Gardner Jr. (Mike), 1910. *Courtesy of the Gardner Cowles Jr. Collection, Cowles Library, Drake University, Des Moines.*

a paper long on reputation but short on readers when compared with two larger dailies in Des Moines. To turn the ailing paper around, Cowles and Ingham implemented a series of sound managerial practices.[1] They adopted ambitious long-range plans and coordinated day-to-day activities to attain those goals. Together, they made the *Register* successful by building on the strengths of its heritage while incorporating innovations.

Under Cowles and Ingham, the paper grew along lines both familiar and unfamiliar. Following in the Clarksons' footsteps, the new management team expanded on the strategy of making the paper a statewide institution. After putting the financial house in order, Cowles devoted most of his energy to building circulation on both the local and state levels. Indeed, expanding circulation became the backbone of his business strategy. Former newspaper publisher and later professor of journalism Frank Rucker saw newspaper sales as central: "Circulation ... is the foundation of a newspaper's success."[2]

Cowles clearly understood that growing circulation numbers were crucial. He once explained circulation's role in the newspaper business in this circular way: "We need to get more circulation to get more advertising to get more money to make a better newspaper to get more circulation."[3] While a larger readership meant increasing circulation income, it was also critical to expanding the more important advertising revenue. By 1904, advertising revenue made up 56.7 percent of American newspapers' total income; subscriptions and sales accounted for 43.3 percent.[4] Cowles justified his near fanatic interest in circulation to an editor: "It does you no good in a business way just to put out a good paper. You have to go out and sell it."[5] Besides increasing circulation through selling more subscriptions, the publisher also pursued expansion through the acquisition of competitors.

To differentiate the paper from its rivals, news coverage from around the entire state was expanded and cultivated. Agricultural news that appealed to rural readers remained prominent. The *Register* continued to provide in-depth reporting about state politics. Unlike the former owners, Cowles and Ingham expanded the daily dose of national and international news by always trying to present an Iowa angle in every story. They also decided to drop the *Register*'s extreme Republicanism and to move toward a more independent political position. Likewise, Ingham followed other contemporary editors by emphasizing objectivity in reporting and the separation of news and opinion. Overall, the new management team viewed the newspaper primarily as a business enterprise.

Other changes in the paper's content were designed to attract new readers. As larger newspapers in other cities had been doing since the turn of the century, the *Register* introduced a number of features in an effort to separate itself from competitors in both local and statewide markets. For example, the paper added a color-print comic section as a regular Sunday feature. In a similar move, management included political cartoons on the paper's front page and in the editorial section. One staff cartoonist, Jay N. "Ding" Darling, later won two Pulitzer Prizes; he gained national prominence when his drawings were syndicated. With the increasing popularity of illustrations, American newspapers ran a growing number of photographs, and the *Register* followed this path as well. In 1919, it initiated a "rotogravure" (photographic) section as a standard offering in the Sunday paper.

Under the Clarksons, the *Register* had tended toward political conservatism and a maintenance of the status quo, but under Ingham's direction, the editorial page took on a more liberal stance. It actively supported the Progressive movement and took up such causes as a reform plan for Des Moines city government, black civil rights, women's suffrage, and an internationalist foreign policy.

Cowles Comes In

By the early 1920s, the success of the Cowles-Ingham strategies was evident. As of 1924, only one Des Moines paper remained outside the Cowles fold, and readership had vastly increased. In November 1917, the combined daily circulation topped 100,000 for the first time; the Sunday edition reached that mark in 1921. Profits climbed as well. The company paid its first dividends in 1906 and continued to do so throughout the period.[6]

Between the Clarkson and the Cowles era was a 17-month period when the paper was held by George Roberts and Samuel Strauss. Their ownership began in June 1902, and once the deal was settled, Roberts surveyed the difficult task that lay ahead. He wrote George Perkins, publisher of the *Sioux City Journal*: "I feel I have launched upon a pretty big undertaking [buying and trying to rebuild the paper], but you know a man must keep trying something larger than he is accustomed to, if he is to satisfy himself and bring out the best there is in him."[7] Roberts had responsibility for the paper's editorial policy, but because he was director of the U.S. Mint, he remained in Washington, D.C. To oversee editorial matters on a day-to-day basis, he hired fellow Republican Harvey Ingham, the 43-year-old editor and publisher of a small Algona weekly, *The Upper Des Moines,* to serve as associate editor in Des Moines.

After a year, however, Roberts realized that while living on the East Coast, he could not devote the time necessary to turn around the fortunes of the *Register and Leader* (*R&L*). The paper was losing money, and within a year, Roberts was looking to unload the property. But much like the Clarksons before him, he wanted the paper continued by owners sympathetic to the Dolliver camp.[8] Meanwhile, Samuel Strauss sold a portion of his stock—Ingham purchased 545 shares, Roberts the other 300—and left to become involved in publishing the *New York Commercial Advertiser.*[9] By late October, Roberts found a group of acceptable buyers and closed a deal. Three prominent Iowa Republicans, all of whom had served together in the state senate—Abraham Funk, editor and publisher of the weekly *Spirit Lake Beacon;* Fred Maytag, the Newton farm equipment maker (later the successful appliance manufacturer); and James Smith, the Osage lumberman—agreed to purchase 1,500 shares, or 50 percent ownership, of the paper. Roberts planned to retain 300 shares and remain as president of the company.[10]

But the new arrangement was not satisfactory to Ingham. He was unwilling to share editorial duties with Funk. Ingham persuaded Roberts to give him a chance to solicit another offer, and he sought help from a friend, Algona banker and businessman Gardner Cowles. During their years together in Algona, the two had apparently mused about buying the *Register.* With the opportunity at hand, Ingham telegraphed Cowles in early November, suggesting that there might be "some things to be adjusted [in the deal between Roberts and Funk, Maytag, and Smith] that may cause a hitch." He then pitched his friend: "Would you put $50,000 into the R&L and get control with me, or put $75,000 and get control yourself, and take the business management of the paper?"[11] Cowles was interested and took the train to Des Moines to discuss the situation with Roberts.

On November 7, 1903, the *Register and Leader* announced the abrogation of one deal and the consummation of another. It reported that the new publisher, Gardner Cowles, would concentrate on the business side of the paper, while Ingham would continue as editor. Cowles purchased the 1,500 shares originally earmarked for Funk, Maytag, and Smith. Together Cowles and Ingham controlled 2,045 of the company's 3,000 shares.[12] The new owner explained what led to his apparently sudden decision to buy the *Register*: "Both Harvey [Ingham] and I always had the feeling that it was possible to build a strong daily newspaper in Des Moines. We probably thought more of the opportunity than of the discouraging condition of *The Register and Leader.*" Besides seeing possibilities for the paper, the banker later remarked that he "had no pressing need for the money. ... It seemed to be a good thing to do on the theory that something would arise."[13]

At the date of purchase, the newspaper was the smallest daily in Des Moines. Although the sellers had assured Cowles that circulation stood at 32,000, it actually was somewhere around 14,000, with paid up subscriptions only about 8,000. Two afternoon papers, the *Capital* and the *News,* had larger circulations.[14] Cowles later recalled, "The first five or 10 years with the Register & Leader ... were mighty strenuous." Like his predecessors, he thought seriously about selling out.[15] But Cowles stuck it out, and the tight market forced him and editor Ingham to adopt innovative business and editorial practices.

Initially, the afternoon papers were unconcerned about the ownership change at their morning competition. In a rather dismissive editorial, the *Capital* greeted the new publisher at the *Register and Leader*: "We welcome Gardner Cowles as one of our 'hated rivals' and wish him success."[16] Although a successful businessman, Cowles had only limited journalism experience and thus was not viewed as a threatening figure to the publishers of the city's larger papers. Hindsight, however, proved the other newspaper owners wrong: Cowles' varied background was a huge asset for revitalizing the troubled company.

The son of a Methodist minister, Cowles was born in Oskaloosa, Iowa, in 1861. Because his father was frequently transferred from church to church, Cowles lived in many parts of the state. In his youth, summers were spent working; several years he traveled from farm to farm selling maps, and during one vacation, he worked on a survey crew planning a railroad through central Iowa. His interest in railroads led him to take a summer job between his junior and senior years in college working on the Union Pacific's Oregon's Shortline from Portland to Utah. After graduating from Iowa Wesleyan College in 1882, he took a job as superintendent of schools in Algona. While remaining in that position, Cowles bought half-interest in the weekly *Algona Republican* in 1883. As co-owner, he successfully managed the business side of the operation. This move, however, prompted a biting editorial from Harvey Ingham, part owner and editor of a rival paper, the *Upper Des Moines*. Seeing Cowles' newspaper ownership as a conflict of interest with his job at the Algona schools, Ingham demanded the superintendent be relieved of his duties and replaced by someone "old enough not to be attracted by side speculations and smart enough to only try to do one thing at a time."[17] Cowles disregarded the jibe, and the two men soon became good friends. Cowles stayed with the paper until a dispute with his partner led him to sell out just one year later.[18]

Free of the newspaper and deciding that two years was enough as superintendent, Cowles went into banking and real estate investment. He ultimately became a major shareholder in 10 banks and president of County Savings Bank, the principal bank in Algona. During his Kossuth County career, Cowles amassed a net worth of $200,000. However, the most pertinent lesson for later expanding the *Register* came when he went into business with his father-in-law, Ambrose Call. Their firm solicited government contracts to run mail by horseback or wagon to small towns not served directly by railroads. They soon maintained more than 30 routes in Iowa, Kansas, and the Dakotas. Taken as a whole, this background introduced Cowles to various parts of Iowa, gave him an understanding of small towns, exposed him to sales in rural areas, and created an awareness of the importance of a state's rail network. In addition, by the time Cowles acquired the *R&L*, he was a mature and experienced businessman who was already familiar with the newspaper world.[19]

To restore the paper to financial health, Cowles first concentrated on monitoring company costs. He tightened budgetary controls by personally approving every bill paid and signing every check. Spending was slowed by delaying purchases—the acquisition of two typewriters, for example, was not immediately made until absolutely necessary. Although circulation was growing, unpaid bills continued to mount; to cover these accounts, Cowles ordered assessments on the firm's capital stock: a 3 percent assessment in February and another 1 percent assessment in June 1904. Unwilling to put any more money into the *Register and Leader*, Roberts and Strauss sold their stock to Cowles in March. By July, Cowles' austere management began to pay off; just eight months after purchasing it, the company was in the black. At the end of his first year of ownership, the paper had earned $9,000.[20]

Building Circulation

Cowles' primary interest and genius were in the area of circulation. Guided by the belief that "the more honestly a paper is conducted, the more successful it will be," Cowles was uncomfortable with the fairly standard practice of inflating circulation figures to increase advertising rates. He therefore determined not to give out circulation figures until he could provide a sworn statement that the paper's readership stood at 25,000. Along this line, the publisher culled out a couple of thousand unpaid subscriptions—sometimes two, three, or four years past due—and announced that the delivery would be stopped unless accounts were paid up. By 1908, Cowles eliminated the bad debts problem altogether by announcing that future subscriptions would be accepted only on a cash-in-advance basis.[21]

The highly competitive newspaper environment in Des Moines led Cowles to look to the entire state as a potential market. He believed the key to increasing circulation was expanding subscription sales. After hiring and firing several circulation managers, he assumed this responsibility himself. Because much of rural and small-town Iowa lacked ready access to a daily paper, Cowles chose to focus attention on this virgin territory. His interest in railroads proved invaluable. Because trains provided the only efficient means of distributing the paper outside of Des Moines, Cowles studied maps and memorized railroad timetables. Printing schedules for various editions were adjusted to fit the departure times of various trains out of Des Moines. The publisher's obsession with getting up-to-date, quality newspapers into the hands of readers paid off handsomely. By 1906, circulation had nearly doubled, and Cowles could finally provide a sworn statement that the paper had 25,000 readers. That same year, he found a solid circulation manager in William Cordingley, but he continued to keep close watch over this end of the business.[22]

Cowles' background in small-town Iowa and his work as a mail contractor further assisted him in distributing the paper. Because many of his newspapers sold outside of Des Moines were sent through the mail, the system worked for the Monday through Saturday daily editions. To get the *Sunday Register* to readers throughout the state, however, Cowles and Cordingley relied on local news dealers and agents in small towns to sell the Sunday paper. But for the growing number of farm subscribers located on the many rural, free delivery routes, that system was inadequate. Cowles and his circulation manager circumvented this problem by developing an efficient network of youthful carriers and adult rural route sales representatives to deliver the Sunday edition to farmers' doors. This service became a big selling point, and company advertisements frequently played up this competitive advantage: "No other newspaper covers the news of Iowa as does *The Register and Leader* each morning. No other daily newspaper is delivered to all Iowa towns and on almost all rural routes on the morning of issue as is *The Register and Leader*."[23]

Building circulation required more than getting papers to readers. By the 1890s, newspapers around the country were making use of contests, coupons, and premiums to boost circulation.[24] Under Cowles, and then Cordingley, at least three different types of promotions were used to increase subscriptions: premiums were offered to attract potential subscribers; the uniqueness of the paper was stressed; and a direct-mail campaign was launched.

One of the most common methods employed to bring in new readers was the premium. A variety of items were offered to new subscribers, including a wall map of Iowa, a world atlas, or a book of the best political cartoons by *Register* artist Jay "Ding" Darling. Special gift supplements were included in certain issues. For example, beginning in the June 17, 1906, issue and running over the next 20 weeks, the *Sunday Register and Leader* contained a pen-and-ink drawing "on heavy eggshell paper especially suitable for framing" of one of artist Charles Dana Gibson's famous "Gibson Girl" illustrations. Premiums were offered to those who brought additional subscribers to the paper. In 1907, the paper pitched children: "If you will get one person not at present receiving THE REGISTER AND LEADER to sign the following coupon and pay you fifty cents for the first month's subscription, we will mail a TEDDY BEAR to you, free of charge." Meanwhile, current subscribers were not overlooked. At the end of 1906 and early the following year, Gardner Cowles sent letters to his present readers promising them that "for every new subscription to The Register and Leader for one year which you send us accompanied by remittance, we will advance your own subscription six months without charge to you. Each new six months subscription entitles you to three months' extension on your own subscription."[25]

In addition, through newspaper advertisements, posters, and pamphlets, the *Register and Leader* explained how it was superior to other available newspapers. Cowles and the promotion staff highlighted the Sunday color comic section, the inclusion of serialized novels by such contemporary authors as Robert Barr, Ian MacLaren, Max Pemberton, and Mary E. Wilkins-Freeman, and in 1907, the addition of a Sunday women's page. Furthermore, the paper boasted about its 300 correspondents who provided news from all over the state; its baseball coverage, reporting the full box scores of the Western and Iowa Leagues as well as the American and National Leagues; and its complete market coverage, including news from a special correspondent who provided a daily "detailed report of the great Chicago live stock market."[26]

The company's most aggressive technique to hike readership was a direct-mail campaign. By 1906 and likely earlier, letters were sent out to people in at least three different categories: daily subscribers were offered the Sunday paper; former readers were enticed to resubscribe; and nonreaders were induced to try the *Register and Leader.* The promotional letters almost always promised some type of premium to persons who subscribed and usually included a tear-off coupon to return with the remittance. While subscription rates were $4 a year for the daily or $6 for the daily and Sunday issue, the mail campaign's standard pitch offered people the daily for $1 for three months or $1.50 for the daily and Sunday editions.[27]

Increases in circulation confirmed the soundness of the Cowles approach. By the end of 1907, circulation topped 30,000. Even more impressive were the figures published in a promotional brochure. Of the total circulation for the first week of October 1907, over two-thirds of the Cowles papers went to parts of Iowa outside the city of Des Moines. The publisher's strategy of selling his product beyond the state's capital was clearly working. As a letter from a subscriber in Dubuque—a city on the Mississippi River, 180 miles east of Des Moines with easy access to the *Chicago Tribune*—suggested, readers from around the state found the paper indispensable: "I send you a draft to pay my subscription to Nov. 30, 1908. I rely upon the Register and Leader to keep me informed of the news of the state and would not like to do without it."[28]

Attracting Advertisers

Yet, Cowles was also aware that in addition to appealing to readers, his newspaper needed to attract advertisers.[29] Indeed, the rapidly expanding volume of retail advertisements appearing in turn-of-the-century newspapers led one merchant to explain in 1904: "The newspaper of today is largely the creation of the department store."[30] Across the country, local merchants generally bought the majority of advertising space in their respective cities' newspapers. Midway through 1908, for instance, the *Register and Leader*'s local display advertising surpassed foreign display advertising by nearly a four-to-one margin.[31] To entice this important segment of advertisers, Cowles concentrated on "home base" circulation of the *R&L*—newspapers sold within the regional business zone of Des Moines. The more newspapers sold within this area, the more potential customers local business operators could reach with advertisements in the *Register and Leader.* To court this critical business, Cowles labored to beef up *R&L* sales in towns and rural areas surrounding the capital city. While the publisher continued working toward statewide circulation, his successful efforts in building circulation in the more profitable close-in market soon became clear. In a 1908 promotional pamphlet, the company declared that over 82.5 percent of the *Register and Leader*'s circulation came within a 100-mile radius of Des Moines.[32]

As the *Register and Leader*'s circulation numbers rose, so too did the paper's advertising linage. In 1905, its advertising as measured in column inches outpaced the Des Moines *Capital* but still trailed the Des Moines *News.* By 1907, however, the *Register and Leader* carried the most column inches of advertising in the capital city. With such robust growth, Cowles soon felt comfortable about being more selective in the advertising he accepted. At particular issue were the area liquor interests. Both Cowles and editor Ingham were nondrinkers and opposed to liquor in principle. But in the early Cowles years, liquor ads accounted for approximately 30 percent of the paper's total display advertising, and the company could not afford to turn down these advertisers.[33]

From 1903 to 1908, the *Register and Leader* squared off against alcohol manufacturers and retailers. When Cowles' paper printed editorials or news stories that the liquor lobby deemed detrimental to its interests, it threatened to withdraw its advertising from the paper in favor of the *Capital* and *News*. Long opposed to liquor, and emboldened by the increasing number of readers and advertising, Cowles pulled the plug on all liquor advertising. On January 1, 1909, he announced that the *Register and Leader* would no longer accept liquor or beer ads; it thus became one of the first papers to put such a policy into effect. Although many publishers were skeptical about his resolve, Cowles stuck with the policy and later called the decision "one of the wisest he had ever made." He believed it elevated the people's perception of the *Register and Leader* because "the public came to realize ... that advertisers could not control the paper."[34]

Expansion through Acquisition

In order to improve still further his position in the Des Moines daily market, Cowles followed two additional strategies: he spun off the company's weekly publication and pursued expansion through acquiring the rival papers. The *Register* weekly edition dated back to the paper's origins and was continued after the daily was established. In 1905, the weekly *Iowa State Register* changed its name and format. It became the *Iowa State Register and Farmer* and focused largely on agricultural issues. The following year, however, competition for the city's daily readership increased when Charles D. Hellen founded the afternoon *Tribune*. In response, Cowles decided to concentrate all the company's energies on the increasingly competitive daily field, and he sold the weekly in December 1906.[35]

Although the *Tribune* never attained great circulation and did not prove a real threat to the other three Des Moines papers, Cowles recognized it as a possible entree into the evening market and became interested in acquiring it. As an afternoon paper, it would attract a segment of advertising that the morning paper missed. In early 1908, Hellen sold the paper to George Rinehart and G. A. Huffman, who turned the paper into a Democratic daily. Following the Republican victory that fall, the *Tribune* owners sold their declining paper (circulation estimates ranged from 2,000 to 10,000) to Cowles on November 12 for less than $30,000. In announcing the acquisition, Ingham wrote that the *Tribune* would be "entirely independent of the *Register and Leader* in its news service" and that "politically it will be a Republican paper with considerable emphasis on the word newspaper."[36] With this purchase, Cowles obtained an established paper possessing a valuable Associated Press afternoon franchise. Of equal importance, with both a morning and evening offering, Cowles could attain economies of scale by running his presses around the clock rather than having them stand idle overnight after printing the morning *Register and Leader*.[37]

The addition of the *Tribune* furthered the company's expansion. While the *Register and Leader* concentrated on becoming an Iowa newspaper, the *Tribune*'s circulation and coverage focused largely on Des Moines. In 1912, the *Register and Leader* led all Des Moines papers in advertising linage, while the evening *Tribune* ranked third. The combined daily circulation of the firm's morning and evening papers reached 50,000. The increases in readers and advertising translated into greater profits: net earnings rose from $23,880 in 1906 to $38,480 six years later, while return on investment increased from 8 percent to 9.6 percent.[38] Such growth was also reflected in a larger staff—in 1911, the papers employed 20 reporters and an editorial department of 35, up from five in 1890. In November 1908, the company added a $38,000 high-speed Hoe printing press, which it claimed was the "largest and best in use." The new press could "print, paste, cut, and fold a 48 page paper."[39]

For the next 12 years, the business grew through greater subscription sales. Dedicated to getting his papers to readers on time, Cowles once explained: "It appeared obvious to me that every house where I could deliver a morning or evening newspaper on the date of issue housed a potential subscriber; and especially when I could deliver the paper before breakfast and before supper. ... A good newspaper delivered promptly within easy distance of the front door can scarcely shake off its subscribers with dynamite."[40] During this period, he and his circulation staff continued to improve their distribution network. Trucks were used to transport the *Register and Leader* where railroads did not reach. By 1920, the trucking industry had become a serious challenger to the railroads for freight traffic. With more and more newspapers distributed via truck, Cowles became an early and ardent advocate of the "Good Roads Movement." Although, of course, from a circulation standpoint his interest in improving Iowa's roads was self-serving, the state's road system was indeed abysmal. In 1904, for example, the state had over 100,000 miles of road, ranking it third in the nation; but with less than 2 percent of it improved road, Iowa had a reputation as being one of the worst mud-road states in the nation.[41]

As early as 1906, the paper was campaigning to "get Iowa out of the mud." Six years later, the *Register and Leader* ran a series of stories and editorials calling for the passage of a $25 million state bond issue to finance road improvements. The bond issue failed, but the paper continued to battle for better roads. In 1916, the topic came up again in the gubernatorial election campaign. The paper, which usually supported Republicans, came out for Democratic candidate E. T. Meredith over Republican William Harding (who went on to win the election), largely because of the Democrat's support of road bonds. Although Iowa was relatively slow to pave its roadway system, more and more of its roads were improved; and from 1913 to 1919, the state made great strides in constructing concrete bridges and culverts. Finally, in 1919, the paper's long fight for better roads appeared successful. That year the Iowa Legislature designated 6,500 miles of state highway as primary routes and in need of paving.[42]

Better roads, coupled with the nationwide phenomenon of large circulation increases associated with World War I and local population growth—from 1910 to 1920, Des Moines grew from 86,000 to 126,000—led to big readership gains and handsome profits for Cowles. By March 1920, combined daily circulation of the morning and evening papers reached 112,000, while *Sunday Register* (the name *Leader* was dropped from the paper's masthead in the beginning of 1916 and the company was renamed the Register and Tribune) stood at 82,000. These advances were made in spite of increases in subscription prices to cover spiraling costs associated with wartime inflation. Over the course of the decade, net earnings nearly quadrupled, increasing from $52,098 in 1910 to $206,766 in 1920, while the return on investment rose from 13 percent to 22 percent.[43]

In the midst of this growth, the company suffered a setback when its building, located downtown on the southeast corner of Fourth Street and Court Avenue, was badly damaged by a fire on Sunday morning, February 21, 1915. Losses were estimated at $200,000, but the building was insured, and Cowles' primary concern was getting out the Monday paper. The resourceful publisher made immediate stopgap arrangements to print the paper at the *Capital*'s plant, and the *Register and Leader* did not miss an issue. Within weeks, temporary offices and printing facilities were set up in a building east of the paper's fire-ravaged home, and plans were readied to erect a new "ten to twelve story building on Locust Street between Seventh and Eighth Streets." When completed in the spring of 1918, the *Register*'s new 13-story building was the tallest in Iowa. Centrally located in Des Moines's business district, its modern, fireproof facilities were opened 24 hours a day and featured elevator service. Originally over half its office spaced was leased to tenants, but over the years the paper came to occupy the entire building.[44]

Now highly successful and clearly the dominant paper in Des Moines, the *Register* rarely compared itself to the other two papers in the city. A 1922 advertisement, for example, barely mentioned its local rivals. Instead, the *Register* boasted that it was the "largest Iowa daily newspaper by many thousands."[45] Cowles, however, was still keenly aware of local competition. Inflation related to World War I had, in fact, made many publishers across the country more concerned with their competitive position and led to an increase in newspaper mergers and consolidations. This trend led to a growing concentration of newspaper ownership. From 1910 to 1930, 362 dailies merged with rival papers, and an increasing number of cities had only one daily or one company owning all local papers.[46]

Through the mid-1920s, competition among the city's three evening papers was particularly intense. In the fall of 1924, Roy W. Howard, chairman of the board of the Scripps-Howard chain, which owned the *News,* came to Des Moines to discuss the situation with Gardner Cowles. The two men met at the Hotel Fort Des Moines, and the encounter soon turned into a negotiation for the sale of the Scripps paper to the R&T. Ultimately, the deal was signed in Chicago, where Cowles bought the *News* for $150,000. He then combined it with his *Des Moines Tribune.* The *Sunday Register* explained the acquisition on November 9: "The Tribune-News is made with the expectation and purpose of better serving the people of Des Moines and Iowa. This consolidation is in keeping with the nationwide trend toward fewer and better newspapers." After promising that the new, enlarged paper would maintain the popular features of both the *News* and the *Tribune,* the editor noted that "the consolidated paper will strive always for fairness in its news and editorial columns and to show sympathy for the average man."[47] Besides eliminating a rival paper, the merger added new readers for the *Tribune.* The R&T's combined daily circulation rose from 144,011 in 1924 to 160,740 in 1925. Only one Des Moines newspaper, the *Capital,* remained outside of Cowles's control.[48]

Cowles and Ingham: A Successful Partnership

Gardner Cowles had overseen the 20-year rise of the *Register* through adept management. In his first years at the paper, Cowles usually arrived at the office before 7 a.m. and remained until 6 p.m. Weekends were also often spent at the Register building reading and sorting mail and developing circulation campaigns. Ambitious and energetic, yet also stern and forbidding, Cowles was ideally suited to revive the ailing paper. Although detail-oriented, he was also a visionary and a builder who saw the entire state as virgin territory for his small newspaper. Early on, he was very much the hands-on manager; he made all business decisions, paid all the bills, dealt with advertisers, and ran the circulation department. Gradually, after hiring conscientious and competent people to head up the various departments—William Southwell as business manager or Cordingley in circulation, for example—Cowles gave them the necessary latitude to do their jobs effectively. Yet he remained closely involved in the decision-making process. Once the management team was in place, department heads were gathered together in weekly conferences with Cowles and the editors. Managers presented progress reports, and out of these meetings came day-to-day policy as well as corporate strategy. Whenever Cowles was out of town, he insisted on being kept informed by a constant flow of daily reports.[49]

Cowles continued to spend long hours at the office. Besides his weekly meetings with top management, he kept a close eye on company operations by wandering the building. Inquisitive by nature, Cowles peppered his staff with questions and encouraged them with a variety of slogans such as: "Things don't just happen, somebody makes them happen." A stickler for order, the publisher often walked through the building on Sunday mornings after church. During these "inspection tours," he often left employees notes chiding them for such minor infractions as leaving lights on in unattended rooms or failing to return reports to their proper place. This focus on the smallest detail may have been counterproductive, and Cowles certainly intimidated many employees with his questions, exhortations, and notes. At the same time, however, he led by example, showing his staff a diligence and willingness to work hard. By giving an impression that he and his employees were in the enterprise together, Cowles built an esprit de corps in the company. He emphasized this idea in an internal publication in October 1915: "Co-operation will win in building up a business just as it will win in a football game."[50]

The publisher also monitored the business by reading "every line of type that appeared on the editorial page."[51] But Cowles made no effort to direct or influence the editorial stance of the paper. He gave editor Harvey Ingham free rein over this phase of the business. In fact, the working relationship between Cowles and Ingham established an owner-editor tradition that would remain in place until the paper was sold in 1985. From this point forward, Cowles family members oversaw the business side of the enterprise, while salaried editors were left to determine editorial positions.

On the surface, Cowles and Ingham appeared to be opposites. While the publisher was quiet and reserved with a penchant for conservative Republicanism, the editor was talkative and affable with leanings toward liberal and progressive causes. But the shared ideas of building an independent newspaper that stressed objective reporting and covered the entire state bound the two men together. As son Gardner "Mike" Cowles Jr. recounted, "Their [Cowles and Ingham] individual talents were perfectly complementary. Father was the quintessential business manager, who delighted in the minutiae of circulation and accounting. Ingham was the quintessential editor who delighted in rooting out the news and advocating ideas."[52]

While the elder Cowles was streamlining business operations, Ingham improved the quality of the *Register and Leader* by stressing objectivity in reporting. As early as 1902, Ingham had established his editorial vision: "The first and supreme purpose of everyone concerned is to make a worthy newspaper in the broad and modern meaning of the word. This requires that the news service shall be ample and reliable, and maintained scrupulously independent of the editorial opinions of the paper." Although Ingham noted that the owners were dedicated to supporting the Republican Party in its editorials, the staff saw "its first responsibility to be to its readers, and that every choice will be a free one, made when the occasion arises, and not predetermined by factional alliances or considerations." The editor added that the "field of the paper is Iowa" and "special efforts will be made to cover the news of this state and to make a paper more satisfactory to Iowa readers than any paper published."[53]

Ingham's policy statement sounded at once both old and new. With his notion of running a paper that covered the entire state, he was following the path already laid out by the Clarksons. But with his pledge to separate news and opinion, the editor was breaking with the partisan past of the *Register and Leader.* Ingham was right in line with the "new journalism" beginning to take hold across the nation at the end of the 19th century. Advocates of this new form "believed in the news function as the primary obligation of the press; they exhibited independence of editorial opinion; they crusaded actively in the community interest; they appealed to the mass audience through improved writing, better makeup, use of headlines and illustrations, and the popularization of their contents."[54]

Under Ingham's direction, the *Register and Leader* moved away from the extreme partisanship of the Clarkson years, but complete independence and objectivity were not immediately accomplished. By 1905, the paper was referring to itself as "independently Republican—not allied to any faction."[55] And although the paper sometimes backed Democrats—as it did in 1916 when it supported Meredith for governor—or sometimes refused to endorse any candidate—as it did in the 1920 and 1924 presidential elections—the *Register* tended to have a moderate Republican cast through the 1920s. The paper's political leanings were clear, for example, in its coverage of the state political conventions of 1906. It described the Progressive Republicans' triumph over the conservative elements in the party as the "greatest victory ever recorded" and added that the party was now "invincible." A month later, in referring to the rival party's state convention to be held in the northern Iowa town of Waterloo, a headline proclaimed: "Democratic Invasion of New Waterloo."[56]

Meanwhile, Ingham emphasized accuracy and objectivity in reporting. In 1904, his principles were put to the test. Reporter Don Berry, who was covering a local school board election, was told by Cowles to be "very careful" and "go slow" on the story because subscribers and advertisers had sharp differences of opinion on the subject. Troubled by the publisher's comments, Berry went to Ingham, who gave him this order: "Write the truth and let the chips fall where they may." The reporter followed his editor's instructions and heard no more from Cowles. Sometimes, however, these higher journalistic standards were ignored; the paper's coverage of the company's purchase of the *Tribune* is illustrative. Instead of merely reporting the acquisition, the *Register and Leader* could not avoid hyperbole and self-promotion: "With the greatest staff of news writers ... ever assembled in Iowa. ... The Evening Tribune and the Register and Leader will be published under the same management." The story then continued to list all the "firsts" of "the *Register and Leader* [which] has been a long leader in Iowa newspapers."[57]

Even though the *Register and Leader* did not immediately live up to Ingham's ideals, he continued to prod it in the direction of independence and objectivity. In 1915, he explained that such a policy was not only good journalism, it was also good business: "Two avenues of popularity are open to the newspaper. The first is to yield, to flatter, to cajole. The second is to stand for the right things unflinchingly and win respect. A strong and fearless newspaper will have readers and a newspaper that has readers will have advertisements."[58]

Differentiating the *Register*

Besides encouraging the ideas of the new journalism, Ingham knew that because the Des Moines market was small, the *Register and Leader* needed additional ways to differentiate itself from other local papers. Product differentiation was a distinct business strategy applied by some publishers to separate their offerings from those of their rivals.[59]

Statewide Coverage

One of Ingham's key strategies was to build upon the Clarkson heritage of statewide coverage. Longtime sports reporter and editor Leighton Housh once explained that the *Register*'s goal was "to cover the state as would a local newspaper."[60] This goal was accomplished by establishing a state news department that coordinated stories from some 300 local correspondents scattered throughout Iowa. With this unique service, the paper featured daily reports from around the state. The company promised that "day after day, month after month, THE REGISTER AND LEADER prints more

REAL IOWA NEWS than any other paper."[61]

Ingham took advantage of his Des Moines location to provide detailed reporting on affairs at the statehouse. A 1906 advertisement stressed that coverage: "The *Register and Leader* will be indispensable to Iowans who wish a complete, accurate report of its [the Iowa Legislature's] sessions day by day."[62] While Cowles labored to distribute the paper to all rural Iowans, Ingham made every effort to provide timely news of interest to them. Coverage of agricultural issues was enlarged, including the most extensive daily report of the Chicago livestock markets of any Iowa newspaper. A full-time farm editor was added during World War I, and beginning in 1920, a full-page agricultural section covering farming issues throughout the entire state appeared every Saturday. Finally, to make national and international news more readable for Iowans, these stories always sought an Iowa angle. Sometimes an Iowa perspective had to be created. In an August 1914 editorial, for example, Ingham brought the war in Europe home to Iowans by comparing Belgium (which had just been invaded by Germany) in size, population, and economy to the state of Iowa.[63]

Comics and Cartoons

Besides tailoring the paper specifically for Iowa readers, Ingham and Cowles continued to improve their product to set it apart from competitors. In September 1904, the company announced the addition of a new, four-page, color comic strip supplement to the Sunday paper: "The Register and Leader has taken an unusual step in newspapering in Iowa, for it is the first and only daily in the state to adopt such a feature."[64] The original strips included "Professor Hypnotiser," "Simon Simple and Mose," "Herr Spiegleberger," "Uncle Pike," and "Billy Bounce." The first regular comic section had appeared 15 years earlier in the *New York World*. Seen as a way to attract young readers, comics were soon added to other New York papers, and they spread to large dailies across the country after the turn of the century. As Ingham noted in an editorial, however, "The Register and Leader will be one of the pioneers [in its use of comics] in cities of less than 100,000."[65]

The Sunday comics clearly gave the *Register and Leader* a competitive advantage over its local Des Moines rivals. Neither the *Capital* nor the *News* carried comic strips, although the latter had a humor page in its Sunday morning edition. While this page included several one-cell cartoons, they lacked the two key elements of the comic strip: they were not a sequence of drawings about a single amusing incident, nor did they present characters that reappeared in successive issues from week to week.[66]

The *Register and Leader* again differentiated itself from other papers by hiring the talented political cartoonist Jay N. "Ding" Darling.[67] Prior to coming to Des Moines, he had spent six years at the *Sioux City Journal.* There, Darling's reputation as a cartoonist grew, and several Iowa newspapers, including the rival *Capital,* tried to hire him. But Cowles succeeded where the others had failed, and Darling's first cartoon appeared on the front page of the Sunday *Register and Leader* in December 1906. A week prior to Ding's arrival, the paper advertised: "The Des Moines Register and Leader announces that it has contracted for the exclusive services of J. N. Darling, better known as 'Ding,' who won wide popularity as cartoonist for the Sioux City Journal. 'Ding's daily cartoons dealing with the affairs of the state and nation will be warmly welcomed by the readers of The Register and Leader. ... The addition of Mr. Darling to its staff will further strengthen the position of The Register and Leader as the best newspaper in the state."[68]

Darling's first *R&L* cartoon sparked immediate controversy and upset several groups. It consisted of an overweight monk smoking a pipe inscribed "soft coal." "Catholics were offended at the notion that the monk was responsible for the heavily polluted air in the city. Darling had mistakenly assumed that 'Des Moines' was derived from the French word for monk. Des Moines coal dealers were also angry."[69] Despite his rocky beginning, Darling's works quickly became popular, and his cartoon on the front page of every *Register and Leader* was "a trademark of the paper." After five years in Des Moines, Ding was ready to try his hand in a larger market, and he took a job at the *New York Globe* in November 1911. While the *R&L* felt the loss of Darling's artwork, matters were made all that much worse when to management's horror, Ding's cartoons began to appear on the front page of the *Des Moines Capital* (which had purchased them from the *Globe* syndicate). In 1912, *R&L* business manager William Southwell began talking to Ding, who was not happy with his situation in New York, about coming back to Iowa. After Cowles and the cartoonist ironed out the details, Ding returned to the *Register and Leader* in February 1913.[70]

Back on the *Register and Leader*'s front page, Ding was given complete freedom to deal with any topic in any way he wished. Such leeway led to battles between the conservative artist Ding and liberal editor Ingham. These disputes were mediated by Cowles, who always stressed teamwork. Because Darling and Ingham were each important members of the *R&L* team, Cowles often had to remind the former to stick to cartooning and the latter to concentrate on the editorial page.[71] Given the control the cartoonist and editor wielded over their respective domains and their contrary political outlooks, it is not surprising that Ding's cartoons sometimes presented different opinions from those expressed on the editorial page. Biographer David Lendt notes, "In 1915, for example, Darling argued for national military preparedness while the editorial page condemned the worldwide arms race."[72]

Happy to be back in the Midwest, Darling still wanted to reach a larger audience than the *Register and Leader* offered. In 1916, the ideal opportunity came; Ding signed on with the *New York Herald Tribune* syndicate while remaining on the staff of the Des Moines paper. In addition to gracing the pages of the *Register,* Darling's cartoons appeared in more than 100 newspapers from coast to coast. Thousands of new readers across the country now became familiar with Ding's simple drawings that conveyed a "gentle but unmistakably barbed ridicule."[73] In 1924, his fame grew when he was awarded a Pulitzer Prize for the previous year's cartoon entitled "In the Good Old U.S.A." His winning drawing emphasized hard work and opportunity by depicting the rags-to-riches success stories of Herbert Hoover, Dr. Frederick Peterson, and President Warren G. Harding.[74]

When Cowles hired Darling, he had high hopes that the cartoonist would help attract readers to the *Register*. By the 1920s, Darling had surpassed the publisher's greatest expectations and was a major reason for the paper's success. John M. Henry, a friend and colleague of Ding, felt that the cartoonist "did more for the *Register* than Cowles did."[75] Although probably an overstatement, Henry's remark was correct in suggesting that Darling was a critical part of the paper's rise to prominence in Iowa and across the nation.[76]

Photojournalism

The *Register* set itself apart from other newspapers in Iowa by being the first to include a rotogravure (photographic) section in its Sunday edition. Although the R&T did not originate the idea, the company beat out the local competition in its commitment to photojournalism. After the *Capital*'s announcement in early 1919 that it planned to provide the state's first photo section, Cowles moved quickly to meet the competition. His rapid action paid off; on March 30, 1919, the *Register*'s eight-page rotogravure supplement appeared, one week earlier than the *Capital*'s four-page section. From its beginning, the *Register*'s weekly offering consisted of a large number of photographs covering several themes, plus advertisements; little copy accompanied them.[77]

Register Editorial Positions

While R&T management was continually trying to attract readers by adding new features, Ingham moved the *Register*'s editorial stance from the conservative position of the Clarkson era to a more liberal tone. He was among a growing number of editors who demanded a wide variety of reform. Others included, for example, Frank L. Cobb, the brilliant editor of the *New York World*; William Allen White, the small-town Kansas editor and publisher of the *Emporia Gazette,* who became a close friend and advisor to President Theodore Roosevelt; and newspaper magnates such as E. W. Scripps and William Randolph Hearst.[78] Like those of many of his contemporaries, Ingham's editorials actively supported the Progressive crusade for regulation of the railroads, restraints on big business, primary elections, the direct election of U.S. senators, the creation of a federal income tax, and Prohibition. Over the span of his first two decades as editor, Ingham focused much of his paper's attention on four additional issues: the reorganization of Des Moines city government, civil rights for blacks, women's suffrage, and the cause of internationalism.

City Government Reform

The movement to rid cities of political machines and replace them with nonpartisan experts trained in management had been mounting since the public exposure of massive corruption among city officials around the country. Given the clear shortcomings of urban administrations, Progressive reformers looked to the private sector for managerial models that could be applied to a municipal setting. In 1901, following a devastating hurricane that destroyed much of Galveston, Texas, local business leaders overhauled the city's standard governance system. An elected five-member commission assumed power. Each commissioner headed up one executive department, and if residents were unhappy with services under his jurisdiction, they could vote a particular commissioner out of office. The "Galveston Plan," as it was called, made city government more responsive to voters and soon became a model that other cities emulated.[79]

Des Moines was clearly not immune to the civic corruption that plagued many of the nation's urban centers. Journalist George Mills quoted one historian who referred to the turn-of-the-century government in Iowa's capital as having "the worst reputation for rottenness and inefficiency of any administration in the history of Des Moines."[80] At that time, the city was run by a mayor and a council of nine aldermen. A Board of Public Works, appointed by the mayor with the approval of the council, had charge of many city services, while police and fire departments were overseen by other quasi-independent boards not subject to voter approval.[81]

In 1905, Ingham and the *Register and Leader* noted "a general feeling of dissatisfaction over the present management of municipal affairs has been manifest for sometime." Over the course of that year, Ingham discussed the need to reform city government with businessman James G. Berryhill. Berryhill's business had often taken him to Galveston, and he told the *R&L*

editor about the success of the Texas city's new governmental structure. Ingham offered to publish a story about Galveston's new municipal system based on Berryhill's next visit to the city. Thus began Ingham's 18-month effort to get Des Moines to adopt a similar form of government.[82]

In November 1905, Berryhill addressed the Des Moines' Commercial Club on the many benefits of the Galveston Plan. Following the report, the club organized an effort to persuade the General Assembly to approve the use of a commission form of city government in Iowa. The *Register and Leader* headed the campaign, followed by both the *Capital* and *News,* which advocated reform. By January 1906, the *R&L* reported that there "was little doubt Des Moines wants change in city government," but the following month the bill was killed by a joint committee of the Iowa House and Senate.[83]

Seeing the defeat as only a "temporary setback," the *Register and Leader* promised to continue the fight for the commission system. A year later, the paper encouraged its readers to lobby for passage of the commission bill: "Now is the time for those who believe in popular government and honest and efficient government to be active."[84] In March 1907, the General Assembly passed the law, which had become known as the "Des Moines Plan." It gave Iowa cities the option of adopting a commission style of municipal government. In addition to offering basically the Galveston system, it added elements of direct democracy such as the initiative, referendum, and recall. Several months later, the plan was put before the city's voters and adopted by a 2,300-vote plurality. The *Register and Leader* called the victory "a mighty stride forward."[85]

The Des Moines Plan was to take effect following municipal elections in April 1908. But when the commission government finally went into effect, it was not with the reform slate of candidates the *Register and Leader* had supported. Of this defeat, Ingham wrote: "The people will not always accept the judgment of a civic league or good-government club, just as a jury will not always accept the view of an able and honest lawyer."[86] Although the editor lost the battle over the first elected officials to sit in the new governmental body, he had succeeded in pushing Des Moines to adopt the commission system and to begin cleaning up city government.

Black Civil Rights

Besides leading the fight to reform local politics, Ingham's editorials constantly pointed out the pervasive racism in society and demanded full civil rights for blacks. On one occasion, he noted: "I have seen at every athletic contest of the state, paths carefully marked that colored boys might run unobstructed. I have yet to learn of a colored boy who left an athletic contest feeling that he might have won and was not permitted to win. Can you name another competition in life where that is true?" He made his position clear in 1906 when Des Moines was hosting a national conference of the Presbyterian Church. The meeting brought together the organization's northern and southern branches for the first time since the Civil War. During the convention, a black minister was not allowed to attend a session in a local hotel. While the minister suggested that he understood that his presence might anger Southerners in attendance, Ingham wrote a blistering front-page editorial charging the church with condoning the action. He asked: "What is to be the effect on society when the church refuses to stand without flinching?"[87]

In 1912, Ingham followed the story of a black attorney in Boston who had been disbarred by the executive board of the American Bar Association (ABA). Although he was eventually reinstated, the editor noted that the ABA had no intention of allowing all eligible blacks to join the organization. The ABA, he wrote, "looks upon color as a test for admission." After chiding the national bar association, Ingham expressed hope that the reinstated lawyer would prove that blacks were fully capable of succeeding in the profession.[88]

When a Des Moines branch of the National Association for the Advancement of Colored People (NAACP) was formed in 1915, Ingham became one of its most prominent members. Besides speaking out against discriminatory policies, he used the power of the paper to aid the organization's cause by seeing to it that "fair, if still limited stories" about blacks were included in the *Register.*[89] In the early 1920s, the editor was disturbed by the growing membership of the Ku Klux Klan (KKK) in Iowa. Initially, the paper did not appear to take a strong stand against the Klan. In fact, the *Register* actually provided a medium for a Klan organizational drive by running a large KKK recruiting advertisement in late 1922.[90] Several months later, the resurgent Klan claimed 2,500 members in Des Moines and boasted that it was growing at a rate of 200 new members per week.[91]

By 1924, the local Klan had moved into politics. In the municipal elections that year, KKK-backed candidates (who were either members of or sympathetic to the organization) ran for mayor, public safety commissioner, and park commissioner. Prior to the election, the *Register* indicated its distaste for the group in an indirect fashion. As scholar Kay Johnson points out, the *Register* correctly identified the Klan as " 'the leading issue in the election' but failed editorially to take a stand on the organization. A subtle indication of its preference, however, could be found in the juxtaposition of its lead article on the Des Moines Klan and the newspaper headline, 'MAdoo Assails Klan's Stand.' "[92]

Only one of the three Klan candidates won, but the *Register*'s antipathy for the organization was again subtle: in wishful tones, the paper overstated the election results, claiming that the returns represented a clear defeat for the Klan.[93] Later, the Klan suffered a major setback when its candidates lost a school board election in early 1926. With its power apparently waning, KKK members returned to more traditional activities—cross burnings, intimidation, and parades. At this point, Ingham changed his tune. He made a distinction between standing before the voters in elections and the Klan's usual operations. His previously subdued statements against the Klan gave way to sharp attacks.

He denounced the KKK for taking the law into its own hands: "History makes it plain as daylight that no society can be either safe or sound where justice is not administered in the orderly manner of a public tribunal."[94] Furthermore, the editor lectured his readers on the necessity of racial harmony: "A man who does not know that the races are all here and are all going to be here, and until their common rights are recognized there can be no peace and security for anyone, is not yet out of the international kindergarten."[95] By 1927, the Des Moines Klan was on its last legs, and Ingham's continued crusading for blacks was recognized when in 1929 he was named honorary president of the Des Moines NAACP.[96]

Women's Suffrage

The women's movement also benefited from the support of the liberal Ingham.[97] Nationally, the cause of women's suffrage had slowed by 1900. Already having the vote in Wyoming and Utah, women gained the franchise in Colorado and Idaho in the 1890s. Further progress was stymied until 1910, when Washington became the fifth state granting women the vote. From that point on, the movement gained strength. In Iowa, the 1913 election of Flora Dunlap, a social worker and friend of Jane Addams, to the presidency of the Iowa Equal Suffrage Association led Ingham and the *Register* to applaud: "In naming Miss Dunlap the woman suffrage movement of the state has taken a very important step toward realization of their hopes. The newly elected president combines with a tactful disposition and perfect poise and self control, a much more thorough knowledge of the practical phases of the woman problem than any woman could possibly have who had not been meeting the world on its practical side as Miss Dunlap has been meeting it."[98]

By 1915, six more states were admitting women to the polls, while in Iowa, the General Assembly approved—for the necessary second time—the women's suffrage amendment. The issue was to be put before male voters in June 1916. To show its support for the cause, the *Register and Leader* published a special 16-page Woman's Suffrage Edition on May 12, 1915. Written and edited by the Iowa Equal Suffrage Association in concert with the Votes for Women League of Des Moines, the paper provided a history of the suffrage movement, carried stories by and about leading women's rights advocates, and called for passage of the amendment in Iowa. In the introduction to the special paper, its editors said they hoped to "show by the variety of arguments and the personality and standing of their contributors that woman's suffrage is a live issue in Iowa: that progressive men and women of the state believe in suffrage and that every man and woman who believes in the future of the state and in the success of democracy should join the suffrage ranks."[99]

The same day the special issue was published, Ingham devoted editorial space to the women's cause in the regular edition of the *Register and Leader*: "It is not primarily a question of the ballot, it is not even a question of wise or right use of suffrage, it is not the immediate effect on government by the woman voter. It is a question of liberty as a foundation of all human relations." The editor went on to argue that since no "sex line" existed when it came to liberty, no line should exist at the polling place.[100]

In June 1916, male voters defeated the suffrage amendment, but Ingham and the *Register* continued to argue for its adoption. In April 1919, the state legislature passed presidential suffrage for women. Nearly a year later, Ingham continued to point out the lack of logic embodied in the measure: "Coming to America, we find nationwide presidential suffrage sprinting down the last lap, and we see in Iowa a situation which will allow women to vote for presidential electors next fall, but which will disallow voting by women in the state primaries this spring. What could be more indefensible than the granting of this kind of half-hearted political 'equality?' "[101]

Two months after Iowa granted presidential suffrage to its women, Congress approved the 19th Amendment, providing women the right to vote once it was ratified by three-quarters of the states. As the amendment closed in on the needed majority, Ingham acknowledged the difficulties the suffragists faced: "The women have themselves to thank for the ballot, their own persistency and leadership, and they know how hard it has been to persuade the party leaders on either side to do anything, and how reluctantly it was done even after the handwriting was on the wall."[102]

Internationalism

With the suffrage issue fading by 1919, the *Register*'s editorial page was dominated by Ingham's crusade for internationalism. When World War I began, Ingham had sounded like an isolationist. In August 1914, the editor referred to the war as a "cocaine fiend who runs amuck in the community" and heartily endorsed President Woodrow Wilson's policy of neutrality: "Now is the time to accept a bit of homely advice and tend to our [own] knitting." Nine months later, following the sinking of the *Lusitania,* the *Register and Leader* held to its position and cautioned its readers to stay out of the war zone: "There is but one place for Americans [during the war] and that is on the American side of the ocean." Even after Germany announced unrestricted submarine warfare in early 1917, Ingham still preached remaining aloof from the conflict: "There is, of course, tremendous sentiment in favor of making the cause of the Allies the American cause and joining the war. ... But the cool judgement of the people has been for neutrality and will continue to be for neutrality unless the Germans' assault on us is so plainly intentional as to force us into war." But he added: "The problem for America is not Germany and German motives, it is putting America in a position when the time comes to exert the greatest influence possible on world readjustment." Belligerency, Ingham feared, might hinder America's opportunity to shape the postwar world.[103]

But in March 1917, following the announcement of the Zimmermann telegram and the German sinking of three American ships, Ingham acquiesced to the idea of American entry into the war. On April 7, 1917, the day after Congress declared war on Germany, Ingham wrote: "The time for internationalism has come, and the U.S. might as well recognize now as later that our fortunes are tied up with the fortunes of the other democracies of the world."[104]

Thereafter, Ingham consistently supported an internationalism foreign policy. Contrary to popular belief, the *Register* was not an anomaly championing such a perspective in a sea of midwestern isolationism. Despite the long-standing myth, the Midwest was not a bastion of post–World War I isolationist sentiment. Indeed, many other regional papers backed internationalism.[105] Ingham's position became clear in his endorsement of Wilson's "14 Points" speech in January 1918 that outlined a sound basis for postwar peace. On November 11, when the war came to an end, Ingham referred to Wilson's League of Nations as "practical internationalism" designed to "protect the legitimate rights of nations." For the remainder of the year, the *Register* was one of Wilson's biggest supporters, cheering him as he left for the Paris Peace Conference.[106]

By the spring of 1919, U.S. Senate opposition to Wilson's League of Nations was growing because of a perceived threat to American sovereignty. The major area of contention was Article 10 of the League Covenant. In essence, it stated that the League of Nations would protect all member nations against aggression with force if necessary. To some members of the Senate, that was tantamount to surrendering control over the American military to the international body. But the *Register* remained confident that, while amendments might be added, the League would be ratified.[107] As summer neared, Ingham's editorials became more adamant and even prophetic:

> There can't be a balance of power without America. No matter what America does or says the balance will include her. ... The fact is European power no longer dominates the world. Asiatic power is a factor. American power is the greatest factor of all. We cannot change that by denying it. ... There is no hope for America in telling the rest of the world to organize for war or peace as they chose and to count us out. ... If she [America] doesn't want to be called upon time and again to put out fires, she has got to see that fires don't start.[108]

In order to get around Henry Cabot Lodge, the chief opponent of the League and head of the Senate Foreign Relations Committee, President Wilson chose to take his case to the people. In the fall of 1919, Wilson embarked on a whistle-stop tour across the country to rally support for the League. Exhausted by the rigorous trip, Wilson collapsed in Colorado and returned to Washington, where he suffered a massive stroke. As the treaty neared a vote in the Senate, the *Register* argued forcefully that the treaty—with reservations added by the Senate—was like an insurance policy whose promises were actually made void by the fine print. "The United States will appear contemptible in the eyes of the world if it apparently agrees to the covenant of Paris in the words in which it is written, and then tries to avoid the liability by crossing its fingers when it signs."[109]

When the treaty came up for a consideration in November 1919, Wilson ordered all Democrats to reject the treaty with any reservations. The Senate then voted on the treaty twice, once on a version with reservations and once without. Both times the treaty went down in defeat. In March 1920, the Senate rejected the treaty again. Disgusted at the result, the *Register* blamed the Senate for the treaty's failure and suggested its motive was to "get even with the president."[110] Clearly, however, Ingham and the paper were biased by their early support for Wilson's internationalist vision. Although the Senate and political partisanship certainly deserves part of the blame, Wilson, given his conceit and inability to compromise, must bear responsibility for the treaty's failure as well. Diplomatic historian Thomas Paterson suggests the League's defeat was caused by a more fundamental rift between the League's ideas of collective security and unilateral action: "In essence, then, traditional American nationalism and nonalignment ... decided the debate against Wilson."[111]

Stung by the League's defeat, Ingham continued to crusade for an internationalist foreign policy. Considering possible presidential candidates early in 1920, the *Register* suggested Herbert Hoover because, among other things, he believed in sustaining American world leadership. For similar reasons, Ingham opposed Senator Hiram Johnson of California: "Do the Republicans wish to enter the campaign with a platform definitely declaring against the League of Nations?" When Warren G. Harding, who waffled on the League of Nations issue and pledged a "return to normalcy," received the Republican nomination for president, Ingham and Cowles for the first time refused to support a GOP presidential candidate.[112]

Once elected, President Harding showed little interest in foreign policy, but Ingham had high hopes for the secretary of state, Charles Evans Hughes. The secretary invited major naval powers to a disarmament conference in Washington in November 1921. Here Hughes proposed that the world's three largest navies—those of Britain, the United States, and Japan—scrap nearly 75 naval vessels, sign a naval limitation pact, and agree to a tonnage ratio for capital ships. Seeing the plan as a step toward assuming international leadership, Ingham wrote: "One of the chief gains made by Secretary Hughes' bold announcement of America's radical proposals for armaments reductions is that it immediately challenges the attention and wins the backing of the American public."[113]

The conference ended in February 1922 with diplomats putting together two treaties that incorporated most of Hughes' roposals. The internationalist-minded editor cheered the outcome as marking "the turning of the way in our American relations to the world. They break the precedent of isolation." Encouraged, he argued for still more international involvement: "Does it not come home to everybody as striking that the further we go for world organization the more persistent the other nations are for the league of nations? Why should they have so much confidence in what was done at Paris and we so little? Is it not about time for us to drop the divisions of our domestic policies and take inventory of the league, and ask ourselves seriously what machinery the world is likely to set up that will better work [toward] the ends we have sought in the Washington Conference?"[114]

The Senate ratified the naval treaties, and the United States became more active in the international arena. The Dawes Plan, enacted in 1924, provided loans to Germany to assist in the payment of reparation debts. Ingham, however, remained troubled by America's isolationist stance, and he continued to argue for greater engagement. In 1924, he predicted: "We are either going to accept leadership of those who believe in a league of nations or we are going to get ready for a bigger war than the world has ever known."[115] Ingham was prescient, but few politicians heeded his warnings.

Publishing Powerhouse

After purchasing the paper in 1903, Cowles and Ingham reversed the fortunes of their small, ailing paper and created a publishing powerhouse that far exceeded the modest achievements of the Clarksons. By 1924 the company had absorbed all but one daily newspaper in Des Moines, and with the *Register's* ever-growing circulation throughout Iowa, it was fast becoming a statewide institution. The success of these years was the result of Cowles' sound management, his genius for circulation, his ability to hire talented individuals and give them latitude to work, and his willingness to innovate. Meanwhile, Ingham vastly improved the news product. He and his staff expanded the paper's all-Iowa coverage, moved it away from a highly partisan past toward a more independent political stance, stressed the separation of news and opinion, and added a number of features to differentiate the *Register* from its competition.

By the mid-1920s, both Cowles and Ingham were in their early 60s, and management succession was a pressing issue that required attention. The two men remained in charge of the paper for several more years and then relinquished control to the next generation. Cowles' sons, John and Mike, and two new editors, William W. Waymack and Basil "Stuffy" Walters, became the new management team. Following the example of Cowles and Ingham, they continued to flourish by preserving past successes and embracing innovation.

Register and Leader Building at Fourth Street and Court Avenue, Des Moines, ca. 1905. *Courtesy of the State Historical Society of Iowa, Des Moines.*

Chicago and Northwestern train at Des Moines depot, ca. 1906. Gardner Cowles used the railroads to distribute his papers throughout the state. *Courtesy of the State Historical Society of Iowa, Des Moines.*

Cartoonist Jay N. "Ding" Darling, ca. 1918. *Courtesy of the John Cowles Collection, Cowles Library, Drake University, Des Moines.*

CHAPTER 5

The Cowles Brothers Take the Reins

1925–1939

Under the business leadership of John and Mike Cowles and new editorial heads William Waymack and Basil "Stuffy" Walters, the Register and Tribune expanded during the 1920s. Despite the Great Depression, company profits grew throughout the 1930s. Circulation of the Sunday *Register*, for instance, increased from 146,751 in 1925 to 368,487 in 1939; meanwhile, net revenue more than doubled, rising from $483,000 to

Des Moines Register and Tribune airplane, the *Good News II*, ca. 1930. *Courtesy of the State Historical Society of Iowa, Des Moines.*

$932,600.[1] The firm's continued success resulted from a two-pronged strategy of building on the winning formula of Gardner Cowles and Harvey Ingham while at the same time adopting new ideas. The brothers' achievements in Des Moines led to a search beyond the R&T for other undertakings.

A growing circulation base remained the key ingredient. Rising circulation revenue, in fact, played a significant role in sustaining the paper during the depression years. Like other American newspapers, the *Register* worked to attract new readers by expanding its already popular features. Its sports section, headed by editor Garner "Sec" Taylor, was enlarged. Under new farm editor J. S. Russell, an agricultural page graced the paper twice a week rather than once. With the purchase of the *Capital* in 1927, the R&T obtained still more readers and pressed forward its drive to eliminate local competition in the Des Moines market.

Beyond following tried-and-true strategies, the Cowles brothers further modernized the paper, often applying and adopting the latest technology. They ventured into the radio business, made use of readership studies, and pioneered the area of photojournalism; in the late 1920s, they acquired their first airplane to facilitate statewide news coverage. Sometimes the successful strategies of other news organizations were adopted by the R&T. The company, for instance, set up a syndicate to sell stories and cartoons and established its own Washington news bureau. Innovation was not confined to the editorial side of the operation, however. The circulation department also continued to perfect its operations. In the midst of the depression, it introduced a weekly payment plan, added a creative, cost-cutting technique for distributing the *Register* to small towns, and started an annual carrier convention.

The paper's editorial positions, meanwhile, remained much the same. The *Register* usually backed Republican politicians and continued to support an internationalist foreign policy. From the mid-1920s through the 1930s, the paper devoted a growing amount of editorial space to the plight of the nation's farmers and applauded the efforts of the federal government to assist them. The depression was given widespread coverage, and President Herbert Hoover, a Republican and an Iowan, received favorable comment from the editorial pages. Following Franklin Roosevelt's 1932 presidential victory, the *Register* initially gave him high marks. After the brief honeymoon, however, the paper turned against Roosevelt and his New Deal, but it remained supportive of FDR's moves toward greater international involvement.

By the 1930s, the R&T's continuing success led the Cowles brothers to seek new journalistic challenges. With profits from their Des Moines enterprises, John and Mike chose to enter the newspaper business in neighboring

Minnesota. In 1935, the family purchased the ailing evening daily, the *Minneapolis Star.* The brothers successfully turned it around by using many of the same techniques already employed in Des Moines. They bought up competing papers and built circulation by solicitation and acquisition. Within six years, the Cowles' operation had attained a monopoly in the Minneapolis newspaper market.

In a second innovative thrust, the brothers ventured into a new sector of print media—the nationally distributed picture magazine. Mike made use of his interest in photographs and his experience with the *Register*'s rotogravure section to launch the nationwide *Look* magazine in 1937. *Life,* and then several months later *Look,* took advantage of the rising popularity of photojournalism in newspapers and adapted the concept to the magazine format. The early success of both these pioneer publications led to a series of imitators, including such magazines as *Click, Pic,* and *See.*

By the end of the 1930s, John and Mike Cowles had not only expanded the family's newspaper business in Des Moines, they had also laid the groundwork for a nascent media empire. Arthur Gormley, R&T business manager from the mid-1930s through 1960, explained their role: "Gardner Cowles built a solid newspaper foundation, but he was fortunate to have his sons coming up. ... The old gentleman and Harvey [Ingham]were good, but the boys gave the paper[s] a push that kept them going upward."[2] Although the brothers' next moves remained unclear, their impressive achievements and bright futures were heralded in the contemporary press. In 1935, for example, *Time* magazine ranked John and Mike with some of the leading figures in publishing: "With 30 years of actively publishing ahead of them, with William Randolph Hearst settling into old age, with Scripps & Howard in their prime, the youthful Brothers Cowles of Iowa may yet step out as one of the great chain newspapers publishers of tomorrow."[3]

Changing of the Guard

During the late 1920s, a changing of the guard occurred at the Register and Tribune. After spending more than 20 years building the newspaper, Gardner Cowles and Harvey Ingham decided to step down in favor of the next generation. On the publishing side, the mantle was passed to Cowles' two youngest children, John and Mike.[4] Both literally grew up with the newspaper and apparently did not consider any career options other than going into their father's business.

John, the elder of the two brothers, was born in Algona, Iowa, on December 14, 1898. He was nearly five years old when his father bought a controlling interest in the *Register and Leader* and moved the family to Des Moines. As a youngster, John's summers and Sunday mornings were consumed working at the Register building sorting mail and counting the number of new subscriptions. Later, as a prep school student, he spent hours of his vacations at the newspaper, and much like his father, he constantly asked questions: "Home on holiday from Phillips Exeter ... small John would often go with his father to the ... office, perch himself on the desk of his father's secretary, Agnes MacDonald, [and] spout a stream of questions: What does so & so do? Is he smart? ... What's that voucher for? ... Why is there a two per cent discount marked on it? ... How much does newsprint cost? ... How fast can the presses turn out 1,000 [newspapers]?"[5]

Graduating from Phillips Exeter with honors in 1917, John enrolled in Harvard. After his college career was interrupted by a brief period of army service during World War I, John completed his bachelor's degree in three rather than four years. In addition to graduating cum laude, he became the first undergraduate to serve as an editor of all three campus publications—the *Crimson,* the *Lampoon,* and the *Advocate.* Following a grand tour of Europe, John returned to Des Moines in 1921 to take a job as a reporter for the R&T. His first assignment was covering a session of the Iowa Legislature. A stint as a business reporter followed. From there, John's rise at the paper was nothing short of meteoric; within three years of his arrival, he was named vice president, general manager, and associate publisher. His work at the R&T soon captured the attention of others in journalism, and John's advance in the industry's professional associations was equally impressive. From 1929 to 1933, John was a director of the national Audit Bureau of Circulation. Meanwhile, he was elected a vice president of the Associated Press organization and served as a member of its board of directors from 1934 to 1943.[6]

John's younger brother, Mike, was also eager to work at the *Register.* Born January 31, 1903, he was named Gardner Cowles Jr. A day or two after the birth, however, his father looked at his newborn son and said: "He looks like an Irishman. Let's call him Mike."[7] The nickname stuck and remained with him the rest of his life. Young Mike was soon following in his brother's footsteps. Endless hours of his childhood were spent at the Register building. Looking back on these years, Mike remembered: "When I was only five, I used to watch the activities in the newspaper's cashier cage. Employees were then paid with metal coins. ... My father, who made up the payroll used to put the money in manila envelopes." Three years later, at age eight, he was proofreading newspaper editorials and earning 25 cents apiece.[8]

Like his brother John, Mike attended Phillips Exeter and went on to Harvard (where he also served as editor of the *Crimson*). During college, he spent summer vacations back in Des Moines working as an R&T reporter. He completed his degree a semester early and then, disregarding his mother's advice of continuing his education at Oxford, Cambridge, or the London School of Economics, he joined the staff of the family's *Tribune* in 1925. Mike subsequently switched to the *Register.* One of Mike's first assignments was covering the Iowa Legislature's efforts—which were strongly supported by the *Register*—to improve the state's system of roads. Finally, much like his older brother, Mike was not at the paper long before he began moving up through the ranks. From reporter, he advanced to city editor, assistant managing editor, executive editor, and then vice president and associate publisher.[9]

Together, John and Mike shared ambition, energy, and a passion for journalism. The brothers remained best friends throughout their lifetimes, and according to John, their views were "98 percent identical on any major subject."[10] In other ways, however, they were different. John proved to be a fine reporter—of particular note was the 14-part series he wrote describing his firsthand look at revolutionary Russia in 1923—but his real talents were on the management side of the business. His intellect led the *New York Herald Tribune* to describe him as "an egghead—and about as sharp as a razor." Much like his father, John was a conscientious, detail-oriented manager who demanded to be kept informed about the smallest elements of the enterprise. His wide-ranging knowledge of all the aspects of the newspaper business led one executive to remark, "He probably knows more details about every operation, right down the line, than the men doing the jobs."[11]

Mike's personality, interests, and skills complemented those of his brother. "Breezier [and] more imaginative than Brother John," Mike was more of a visionary and promoter. He was sometimes flamboyant and much more of a risk taker than his elder brother. Innovative ideas, for example, were more likely to come from Mike, while John acted as a stabilizing force. As John became ensconced in his father's old business office on the first floor of the R&T building, Mike, who was a good writer and reporter, chose to move up the ladder on the editorial side. He had an office overlooking the second-floor newsroom.[12] Although nepotism had clearly played a role in getting John and Mike into the family business, they soon distinguished themselves. Together the brothers took the company to new heights.

With John and then Mike assuming leadership roles at the R&T, Gardner Cowles began spending more time away from the paper. Although he kept in close touch with Des Moines, by the mid-1920s, Gardner and wife Florence were wintering in Phoenix and took extended vacations to exotic locales such as Egypt and the Far East. Confident in both his sons and the fine staff, Cowles accepted a presidential appointment from Herbert Hoover to serve on the Board of Directors of the Reconstruction Finance Corporation (RFC) in July 1932. Cowles remained at the RFC until April 1933.[13]

Meanwhile, back in Des Moines, the Cowles brothers relied heavily on the services of two important editors, William Waymack and Basil Walters. Following graduation from Morningside College in Sioux City, Iowa, Waymack became a reporter for the *Sioux City Journal* in 1911. Over the next seven years, he was promoted to city editor and then chief editorial writer. In 1918, Waymack joined the R&T as associate editor and editorial writer; by 1921, he was managing editor. He served in that position until 1931, when Ingham stepped aside and Waymack assumed full responsibility for the editorial pages. Under his guidance, the *Register*'s editorial pages continued in the progressive tradition established by Ingham. According to Waymack, the editorial page was supposed to help the public "see things whole." To that end, in addition to offering the *Register*'s opinions, Waymack expanded the editorial page to include columns presenting a variety of viewpoints. Essays by prominent writers such as Walter Lippmann, Jay Franklin, Ernest Lindley, Frank Kent, Mark Sullivan, David Lawrence, and Dorothy Thompson appeared regularly. In addition to furnishing the views of others, Waymack was awarded the paper's second Pulitzer Prize in 1938 for his own editorial writing the previous year. Ingham, meanwhile, was not ready to retire completely; he continued writing a signed column on the editorial page for 12 more years and retained the title of editor until 1943.[14]

Regarded as tough-minded but fair, Waymack elaborated further the paper's editorial mission laid down by Ingham in 1902. Calling his principles "The Three Commandments Guiding the *Des Moines Register* and *Tribune*," Waymack wrote:

1. We believe in presenting ALL the news impartially and objectively in the news columns.
2. We believe in expressing our own opinions as persuasively and forcefully as possible, but confining those expressions to the editorial pages.
3. We believe in giving our readers the opinions of other competent writers presenting ALL SIDES of important controversial issues in order that our readers may form their own judgments.[15]

Waymack's words soon graced a plaque hung in the R&T building and over the years appeared in a number of advertisements for the paper. The Three Commandments remained a guiding force at the R&T long after Waymack left in 1946 to accept an appointment to the new Atomic Energy Commission.[16]

While Waymack was making his mark on the editorial page, Basil "Stuffy"

Walters was making his presence felt in the newsroom. He had been called Stuffy since childhood because his baseball skills were reminiscent of Boston outfielder Stuffy McInnis. With a short and stout physique, Walters was "nearly as round as he was tall," and the nickname Stuffy fit him perfectly.[17] He attended Indiana University, but military service in World War I intervened, and he never finished college. Breaking into journalism at the *Indianapolis Star*, Walters in 1921 moved to the *Milwaukee Journal*, where he served as telegraph editor. In 1928, Mike Cowles brought the 32-year-old Walters to Des Moines as news editor of the *Tribune*. Three years later, Stuffy was managing editor of both the *Register* and the *Tribune*. Although not known for his own writing, Stuffy was a renowned editor. Because he believed that people had short attention spans, Walters stressed "crisp writing, short sentences, and snappy page layouts that commanded readers' attention."[18]

Expanding Readership

In the midst of these years of leadership transition, the R&T moved to expand readership by improving its various departments. John and Mike both took an interest in the sports page. Sports coverage in large metropolitan dailies had become a fixture by the beginning of the 20th century. The *Register and Leader* decided to add its first sports editor. Garner W. "Sec" Taylor was hired to cover sports as well as affairs at the Iowa Statehouse. Taylor took the job on the condition that he cover sports exclusively, and along with Jack North, sports editor of the *Tribune*, they made up the entire sports department. By the 1920s, the hardworking Taylor had developed a national reputation for baseball and boxing coverage.[19]

As interest in college and professional sports boomed following World War I, newspapers came to see sports news as a "'safe' means of exciting and holding reader interest."[20] John and Mike Cowles were both avid sports fans, and arriving at the same conclusion, they moved to beef up the R&T sports page. With the growing popularity of sports columns across the nation, John pushed Taylor to start his own column. Titled "Sittin' In with the Athletes," Taylor's column first appeared in February 1926. Meanwhile, the Sunday sports section, which, to make it stand out, had been printed on green paper since 1922, was expanded to eight pages in September 1925. The "famous Green Sports Section" (which, several years later, printed on light-orange paper, would become the "Big Peach") of the Sunday *Register* proved to be a real circulation builder. In April 1926, the brothers expanded the daily dose of sports coverage and, to attract readers' attention, the new daily section was printed on pink paper.[21]

Changes were also made in the *Register*'s coverage of agriculture. Although the paper provided a page of farming news once a week, Gardner Cowles pushed for an even greater focus on agriculture. J. S. Russell was hired in 1925 to edit the paper's farm section on the condition that the job would only become permanent if he "could deliver."[22] A 1913 Grinnell College graduate, Russell had farmed near Newton (a town 30 miles east of Des Moines) before shifting careers and becoming the co-publisher of the weekly *Sac City Bulletin* (located in a town 130 miles northeast of Des Moines). Soon after Russell joined the R&T, the paper's agricultural coverage, "Iowa Farm Register," began running in the *Register* twice a week rather than on Saturday only. In addition to more news, farm page layouts became more eye-catching through an increasing use of photographs.

When the new farm page format was introduced, the *Register* announced it would not try to "teach farmers to farm." Rather, it pledged to present "unbiased news about farming and farmers, and their ideas and methods." Russell's reporting lived up to the paper's promises and surpassed Cowles' expectations: his hands-on knowledge of farming gave him an understanding of and sympathy for the subject. Led by Russell, who became one of the nation's leading farm editors, the *Register* "treated all news about agricultural problems as the biggest possible news for Iowans." This type of coverage successfully catered to the large rural readership.[23]

Additional efforts to win readers included improving other favorite *Register* offerings and buying out the last remaining competition in Des Moines. A full page of comics became a daily staple in 1926. To accommodate this addition, features such as "Health and Diet" or "Beauty Chat" that had previously shared the cartoon section were moved to a "Double Women's Page."[24] The following year, John Cowles completed the effort begun by his father to monopolize the Des Moines newspaper market. When the two major department stores in the city, Harris-Emery and Younkers, merged, advertising revenue in local newspapers fell significantly. Given the revenue loss, Lafayette Young Jr., publisher of the afternoon *Capital,* proposed consolidating his property with the *Register.* With Gardner Cowles on a cruise to the Far East, John Cowles conducted the negotiations. When the deal was signed in February 1927, the R&T paid Young $552,200 for the *Capital,* which was then merged with the R&T's *Tribune.*[25]

With the R&T's acquisition of the *Capital,* Des Moines joined a select group of only six cities—the others being New Bedford and Springfield, Massachusetts; Duluth, Minnesota; Wilmington, Delaware; and Charleston, South Carolina—in which one company owned all the dailies published.[26] Much like the other newspaper companies that held monopolies, the Register and Tribune made a special effort to provide "fair and full news service." Following the purchase of the *Capital,* Ingham noted, "We must now be far more careful than ever before to give both sides of all questions; we are our own competition." Indeed, that soon became the case, as a rivalry between the news staffs of the morning and evening papers developed. Further, to avoid criticism of biased coverage, the R&T created an internal Bureau of Accuracy and Fair Play. Fred Pownall, former editor of the *Capital,* was selected to head it. The bureau quickly blunted attacks by adroitly handling complaints about advertising, news coverage, and subscription problems.[27]

This merger and management's efforts to make the paper more reader-friendly proved successful. Combined morning and evening circulation grew from 170,131 in 1925 to 234,323 in 1928. Advertising revenue rose 50 percent, while total net profit nearly doubled, moving from $483,542 to $918,035. The profit margin on newspaper operations rose from 13.5 percent to 18.7 percent, and healthy dividends, which had been paid since 1906, continued.[28] But the Cowles brothers were not content to sit back and merely reap the rewards of their family business. They continued working to upgrade their news product and expand the company's horizons. As a 1936 *Register* advertisement explained, "The Register and Tribune [managers and editors] for a generation have realized that newspapers ... never stand still. If the service they render their readers is constantly improved, the newspapers gain."[29]

A New Medium

Even before the Cowles brothers joined the R&T, people across the nation were fascinated by the marvels of a new medium—radio. By the early 1920s, interest in this new technology had reached fad proportions. The *Review of Reviews,* for instance, observed: "The rapidity with which the thing [radio] has spread has possibly not been equaled in all the centuries of human progress. Never in the history of electricity has an invention so gripped the popular fancy." Similarly, the *New York Times* described the craze: "In 12 months radio phoning has become the most popular amusement in America. If every boy does not possess a receiving outfit, it is because he lacks either the imagination or money. ... In every neighborhood people are stringing wires to catch the ether wave currents."[30] Like a handful of other newspaper companies, the Register and Tribune Company was drawn to the early potential of radio as a mechanism for expanding the news audience and hence increasing circulation. In 1920, the *Detroit News* became the first newspaper to establish a radio station. Several others soon followed. As of May 1922, there were 11 newspaper-owned radio stations in the country; by the end of the year, there were 69.[31]

In the spring of 1922, the R&T launched its own radio station, WJB (the call letters were soon changed to WGF). On March 10, the maiden broadcast opened with an address by Iowa Governor Nathan E. Kendall, who "stepped up to the 'receiving horn' of the five-watt transmitter on the 13th floor of the Register and Tribune building and told those listening that 'We live in a mighty age, but the age which follows will be mightier still.' " An estimated audience of 10,000—many of whom listened on radios in stores and theaters—heard the governor's speech and the live music that followed. The station was on the air every Friday evening from 7:30 to 9:00. Its original 5-watt transmitter could reach listeners in 30 states; by November 1922, the transmitter's power was increased to 100 watts, and the station could be heard "by ships on both oceans."[32]

Like other radio stations owned by newspapers, WGF was created for the purpose of promoting the company's papers and their circulations, and it did not sell advertising spots. That, of course, meant that all broadcasting costs were borne entirely by the parent newspaper firms. With mounting expenses—in 1922, for example, a 100-watt transmitter cost approximately $8,500—and the difficulty of measuring the benefits accrued by their radio properties, newspapers began to reassess their broadcasting interests. Upon reflection, R&T management decided to pull the plug on WGF, apparently because there was little evidence to suggest it generated greater newspaper circulation or increased advertising revenue. The station was suspended just 18 months after its first broadcast. Clearly, the Register and Tribune was not alone in getting out of the radio business. Along with WGF, 93 other stations, or 14 percent of all stations operating across the nation, ceased broadcasting in 1923.[33]

Over the next few years, the radio industry matured, commercial networks were developed, and a growing number of Iowans owned radios. By 1931, 48.6 percent of Iowa families had a radio, while in Des Moines, the number was 51.4 percent.[34] Given these changes, the Cowles brothers moved the firm back into the radio business. The R&T created the subsidiary Iowa Broadcasting Company to operate new radio properties. Initially headed by Mike Cowles, it purchased three Iowa radio stations in the spring and summer of 1931: KWCR (Cedar Rapids), KSO (Clarinda), and WIAS (Ottumwa). In November of the following year, KSO was moved to Des Moines. Its studio, "the most complete and modern of any radio station west of Chicago," occupied the entire 13th floor of the Register building. The new Des Moines station was affiliated with the blue network of the National Broadcasting Company (NBC), and it was on the air weekdays from 6:30 a.m. to midnight and Sunday from 7 a.m. to midnight. Although the broadcasting division lost money for the first three years, the brothers remained sanguine about the future of radio.[35]

After closing WIAS in February 1934, Iowa Broadcasting purchased WMT in Waterloo that fall. The following spring, two of the company's stations were moved. To bring the last remaining network, the Columbia Broadcasting System (CBS) to Des Moines, Mike moved KWCR from Cedar Rapids to the capital city and renamed it KRNT (the new call letters were in honor of the parent company, the R&T).[36] With twice the power of KSO, the Register's second Des Moines station shared the expanded studio and office facilities atop the R&T building. But, so as not to lose out on the growing radio market in east-central Iowa, WMT was moved to Cedar Rapids. By 1935, their radio holdings had expanded to the point where the attention of a full-time manager was needed. Mike Cowles stepped aside as head of Iowa Broadcasting in favor of Luther L. Hill. A longtime family friend of the Cowleses, Hill was an affable and competent manager. After beginning a career in the military, he established a successful brokerage house in Des Moines (until the depression) and then went on to work for the Reconstruction Finance Corporation (RFC) in the early 1930s. But there was another reason Hill was hired: he was the brother of Joseph Lister Hill, then a congressman and later a U.S. senator from Alabama. Given the many problems broadcast properties might encounter with the Federal Communications Commission (FCC), Mike Cowles considered friends such as Lister Hill on Capitol Hill a huge asset.[37]

Under the new manager, the Register's radio holdings expanded in 1938 with the purchase of WNAX in Yankton, South Dakota. Meanwhile, Iowa Broadcasting enjoyed its first profits in 1934. From that point on, the subsidiary remained a solid profit center. Net return on investment, for instance, rose from only 3 percent in 1934 to 19 percent in 1939.[38]

Changes in Content and Layout

Even before Mike Cowles became involved with R&T radio properties, he employed an innovative technique to analyze the *Register*'s readability. In 1928, while Mike was teaching a journalism class at the University of Iowa in Iowa City, 100 miles east of Des Moines, he met graduate student George Gallup. Several years earlier, Gallup's research in the scientific measurement of reader interest in news stories had caught the attention of the Cowles brothers. Mike was so intrigued by Gallup's dissertation on newspaper readership studies that he persuaded the doctoral candidate to come to Des

Moines and head up Drake University's new department of journalism. As part of the deal, Gallup was allowed to attend all R&T staff meetings and send his students to the newspaper for hands-on work experience. While serving as the sole member of Drake's journalism department from 1929 to 1931, Gallup spent his summers conducting some of the nation's first readership surveys at the *Register* and *Tribune,* trying to identify which stories had the greatest appeal.[39]

The studies' findings led to significant changes in the *Register*'s and *Tribune*'s content and layout. First, Gallup's surveys found that the *Register*'s lead stories, usually national or international in content, were the poorest-read articles in the paper. Furthermore, readers often did not understand all the words used in the paper's banner headlines. Rather, Gallup contended, readers preferred local and state news written in simple language. Finally, the scholar discovered that newspaper stories accompanied by pictures or graphics received the highest readership. These assertions did not sit well with Stuffy Walters, who hotly contested their validity. To prove the young Ph.D. wrong, Walters and several editors took Gallup across the street to a local restaurant; there they asked diners to define words in banner headlines. Much to Walters' surprise, the restaurant patrons confirmed that Gallup was correct. This research "helped revolutionize the techniques Walters used to edit the *Register* and *Tribune.*" Once influenced by Gallup, the managing editor told reporters "to write their stories in the same way they would tell their story to a friend. First person was used when it added anything to the story."[40]

Photojournalism

Gallup's studies also found that readers preferred stories supplemented with photographs. In addition, in sections with several photographs and little copy, readers favored pictures that were connected in a series, compared to groups of photos on unrelated topics. Gallup had confirmed the popularity of the photographs that Mike Cowles and rotogravure editor Vernon Pope were already running in the Sunday paper. It also encouraged Cowles to set up a group under Pope to experiment with the idea of telling a story through a sequence of pictures. These "pictures stories" tested well in the Sunday *Register*'s rotogravure section, and Sunday circulation increased from 312,072 in 1930 to 333,125 in 1937.[41] Now knowing the power of pictures, the paper ran a series of advertisements that stressed its frequent use of photographs. In January 1930, for instance, the *Register* boasted it had "a million pictures on file." It then explained: "Only large metropolitan newspapers like The Register can afford to assemble and keep up to date such an enormous file of pictures. Pictures are easy to read. They tell the story at a glance.

Because the world's news in The Register is so fully illustrated each day, you will want it during the coming year."[42]

The *Register* gave photojournalism another boost when in 1934 Stuffy Walters and R&T photographer George Yates were examining a series of photos depicting the assassination of King Alexander of Yugoslavia. When Walters asked Yates if he could take similar play-by-play pictures, the photographer observed that the photos out of Europe were produced with a newsreel camera—which explained the blurred quality of the photographs—not a still camera. Such a rapid-fire still camera with fast shutter speed did not yet exist, therefore Yates told Walters he could not capture comparable photos because "I couldn't have changed the plates fast enough." Several weeks after this discussion, Yates developed what was later called the "machine gun camera" with an extremely fast shutter. The innovative camera could frame 16 shots per second.[43]

With the new camera available, Yates saw tremendous possibilities, especially for sports photography. He boasted, "Now we'll be able to show the way a winning play puts the ball over the goal line, motion by motion. Sports fans can see the interference clearing the roads, tackles missing by a hair, the ball sailing through the air from one gridster to anther." Amid much fanfare in the *Register* and *Tribune,* pictures from the "machine gun" debuted during the 1935 football season. The camera's pictures surpassed the photographer's highest hopes, and continuity or sequence pictures were soon widely used in sports coverage. Readers of the Sunday morning sports section were thrilled with the advent of these action pictures.[44]

Several years earlier, based on John Cowles' initial proposal, the R&T became one of the first newspapers in the nation to own a plane when it purchased a Fairchild FC-2 in 1928. A statewide contest to name the plane produced *Good News,* the first of 11 planes to be owned by the firm. With full-time pilot Charles Gatschet at the controls, the plane was initially used for publicity; it made a number of promotional flights putting in appearances at events such as county fairs and festivals. Soon, however, the *Good News* was shuttling reporters and photographers to events and breaking stories in all corners of the state. Equipped to carry four passengers in addition to the pilot, the plane had a circular trapdoor for vertical aerial photography and a darkroom to develop pictures in flight. After 1934, the *Good News,* in concert with the unique camera, vaulted the *Register* and *Tribune* to national prominence in the early days of photojournalism.[45]

With the R&T becoming increasingly interested in the use of photographs, management jumped at the opportunity to join 23 other papers as the first in the country to receive the wirephoto service of The Associated Press. The technology transmitted photographs via electrical signals over first telegraph and later telephone lines. "Hailed as one of the most revolutionary inventions in newspaper history," according to a pamphlet for *Register* employees, wirephoto service began on January 1, 1935. As part of the new AP network, the *Register* and *Tribune*'s newsroom received pictures from around the world in as little as eight minutes. Over the next few years, the AP wirephoto service provided the R&T between 50 and 60 photos a day. Among the initial group to obtain wirephoto nationally, the papers were the first to have the service in Iowa.[46]

Syndication

Sometimes copying the moves of other newspapers paid off as well. In 1922, just a year after he joined the staff of the R&T, John Cowles made an important decision. Following other dailies, such as the *Chicago Tribune,* he launched the Register and Tribune Syndicate. It was designed to sell news stories, serialized fiction and nonfiction, cartoons, and photographs to other newspapers worldwide. This division received nationwide attention in 1933, when it offered an adaptation of Laurence Stallings' *The First World War,* which included a moving series of photographs. The success of the Stallings' piece led to other popular picture features, such as "Hollywood Uncensored" and the "Life of Shirley Temple." By 1935, the syndicate's features were carried in 453 newspapers in 44 states and 10 foreign countries. Besides bringing prestige to the R&T, the syndicate proved a moneymaking operation from the beginning. "At its peak, the syndicate offered 60 to 75 features—including such comics and cartoons as 'The Family Circus' and 'Spiderman' and commentaries by David Horowitz, Stanley Karnow, political cartoonist Herblock and others."[47]

Washington Bureau

By 1933, Mike Cowles and Stuffy Walters thought another addition was necessary. The onset of the Great Depression in 1930 suggested that the federal government's role in people's everyday lives was likely to grow. With the election of Franklin Delano Roosevelt and the coming of the New Deal, events in Washington became much more important to all Americans. As Walters noted, Iowa was "no longer being run out of the Statehouse but out of Washington."[48] In a year where the circulation of the Sunday *Register* fell by 9,000 and talk of belt tightening was pervasive, Mike Cowles, a gambler by nature, chose to expand the paper's operations.[49] In September 1933, the R&T initiated a Washington Bureau and sent a city editor, 28-year-old Richard Wilson, to act as correspondent. The *Register* explained the creation of the Washington Bureau: "In recognition of the tremendous importance of Washington news to the people of Iowa in this extraordinary period ... the Register and Tribune have expanded ... to cover Washington news from the Iowa angle."[50] This explanation placed the bureau squarely in the journalistic tradition of the *Register*: providing coverage of the nation for its readers through the prism of Iowans' concerns.

According to Kenneth MacDonald, a former classmate of Wilson's at the University of Iowa and then news editor of the *Register*: "His [Wilson's] going to Washington for us was one of the crucial moves we made in those days. It was a sign to our readers and the rest of the staff that the paper was going someplace."[51] Once in the capital, Wilson's aim was to cultivate two new sources and write two stories daily—one presenting an Iowa angle and one of national importance. Often, his reports blended both perspectives. Some of Wilson's first stories, for example, dealt with agricultural developments and New Deal farm policies. Publicly reserved, Wilson's first sources in Washington were Iowans—James LeCron, a son-in-law of Gardner Cowles and former *Register* editorial writer, who worked for the Department of Agriculture; Harry Hopkins, close advisor to FDR and soon-to-be head of the Works Progress Administration (WPA); and Secretary of Agriculture Henry Wallace, with whom Wilson regularly played tennis.[52]

Within months of moving to Washington, Wilson was beating the wire services to exclusive stories. His work soon led President Roosevelt to refer to Wilson as "one of the four best reporters in Washington." Although he disregarded the president's compliment as "standard Washington persiflage," readers of the Sunday *Register* apparently agreed. In March 1934, just six months after founding the Washington Bureau, the R&T circulation numbers were looking up. Cowles and Walters had correctly assessed what Iowans wanted: they were eager to read news out of Washington. Circulation of the Sunday *Register* rose by nearly 30,000, and the bureau, which cost the paper $3,600 in 1933 and $8,500 the following year, proved a very wise investment.[53] Wilson later broke such stories as FDR's attempt to purge congressional leaders who had opposed his court-packing plan, and in 1954 he won a Pulitzer Prize for national reporting with his story on Soviet espionage in the United States prior to World War II.

These various changes, upgrades, and innovations in the *Register*'s layout and content were designed to build readership, but they took place in the midst of the Great Depression. The early years of the 1930s were particularly hard on Iowans. Historian Dorothy Schwieder noted that by 1932, "farm products were selling for about one-half or even one-third of their 1922–1929 value. ... At the same time, the cost of necessities purchased by farmers declined only slightly or remained the same." The farm crisis had a ripple effect on other sectors of the state's economy, and unemployment became a growing problem in Iowa's cities. Given this dismal climate, the

R&T would likely have struggled if not for the continuing improvements in the company's circulation department and gradual improvement in economic conditions.[54]

Importance of the Circulation Department

From the beginning of the Cowles ownership, company management well understood the importance of a strong circulation department. Circulation manager Cordingley and his team had organized such an efficient delivery system that by the end of the 1920s, two-thirds of the papers' combined daily circulation went to readers outside of Polk County, where Des Moines is located. The paper reported in 1929 that "two out of every three families in the Central two-thirds of Iowa read The Register and Tribune."[55]

During the first three decades of the century, the R&T had developed one of the largest circulation departments in the nation. It consisted of five divisions: traffic, which was responsible for transporting papers to distribution points for pickup by carriers, dealers, and rural route sales representatives; city circulation, which handled sales in Des Moines and vicinity; agency sales, which managed circulation in the state's 50 larger cities and towns outside Des Moines; independent dealers and carriers, which was responsible for circulation in all other towns and rural villages; and mail subscriptions, which took care of paid-in-advance sales through the mail.[56] The system worked well until the early 1930s, when subscriptions by mail began to decline sharply. Iowa farmers made up the bulk of this division's business, and in the midst of the depression, many farm families could not come up with the six-dollar, paid-in-advance, yearly subscription fee. In March 1933, the farm service division was added to win back farmers who had stopped taking the paper. The brainchild of E. P. Schwartz, manager of mail subscriptions, it was "the greatest single marketing first of the Register." Taking the idea from a small Texas newspaper, Schwartz introduced a rural weekly pay system. Rather than requiring mail subscribers to pay a yearly, up-front rate, patrons could pay by the week. Customers put their 12-cent weekly payment in small metal cups attached to their mailboxes; the fees were then collected by the rural route sales representatives who delivered the Sunday *Register.* Even struggling farmers were often able to afford the paper under the new payment system, and the company won back many of its former rural readers.[57]

In addition to coming up with the more convenient payment plan for rural customers, the R&T actively sought better, more cost-effective means of delivering the paper to customers statewide. As Kenneth MacDonald remembered, the *Register* was "delivered in every conceivable way." One especially innovative technique to cut the transportation costs involved a deal with a company called Iowa Film Delivery. Because Des Moines was centrally located, the city became the hub for motion-picture film distribution throughout Iowa. Every night trucks from Iowa Film Delivery carried new films out to Iowa towns and transferred reels from one town's movie theater to another. In the mid-1930s, the R&T traffic department worked out a deal with the film distribution firm: trucks carrying films would also carry copies of the morning *Register* to the theaters in towns in certain sections of the state. These theaters then served as mini–distribution centers for the surrounding areas. Because most Iowa towns had a movie theater, the shared film-and-paper delivery plan helped keep R&T traffic costs down.[58]

As circulation grew, Cordingley needed more and more young carriers to deliver papers to the homes of readers. By the early 1930s, more than 4,000 young boys in towns and cities throughout Iowa were part of the R&T distribution effort. Like many other newspapers, the Register made effective use of a "little merchant plan." Under this system, carriers operated as independent contractors, responsible for selling and delivering papers as well as collecting payments along a specific route. The paper actively recruited carriers through advertisements that often appealed to parents of potential paperboys: "The boy who handles a newspaper route successfully must bring into practice the same business principles that apply to the successful merchant. He must know how to handle customers—how to keep up with his collections—how to get new customers—and how to give good service. The boy who learns these services while handling a paper route will become a successful businessman in later years. Let your boy get the value of business training by handling a Register and Tribune route in your town."[59]

To reward its carriers and build loyalty to the company, the R&T initiated a carrier convention in 1930. The annual event was held in Des Moines for carriers and their families. The convention not only recognized outstanding performance, it also provided entertainment and fellowship for the paperboys. In addition to the fun, which included marching in a carrier parade through downtown Des Moines, the youths were treated to a tour of the Register and Tribune plant. Similar to other newspapers' activities for their carriers, the R&T convention was held yearly through 1941. It was discontinued because of World War II. The event successfully acquainted the youngsters with the company, built morale and interest, and sought to increase the goodwill of carriers' parents toward the R&T.[60]

The importance of the *Register*'s circulation department became clear as the Depression led many companies to pare advertising costs. Nationally, total expenditures on all forms of advertising fell dramatically, from

$3.4 billion in 1929 to $1.3 billion in 1933.[61] Like most other newspaper firms, the R&T was hurt by the advertising cutback: its net revenue from advertising, which had risen from $2.1 million in 1925 to $3.4 million in 1929, sank to $1.9 million in 1933. Meanwhile, although the nation's population rose 7 percent during the 1930s, aggregate newspaper circulation remained relatively constant throughout the decade. In this area, however, the Cowles' papers did not follow the industry. Over the course of the 1930s, Iowa's population increased 2.7 percent, but combined daily circulation of the *Register* and *Tribune* rose by 29 percent, while that of the Sunday *Register* increased a whopping 74 percent. Editorial upgrades, concern for the customer satisfaction—as exemplified, for instance, by the creation of the Bureau of Accuracy and Fair Play—and the improvements in distribution and billing appeared to be paying off.[62]

As advertising income fell, net revenue from circulation—$1.1 million in 1925 and $1.6 million in 1929—remained relatively steady and by 1933 stood at $1.7 million. Because the company had relied on advertising for as much as 70 percent of its revenue, total net profits, which had risen to $1.1 million in 1929, fell to a Depression low of $470,000 in 1932, while the profit margin on newspaper operations declined from 20.8 percent to 16.6 percent. From this nadir, however, net profits quickly climbed back up, exceeding $1 million in 1936 and 1937, before dipping slightly the last two years of the decade. Although advertising revenue began to recover in 1935, the rebound in profitability was led by a change in net circulation revenue, increasing from $1.9 million in 1934 to $2.7 million in 1939. By 1938, in fact, net revenue from circulation exceeded that of advertising for the first time; subscriptions accounted for 52.6 percent of net revenue from the company's newspaper operation. Relatively unique in the newspaper industry, where ads usually covered most costs, this situation prevailed into the mid-1940s.[63]

Clearly, an improvement in economic conditions also affected the R&T's fortunes. Various New Deal programs provided relief to Iowans, but the Agricultural Adjustment Act (AAA) of 1933 had the greatest impact. Nationally this program helped lift farm income from $5.5 billion in 1932 to almost $8.7 billion in 1935. In Iowa, nearly three-fourths of the state's farmers voluntarily participated in the AAA. By mid-decade, the situation in both rural and urban areas of the state had eased, and "many Iowans talked in terms of the Depression coming to an end in 1938."[64]

Company prosperity provided the Cowles family with ample salaries plus dividends. In 1934, for instance, Gardner Cowles and sons John and Mike each took down a salary of $48,000. Although this put them in a three-way tie for the second highest salary in Iowa, their incomes were lower than those of other important publishers. That year William R. Hearst earned $500,000, Joseph Pulitzer got $134,000, and Frank Knox, publisher of the *Chicago Daily News,* received $75,000. Dividends, meanwhile remained solid and augmented the brothers' hefty (by Iowa standards) salaries.[65] Besides accommodating lavish lifestyles, company profits led the Cowles brothers to expand their papers and invest in the radio industry. Such success also allowed them to consider bigger ventures beyond Des Moines.

Branching Out

Having taken their family papers to new heights, the still young and ambitious Cowles brothers hankered for still greater challenges. In 1935, this process began with the family's entrance into the Minneapolis newspaper market; two years later, the Cowleses went into magazine publishing with the introduction of *Look.*

John's Rising *Star*

By the early 1930s, the Cowles brothers were ready to try running a newspaper operation of their own. In 1933, they began a methodical search for an evening paper with solid reader loyalty and a large home-delivery circulation. They hoped to find a paper in a community with high literacy rates. One year later, John and Mike tried to buy two papers in Duluth, Minnesota, but when no agreement on price was forthcoming, the brothers resumed their search. In the spring of 1935, they located another paper that met all their criteria—the *Minneapolis Star.* The weakest of three newspapers in Minneapolis, the *Star* was considered the city's most liberal, with appeal to the working classes. With a circulation of 79,000, it struggled against two larger papers: the evening *Journal,* which had 115,000 daily readers, and the morning and evening *Tribune,* whose combined circulation stood at 140,000.[66]

In June 1935, John purchased the *Star* for $1 million, but within less than three months, the R&T and then Mike were brought into the project financially. Immediately after acquiring the paper, John reorganized its corporate structure. The new capitalization was 8,000 shares of preferred and 20,000 shares of common stock. In August, the R&T bought 7,000 of the preferred shares at $100 per share. The following month, John and Mike equally divided the remaining 1,000 preferred shares and all the 20,000 shares of common stock.[67]

Even as the financing was being worked out, John moved quickly to revive the Minneapolis paper by introducing the successful strategies already employed at the R&T. Although Davis Merwin, a friend of the brothers and publisher of the *Bloomington* (Illinois) *Pantagraph,* was installed as publisher, John headed the *Star* operation and commuted regularly between Des Moines and Minneapolis. To turn the paper around, he adopted what *Newsweek* referred to as the "Des Moines formula." John stressed the use of "pictures, features, bright writing, honest and thorough reporting, and small shots of well-deplored sin. All this ... [was] topped off with an icing of promotional razzmatazz that would let no Minnesotan forget the *Star.*"[68] By the fall, Cowles asked R&T managing editor Stuffy Walters to divide his time between the Des Moines papers and the *Star.* For the next two years, Walters traveled between the two cities. Success, however, was not immediate; in fact, the *Star* suffered losses of $225,000 in 1935 and $325,000 in 1936. The company was able to sustain these large losses only through loans from the R&T. Mike Cowles later confessed that he and his brother were "a bit overconfident on how quickly we would be able to put the *Star* in the black."[69]

Their new paper was struggling and, at Gardner Cowles' urging, John and his family moved to Minneapolis, where he became the *Star*'s full-time publisher in 1937. From that point on, the brothers divided their responsibilities: John stayed in Minneapolis to supervise the new paper, and Mike remained in Des Moines to oversee the R&T. Once established in Minnesota, John moved Walters, then the R&T's managing editor, to Minneapolis permanently as editor. Although the first two years were not successful financially, real gains were made in circulation. By 1937, the *Star*'s readership exceeded that of the *Journal* and was closing in on the *Tribune.* In advertising linage, however, the paper's performance remained stagnant. Advertisers were wary of the *Star*'s liberal tendencies and unattracted by its largely blue-collar audience. However, possibly most damning in the eyes of the business community, the *Star* maintained a policy of honest news reporting regardless of who or what was involved. Such aggressive journalism led to circulation increases but tended to anger some powerful advertisers. For example, when Minneapolis banker C. T. Jaffray was arrested for bagging more ducks than the hunting limit permitted, he was able to dissuade the *Journal* and *Tribune* from printing the story, but the incident made the front page of the *Star.* As John later recounted, "It took many years for the business community to get used to the idea that news would be printed regardless of whose interests might be harmed."[70]

Yet progress continued at the *Star,* in large part because of the fresh writing and dramatic layouts stressed by Stuffy Walters. Equally important to the *Star*'s rise was its massive promotional effort. Like its local competitors, the *Star* employed a variety of fairly standard advertisements and contests to expand readership. The paper also employed radio to boost circulation. Making an agreement with Minneapolis station WCCO, the *Star* broadcast its own daily radio program that dramatized three or four top news stories. In addition, the paper established a special carrier radio network that broadcast to forty-four paperboy stations across the city. Set up to build morale, it broadcast announcements, interviews with staff members, music, and drama. Besides using radio to its advantage, management realized that company trucks used to distribute papers could serve as moving billboards, and the newspaper's name was soon prominently displayed on the vehicles.[71]

By 1938, editorial improvements and aggressive promotion boosted the *Star*'s daily circulation to the largest in the city.[72] In the midst of that year, John and Mike apparently wanted to liquidate their equity in the Minneapolis paper. They sold their common stock to the R&T. In 1940, when the Register and Tribune had completed its payments to John and Mike for their *Star* shares, the Des Moines company immediately turned around and began divesting itself of the Minnesota operation. Half the common stock, by that time 50,000 shares, was distributed to R&T stockholders (20,000 shares on the basis of one share of Minneapolis stock for every three of Register stock held, and several months later, 30,000 shares on the basis of one of Minneapolis for every two of Register stock). At the same time, John and Mike were both permitted to buy 20,000 shares each of Minneapolis paper's stock (at $10 per share), and the remaining 10,000 shares were purchased by John Thompson, former publisher of the *Star.* [73]

Meanwhile, the *Star* followed in the path of its Des Moines parent; it started down the road of consolidation by acquiring the evening *Journal* for $2.270 million.[74] Two years later, on April 29, 1941, the *Star* acquired the *Tribune* in a deal that involved a stock swap. According to the agreement, the *Star*, which then had 100,000 shares of common stock outstanding, issued an additional 50,000 shares, which were then transferred to the Murphy family, owners of the *Tribune.* In addition to owning one-third of the new consolidated newspaper company, the Murphys also received $1.425 million in notes payable. As a final part of the acquisition, the new firm, the Minneapolis Star Journal and Tribune Company, bought back its preferred stock from the Register. With this action, the R&T, although it still held $2.9 million in notes receivable from the Minneapolis paper, ceased owning any of its stock. When the transaction was complete, John had attained a monopoly in the Minneapolis newspaper market.[75]

Fortune magazine explained the takeovers rather simplistically by stressing the *Star*'s superior business management: "The Cowles papers were run with that extra pinch of business ability, which in the old days meant the difference between pleasant and prodigious profits."[76] Two years after gaining control of all newspapers in the city, John Cowles provided a more detailed account of his company's rapid success.

> The greatest obstacle that had to be overcome in attaining control of the field was reader habit. Our formula was simply this, give them a superior product; deliver it better and promote it effectively. During all this expansion program we placed our major emphasis on the editorial content and sound promotion, in addition to enlarging our circulation revenue. By giving our readers a good editorial product and breaking their habits of reading other Minneapolis newspapers, we were able to offer our advertisers a productive medium. They too, however, had to learn to change their habits in favor of our paper, but they eventually wanted to buy space from us. The important thing about a publication is its editorial content and how it is distributed.[77]

Holding a newspaper monopoly in a growing metropolis, the Cowles papers in Minneapolis became highly profitable. Immediately prior to the merger in 1940, net earnings stood at $76,257. Once the *Star Journal* and *Tribune* were combined the following year, net profits jumped up to $296,949, and then soared to $1,194,706 in 1942.[78] But to John, such dominance also meant something else; it provided an opportunity to establish a fine newspaper. He once explained in a speech: "The best newspapers in America are those that do not have newspapers competing with them in their local field. [They are] the most responsibly edited, the fairest, the most complete, the most accurate, the best written, and the most objective."[79] In later years, high regard for the Minneapolis Star and Tribune seemed to bear out John's views. In 1961, for instance, "Minneapolis was only one of four cities to have two newspapers [the morning *Tribune* and the evening *Star*] cited among the top 20 dailies in the *Saturday Review* poll of 1961; the others were New York, Chicago, and Washington."[80]

A New *Look* for Mike

While John was becoming active in Minneapolis, Mike was eager to do something beyond minding the family shop in Des Moines. Although he had played a prominent role in improving the R&T, Mike knew it was his father who had built the business. John had a similar opportunity at the *Star*, and Mike yearned to prove to himself and others that he could make it on his own.[81] As early as 1933, after the success of Laurence Stallings' series of World War I photographs that appeared in the Sunday rotogravure section and then as a R&T syndicated feature, Mike believed immense opportunities existed in the new field of photojournalism. He and R&T rotogravure editor Vernon Pope continued experimenting with ideas in the Sunday *Register.* The popularity of the photo section grew, and Mike felt the concept of storytelling through pictures could be introduced successfully in magazine form.

By 1936, he and Pope had pasted up dummies for a picture magazine to be called *Look.* The name was the brainchild of John and Mike's mother.[82] Upon hearing a rumor that Henry Luce and Roy Larsen of Time Incorporated were planning a similar type of publication, Mike took his mockup to them for advice. Luce was intrigued with Cowles' proposed publication, and after examining it, he pulled out his company's intended magazine called *Life.* Because the two magazines appeared to target two separate audiences—*Look* was to be a feature-oriented monthly, while the weekly *Life* would focus more on news and cater to upscale readers—both projects went ahead. Luce even invested $25,000 in *Look.* On John's suggestion, Mike delayed the premiere of *Look* to see how the public received *Life.* It proved an instant success, and Mike soon followed with the first issue of *Look.* It hit the newsstands five weeks later, on January 5, 1937.[83]

Look also caused an immediate sensation, but not for the same reasons as *Life.* After selling out its initial press run of 400,000 copies, the Cowles company began another printing. As sales topped 700,000, Mike and his colleagues discovered a major reason for the magazine's immediate popularity. The first issue's back cover consisted of a photograph of film star Greta Garbo. When folded in half, however, the photo resembled female genitalia. News of the oddity spread quickly, and the Montreal police actually seized several hundred copies of the magazine. Cowles responded by rapidly recalling all unsold copies at a cost of over $100,000. Meanwhile, interpreting the folded Garbo picture as obscene, the U.S. postal service threatened to prohibit the publication from the mail. Mike sent Luther Hill to Washington, D.C., to prevent the postal ban. There Hill's brother in Congress came in handy. Lister Hill set up a meeting between his brother and postal officials and apparently put in a good word for the Cowles family. After Luther described "the unfortunate incident," the Post Office Department accepted the explanation and chose to back down. Yet the unintentional faux pas proved to be tremendous publicity. Circulation of the March issue rose to 1.2 million, and in April it increased another 100,000. That month, *Look* became a biweekly, and by October circulation stood at 2 million per issue.[84]

Soaring readership did not necessarily mean a profit, however. Initially *Look* was an "ad-less" magazine because Mike wanted to concentrate on building circulation. It began to accept advertising in November 1937. The advertising rates were based on a guaranteed circulation of 2 million, but because of the brief 1938 recession, *Look* circulation tumbled to 1 million. Competition from additional picture magazines and reduced newsstand sales (on which *Look* relied almost exclusively) were also to blame. Unable to sell the promised number of magazines, *Look* was forced to discount its advertising rates. Losses mounted, and much like the *Minneapolis Star*, the R&T rapidly increased its stake in the venture. *Look* lost $608,000 between 1937 and 1940; the Register's investment in the magazine rose from an initial $25,000 to $453,000. These problems were not unique to the Cowles magazine. While *Look* struggled, *Life* was losing $3 million a year, and in 1937, its parent, Time, Inc., recorded its lowest profits since 1928.[85]

In the midst of *Look*'s decline, Mike concentrated his efforts on rebuilding readership by increasing mail subscriptions and lessening the magazine's dependency on erratic newsstand sales. To do so, he hired two magazine circulation experts: Lester Suhler from Rand McNally and S. O. Shapiro of MacFadden Publications. Within three months, circulation rebounded, moving up from 1.1 million to 1.24 million; a year later, the portion of circulation from subscriptions jumped from 4 percent to 20 percent. While *Look* did not begin to show a profit until the next decade, the magazine's future appeared brighter. Symbolic of the turnaround and with the realization that it must be located closer to national advertisers, the magazine moved its headquarters from cramped offices in the R&T building to New York in 1940.[86]

Register Editorial Positions

During these years of change and expansion, the editorial position of the *Register* remained relatively consistent. Even after Waymack replaced Ingham as head of the editorial pages, the paper continued its general support of Republican candidates and remained committed to involvement in world affairs. During the period, most of its editorial energy was focused on the farm problem, the New Deal, and growing foreign policy concerns.

When Republican incumbent President Calvin Coolidge, who failed to receive the *Register*'s endorsement in 1924, chose not to seek office in 1928, the paper heartily threw its support to native son presidential candidate Herbert Hoover. After his election victory over Democrat Al Smith, Hoover appeared ready to lead the country toward even greater prosperity, and the *Register* was confident of his abilities. A couple months before the October 1929 stock market crash, it noted: "President Hoover knows how to do it [lead the nation] and he has made a success of everything he has undertaken."[87] Even as the country fell into depression, the paper remained pleased with Hoover's performance, especially on the farm issues and in foreign policy.

Unlike workers in most other sectors, farmers had not been enjoying the benefits of the 1920s economic boom. Following the brief upsurge in demand and prices associated with World War I, American farm income had dropped below prewar levels by the early 1920s. A resurgent European agricultural sector again supplied most of the continent's food needs, and world commodity prices fell. Iowan Henry C. Wallace, secretary of agriculture under Presidents Harding and Coolidge, explained the postwar bind confronting American farmers: "In the Corn Belt the value of an acre of corn in 1920 was 20 percent under pre-war value, whereas monthly wages of farm labor were 34 percent higher ... implements [ranged] from 66 to 92 percent higher, and freight rates about 60 percent higher."[88]

Congress tried to help by enacting temporary tariffs on farm commodities that raised agricultural prices, but that led to foreign retaliation and the effort proved ineffective. By mid-decade, the usually internationalist Ingham began arguing that since tariffs were used to protect American industry, they should also be employed to support farm prices. He explained that because "manufactured products are sold at home on a protected price basis while farm produce is sold on a world price basis," some type of adjustment was needed to give farmers a level playing field.[89]

In the mid-1920s, Ingham backed the McNary-Haugen bill. This proposed legislation called for the creation of a federal corporation to purchase U.S. agricultural surplus at a set, artificially high price and sell the products at whatever price prevailed on the world market. Government losses in the transactions were to be made up through a tax (or equalization fee, as it was called) on farmers. Congress passed the program twice, only to see Coolidge, largely on the advice of Secretary of Commerce Hoover, veto it both times. After the second veto in February 1927, the disappointed *Register* charged that Coolidge had been captured by the industrial East. The paper later quoted Henry A. Wallace—son of Henry C. Wallace and editor of *Wallace's Farmer*, who went on to become secretary of agriculture and then vice president under Franklin Roosevelt—who suggested that "Coolidge and Hoover stand for industrializing the United States" and were against "giving farmers a fair share of the national income."[90]

Once in the White House, Hoover dealt with the farm crisis by proposing the Agricultural Marketing Act. When enacted, the law established a federal farm board, which was authorized to loan money to agricultural cooperatives and purchase surplus crops. It also urged farmers to reduce voluntarily their planted acreage in an effort to lessen supply and thus raise commodity prices. The *Register* applauded Hoover's efforts "toward farm stabilization" by "giving the farmer a working organization" while concurrently "holding tariff legislation down to the farm schedules."[91] But by 1931, the farm situation had not improved, and *Register* farm editor J. S. Russell reported that between March 1926 and March 1931, one-seventh of Iowa's farmers had lost their farms through foreclosures. That translated into 33,000 farms and more than 5 million acres ending up in lenders' hands.[92]

When rural problems continued to mount, agrarian radicalism rose among Iowa farmers, as evidenced in the "Cow War" and the creation of the Farmers Holiday Association. In 1931, Iowa was in the eighth year of its program to eliminate bovine tuberculosis through statewide testing to identify and then eradicate all diseased cattle. When farmers failed in their attempts to make testing of their herds optional, violence broke out in Cedar County (140 miles east of Des Moines). After farmers attacked state veterinarians and blocked further testing, Iowa Governor Dan Turner declared martial law in the county, sent in the National Guard, and resumed testing. Although the *Register* stood for Iowa's farmers, it opposed violence: "Iowans throughout the state will regret the resort to martial law. Yet no other course was open to the governor. ... The law requiring the testing of cattle for tuberculosis resulted not from despotism but from democratic procedures. It was intended not to oppress farmers but to protect the milk consumers of the state, including the farmers and their families."[93]

In the wake of the "Cow War," Miles Reno, president of the Iowa Farmers Union, prepared to implement a farm strike. Led by the new Farmers Holiday Association, the plan called for a withholding of agricultural goods from the market in an attempt to boost prices. In August 1932, the strike began peacefully; for instance, milk was dumped in ditches rather than taken to a creamery. It soon turned violent, however, when strikers moved to stop nonparticipating farmers who were taking their goods to market to be sold. Rapidly put down by widespread arrests, the strike was a failure, but it led both Hoover and Roosevelt to come to Iowa and campaign in the fall of 1932. In October, Hoover spoke in Des Moines, hoping to convince farmers that he understood their plight. But as the *Register* reported, while the president discussed the need to develop a plan to refinance farm mortgages, he emphasized the importance of the farmer's rugged individualism. He promised not to let the federal government do anything to impede the initiative of rural Americans.[94]

Meanwhile, the *Register* approved of Hoover's moves, albeit timid, toward greater involvement in the world. In 1930, the paper lauded the president's foreign policy for heading "toward world organization." By late 1932, it commended Hoover's "fine and high statesmanship" and suggested he should receive "an historic place ... [for] his contributions to world peace."[95] Specifically worthy of praise, editor Waymack singled out the Kellogg Peace Pact, the Stimson Doctrine (which he referred to as the Hoover-Stimson Doctrine), and the repudiation of the Roosevelt Corollary to the Monroe Doctrine.

During the first months of Hoover's administration, the United States formally joined in the Kellogg-Briand Treaty—a rather innocuous, multilateral treaty that condemned war as a means of settling international disputes. In addition, under Hoover, the United States was working more closely with the League of Nations. Although much to the chagrin of Ingham and Waymack, the United States never joined the League of Nations but, by 1930, American "observers" were participating in League conferences on such international issues as health. The following year, an American diplomat took part in the League's meetings regarding the Japanese invasion of Manchuria. When the League chose only to investigate the crisis, Secretary of State Henry Stimson did all within his power by issuing the so-called Stimson Doctrine. It pledged that the United States would not recognize Japan's territorial conquests. Finally, Waymack was pleased that the "Monroe Doctrine was reinterpreted back to its original nonaggressive meaning." Under Harding, Coolidge, and then Hoover, American troops were withdrawn from Haiti, the Dominican Republic, and then Nicaragua, although a civil war in Nicaragua brought the U.S. Marines back from the mid-1920s until the early 1930s. Besides the removal of troops, in 1930, the State Department formally disavowed the Roosevelt Corollary, which had reserved for the United States the right to intervene in Latin American states. That was the beginning of what Franklin Roosevelt would later term the "Good Neighbor Policy."[96]

As the presidential election of 1932 approached, the *Register* found itself siding with a majority (59 percent) of the nation's dailies in giving its endorsement to Hoover. Once elected, however, Franklin Roosevelt enjoyed the R&T's editorial support during his first few months in office. The paper was encouraged by FDR's "prompt and cheerful assumption of the responsibility," and it assured its readers that the banking crisis would "be met by satisfactory emergency measures."[97] It was further impressed with Roosevelt's rapidity of action, especially on farm relief. As FDR's agricultural adjustment bill began to take shape, the *Register* referred to its plan to restore farm prices through crop reductions as "bold." The bill proposed to pay farmers not to plant. They were to be paid based on an artificially high price that would provide farmers with the same purchasing power they had enjoyed from 1909 to 1914.[98]

As the agricultural bill neared passage, Waymack was uneasy with its pathbreaking nature: "The bill carried the idea of a planned national economy farther beyond all comparison that it has ever except in war been carried before, setting up a large degree of government control not only of agricultural production but of processing and marketing as well." Yet, even after suggesting that it might not work, he thought it was worth a try. The editor called on "every class in the country now to give every possible assistance in trying to make it work, and certainly no group so much as farmers themselves." The "epochal" farm bill passed the following day.[99]

Meanwhile, the *Register* was watching what it called an "extremely radical plan" for industry make its way through Congress. The bill—which upon passage in June 1933 was to become the National Industrial Recovery Act and create the National Recovery Administration (NRA)—exempted businesses from antitrust laws and called on all industries to draw up codes of fair competition. While it was being considered, Waymack told readers that the industrial bill was nothing short of revolutionary. "We shall never go back to the theoretically 'free competition' days that trust busting aimed to perpetuate. We shall never go back to industry functioning without some degree of government supervision—if we set up within the separate industries new powers and machinery to control production, prices, employment, and wages. In any case, the hint is that we have ended an era and are about to start a new one."[100] Other midwestern editors shared Waymack's view of the bill. In May 1933, the *Omaha World-Herald* referred to the proposed law as "a program for tremendous change," while the *Kansas City Star* saw it as a "revolution in the American industrial system."[101]

Waymack's concern over the National Industrial Recovery Act soon turned to opposition. By June 1933, he worried that the law gave government too much control over the country's economic life. On this point, the *Register* said the NRA was "an acceptance, to a considerable degree, of the Fascist view." Ten months later, the editor suggested that problems were created with NRA because it was set up "in a rush ... ignor[ing] the complexities of industry." When the Supreme Court struck down the legislation in May 1935, Waymack was elated, writing that of the New Deal programs, "the worst and foolishest was NRA."[102] Neighboring editors agreed. The *Omaha World-Herald* claimed it "went too far, attempted to do too much, and imposed too onerous restrictions." Similarly, the *Kansas City Star* wrote that the law had been a "genuine detriment to business as well as the public."[103]

The AAA also soon became a favorite target of the *Register* because it allegedly expanded federal powers too far. Although the program provided much-needed assistance to farmers, its means—specifically production controls—were particularly distressing. By April 1934, the *Register* was pleased that FDR's secretary of agriculture, Iowan Henry A. Wallace, seemed to have second thoughts on this issue and "look[ed] with reserve on the experiment with compulsion in crop reduction."[104] Two years later, the Supreme Court's decision invalidating AAA received Waymack's approval. Yet the *Register* remained convinced that agriculture could not "go back to ... individualistic competition," and the paper hoped for some type of program to uplift American farmers.[105]

From the mid-1930s, Waymack grew increasingly hostile to the New Deal. In the 1936 presidential election, the paper supported FDR's challenger, Republican Alf Landon.[106] In its editorial opposition to Roosevelt, the *Register* found itself in league with the *Chicago Tribune,* the *Detroit Free Press,* the Hearst papers, the *Los Angeles Times,* the *New York Herald-Tribune,* and the *New York Sun.* In fact, only 37 percent of the nation's dailies supported the president in his bid for a second term.[107] Yet while Waymack objected to FDR's overreliance on governmental power to deal with the Depression, he defended the president's attempts "to limit the nation's retreat into isolationism."[108]

Ever since the United States refused to join the League of Nations in 1919–1920, political leaders remained wary of active involvement in world affairs. Roosevelt, however, had internationalist leanings, and the *Register* was quick to praise his moves in that direction. In 1934, Roosevelt renewed the efforts of the previous Republican administration to join the World Court. Although membership in this international body was largely symbolic, the Senate rejected the association the following January. The *Register,* which had for years called for joining the organization, saw the outcome as a defeat for FDR and condemned its failure as damaging to U.S. foreign policy: "The inability of the president to get through so innocuous a treaty is a rebuff to President Roosevelt and a weakening of his position in dealing with other nations. ... It is most deplorable."[109] In 1935, Congress passed and FDR signed the first of several neutrality laws designed to avoid entanglements with belligerents. The new law banned the sale of weapons to belligerents and warned Americans to stay off ships of warring powers. After Italy invaded Ethiopia later that year, the president invoked the Neutrality Act and pledged "to avoid those perils that will endanger our peace in the world."[110] Here Waymack and the paper strongly condemned the president as someone "who ought to know better." The editor felt FDR was "guilty of encouraging the belief that by just resolving to stay isolated and by passing 'neutrality laws' we are really assuring ourselves against being drawn in [to war]." To emphasize the naïveté of such a policy, the editorial concluded with a history of the nation's failed attempts at neutrality.[111]

Much to *Register*'s dismay, two additional neutrality acts had passed by 1937, but in October, the paper cheered what it believed was a change in presidential course.[112] When Japan invaded China, FDR did not invoke the neutrality act (which allowed the Chinese to purchase arms from the United States) and, in a stirring speech, he called for an international "quarantine" of "aggressive treaty-breaking nations." He went on to talk about an "interdependence in the modern world" and then told his listeners that "America will not escape [if war comes]." Pleased by Roosevelt's speech, Waymack reminded readers that "the only way for a major nation to keep out of general war is to see that it doesn't happen." He concluded the piece by affirming that "isolation is a dream."[113]

On September 1, 1939, war broke out in Europe with Germany's invasion of Poland. While the *Register* hoped the United States could stay out of the conflict, it had "no illusions how hard this will be."[114] The paper did not advocate isolation as a means to avoid war. Earlier that summer, President Roosevelt had attempted unsuccessfully to get Congress to repeal the arms embargo. Following the outbreak of hostilities, he renewed his efforts to have the ban lifted, and the paper supported him. The *Register* argued that a German victory would likely draw America into the war, and the Germans held an advantage over the British and French because they were much better prepared for the conflict. To lessen the likelihood of German victory and America being sucked into war, the sale of arms—to the British and French—on a cash-and-carry basis was necessary. In early November, when Congress enacted the modified neutrality law Roosevelt wanted, the *Register* commended the legislative body with the editorial headline "Wisely Done." Yet Waymack understood that the cash-and-carry provision did not ensure an avoidance of war. While he felt Congress had taken the prudent step, the international situation was still highly dangerous, and U.S. involvement in the war remained possible, but the revised law had, Waymack thought, "slightly reduce[d] the danger of that."[115]

The Cowles Touch Continues

By 1939, Gardner Cowles Sr. could look back on the past 15 years with tremendous satisfaction. The paper he and Harvey Ingham had revived and made a statewide institution had been made even bigger and better by his two youngest sons, John and Mike Cowles. From an early age, the brothers had been groomed to take over the *Register.* Each possessed skills that complemented the other; together they made a fine management team. John and Mike worked with several fine editors and staff members to strengthen the Des Moines paper and further expand its circulation. Their success translated into increasing R&T profits and provided the means for branching out into radio ownership, moving into the Minneapolis newspaper market, and introducing *Look* magazine. During World War II, John and Mike would leave to serve the federal government briefly, but the media empire would be managed in their absence. The high demand for war news would generate new readers for newspapers across the nation. During the postwar years, new media—television and free shopper newspapers—would emerge and challenge the R&T's monopoly of the Des Moines advertising market.

Editor Harvey Ingham and publisher Gardner Cowles Sr., 1937. *Courtesy of the State Historical Society of Iowa, Des Moines.*

Circulation manager William Cordingley holding "Ding" Darling's cartoon heralding the Sunday *Register* reaching the 300,000 circulation mark, 1936. *Courtesy of the John Cowles Collection, Cowles Library, Drake University, Des Moines.*

CHAPTER 6

Growing Pains

1940–1959

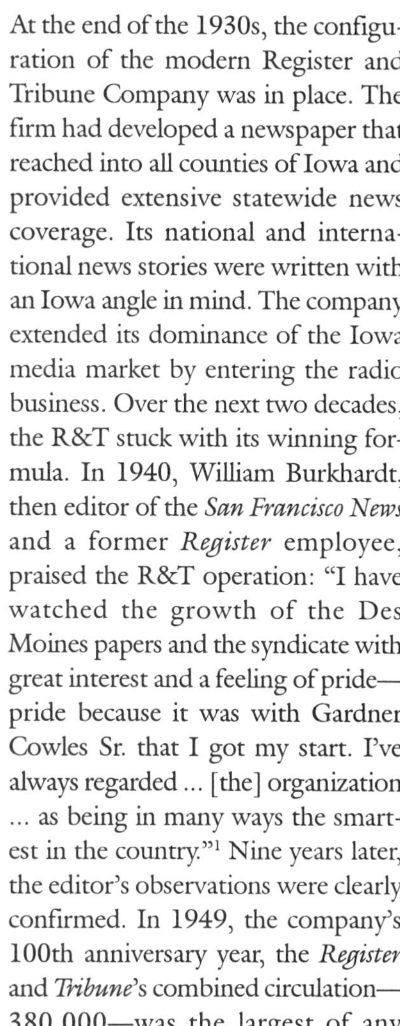

At the end of the 1930s, the configuration of the modern Register and Tribune Company was in place. The firm had developed a newspaper that reached into all counties of Iowa and provided extensive statewide news coverage. Its national and international news stories were written with an Iowa angle in mind. The company extended its dominance of the Iowa media market by entering the radio business. Over the next two decades, the R&T stuck with its winning formula. In 1940, William Burkhardt, then editor of the *San Francisco News* and a former *Register* employee, praised the R&T operation: "I have watched the growth of the Des Moines papers and the syndicate with great interest and a feeling of pride—pride because it was with Gardner Cowles Sr. that I got my start. I've always regarded ... [the] organization ... as being in many ways the smartest in the country."[1] Nine years later, the editor's observations were clearly confirmed. In 1949, the company's 100th anniversary year, the *Register* and *Tribune*'s combined circulation—380,000—was the largest of any

Register and Tribune Building at Eighth and Locust streets, Des Moines, ca. 1947. *Courtesy of the State Historical Society of Iowa, Des Moines.*

newspaper published in American cities the size of Des Moines or smaller. Des Moines was the 53rd largest U.S. city, but only nine other cities had Sunday newspapers with a circulation larger than the *Des Moines Sunday Register.* The paper was distributed by more than 7,500 carriers and some 400 trucks traveling over 80,000 miles a week to all sections of the state. News coverage was conducted by an editorial staff of 115 plus 300 state correspondents.[2]

Not everything at the firm remained the same, however. John and Mike Cowles had both used the R&T to launch their own nascent media empires. As World War II came to a close, most of John's energies were focused on the Minneapolis papers, while Mike concentrated on *Look* magazine. Although the brothers remained involved in all strategic planning decisions in their family's Des Moines holdings, they were no longer involved in the day-to-day affairs of the company. Meanwhile, their involvement in these communication holdings beyond Iowa meant that the R&T remained financially interested in both the Minneapolis papers and *Look* magazine. As the brothers devoted less time to Des Moines operations, the leadership vacuum was competently filled by several editors. After World War II, managerial responsibility fell to company executive Luther Hill and executive editor Kenneth MacDonald.

Managers at the *Des Moines Register* continued to cultivate the paper's special relationship with its Iowa readers. Like other newspapers, the *Register* capitalized on the demand for war news by sending its own reporter to cover the conflict firsthand. But instead of concentrating on the travails of the American military generally, the *Register*'s war correspondent told the story of World War II through the eyes and ears of Iowa soldiers. As the war increasingly focused people's attention on the federal government, the R&T expanded its Washington Bureau. To serve its readership even better and provide a mirror of the Iowa experience, the R&T created the first statewide opinion poll owned and operated by a newspaper. Correctly believing there was "a hunger for statewide news," Ken MacDonald and the editorial staff expanded and improved the already extensive coverage of major news events throughout the state.

Besides adding new and innovative sections to the paper, the company remained interested in radio. During the 1940s, the *Register* increased its radio holdings from four up to six stations. When plans to build a regional network fell through, the company retreated to merely maintain a strong radio presence in Des Moines. As the power of television became more apparent, the R&T joined with other newspapers around the country in entering that medium as well. These moves into radio and television notwithstanding, the firm remained committed to its core business of publishing Iowa newspapers.

The R&T's reputation, combined with its newspaper monopoly in Des Moines and continued dominance in the Iowa newspaper market, strengthened its ability to attract quality editors, reporters, and photographers. The paper's staff won six Pulitzer Prizes from 1942 to 1958. Success was also reflected in the company's increasing revenues. Despite the challenge of television and the advent of free "shopper" newspapers (which cut into advertising revenue and were factors in declining circulation), the R&T remained profitable, but the growth fell to an annual rate of only 3.5 percent. Yet, in an industry that as a whole struggled with rapidly rising production costs and stagnant revenues, the company's performance was understandable. From 1940 to 1959, net profits nearly doubled, rising from $912,549 in 1940 to $1.7 million in 1959.[3]

While R&T managers kept the company profitable, the editorial voice of the paper remained what some referred to as "liberal Republican" or what John Cowles described as "intelligently conservative."[4] Editors William Waymack, Kenneth MacDonald, Forrest Seymour, and Lauren Soth maintained the paper's tradition of supporting of Republican candidates (Mike and John were, in fact, among Wendell Willke's earliest supporters in his 1940 bid for the presidency), fighting for civil rights, and advocating involvement abroad. As the cold war came to dominate the news, the paper called for moderation.

Less Involvement for Mike and John

By the late 1930s, Mike and John Cowles were already moving away from day-to-day affairs of the R&T. The firm had been a training ground and a foundation for both brothers' own journalistic ventures outside of Des Moines. Their separation from the family's Iowa business was further hastened by two events: the presidential election campaign of 1940 and the Second World War.

In the spring of 1940, the Cowles brothers became key figures in Wendell Willkie's bid for the presidency. Mike and John met Willkie at a dinner in April of that year. Holding similar progressive Republican views on international affairs and civil rights, the three men began to discuss Willkie's interest in running for the presidency. During the next couple of months, the Cowleses worked long hours helping Willkie secure the Republican nomination.[5]

Roosevelt defeated Willkie in November, but the Cowles brothers continued to believe their candidate was presidential material and looked forward to the 1944 election. The connection between Willkie and the Cowleses grew even stronger, and these ties distracted the brothers away from the Des Moines business. In January 1941, Willkie and John were asked by President Roosevelt to travel to Britain to boost bipartisan support for the Lend-Lease bill. Upon his return, Willkie told Congress of England's desperate need for U.S. military equipment, while John carried on the campaign in a series of eight articles entitled "Britain under Fire." This series ran in over 30 U.S. newspapers, including the *Minneapolis Star.* In July, in part because of the work of Willkie and Cowles, the Lend-Lease law was enacted.[6]

During the summer of 1942, Willkie took Mike Cowles and foreign correspondent Joseph Barnes—both of whom were then working for the Office of War Information (OWI)—on a 49-day, 31,000-mile flight around the world. Backed by President Roosevelt, Willkie's "One World" tour was intended, among other things, to assure the Allies that America's war effort was bipartisan. Several months after the trip, Willkie published the best-selling book *One World,* which described the journey and called for postwar cooperation between nations.[7]

Mike's position at the OWI, in fact, kept him away from the *Register* and *Look* for over a year. In July 1942, Elmer Davis, director of the OWI, offered Mike the post of deputy director with responsibility of the domestic branch. At the president's personal request, Mike accepted the position.[8] Before the end of the year, John, who had earlier worked to enact the Lend-Lease program, was named special assistant to the Lend-Lease administrator, Edward Stettinius. With Mike already in Washington, Gardner Cowles Sr. became concerned about who would be "look[ing] after the family businesses."[9] Although the Des Moines papers were left in the capable hands of William Waymack, John understood his father's concerns and tried to ease the aging publisher's worries:

> Obviously under normal conditions, it would be extremely undesirable for both Mike and me to be away from our various business enterprises at the same time, but these are not normal times. ... So long as he [Mike] is in Washington in his OWI job, he can spend a couple of hours a week checking on the Register and Tribune, on LOOK, and on Minneapolis, and make such final policy or personal decisions as are necessary. While it is undeniable that probably our various companies won't run quite as well as they would if Mike or I were on the job running them full time, nevertheless, we have a lot of extremely competent people in the different companies, and things may go relatively a good deal better than you might expect.[10]

Whether John's letter lessened his father's anxiety or not, it turned out to be fairly prophetic. Although Mike remained in Washington during most of his year at the OWI, he kept in close touch with his Des Moines managers through telegrams, letters, calls, and visits. John, in contrast, was unable to stay as closely involved with his family's enterprises. He was sent by Stettinius to North Africa and then to England to evaluate the progress of the war and the Allies' needs. John's stint at Lend-Lease lasted until the summer of 1944, and he received a Presidential Certificate of Merit for his service.[11]

Challenges during World War II

With the brothers away from Des Moines during the war years, the R&T was headed by editor William Waymack, acting managing editor J. S. Russell (managing editor MacDonald served in the military in 1943 and 1944 and was on leave from the paper), and editorial page editor Forrest Seymour. Through the early 1940s, the newspapers held their own. Combined morning and evening circulation rose gradually from 326,048 in 1940 to 360,995 in 1945, and net profits inched up from $914,978 to $937,377. In light of higher tax rates, which soared from 26 percent in 1940 to 63.7 percent in 1945, these modest increases in profit appeared reasonable. Labor shortages caused wages to rise, and the R&T's total payroll increased by nearly one-third, jumping from $1.85 million in 1940 to $2.4 million in 1945.[12]

Newsprint Shortages

Newsprint shortages led to a steep increase in cost, and ultimately rationing became necessary in 1943. Several months before this rationing policy went into effect, John Cowles explained the situation to his father: "If a substantial reduction in newsprint is ordered, I assume newspapers like the R&T and the Star Journal and Tribune would react in a combination of three ways: first, by reducing editorial content; second, by raising some advertising rates and possibly rationing or limiting advertising space; and third, by raising some circulation rates, which would result in a decline in circulation volume."[13]

Much as John had predicted, newspapers around the country experimented with various strategies to deal with the rising cost and decreasing supply of newsprint. As the number of pages in newspapers declined, advertising space was carefully allotted, classified advertising was reduced, margins were narrowed, editorial content shrank in favor of advertising, and circulation rates jumped.[14]

The *Register* dealt with mounting paper prices—which had risen from

$51 per ton in 1938 to $62 in 1945—and a decreasing supply of newsprint by printing a smaller newspaper. The morning *Register's* size, for instance, declined nearly 20 percent. Amid these troubles, Mike Cowles feared that it could become "necessary to take steps to curtail advertising and circulation volume" with the result that "the net earnings of the corporation might be reduced considerably."[15] Although the situation never became that dire, the shrinking number of pages in the *Register* meant less space for advertising. The percentage of the newspaper devoted to news declined as the portion for advertisements rose. From 1940 to 1943, advertising content rose from 29 to 36 percent. Regardless of the increased ratio of advertising to news, the smaller paper had an adverse impact on advertising linage. From 1940 to 1945, advertising linage declined. To cover the loss in volume, advertising rates were raised 5 to 10 percent.[16]

Higher costs also led the *Register* to hike its circulation rates. John was hesitant because he feared that increasing the paper's price might lead to falling circulation. In February 1942, the R&T increased its city circulation rates from 30 cents to 35 cents (this was the weekly rate for receiving the morning *Register,* the evening *Tribune*, and the *Sunday Register*). A month later, a relieved Mike Cowles was happy to note that the higher rate had not driven away readers: "The raise in City Circulation rates has apparently gone over without severe opposition, and the increase in circulation income will be a real help. We had a severe loss in advertising in February, and indications are not too favorable for March advertising. I am very glad that the raise in circulation prices in Des Moines was made several weeks ago."[17] The subscribers' acquiescence to the increase led to the company's strategy of offsetting its rising costs with several wartime rate hikes. City prices were bumped up again in 1943, while the cost of carrier service to those outside Des Moines rose in both 1943 and 1944. Charges for the farm service, which had risen in 1941, were also increased in 1943.[18]

War Reporting

As was the case with other newspapers around the country, reports and stories about World War II dominated the *Register.* R&T readers craved news of the war, and the paper responded by filling its pages with detailed maps of the battlefronts and extensive coverage of both the European and Asian theaters. But as journalist Malcolm Browne noted in a 1995 book review, "The human dimensions of any war—World War Two more than all others—become perceptible only when the grand tableau is broken up into digestible vignettes."[19] Major news agencies and the larger newspapers realized the importance of humanizing the conflict; to get these stories, they sent reporters to the front lines. Some correspondents, such as Ernie Pyle of the Scripps-Howard organization, gained national attention. Pyle won a Pulitzer Prize in 1944 for his syndicated column that followed the everyday life of the American soldier.[20] The *Register* soon followed suit and dispatched its own commentator to cover the war.

In October 1943, the R&T sent veteran reporter Gordon Gammack to North Africa, where he was assigned as a war correspondent to the 34th Infantry Division (many divisions were created on a regional basis, and the 34th consisted of many troops from Iowa). The *Register* told its readers: "Gammack ... is on assignment in the Mediterranean theater of war, charged with reporting the activities of thousands of Iowa fighting men who are engaged there."[21] He was to seek out Iowa soldiers and tell their personal stories to readers back home. With Gammack at the front, the paper successfully adapted its proven formula of providing the Iowa perspective on national and international events. Wes Gallagher, who covered the war for The Associated Press, suggested that what Ernie Pyle did by reporting the "little picture of the war by providing the G.I.s' view" to a national audience, Gammack did for Iowans. Regardless of the topic, Gammack always crowded his articles with names and addresses of his Iowa subjects."[22] For the thousands of R&T readers searching for tidbits of information about loved ones and neighbors in the war, the column was always popular.

Washington Bureau

With the war dominating the news, more attention was focused on Washington, D.C. The R&T responded by expanding its Washington Bureau. Richard Wilson, who had been the bureau's sole member since its founding in 1933, was joined by Marr McGaffin, formerly of the *Omaha World-Herald,* in 1940. The following year, Nat Finney, a reporter for the *Minneapolis Star Journal,* came on board. With the addition of Finney, the bureau began serving the Cowles papers in both Des Moines and Minneapolis. From the end of 1943 through early 1944, two more correspondents joined the team and its functions were expanded. The new reporters were William Mylander, formerly of The Associated Press, and John Wilson, an experienced reporter from the *Minneapolis Tribune.* Headed by Richard Wilson and managed by Finney, the bureau was enlarged to serve all the Cowles media concerns—the R&T, the Minneapolis papers, *Look* magazine (all of which were connected to the bureau through a leased wire), and the radio stations.[23]

As the Washington Bureau's duties grew, John and Mike decided in late 1944 to incorporate the entity as Eastern Enterprises. Expenses for the Washington news-gathering operation were now shared by all the Cowles companies. By 1949, the Minneapolis papers shouldered 40 percent of Eastern Enterprises' expenses; the R&T paid for 30 percent; *Look*'s share was calculated at 27 percent; and the Cowles radio stations chipped in the remainder.[24]

Iowa Poll

In 1943, the *Register* became the first single newspaper to sponsor a statewide public opinion poll. The Iowa Poll, initiated by Mike Cowles when he returned to Des Moines after working for the Office of War Information, was originally intended to act as a public service for the state and to provide the *Register* with yet another feature that its competitors lacked. Cowles, of course, had been introduced to scientific polling techniques by George Gallup in the late 1920s. His OWI experience once again exposed him to the benefits of public opinion research and rekindled his interest.[25] John explained its value to their parents: "I am greatly sold on the potential value of these public opinion surveys. They will provide us with lots of ... information which we can both publish and use on our own."[26]

Because the R&T was an early entrant in this field, the creation of the poll required extensive preparation. After lengthy discussions with the two major polling organizations—the Gallup Poll and the Denver Poll—the company created a research department to set up and conduct the public opinion surveys. Originally headed by Seymour Morris, with whom Mike Cowles had become acquainted in Washington, D.C., the department was soon turned over to Henry Kroeger, a former advertising executive. Kroeger remained head of the research department for the next 17 years. The paper then hired University of Iowa psychologist Norman Meier, an expert on sampling techniques, to serve as the Iowa Poll's technical adviser. Finally, an advisory committee, originally consisting of "14 widely known Iowa men and women," was created to review questions that were to be asked in upcoming polls.[27]

Since polling was relatively new, the *Register* included an explanation of scientific sampling with its first Iowa Poll in December 1943: "The IOWA POLL is operating under the auspices of The Des Moines Register and Tribune. Its findings will be published weekly in The Des Moines Sunday Register. Polling only residents of Iowa, it is a scientific, impartial, weekly survey which samples a typical miniature of the population of Iowa, with the proper proportion of farmers, city and town persons, of rich and poor, young and old, men and women, voters and non-voters, all sampled proportionately in the various parts of the state."[28]

On December 19, 1943, the first Iowa Poll reported that Iowans narrowly preferred maintaining farm subsidies to increasing food prices at grocery stores. From that point on, the poll was a weekly *Register* feature revealing what Iowans thought on any number of issues. Early surveys, for instance, dealt with a wide variety of topics, including approval of presidential policies, the atomic bomb, labor issues, religious beliefs, women's hairstyles, and war bonds.[29] The poll, then, fit perfectly into the R&T's longtime strategy of reporting on what the people of the entire state thought. The power of the new feature was not missed by readers. Following a poll on religious questions, a subscriber wrote: "We appreciate the service you render in the Iowa Poll, for it does a great deal of good, a very good way to crystallize the thinking of the people of the state."[30] The poll's influence also became clear in more concrete ways. In 1946, for example, the Des Moines city council was considering whether to install parking meters in the downtown area. When the Iowa Poll queried a sample of automobile owners on the issue, it found that 54 percent approved of having downtown parking meters. Armed with this information, the city council voted to support parking meters, and installation began in late 1947.[31]

Besides impacting Des Moines and the state, the Iowa Poll (and the research department that administered it) soon proved beneficial in several other ways. In an era when few public opinion polls existed, the Iowa Poll increased the prestige of the *Register.* Syndicated columnist Marquis Childs, for example, mentioned the Iowa Poll in a 1946 article calling for the continuance of price controls. Childs noted that "every poll without exception reported a large majority in favor of keeping controls. This was true of The Gallup Poll, of the National Opinion Research Center in Denver, and of such reliable local polls as those conducted by the Des Moines Register in Iowa and the Minneapolis Tribune in Minnesota."[32] Its existence was a key element in an advertising campaign to convince national companies to advertise in the paper. Kenneth MacDonald, a longtime editor and later publisher of the R&T, noted, "At the time [1940s] this poll was unique. ... The motivation was to advertise the *Register* as a progressive newspaper that was trying to cover the state in all ways possible, including by polls of what its readers thought." Finally, the paper's research department conducted market surveys that were used internally by the paper, particularly the company's advertising department.[33]

Radio Growth

The Iowa Poll was not the only change Mike Cowles introduced to the company once he returned from the Office of War Information. Having earlier taken the family business into radio, Mike looked to expand the firm's holdings in this growing medium. According to James Baughman, "By 1945 an American home or apartment was more likely to have a radio than indoor plumbing or a telephone."[34] Many medium-size to large daily newspapers, including the *Register,* had been active in establishing or acquiring radio stations in their market areas during the 1930s. Newspaper entry into the radio business was fomented by both the prestige that accrued by using the latest technology and a fear that radio might lure advertisers away from the print medium.[35] Through its wholly owned subsidiary, the Iowa Broadcasting Company (IBC), the R&T held four radio properties: two Des Moines stations, KRNT and KSO; a Cedar Rapids station, WMT; and a South Dakota station, WNAX. A moneymaker since 1934, the radio division continued to be profitable. From 1939 to 1943, IBC's net profits nearly doubled, rising from $125,416 to $207,300.[36]

Although Mike was by nature an empire builder, his interest in increasing Iowa Broadcasting's holdings was first apparently prompted by the duopoly order of the Federal Communications Commission (FCC). This ruling disallowed one company from owning two radio stations in the same city and/or market. The Cowles' properties were, of course, not the only ones affected, and in response to the FCC's mandate, several radio stations changed hands in the spring of 1944.[37] One of the stations sold was the *Register*'s KSO. It was purchased in early May by Kingsley Murphy, a newspaper executive and minority-share owner of the Minneapolis Star Journal and Tribune Company, for $275,000. Even as this deal was being worked out, Mike targeted several more stations for acquisition.[38]

On May 5, just three days after the KSO sale, Iowa Broadcasting bought WHOM in Jersey City, New Jersey, from Paul Herron, Joseph Lang, and their families for $350,000. Although located in New Jersey, it had the range to cover the New York City area.[39] While media watchers were digesting these two transactions, Cowles pushed forward by announcing the hiring of T. A. M. Craven to help manage the radio properties. Regarded as an expert in radio and television, Craven had served on the FCC since 1935. By engaging such an industry heavyweight, Cowles signaled that the company's broadcasting holdings would be dramatically expanded. With his office located in Washington, D.C., Craven headed up the firm's eastern holdings. Many speculated that other deals were in the works.[40]

By the end of May, Cowles had purchased Arde Bulova's (of the famous watchmaking family) Massachusetts Broadcasting Company, which owned WCOP Boston, for $225,000. Like the Cowles' earlier sale of KSO, Bulova's divestment of WCOP was prompted by the FCC's duopoly ruling.[41] Before this acquisition, Cowles was involved in discussions with the owners of WOL in Washington, D.C. At issue was the possible exchange of the R&T's Cedar Rapids station, WMT, for WOL. Iowa Broadcasting already had plans to expand the power and improve the facilities of its Des Moines–based

KRNT. But more power would also push its signal into the Cedar Rapids area. Such overlapping, Mike Cowles thought, might violate the duopoly ruling. He was worried that the FCC would not allow KRNT's expansion unless WMT was divested.[42]

In an internal memo, Cowles reviewed the benefits and drawbacks of the contemplated station swap. On the downside, he noted that WMT expected to earn $275,000 before taxes in 1944, compared to WOL's earnings, which were likely to be between $60,000 and $75,000. In a revealing handwritten note to his brother scribbled atop the memo, Mike confessed, "Being a gambler at heart, I think I favor this deal, although the arithmetic certainly doesn't support it." Cowles then suggested that while the Cedar Rapids station was probably at or near peak earnings, the Washington station "should offer very large growth possibilities."[43]

Craven's response to Mike's memo suggested their plans for the immediate future. By the end of 1944, the subsidiary was named Cowles Broadcasting to reflect the new holdings outside of Iowa. After agreeing with Mike's conclusion that the station swap was not equitable since WMT had "less competition and better net earnings" than WOL, Craven supported the proposed trade for two reasons. He noted that WOL was an "important radio station in a world center." Over time, Craven believed "television and FM will tend to increase the advantages of Washington over Cedar Rapids."[44]

On October 1, 1944, WMT in Cedar Rapids was exchanged for WOL, and executives at Cowles Broadcasting Company (CBC) envisioned a regional East Coast network. With this foundation, CBC began expanding the power of the three stations in Boston, New Jersey, and Washington, and added FM to all these operations. The changes required the construction of new transmitting towers, more powerful antennae, and studio renovations. Such additions (as well as similar improvements to KRNT and WNAX) were expensive, however. From 1945 through 1947, the R&T loaned its radio companies $930,000.[45] Meanwhile, dreams of running an Atlantic cluster of stations carrying the same network programming were shelved when long-term agreements between two stations and two different networks were too good to pass up. WCOP in Boston signed on with NBC's blue network, and WOL in Washington chose to remain with the Mutual network. Given this situation, the company decided to dispose of the New Jersey station, which had lost $32,000 during the first quarter in 1945, rather than pour more money into it.[46]

When plans for an eastern radio network fell through, Mike Cowles tinkered with the idea of selling the Boston and Washington holdings as well. In the fall of 1946, he held preliminary talks with the recently created American Broadcasting Company to test if it had any interest in acquiring one or both of these properties. Although nothing came of the talks, CBC appeared ready to retreat to its familiar, and more profitable, midwestern markets.[47] Comparative earnings of the company's stations supported the soundness of this policy. While KRNT (Des Moines) net profits rose from $61,500 in 1947 to $93,900 in 1950, and WNAX (Yankton, South Dakota, and Sioux City, Iowa) remained a moneymaker despite a drop in profits from $167,600 to $126,600, the eastern stations struggled financially. From 1947 to 1950, WCOP (Boston) could barely turn a profit, and net earnings of $32,300 at WOL (Washington) sank to a net loss of $31,200.[48]

Besides poor financial performance, the eastern stations' need for expensive upgrades and their increasingly competitive radio markets portended a bleak future. With no turnaround in sight, CBC put its Boston and Washington properties up for sale in 1947. By the spring of the following year, no buyers had been found. Mike took the stations off the public auction block, explaining that their business was "being injured because of the gossip that they are for sale."[49] Still, the company remained interested in disposing of its eastern holdings and it continued, albeit more discreetly, to seek out possible purchasers. In February 1950, Cowles Broadcasting closed a deal unloading WOL for $300,000. Based on internal calculations, this transaction represented a loss of $31,700 from the depreciated value of the station's properties. The following year, CBC succeeded in selling WCOP, but like the earlier transaction, the Boston station was also sold at a loss.[50]

No longer hamstrung by its struggling eastern concerns, Cowles Broadcasting still faced growing competition in the Midwest. The situation in Des Moines was suggestive. In 1944, there were three stations in the city, two of which were owned by the R&T. Three years later, the firm's KRNT was one of four existing Des Moines stations, and three others were in the process of being established. In addition, five new FM stations had recently been authorized. Given this situation, company executive Luther Hill told the board of directors, "We cannot count on increasing the operating profits of the radio stations, but will be doing well to keep them at present levels."[51]

Personnel Changes

As the company was testing the waters of radio with decidedly mixed results, several important personnel changes occurred. In November 1946, Pulitzer Prize–winning editor William Waymack resigned to take up an appointment as a member of the newly formed Atomic Energy Commission.

With his departure, the firm's board of directors heaped praise on Waymack, noting that he had "carried on and added to the tradition of Harvey Ingham." In so doing, they continued, the editor "helped widen the influence of The Register and Tribune beyond the city, beyond the state, and beyond the nation, to Humanity itself."[52] To fill the positions Waymack vacated, associate editorial editor Forrest Seymour was promoted to editor of the editorial pages and managing editor Ken MacDonald was given the title of executive editor.[53]

The month following Waymack's resignation, publisher Mike Cowles decided to devote more energy to *Look* magazine. Faced with "increased costs and lowered profit margins," the magazine required Mike's closer attention. In December 1946, he took up full-time residence at an apartment in Manhattan's fashionable Waldorf Towers. In addition to Mike's move, the Register and Tribune provided a needed infusion of capital to *Look*; the company name was changed to Cowles Magazines, Incorporated (CMI) in 1944. By 1950, the R&T investment in CMI had climbed from $452,000 in 1940 to $1,786,282, and the paper owned approximately 55 percent of the magazine firm.[54]

Although now based in New York, Mike did not completely forsake the R&T. To keep tabs on the paper, he initially made a couple of trips a month to Des Moines. Although the frequency of these trips declined throughout the remainder of the 1940s and 1950s, he continued to visit the R&T on at least a bimonthly basis. When not in Des Moines, Mike generally talked to top R&T managers on the telephone once or twice a week. Yet he recognized his inability to deal with details of R&T operations. He relinquished the title of publisher but retained the company presidency. While not given the title of publisher until 1950, Luther Hill was named general manager in 1947 and assumed the top executive position in Des Moines.[55]

Besides these personnel changes, the late 1940s marked the passing of three key figures who built the Register from a struggling daily to the foundation of a publishing empire. On February 28, 1946, Gardner Cowles Sr., the founder of the publishing dynasty, died on his 85th birthday. The *Des Moines Tribune* editorialized: "We can think of no greater honor to be paid to Mr. Cowles by those of us who have worked with him and who shall follow him than that we continue to be guided by the principles of fairness, and honest dealing, and progressivism, and courageous support of Truth and Right which he himself espoused." Editorial editor Seymour and a special resolutions committee at the 1947 annual stockholders' meeting eulogized Cowles in similar fashion: "Mr. Cowles was truly the founder of these newspapers. It was his tirelessness that put them upon a sound business foundation. It was his high standards of honesty and fair play that earned for them the respect of the state and, indeed, the nation. It was his deep sense of public responsibility and his courage to pursue the truth that made possible their leadership and the winning of public confidence in them." Iowa Senator Bourke Hickenlooper's tribute captured the publisher's wider significance: "No man has left a greater record in the culture and development of our state than he. Coming from a small Iowa city, he met the challenge of metropolitan journalism and established a great middle western newspaper and a great influence reaching far beyond our borders."[56]

Several months later, William Cordingley, the 67-year-old circulation manager who oversaw the *Register*'s spread into every corner of Iowa for 40 years, died unexpectedly. In a front-page story, the paper noted Cordingley's emphasis on superior service, getting newspapers delivered promptly and regularly. The article credited the manager with seeing "the possibility of establishing carrier service similar to that in Des Moines for other towns. It was real pioneering, but it brought home delivery of a daily newspaper [the *Des Moines Register*] to most Iowa homes and to Iowa farms on Sunday."[57] Privately, the company's board of directors recognized his importance and contributions by awarding his widow a lump-sum payment amounting to one year of her deceased husband's salary. The vacancy left by Cordingley's death was ably filled by Ernest P. Schwartz, the longtime head of the farm service circulation division and the architect of the innovative rural weekly pay system.[58]

Along with Cowles and Cordingley, Harvey Ingham was another essential figure at the paper during the first few decades of the 20th century. A month shy of his 91st birthday, Ingham passed away in August 1949. It was Ingham who had established the liberal and progressive tradition at the paper. William Waymack said of the editor emeritus, "Through decades of public education by explaining and debating issues, his intelligence invariably sought the core of things, the causes and reasons behind problems. ... He supported causes that were unpopular because they were not understood. The test of his wisdom and of his service is in the fact that nearly every one of them has come to be recognized as sound." According to the *Register*'s farewell editorial, Ingham did more than educate readers: "Wherever he was, whatever he did, to whatever controversy he set his pen, with whomsoever he associated, he made men think, and made them think more kindly."[59]

Although these deaths marked the end of an era, the firm remained committed to putting out a paper for all Iowans. As executive editor, MacDonald understood that much of the *Register*'s past success was based on its statewide news coverage. Determined to maintain this scope, MacDonald consistently "fought off pressure to 'localize' the *Register*." Under his direction, the company expanded on its tradition of providing news from across Iowa. "During my time," MacDonald noted, "we improved the correspondence network throughout Iowa and increased the amount of travel throughout the state by reporters."[60]

Pulitzer Prizes

Besides building on the paper's statewide news heritage, MacDonald continued to stress journalistic excellence. One of the editor's strong points was his ability to hire talented reporters and then, in MacDonald's words, "give them the latitude in which to work." This type of leadership created an atmosphere for the R&T staff to garner additional Pulitzer Prizes. Several years prior to MacDonald's assuming the executive editorship, the paper won two Pulitzers in 1943: Ding Darling gained his second for an editorial cartoon, and Forrest Seymour was given the prize for outstanding editorial output for the year. With MacDonald at the helm, prizes continued. In 1952, photographers John Robinson and Don Ultang won a Pulitzer for a photographic essay shot with the "machine gun" camera at a Drake University football game. The sequence revealed Drake player Johnny Bright being punched by an Oklahoma A&M player. The blow broke Bright's jaw. Two years later, Washington Bureau chief Richard Wilson received the paper's sixth Pulitzer for his stories "unraveling the case of Harry Dexter White, who was given a post in the Truman administration despite FBI reports linking White with Soviet espionage."[61]

Possibly the most influential items to appear in the *Register* during this period were penned by editorial page editor Lauren Soth. After he read a speech by Soviet Premier Nikita Khrushchev, in which the Communist leader spoke of Iowa's great success of producing feed grain, Soth wrote an editorial on February 10, 1955, inviting the Soviets to come to Iowa to see the state's agricultural techniques up close:

> We have no diplomatic authority of any kind, but we hereby extend an invitation to any delegation Khrushchev wants to select to come to Iowa to get the lowdown on raising high quality cattle, hogs, sheep, and chickens. We promise to hide none of our "secrets." We will take the visiting delegation to Iowa's great agricultural experiment station at Ames, to some of the leading farmers in Iowa, to our livestock breeders, soil conservation experts and seed companies. Let the Russians see how we do it.[62]

In return, Soth suggested that an Iowa delegation of farmers and agricultural experts visit the Soviet Union. Although the editor never believed anything would come of his proposal, he thought that a better Soviet understanding of the U.S. economy "might persuade them that there is a happier future in developing a high standard of living than in this paralyzing race for more and more armaments."[63]

This editorial, for which Soth won the *Register*'s seventh Pulitzer Prize, planted the idea of an agricultural exchange. To the editor's surprise, the Soviets responded favorably to the invitation, and the two governments began working out the details. In June 1955, a 12-member American team of farmers and other agrarian specialists (including the R&T's Soth and four other Iowans) traveled to Moscow and toured various agricultural operations throughout the country. Meanwhile, a Russian delegation flew to Iowa and examined American farming methods.[64] These simultaneous tours not only provided a brief respite of goodwill amid the continuing cold war tensions, they also gave the R&T a boost. As publisher Luther Hill put it, "We are getting a lot of good 'mileage' out of the visit of the Russians. In many ways I think it is the best general promotion we have had for years." Although relations between the two powers soured in 1956 because of the Soviet move to crush the Hungarian uprising, connections made during the Russian trip to Iowa led to Khrushchev's stop in the state during his 1959 United States tour.[65]

Soth's coup was followed by yet another Pulitzer Prize in 1958. Washington Bureau correspondent Clark Mollenhoff won the award for reporting on the federal government's scrutiny of the Teamsters Union and its new president, Jimmy Hoffa. The U.S. Senate Select Committee on Improper Activities in the Labor-Management Field was investigating charges of racketeering within the union as well as its alleged ties to the Mafia. As a result of the investigation, in which "Mollenhoff worked closely with then Senator John F. Kennedy and his brother, Robert, who was then counsel to the Senate committee," the Teamsters were expelled from the AFL-CIO. Several years later, Hoffa was found guilty of jury tampering and began serving his prison term in 1967.[66]

Changes in Circulation

Such superior journalism, together with strong Iowa coverage and statewide distribution, led to continued circulation growth through the late 1940s and into the early 1950s. Combined morning and evening circulation peaked at 382,900 in 1951, while Sunday circulation reached its high point of 553,000 that same year. From that date, however, circulation of the evening

Tribune began a steady decline. Part of the problem was that in the 23-county zone (largely comprising central Iowa) where the evening paper had its highest circulation, its major competition was the *Register.* While the *Register's* circulation continued to inch upward in central Iowa, it often grew at the expense of the *Tribune.* Moreover, the costs of promoting and distributing the evening paper outside central Iowa (where sales of the *Tribune* dropped off precipitously) kept rising. After an extensive study conducted in 1954, management decided to decrease gradually the *Tribune's* distribution area. The thinking was that with the *Tribune* less heavily promoted in distant counties, circulation would decline, and readers would subscribe to the *Register* instead. The idea of planned reductions in readership was economically sound, but it cut against the company's long culture of working to build circulation. Hill and his managers, therefore, did not pursue the strategy with much vigor.[67]

Following a particularly bad 1956, John Cowles suggested cutting back the *Tribune* circulation more rapidly to save money. He called for accelerating "the transfer of Tribune business outside the Des Moines 60-mile or 75-mile radius to the Register, letting the Tribune's total circulation steadily decline but adding that loss, I hope, to the morning Register." Such a plan, Cowles believed, would save the circulation department "a considerable amount of promotion and sales expense." Evening losses, however, were not offset by morning gains. By 1959, a discernible trend was apparent: circulation of the morning paper remained steady, the evening offering was losing readers, and sales of the Sunday *Register* stabilized at approximately 25,000 less than circulation numbers in 1951.[68]

The dip in profits highlighted some long-term problems for the R&T. While circulation began declining, costs, especially newsprint and payroll, continued to advance rapidly. New forms of media, such as television and free "shopper newspapers," challenged the company's market dominance. Although newspaper circulation nationwide rose during the 1950s, it increased more slowly than in the previous decade and failed to keep pace with the rapidly growing number of households.[69] Much like the R&T, newspapers all across the country felt the pressure of increased media competition for advertising dollars.

During the decade following World War II, the R&T's net advertising and circulation revenue rose from $9 million in 1946 to $17 million in 1955, but the newspaper operating profit (after taxes) increased only $100,000, while the firm's profit margin on its newspaper business fell from 10.1 percent to 5.9 percent. Rising expenses were largely to blame. The climbing price of newsprint, coupled with payroll increases, fueled the rapid expansion in expenses. Cost of newsprint, which had begun moving upward during the war, soared in its aftermath. In 1946, the price of newsprint stood at $68 a ton; 10 years later, it had nearly doubled to $127 a ton. Company payroll likewise nearly doubled. The upshot of these discouraging figures was that the R&T's total net profit for the period, which included income from such divisions as commercial printing and its syndicate, edged up from $1.1 million to $1.3 million. One publisher summed up the industry's problems in 1958 by saying, "Standstill productivity and rising costs are the bane of newspaper publishing today."[70]

Amid the lackluster performance, John Cowles continued his close monitoring of the Des Moines situation from Minneapolis. With a fine eye for detail, he examined and commented on all R&T business and financial issues. Although in 1952 he noted that Hill was "in complete charge of our Des Moines papers," it was apparent that John and Mike tried to run the Register and Tribune in absentia. Hill was the on-site manager in Iowa, but he constantly had one or both Cowles brothers looking over his shoulder. Clearly, his managerial prerogative was circumscribed by John and Mike's unwillingness to step aside from the running of the paper.[71]

Frustrated by the company's subpar numbers, Mike Cowles expressed his concerns at the annual stockholders' meeting in January 1953. He argued that, considering "the relative boom conditions prevailing in Iowa and throughout the country," the profits of R&T operations "were not so good as they should have been." He hoped that by "cutting expenses and increasing rates, a much better result would be obtained." Over the next two years, management increased advertising rates twice and circulation rates once. The increase in the circulation rates, however, led to declining sales, and earnings did not dramatically rebound.[72]

New Competition

Besides being hampered by steep cost increases, the R&T was facing new forms of competition. Television, which soon grew to be a serious threat, was originally seen by many newspaper publishers as a good investment opportunity. Much like their earlier move into radio, newspapers saw television stations as a "marvelous form of self-promotion and civic boosterism."[73] Through Cowles Broadcasting, the firm joined a growing number of newspapers that went into television. Company involvement in television dated back to the previous decade, when it had expanded its radio holdings. By 1947, CBC had already applied for a television permit for its Boston radio station (WCOP), and Hill noted at the time that "when television programming is available in Des Moines, it will be imperative, in order to protect our present situation [radio station KRNT], for the company to erect a television station here."[74] The firm was first able to obtain a license for a Sioux City station. It established KVTV, and the station began broadcasting in 1953. Two years later, its KRNT-TV in Des Moines went on the air.[75]

The R&T did not remain in the television industry long, however. In December 1955, John and Mike decided to separate Cowles Broadcasting Company from its parent R&T. Several factors led to the spin-off, in which Register and Tribune stockholders received three shares of CBC stock for every share of R&T stock held. Separating the companies, the brothers believed, would allow each to focus on its core business and lead to better customer service. In addition, dividing up the ventures gave CBC a greater chance of acquiring more television stations under the FCC's diversification policy. According to the regulatory body, when "two or more candidates applied for the same [television] outlet and when 'other things are equal,' the license should go to the nonnewspaper or to the candidate with no other media affiliations."[76]

Even as the R&T divested its broadcasting subsidiary, company officials, as well as other publishers around the country, began to see television as a real media competitor. Its rise, in fact, was nothing short of spectacular. In 1950, roughly 100 stations beamed signals to nearly 10 million television sets nationwide. By 1960, there were 533 commercial stations in operation, while 50 million American homes (approximately 87 percent of the total) boasted a television. This rapid growth, combined with the new medium's wide reach, led national advertisers to use television to sell their products.[77]

As television advanced, newspaper firms watched their share of all advertising expenditures shrink. In 1950, newspapers received 37.5 percent of all advertising, while the nascent television industry's share was only 3 percent. By 1955, newspapers' share had fallen to 33.2 percent, and television had risen to 11 percent. Six years later, advertising in newspapers had dropped to 30.5 percent; advertising on television, meanwhile, had risen to 13.5 percent. Although gross advertising revenue at the R&T (and newspapers nationally) rose throughout the period, the shrinking market share was alarming. Lyle Lynn, longtime advertising manager at the paper, noted that in 1962, for instance, $4 million was spent on television advertising in the greater central Iowa market. If television were not present in the area, Lynn estimated, newspapers, largely the *Register* and *Tribune,* likely would have received 70 percent of this advertising business.[78]

Besides television, the company witnessed the advent of five weekly shopper publications, each distributed free of charge in the Des Moines region. Although these papers contained some local news and other filler material, such as astrological charts, they were dominated by advertising. Nationally, "the growth of shoppers," according to media expert Leo Bogart, "was fostered by chain retail advertisers who wanted saturation coverage of the specific localities from which their customers were drawn and who were dismayed by dailies' loss of market penetration."[79] As the R&T circulation had gradually decreased over the course of the decade, some Des Moines businesses had sought to reach their local customer base through other means. Shopper publications were established to meet this need; by 1962, five claimed a total distribution of approximately 67,000 weekly.[80]

The increasingly competitive market made 1956 a dismal year for the Register and Tribune. Although total newspaper revenue rose by $257,053 because of an increase in both circulation and advertising rates, expenses shot up nearly $1 million. As a result, newspaper operating profits declined $359,084, and the profit margin on this operation dropped to 3.7 percent, the worst performance since 1925, the first year such records are available. Meanwhile, the company's total net earnings fell $272,556.[81]

Reversing the Decline

To reverse the downward turn, the Cowles brothers considered several steps. Besides paring down *Tribune* promotion and distribution, John thought about additional ways to cut costs. Among other things, he went so far as to suggest that the tradition of giving every employee a rose on his or her anniversary date of employment at the R&T be curtailed. Eliminating such a "benefit," he believed, could save "$1,500 a year, and perhaps more."[82] While John was reviewing the company budget line by line, Mike proposed a more radical solution. In late 1956, publisher Luther Hill had mentioned that he might retire at the end of the year. Up to that time, there was no indication that either Mike or John was unhappy with Hill's management. But following the poor performance of that year, Mike wrote John in early 1957: "I have decided that [Hill's retirement] is wise, and I will explain to you my reasons when we are next together." Although the letter did not provide specifics, the brothers very likely had concluded that Hill was unable to hold the line on expenses. Over the course of the decade, John Cowles had flooded Hill with letters discussing his concerns about rising costs in Des Moines, but little improvement was forthcoming. Meanwhile, they promoted David Kruidenier, a young nephew who had started at the R&T as assistant business manager in 1952, to director of sales. In this newly created position, the 35-year-old Kruidenier had authority over circulation, advertising, and promotion and research.[83]

David Kruidenier represented the third generation of the Cowleses at the paper. Although not actively recruited into the business empire, he knew that the various family firms were always an option. During his undergraduate years at Yale, Kruidenier decided to follow in his uncles' footsteps. After serving in World War II and obtaining an MBA at Harvard, Kruidenier was given the choice of starting at the Des Moines paper, the Minneapolis paper, or *Look* magazine. Beginning with the *Minneapolis Star and Tribune* in 1948, he moved to the R&T in 1952. By early 1957, Luther Hill was duly impressed with young Kruidenier's work, noting that he "is very helpful in bringing about a reduction in the operating expenses of the R and T."[84]

This closer scrutiny of expenses was one factor in the company's 1957 rebound. Expenses fell 1 percent while revenues rose 2.9 percent from 1956. Total net profits increased by more than $600,000, and the profit margin on newspaper operations moved up to 5.4 percent. Given the improvement, the discussion of Hill's retirement was put aside, but serious questions remained about the company's long-term financial health. For one thing, profits were boosted by a onetime sale of company-owned securities. For another, although both circulation and advertising linage declined, revenues rose after a hike in rates. While publisher Luther Hill was pleased about the progress made, he told stockholders in early 1958 that raising fees "was not the answer to the sound long-time successful operations of these newspapers." He argued that the firm's future rested with increasing mass sales: "Our present and future corporate health depends upon having large numbers and increasing numbers of advertisers using our papers, and a growing number of families reading them."[85]

Despite the solid financial performance in 1958 and 1959, Hill had identified a growing management concern—the general trend of declining circulation. One way to deal with this situation was to buy other newspapers in expanding areas. Late in the decade, the Cowles brothers considered this move. Other industry leaders, such as Samuel Newhouse or Frank Gannett, for instance, had already been actively buying newspapers throughout the 1950s. Their acquisitions and others by the Hearst or Ridder interests meant that by 1960, 109 newspaper groups controlled 560 of the nation's dailies and 46 percent of total circulation.[86]

Among the newspapers under consideration for acquisition by the R&T were those in Rockford, Illinois, and Montgomery, Alabama. After researching the properties, however, John convinced Mike of inherent problems, and neither company was added to the Register fold. Although the Illinois paper was nearby in the familiar Midwest, John noted in late 1957, "I don't think Rockford has much growth potential and is economically vulnerable because of its dependence on the machine tool and metal working industries."[87] Moving into Montgomery, he believed, would be equally questionable. At issue was the *Register*'s strong, liberal editorial voice demanding full civil rights for African-Americans. John Cowles explained: "If we owned them [the Montgomery papers] either we would be inhibited from expressing opinions on the Register and Tribune editorial pages about race discrimination and school integration, or some competing radio or TV station in Montgomery might broadcast what we were saying editorially in Des Moines in ways that would seriously embarrass the management of the Montgomery papers."[88] In the tradition of his father, John worked to keep the business side of the company completely separate from the paper's editorial position. Unwilling to compromise the *Register*'s stand on civil rights, he argued successfully against buying the Alabama concern.

Editorial Positions

Fighting racism, in fact, remained a prominent feature of the paper. This stance, combined with its traditions of supporting Republican candidates and calling for an internationalist foreign policy, continued to be a consistent theme on the *Register*'s editorial page. In the midst of the cold war, the paper counseled a sensible and moderate course in dealing with communism. Similarly at home, it strongly opposed the red-baiting of Senator Joseph McCarthy, the Wisconsin Republican.

Civil Rights

As it had done in 1940 and 1944, the *Register* endorsed the Republican challenger in the 1948 presidential election. But soon after Thomas Dewey was defeated by incumbent Harry Truman, the paper was heartened by the reelected president's continued strong stand on full civil rights for African-Americans. In January 1948, Truman became, according to historian William O'Neill, "the first president to attack racism head on," by announcing his 10-Point Program. Most important, Truman's plan called for an antilynching law, elimination of the poll tax, a ban on racial segregation in interstate transportation, and the creation of a permanent Fair Employment Practices Commission (FEPC) to thwart discrimination against African-Americans in the workplace. Although the *Register* correctly believed that the bills would not get through Congress, it applauded Truman for proposing the "long-needed" program. Calling racial discrimination the "biggest single blot on American democracy," the paper thought "the civil rights committee report on which it [the 10-Point Program] was based will remain a challenge and a goal."[89]

Even as Truman's civil rights bills were blocked by a coalition of Republicans and conservative Southern Democrats, the *Register* began a series of editorials commenting on the "experimental" civil rights legislation recently passed in several states. Writing in August 1948, the editorial staff reported: "Now there is a strong countermovement for justice to racial minorities in the interest of everybody. The recent wave of antidiscrimination laws and ordinances is only the most conspicuous evidence of this." The paper felt, however, that while these steps were positive, "for the long pull, other things are more important—the popular sentiment that backs laws like these, the public and private research and education that accompany them, and the new habits of working together, on the job and in social action, that they foster."[90]

As always, the *Register* made every effort to link prominent national events to Iowa. In October 1948, the civil rights issue was brought home with the paper's prominent, front-page story that Katz Drug Store in Des Moines had been found guilty of violating Iowa's civil rights law. Months earlier, in July 1948, Maurice Katz had refused service to three black customers at the store's soda fountain. Although it was the first time a Katz employee was found guilty of violating the civil rights act, charges had been brought against the store three other times over the course of four years. Iowa, it was clear, was not immune from discrimination.[91]

With the election behind him, Truman used his State of the Union address on January 5, 1949, to tell the American people that every individual had "a right to expect from our Government a fair deal." The reform agenda he laid out was later dubbed the Fair Deal, and it included the expansion of Social Security benefits, the creation of national health insurance, an increase in the minimum wage, federal assistance to education, the establishment of a permanent FEPC, and passage of antilynching legislation. Although the *Register* later referred to most of these programs as "the folly of President Truman," it supported his stand on civil rights. At the same time, the paper was troubled by the Republicans' alliance with Southern Democrats; those groups again succeeded in killing the president's civil rights proposals. The *Register* wondered about the gap between the party's rhetoric and its legislative action: "How can the ordinary joe believe the G.O.P. is the party of freedom when it takes so lightly its pledges to work for the major civil right of an industrial age: the right to an equal chance at jobs, regardless of race, creed, color, nationality, or union membership."[92]

With civil rights ordinances stymied by Congress, the *Register* acknowledged the role the courts had played in the past decade "to take the sanction of law away from race discrimination and segregation." Several years later, attention once again focused on the judicial branch. On May 17, 1954, the

Supreme Court overturned segregation in publicly funded schools in the landmark case of *Brown v. Board of Education of Topeka*. Writing for a unanimous court, Chief Justice Earl Warren declared that "in the field of public education, the doctrine of 'separate but equal' has no place. Separate educational facilities are inherently unequal." The *Register* cheered the ruling that had started the process "to erase one of American democracy's blackest marks." While it noted that the decision "will ease America's conscience," it added that "America's conscience will not be *cleared* until her practice measured up to the noble words of the Court's decision."[93]

School desegregation in border states—Delaware, Kentucky, Maryland, Missouri, Oklahoma, and West Virginia—and states that allowed segregation based on local option—Arizona, Kansas, New Mexico, and Wyoming—began peacefully. One year later, in May 1955, the Supreme Court outlined its plans for implementing the *Brown* decision. Rather than calling for immediate integration, as the NAACP had wanted, the Court expected "a prompt and reasonable start to full compliance." In Des Moines, the R&T editors supported this moderate approach: "A titanic social change is underway, and it is off to a good start. It is quite possible to go wrong in two directions: by letting it bog down or by trying to rush it too fast. The important thing is to keep it moving and to keep it based upon a real change of heart, upon respect for the law, and upon following the example of neighbors who have carried out the big change successfully."[94]

Even as the *Register* closely monitored race relations in the South, it also recounted continuing problems in Iowa. In August 1955, the paper described how Eugene Peniston, a young black military veteran who planned to enroll at the State University of Iowa, had been denied private housing in Iowa City because of his race. While the editorial was careful to note that university housing, offered on a "first come-first serve basis" where "no distinction was made as to race, color, [or] creed," was not involved, it found the incident "deplorable." Editors explained the unfortunate episode as "discrimination by people acting on their own." But they concluded, confidently, that "these people are in a disappearing minority."[95]

If the *Register* editors had reason to be hopeful about the situation in Iowa, such optimism was not warranted in the South. The Court's ruling for the gradualist implementation of the *Brown* decision emboldened southern segregationists to oppose school integration. States in the Deep South instituted a policy of massive resistance. Various means were devised to sidestep integrating schools. Virginia, for instance, considered using public money to fund private schools.[96] Such ideas received a boost in March 1956, when 101 congressmen—including most Southern representatives and all Southern senators except Albert Gore, Estes Kefauver, and Lyndon

Johnson—signed the "Declaration of Constitutional Principles" claiming that the Supreme Court had overstepped its bounds with the *Brown* case. According to this Southern Manifesto, the states alone could decide whether their schools should be segregated. It called for employing "all lawful means to bring about a reversal to this decision that is contrary to the Constitution." The *Register* found this turn of events "ominous": "Those who had thought hopefully that progress toward racial justice would continue are brought sharply to recognize a crisis of resistance."[97]

Even as the white South prepared to oppose integrating its schools, the Civil Rights movement had taken a new turn in Montgomery, Alabama. In December 1955, a black seamstress named Rosa Parks refused to surrender her seat to a white person on a local bus. This act violated a city ordinance, and Parks was arrested. Following the incident, black leaders decided to protest by organizing a boycott of the city's bus system. Martin Luther King Jr. agreed to head up the boycott, and car pools were established to provide alternate transportation to those who ordinarily rode the buses.[98] Eleven months later, in November 1956, the Supreme Court upheld a federal district court's decision that racial segregation on a local bus line was unconstitutional. The *Register* applauded: "That settles the law and that is the way the law should be. The fantastic Hindu caste system of 'separate but equal' was a tragic mistake in law, and a confession of a failure in practice." The following month, the boycott ended in victory, and the city's buses were peacefully integrated. Praising the action of African-Americans, the *Register* wrote prophetically: "One event of 1956 may bulk much larger in history than it did at the time: the extraordinary Negro bus boycott in Montgomery, Ala."[99]

This civil rights victory did nothing to discourage white Southerners from fighting integration, and Little Rock, Arkansas, became the next battleground. On September 2, 1957, Governor Orval Faubus announced that he could not maintain order if forced integration were carried out in Little Rock, and he ordered National Guard troops out to block the entry of black students into Central High School. When Faubus defied a court order to proceed with integration, the *Register* worried, "All of the progress made toward equality of Negroes in recent years, including the historic act of Congress this summer guaranteeing the fundamental right of suffrage to Negroes, will be overshadowed by events in Little Rock."[100]

President Eisenhower eventually convinced Faubus to remove the troops and, amid a large mob of abusive whites, the nine black students entered Central High School on September 23. The *Register* admired the young students' bravery: "They faced known danger and the fortitude they displayed deserves the admiration of all who believe in the brotherhood of man." The following day, Eisenhower finally decided to act. To ward off possible violence, enforce the law, and ensure the black students' safety, Eisenhower federalized the Arkansas National Guard and sent 1,000 paratroopers into Little Rock. The crowd outside the school was dispersed, and the black students were escorted to and from classes. With order restored, the *Register* praised the chief executive's action, explaining that he "did not act peremptorily." The paper continued, arguing that the federal government had "no choice but to employ force ... to uphold the law of the land." Finally, the editorial ended on a hopeful note: "Little Rock must become a symbol of a turning point—not back to the dark ages but toward a new age of enlightened racial harmony, with true equality of opportunity."[101]

As calm descended over Little Rock, the *Register* acknowledged the courage of two Little Rock newspapers, the *Arkansas Gazette* and the *Arkansas Democrat*. They had called for the peaceful integration of Central High School, opposed Faubus's actions, and supported the president's use of federal troops to protect the black students. The Des Moines paper saluted the southern newspapers' strength of conviction: "We have had some slight harassment from pro-segregation readers in Des Moines, enough to appreciate what the editors in Little Rock must be undergoing. In Des Moines it is easy for us to be fearless in saying what we think about the introduction of racial equality in public schools in Arkansas. In Little Rock, it takes courage to withstand threats."[102]

Cold War

While the civil rights struggle received significant editorial comment, a larger amount of space in the *Register*'s opinion page was devoted to the cold war. In general, the paper counseled sensible dealings with the Soviets: it refused to view international events in the bipolar cold war framework and analyzed global incidents on a case-by-case basis. Initially, R&T editors threw their support behind Truman's battling communism abroad. In April 1947, the *Register* defended the president's call to provide military and economic aid to Greece and Turkey to prevent communist takeovers. It explained pragmatically, "We choose to take a firm stand ... about Greece and Turkey rather than the Baltic states, Poland, Hungary, Romania, Bulgaria, or Yugoslavia because geography permits us to. ... Greece and Turkey are situated where we can [take action]. Turkey is the screen preventing communist infiltration in the whole Middle East, and the one place from which our sea and air power can most readily scare Russia." The *Register*'s readers were apparently not as convinced. In an Iowa Poll, the paper reported that Iowans were fairly split on the issue—only 53 percent favored aid to Greece and Turkey.[103] Ultimately, the policy succeeded in maintaining the governments in both countries.

The following year, the United States, Britain, and France prepared to merge their three postwar occupation zones in Germany to create the Federal Republic of Germany. The possibility of a rebuilt Germany tied to the Western Powers frightened the Soviets, and they responded in June 1948 by closing off all land access to West Berlin (located within the Soviet occupation sector of eastern Germany). Unwilling to see West Berlin cut off, Truman initiated "Operation Vittles," a massive airlift of food, fuel, and other basic necessities to the people of the blockaded city. A combined effort with the British, the airlift was soon delivering 13,000 tons of supplies daily. Although the *Register* supported Truman's handling of this "purely emergency affair," it expressed concern: "So long as the chasm between us and the Soviets exists, these crises will recur and recur. There is always the possibility that one of them will 'explode' whether either party intended it to or not." This was not, the paper thought, "a 'satisfactory' program for conducting our relations with Russia." Yet when the Soviets finally lifted the blockade one year later, the editorial page conveyed the heady air of success: "For the air forces of the United States and Great Britain, it is the close of a great chapter. Their achievements stand unparalleled in military operations." It then suggested that the airlift marked "a new phase of American determinism" in foreign policy matters.[104]

After the Soviets backed down in Berlin, the *Register* strongly endorsed "making the Rhine the first line of defense" by providing military aid to western Europe and creating the North Atlantic Treaty Organization (NATO). But even as it advocated a defense buildup, the paper continued to push for talks with the Russians. In February 1950, for example, it appealed to Secretary of State Dean Acheson to make another effort at negotiating nuclear arms control with the Soviets.[105]

Several months later, in late June, communist North Korea invaded South Korea in an apparent attempt to reunite the country. Although the incident is now generally considered part of a civil war between the north and south, Truman and his administration viewed the attack as another example of Soviet expansion. Having learned from successful operations in Greece and Berlin that a firm stand could turn back communist aggression, the president chose to use armed force. The United States obtained a United Nations (UN) condemnation of North Korea, and the UN authorized its members to take collective action to defend South Korea. Several days later, U.S. troops were sent into the war-torn peninsula. According to a July 1950 poll, 77 percent of the country approved of American entry into the Korean conflict. Not surprisingly, the *Register* firmly endorsed the intervention and believed the Soviets were behind the attack.[106]

Once the American troops were involved, the R&T covered the conflict much like it had World War II. Maps of the battlefronts were featured almost daily, and the paper concentrated on the Iowa angle whenever possible. Over the course of the war, reports of the heroics of Iowa soldiers and stories about Iowans killed in action appeared frequently. The paper's veteran war reporter, Gordon Gammack, made three trips to Korea to provide the intimate details of the everyday battlefield experiences of Iowans.[107]

While the *Register* remained committed to covering the Korean conflict from the perspective of Iowans, its support for the American war effort did not remain steadfast. When U.S. forces ignored repeated warnings and advanced through North Korea toward the Yalu River (a boundary line separating North Korea from China) in October 1950, the Chinese intervened in the war. American forces were pushed back into South Korean territory, and by January 1951, Seoul was occupied by communist forces. This turn of events forced the *Register* to reevaluate the importance of Korea to the overall U.S. foreign policy.

In fact, even as the paper had backed entering the war in July 1950, it still felt that the defense of Europe was primary: "For if the eastern shores of Asia are important as they certainly are, the land mass and peoples of Western Europe are *absolutely vital.*" On January 9, 1951, the *Register* began to withdraw its support for Truman's Korean policy. It worried that with Chinese entry into the war, America was "suddenly confronted with a global war rather than a local Korean war." Continuing to conduct operations in Korea, especially with the Chinese army involved, might lessen the U.S. ability to defend Europe, which, the paper emphasized, remained the first priority. Therefore, R&T editors suggested the possibility of declaring Korea "strategically futile" and conceivably withdrawing from the peninsula.[108]

As the paper moved away from its support of the Korean War effort, it watched the growing rift between President Truman and General Douglas MacArthur. By March 1951, American forces had succeeded in pushing the communists back to the 38th parallel, and a stalemate near the prewar boundary line ensued. At that point, Truman chose to fight a limited war and try negotiating a settlement. MacArthur, however, wanted all-out victory, and he began challenging the president's position in public. The general called for widening the war, employing nationalist Chinese forces in Korea, and possibly using atomic weapons. The *Register* had no patience for what it termed the "MacArthur feud" and suggested that firing the general was past due. In the midst of the editorial, the paper continued to stress the primacy of Europe over Asia: "General MacArthur is blindly passionate on this subject of attacking Communism in Asia, where his whole career has centered. If we were to do this, we should be playing directly into Russia's hands by so weakening Europe as to make Communist conquest there vastly easier." It went on to explain that MacArthur had overstepped his authority. "Even if the merits of MacArthur's argument were strong enough to warrant debate, *he is not the one to do the debating*. That is for our congress, the United Nations General Assembly, and other national policy-makers to decide. A general in the field has no business trying to dictate to the civilian political institutions which a democracy properly relies upon." On April 11, 1951, Truman fired MacArthur for insubordination. Several days later, the *Register* spoke of the incident as both "damaging and humiliating."[109]

Korea was not the only area of concern in Asia. Indochina looked like a potential problem, and the *Register* was wary of involvement there from the beginning. Following World War II, the French had been fighting nationalist Ho Chi Minh (viewed by Washington as a communist tied to Moscow) in an attempt to regain control of their former southeast Asian colony. Truman saw the battle as a cold war struggle and in May 1950 extended foreign aid to help the French effort. The *Register*, however, was skeptical of offering such support: "We backed an unpopular and corrupt government in China with disastrous results. We had better have strong guarantees from Bao Dai [the French-installed Vietnamese leader] before we commit ourselves too strongly in his support." Then, in an enlightened statement, it suggested that cold war dogma was an inadequate justification for action: "We ought to know by this time that anticommunism is alone not enough."[110]

Four years later, the French forces surrendered at Dienbienphu, and a peace conference ensued in Geneva. During the talks, which ultimately led to a temporary dividing of Vietnam at the 17th parallel and the assurance that national elections in 1956 would reunify the country, the *Register* cautioned American policy-makers that the United States could not "succeed in Indochina acting alone" without the "support of Allies and the Vietnamese people." While the paper did not want to "abandon Southeast Asia," it was reassured that the United States "planned no open intervention."[111]

Although the R&T firmly supported Dwight Eisenhower for president in 1952 and again in 1956, it remained committed to a pragmatic foreign policy, not one tied to cold war rhetoric. In general, it opposed the "fervent anti-Communist absolutes" of Eisenhower's secretary of state, John Foster Dulles, and his ignoring of "evolving power patterns of the world by 'inflexibly' trying to preserve the status quo with treaties and military pacts." The paper, for example, failed to support the president's decision to send 14,000 troops into Lebanon to put down the threat of a coup in 1958. As discussed earlier, it called for improved relations with the Soviets and played a major role in the agricultural exchange that took place between the two countries in 1955.[112]

Communism at Home

Just as the paper outlined a practical approach to foreign policy and dealing with communism abroad, so too did it take a sober position on dealing with the threat of communism at home. In 1947, President Truman instituted a loyalty program for federal employees to root out communists from government. Even though the *Register* agreed that loyalty was required of civil servants, the paper held that the law's vague wording and its methods, which did not allow those accused to confront their accusers, were problematic. It explained, "Invitations to wholesale disqualification on mere grounds of membership in liberal organizations are in the *opposite* direction of personal liberty and respect for democracy. This is the Communist and the Nazi technique—not the democratic one."[113]

Two years later, the issue of loyalty had spread well beyond the federal government. In particular, by July 1949, 27 states required their public school teachers to take loyalty oaths. *Register* editors continued their opposition to such programs. They believed them to be "a little silly" and thought loyalty oaths would "neither reveal or reform a Communist." Worse, however, were the potential abuses: "The investigation is bound to fall into the hands occasionally of petty or unscrupulous persons, who could use it as a terrible club over the heads of teachers." Rather than legislating against communism, the paper instead proposed an alternative to eliminate the internal threat: "We have to make democracy work, every day, in ever-wider areas. If we do, the few Communists and crackpots will simply win no converts."[114]

Anticommunist hysteria was whipped up to new heights when, on February 9, 1950, Senator Joseph McCarthy made his infamous speech claiming to have a list of 205 known communists working for the State Department. From there, McCarthy crisscrossed the country continuing his accusations but constantly changing the number of known communists in government. That was the beginning of a more than four-year pursuit for communists within the United States. On February 14, the *Register* wrote its first editorial dealing with McCarthy: "Thus far the senator has offered little more than his word to back the charges. ... If the senator cannot do better than this in pointing the finger at Communists in government, we suggest he think twice before making such grave accusations." Like many other papers across the nation, *Register* editors apparently had trouble believing "that anyone could make such specific charges without the evidence to back them up."[115]

As 1950 progressed, McCarthy's unsubstantiated statements mounted, and the paper moved from questioning the senator to outright opposition. In July, for example, it denounced McCarthy's "shotgun charges," which were leveled against individuals "without anything like the kind of evidence that a court of law would require." Soon thereafter, it complained, "Seven months of Senator McCarthy's howling 'wolf' have failed to weed out one solitary Communist from a government post. Instead he has merely created uncertainty and confusion."[116]

By the spring of 1954, during the televised Army-McCarthy hearings, the R&T tried to connect McCarthyism more directly to its Iowa readers. The *Register* surveyed 40 editors of Iowa weekly newspapers and reported that the vast majority, "even strong Republicans, denounced the senator." Later, it conducted an Iowa Poll, which found that Iowans supported the Army over McCarthy by a two-to-one margin. The *Tribune,* meanwhile, asked readers how they felt about the Army-McCarthy case. As the hearings wound down in late June 1954, the *Register* ran a story under the headline, "McCarthy's Popularity Sinks to New Low." Finally discredited, McCarthy was censured by the Senate that December.[117]

As the 1950s came to a close, R&T profits were up from the low point in 1956. In fact, a proud Luther Hill reported that in 1959, "the company had had its best year and that prospects looked good for the year 1960."[118] Having overseen the rebound, Hill announced that he would retire as publisher effective in February 1960.[119] But his departure did not break the continuity of leadership at the paper. Although now immersed in their own media

Mike and John Cowles with Dwight D. Eisenhower, 1952. *Courtesy of the Gardner Cowles Jr. Collection, Cowles Library, Drake University, Des Moines.*

concerns, John and Mike Cowles remained involved in the firm's strategic decision-making process. In Des Moines, Ken MacDonald, who had been with the *Register* since 1926, was named chief operating officer, and David Kruidenier, a third-generation Cowles, became the company's general manager.

Struggle and Survival

The period from 1940 to 1959 had been challenging for the Register and Tribune. Important new features, such as the Iowa Poll and the use of its own war correspondent, had been introduced during World War II. Like other contemporary newspapers, the *Register* faced skyrocketing newsprint and inflated labor costs while its circulation began to level off. The firm expanded its interest in broadcasting, only to decide to pull back and spin off its radio-and-television subsidiary. By the mid-1950s, the focus had returned to the R&T's core business of newspaper publishing, but because of new forms of media competition, the company struggled. As the 1950s came to a close, however, R&T officials had succeeded in cutting costs and increasing revenues. Given the turnaround, the new leadership team of MacDonald and Kruidenier were optimistic about the Register and Tribune Company's future.

CHAPTER 7

Clouds Before the Storm

1960–1970

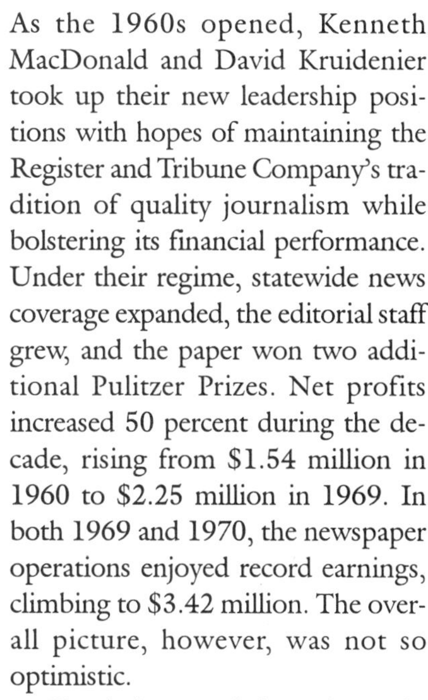

As the 1960s opened, Kenneth MacDonald and David Kruidenier took up their new leadership positions with hopes of maintaining the Register and Tribune Company's tradition of quality journalism while bolstering its financial performance. Under their regime, statewide news coverage expanded, the editorial staff grew, and the paper won two additional Pulitzer Prizes. Net profits increased 50 percent during the decade, rising from $1.54 million in 1960 to $2.25 million in 1969. In both 1969 and 1970, the newspaper operations enjoyed record earnings, climbing to $3.42 million. The overall picture, however, was not so optimistic.

Register and Tribune Building after addition of new exterior, 1962. *Courtesy of the Gardner Cowles Jr. Collection, Cowles Library, Drake University, Des Moines.*

Circulation trends hurt the R&T. Like many other newspapers nationally, the afternoon *Tribune* suffered from a steadily declining readership. This trend was especially worrisome because the *Tribune*'s large advertising revenues had supported the less profitable daily *Register.* Furthermore, as the number of newspapers read per household continued to plummet across the country, the R&T found itself in an uncomfortable bind. Although the two company papers may have enjoyed a monopoly in Des Moines, they competed with smaller city papers for readers throughout the state. Traditionally, the *Register*'s marketing strategy was not to supplant local newspapers; rather, it tried to supplement those papers by providing national and statewide coverage that the locals lacked. As long as Iowans living in such cities as Cedar Rapids, Dubuque, or Sioux City read two newspapers, the tactic worked. But as lifestyles changed, fewer people subscribed to two papers, and a growing number kept their local paper and dropped the *Register.*

Besides declining circulation, the R&T, like other newspapers across the country, faced continuously rising costs. To make up for the loss of revenue and cover increasing expenses, the company boosted both circulation and advertising rates. These actions proved problematic, however; higher rates led to further decreases in subscriptions and encouraged advertisers to seek other means to reach their customers.

By the late 1960s, MacDonald, Kruidenier, and others on the board of directors considered alternatives to rekindle the firm. At issue was whether to forgo statewide circulation and make the *Register* a metropolitan Des Moines paper. While financial projections suggested that such a reduction would have proven profitable, top management decided against this option. Key executives believed that an all-Iowa strategy was important to the paper's prestige. Instead, they chose to expand and diversify the company. Although no acquisitions were made during this period, the seeds were laid for expansion in the 1970s.

The editorial page, meanwhile, remained under the control of Lauren Soth, and the Cowles family continued to steer clear of editorial policy. Soth maintained the paper's tradition of strong support for civil rights and a healthy suspicion of cold war rhetoric. In an unusual move, Mike Cowles put his imprint on the newspaper's endorsement of a presidential candidate in 1960, and the paper backed Richard Nixon. Then in the next two presidential elections, the paper moved away from its general support of Republican contenders.

MacDonald and Kruidenier at the Helm

Long known as "the general" because of his West Point background and military career, Luther Hill had been a commanding presence at the R&T. Nearly two years after he stepped down as publisher of the two Des Moines papers in November 1961, the congenial leader was sorely missed. David Kruidenier, the new general manager, explained to John Cowles that the company lacked "some of the inspiration and imagination of the type Luther Hill has."[1] With Hill gone, the chores of top management were divided between Ken MacDonald, who remained as editor and was given the added title of chief operating officer, and Kruidenier, who oversaw day-to-day business operations.[2]

Although quite different, the elder MacDonald and the younger Kruidenier developed a sound working relationship. Six months into his role as the top R&T executive, MacDonald told John Cowles that he and Kruidenier were "getting along splendidly."[3] Over the years, MacDonald had proven to be an excellent editor by "allowing reporters and writers great latitude in choosing subjects and approaches, so long as the result was fair and literate."[4] A courtly gentleman of great integrity, MacDonald had many of the essential qualities necessary to serve as the R&T's chief operating officer—in essence publisher, although he was not given that title until 1966. Employees viewed MacDonald as generous and fair; in the words of former general counsel Hedo Zacherle, the editor had "the ability to make people feel that he was listening to them and considering what they said." People left meetings with MacDonald believing "that he would give their judgment careful consideration." Major decisions weighed heavily on him. If the 55-year-old MacDonald had a shortcoming as the on-site head of the Register and Tribune, it was his slowness in making decisions.[5]

David Kruidenier, meanwhile, had moved up on the business side. Well aware of being a third-generation Cowles working in the family's Des Moines operation, he was careful to avoid using his familial connection in dealings with other managers. On the other hand, his eagerness to take power antagonized some company executives. Unlike his uncle Mike Cowles, Kruidenier was shy by nature, and some felt he had difficulties in communicating. Yet, in his tendency to delegate authority and make quick, impulsive decisions, he resembled his famous uncle. With these character traits, Kruidenier complimented MacDonald; together, the two made a good team.[6]

Even though top management had changed, Mike Cowles as president and John Cowles as chairman of the board remained in charge of all major policies and decisions. Board meetings were casual affairs and often held at the Des Moines Club whenever Mike or both Mike and John were in town. Very little was recorded at these meetings. Louis Norris, former chief financial officer, remembers that minutes of the board of directors meetings were sometimes fabricated when certain actions needed the support of a written record.[7]

Industry Challenges

When MacDonald took over in 1960, the whole newspaper industry faced troubling times. Nationally, households were subscribing to fewer newspapers. In 1930, for instance, there were 132 newspapers sold per 100 households. Thirty years later, 90 newspapers were sold for every 100 households, a drop of one-third.[8] A number of reasons accounted for the decline. Because of local mergers, fewer newspapers were being published. From 1963 to 1973, the number of cities served by more than one daily newspaper decreased from 51 to just 37.[9] More problematic, however, was a changing American lifestyle, which undermined the newspaper habit. A rising number of two-income families meant that less time was available to read a second newspaper. The continuing expansion of suburbs meant a longer commute to work, which cut down on free time at home. Then, of course, there was the growing tendency of families to sit in front of the television for both news and entertainment. All of these factors combined to cut down the number of people who read newspapers. In 1957, a survey indicated that 75 percent of people in their 20s read a newspaper; 10 years later, it had fallen to 64 percent.[10]

Intercity Competition

In addition to the negative effect these societal changes had on the R&T, other factors in Iowa challenged the company's dominance. Because the *Register* was the only major Iowa morning daily, the paper sold well in Iowa cities outside Des Moines. Some subscribers also took the evening *Tribune* and their own city newspaper. Thus, the R&T situation was what media analyst James N. Rosse defined as intercity competition. According to Rosse's umbrella thesis, although papers in some cities such as Des Moines had monopoly power, these papers actually faced competition on the periphery because their distribution networks often extended hundred of miles beyond the point of origin: "The circulation falls off as the distance increases, but within this circulation area are 'satellite cities,' each with its own daily circulation that goes beyond its borders."[11]

By the 1960s, daily newspapers in the satellite cities of Omaha–Council Bluffs (the *Omaha World-Herald*), Sioux City (the *Journal*), but especially those on eastern edges of the R&T's circulation area such as Cedar Rapids (the *Gazette*), Davenport (the *Times-Democrat*), Dubuque (the *Telegram-Herald*), and Waterloo (the *Courier*) stepped up their aggressiveness in trying to lure more readers and advertisers. By mid-decade, these last four papers showed gains in readership while the combined circulation of the *Register* and *Tribune* remained stagnant.[12]

Compounding this problem of mounting intercity newspaper competition, demographic trends worked against the Register and Tribune. Much of the company's success was built on selling its newspapers to rural readers. Following World War II, the migration from farm to city accelerated. By 1956, urban residents (defined as those living in towns of more than 2,500) for the first time outnumbered Iowans living on farms. This population shift meant that the R&T lost readers in country markets when households moved to urban areas where competition was the norm. In 1960, the *Register* and *Tribune*'s combined rural circulation totaled 73,491, but by 1970, this readership had fallen to 65,745.[13]

Most of this decrease resulted from rural readers dropping the *Tribune*; its country mail and farm service circulation tumbled from 18,394 in 1960 to 9,045 in 1970. This decline was a reflection of the afternoon paper's situation in general. From 1960 to 1970, its overall circulation decreased 15 percent, from 128,948 to 110,253. As early as the mid-1950s, management had tried to deal with the *Tribune*'s shrinking readership by limiting its distribution area to central Iowa. In the 1960 annual report, however, controller Carl Koester noted that "nothing substantial had been done in this respect." He then went on to wonder "whether there is a sufficient demand today for two dailies with statewide circulation."[14]

In the Des Moines metropolitan area, however, the *Tribune*'s circulation was 50 percent greater than that of the daily *Register.* Local advertisers sought at least 70 percent coverage of the metro retail market, and by using the *Tribune,* they could more than achieve their desired goal.[15] The *Tribune* thus became Des Moines retailers' advertising choice, and by mid-decade, it surpassed its sister publication in advertising revenue. In 1960, the two papers brought in roughly the same amount of advertising dollars; five years later, the *Tribune*'s net advertising revenue was nearly 60 percent greater than that of the *Register.* The pattern continued through decade's end and, by 1965, the *Register* was actually losing money. It was sustained by the profitability of the *Tribune* and the *Sunday Register.*[16]

The *Tribune,* therefore, was a valuable property, and its declining circulation worried R&T management. Of special concern was the Des Moines metropolitan area with its lucrative retail advertising market. Retailer interest would be lost if metro circulation was not at the least maintained. After years of halfheartedly trying to trim back the evening paper's distribution, it was decided in 1969 to limit the *Tribune*'s circulation area. The annual report explained: "A basic area of 32 counties [in and around central Iowa] has been established for Tribune circulation. This is an area than can be meaningful to editors, profitable for the advertising departments and capable of maintaining a 100,000 minimum circulation. Evening circulation outside this area will be phased out in the best manner possible as proper timing dictates." Company efforts could now focus on expanding the *Tribune*'s metro circulation, and with this figure up 2 percent by 1970, the strategy appeared to be working.[17]

Increasing Statewide Presence

Acutely aware of these trends, MacDonald called for strengthening and deepening the editorial product and improving advertising coverage. On the state level, he targeted cities where newspaper competition was strongest and established resident R&T news bureaus. In 1967 and 1968, news bureaus were set up in Cedar Rapids, Dubuque, Davenport, and Waterloo. At the time its facility in Dubuque was ready, the *Register* reported: "The news bureau is a recognition of the continuing growth of the area and the need for improved news service to the increasing readership of The Register and Tribune."[18] While this explanation was reasonable, these resident bureaus were also defensive: by providing better coverage of the host cities, the R&T hoped to halt its loss of distant readers to local papers.

Prior to the bureaus' introduction, the company had taken two steps to beef up its statewide presence. In November 1955, it introduced the weekly Iowa-TV Magazine in the Sunday paper. While such additions were becoming common in many newspapers, the *Register*'s provided television listings for all the large cities and communities in Iowa. By the early 1960s, for instance, the television guide broke the state up regionally and provided programming information for Central Iowa (Des Moines, Fort Dodge, and Ames); the West (Sioux City; Sioux Falls, South Dakota; Omaha, Nebraska; and St. Joseph, Missouri); the Northeast (Cedar Rapids; Waterloo; Mason City; Austin, Minnesota; Mankato, Minnesota; Rochester, Minnesota; and LaCrosse, Wisconsin); and Southeast (Ottumwa; Davenport; Moline and Rock Island, Illinois; Quincy, Illinois; and Hannibal, Missouri).[19]

In 1964, another thrust was made to reinforce the firm's position outside the Des Moines metropolitan area, but this time the tactic focused on eastern Iowa and advertisers. On August 16, the *Sunday Register* included a new tabloid section called the Eastern Iowa Advertising Edition. Originally a biweekly offering, it was intended to increase advertising linage in the eastern half of the state, where the Sunday paper had an approximate circulation of 195,000. Lower rates were established for advertisers doing business in the area. The following year, this section was included in every Sunday edition, and, as hoped, it carried a growing amount of retail advertising. With the success of this supplement, the *Sunday Register* began running western and central Iowa zoned advertising sections in August 1966. Advertising rates for the zoned sections were again lowered in 1967 and linage shot up.[20]

Concern over eastern Iowa remained high throughout the decade. MacDonald and Kruidenier considered building a branch printing plant in this portion of the state. Such a plant would greatly simplify distribution of newspapers to the region and significantly cut transportation costs. The proposal to purchase an 18-acre site for the facility immediately west of Cedar Rapids was approved by the board of directors in 1969. To avoid speculation, the acquisition was made quietly and without fanfare by a real estate dealer who turned over the unrecorded title to the R&T.[21]

Besides expanding news and advertising coverage in the state at large, management did not neglect the local scene. On the news side, MacDonald understood what Harvey Ingham had realized years before: the paper's location in Iowa's capital gave it a huge advantage over others in covering news about state government. MacDonald insisted that his news staff provide detailed reporting of the Statehouse as well as City Hall. His high regard for the value of state and local news fit squarely with other prosperous newspapers of the period. In a study of successful papers versus those that failed during the 1960s, media critic Ben Bagdikian found that "successful papers had 21 percent more local and 18 percent more national news [than those that failed]."[22]

Staff and Layout Changes

Better coverage of both the local and state beats could only be accomplished by a larger news staff. And unlike many newspapers that found it economical to cut back on the editorial side of their operations, MacDonald was able to expand because of Cowles family ownership, which, according to former *Chicago Tribune* editor James D. Squires, had the "reputation of quality over profits." Although not as aggressive as Ben Bradlee, who at the *Washington Post* dramatically increased his editorial staff, MacDonald augmented the R&T's editorial personnel over the course of a decade when the company's total number of employees shrank. From 1960 to 1970, the Register and Tribune's editorial personnel—which included subeditors, reporters, columnists, artists, photographers, and copyreaders—grew nearly 15 percent, up to 176; meanwhile, the company's total full-time employment decreased approximately 5 percent, to 1,085.[23]

Improved coverage went hand in hand with new front-page layouts that emphasized summation and synthesis of the news. By the late 1950s, some prominent newspaper people were recommending wholesale changes. In 1959, for instance, Barry Bingham, president and editor in chief of the *Louisville Courier-Journal*, counseled: "Journalists [must] make their product more appealing, more magnetic, more enjoyable for younger readers. If we fail, we in America at least will be confronted in a few years by a generation that absorbs all its information through sounds and pictures." Although the *Register* did not go so far as the *Los Angeles Times* or the *New York Herald-Tribune* in digesting the news for readers, it followed in their wake. More stories in brief, condensed form appeared on the front page, and new sections, such as "The Day in Washington," provided a summary of key events.[24]

Retooling the Classifieds

Besides transforming the way the *Register* presented news, management was interested in retooling the classified advertising section. Since the late 1950s, shoppers had been attracting a growing amount of local classified advertising. To battle these publications, R&T advertising manager Lyle Lynn called for lowering the papers' rate on Family Want Ads (garage sales, for instance). In March 1964, Lynn's idea was implemented, and by the end of that year, the number of these advertisements increased fourfold. Meanwhile, a year earlier, the classified department had installed three Iowa Wide-Area Telecommunications Service (WATS) telephone lines. Rather than charging per minute, the WATS lines charged a flat monthly rate for telephone calls within Iowa. With the introduction of this service came a much more aggressive solicitation of classified advertising. From their introduction through 1964, these telephones accounted for an increase in linage of 650,000 lines. Together these two factors helped boost classified advertising linage 36 percent by 1966, and the classified department replaced national advertising as the second largest producer of linage, following local retail advertising. From the mid-1960s on, classified advertising revenues continued to grow, while national advertising moved more and more to television.[25]

MacDonald, as well as others in the industry, recognized the connection between good journalism and business success. He once noted that the company's profitability had allowed it to put out responsible papers. *Los Angeles Times* publisher Otis Chandler expressed similar sentiments: "You cannot have a good editorial product or provide community service unless you have good profits."[26] The many years of financial success and the efforts in the 1960s to improve the company's bottom line continued to pay off journalistically. In 1961, the *Des Moines Register* was ranked 16th among American dailies in a *Saturday Review* survey of journalism educators. Furthermore, the company's two papers, the *Register* and *Tribune,* were ranked third behind the *Louisville Courier Journal* and *Times* and the *Minneapolis Star* and *Tribune* as the best combination of morning and evening newspapers published by the same organization.[27]

More Pulitzers

Recognition of excellence in journalism continued throughout the decade as the *Register* added two more Pulitzer Prizes to its collection. In 1963, political cartoonist Frank Miller won the prize for his creativity. The Pulitzer judges explained that his body of work in 1962 "was exemplified by a cartoon showing a destroyed world with one ragged figure calling to another: 'I said—We sure settled that dispute, didn't we?' "[28] Miller had joined the staff in 1953. After 40 years of gracing the *Register* with his perceptive cartoons, Ding Darling retired in 1949, and MacDonald began the difficult task of searching for another talented artist to fill the *Register's* trademark front-page slot for editorial cartoons. The R&T was deluged with applications for the position. Finally in 1951, MacDonald offered the job to 26-year-old Frank Miller, then with the *Kansas City Star,* but military service kept the cartoonist from accepting. Two years later, with his tour of duty over, Miller joined the R&T. Soon the artist was delighting *Register* readers with "political commentaries on world events to lighthearted looks at life in Iowa, from roly-poly farmers to top-hatted legislators to wisecracking pigs wallowing in the mud."[29]

Miller's special relationship with his Iowa readers became evident after his sudden death of a heart attack in 1983. The *Register* ran some of the many letters it received from those who felt the loss of their favorite cartoonist. An Iowa City reader commented, "Growing up in the 1960s, I was confused and frightened by the riots, assassinations and war which filled your pages. Miller's cartoons helped me cut through the confusion and ease the fright. He taught me to think critically and laugh heartily." He then lamented that his children and grandchildren would not have the benefit of Miller's wit and wisdom.[30]

Besides continuing its tradition of fine political cartooning, the *Register* remained strong in national reporting. In 1968, Washington Bureau reporter Nick Kotz won the paper's 10th Pulitzer Prize for his 1967 investigative stories on the meatpacking industry. One reason Kotz was able to pursue this story was because of MacDonald's leadership. Unlike many reporters with others papers, the staffers at the Washington Bureau were not bound by the schedule of daily story deadlines. This freedom allowed journalists such as Kotz to dig deeply into important topics and provide thorough coverage.[31]

Throughout 1967, Kotz wrote more than 50 pieces identifying unsanitary conditions in one-quarter of the nation's meatpacking plants that were not subject to U.S. government inspection. Up to that time, those in packing plants not involved in interstate trade were not under federal jurisdiction. So influential were Kotz's stories in encouraging Congress to pass new legislation, President Lyndon Johnson invited him, along with former muckraker Upton Sinclair (author of *The Jungle,* who campaigned for the Meat Inspection Act of 1906), to witness the signing of the bill into law. Consumer advocate Ralph Nadar lauded Kotz's work: "Now that the meat inspection act is law, I want to commend the truly great reporting of the entire prolonged controversy by ... Nick Kotz. By almost any measure of journalistic excellence, Mr. Kotz came through with a classic performance of objectivity, timeliness, stamina, and thorough coverage."[32]

Boosting Profit Margins

Although these awards suggested journalistic success, R&T management, just like many other newspaper leaders around the country, remained concerned about soaring costs and falling profits. The 1960s, in fact, proved a mixed bag for American newspapers as a whole. Rising costs continued to plague the industry, while an increase in labor strife led to work stoppages and newspaper shutdowns in several cities, including Boston, Cleveland, Detroit, Minneapolis, New York, Portland, San Jose, St. Louis, and Seattle. Given these labor problems, some large metropolitan dailies, such as the *New York Herald Tribune,* succumbed and went out of business. Yet medium-city dailies fared well. According to *Editor and Publisher,* the average medium-size daily (with a circulation of 50,000) was enjoying a profit margin of 23 percent before taxes.[33]

While the R&T faced many of the same problems that other newspapers did, it was not forced to contend with labor troubles. Ever since an attempt to organize the newsroom by the Newspaper Guild failed in 1947, no other serious efforts had been made. Except for a one-week strike of its workers in the International Typographical Union in 1945, the company was never beset with strikes. Attorney Hedo Zacherle, who, beginning in 1960 oversaw labor negotiations, explained that the "good attitude of the company" toward its employees played a major role in the exceptionally peaceful labor relations. Zacherle had "absolute free rein" over labor, and he found that adversity could be avoided by personally going down to the department in question and addressing problems as they arose. This informal touch, and the Cowles' willingness to go along with Zacherle's recommendations, led to the long accord between management and workers.[34]

Management thus could concentrate on other problems. It endeavored to boost profit margins by lowering costs and increasing revenues. Because of its large and widely dispersed readership, the newspaper could not realize the high profit margins of the medium-size paper, but as Otis Chandler once suggested, an 8 percent after-tax profit margin was a reasonable goal for a metropolitan daily. From 1960 through 1970, however, the R&T's after-tax profit margin on newspaper operations averaged just 5.7 percent.[35]

In the 1960 annual report, Carl Koester observed that the R&T's "newspaper operating expenses increased at a faster pace than did operating revenues [a 3.9 percent versus a 1.0 percent increase] with the result that pretax profit suffered a decline of $458,000, or 18%, below that of 1959, and $40,000 below that of 1958. And this imbalance occurred even though there was no increase in the price of newsprint." Newsprint, which shot up in price in the 1940s and 1950s, stabilized through the mid-1960s, but other expenses, such as payroll, did not. Worse still, the company had failed to raise circulation and advertising rates to keep up with rising costs. Koester noted, for example, that while wages in the composing room rose 27 percent from 1952 to 1960, the circulation rate charged for the *Sunday Register* delivered by carrier outside of Des Moines remained at the 1952 level.[36]

Managers, of course, were concerned that if the price of their paper went up, readers would stop subscribing. And circulation was an especially sensitive area for the Register and Tribune. Unlike many newspapers, which derived only 25 percent of their income from circulation, the R&T relied on it for 44 percent of total revenue by 1960. Evidence suggests that the company's hesitancy in raising prices was somewhat justified. A study of 300 newspapers between 1965 and 1986 found that a 10 percent price increase on a single-copy issue accounted for a 5.5 percent decline in circulation. Maintaining or increasing circulation was important because advertisers wished to reach the largest audience. However, as their advertising space became more attractive, publishers were reluctant to raise advertising rates for fear of losing business.[37]

Following the poor performance in 1960, MacDonald and Kruidenier bumped up both circulation and advertising rates in January 1961. But this move failed to push up revenues. Advertising linage declined, and instead of meeting the projected increase of $1.145 million in advertising revenue, it declined $232,000 from the 1960 figure. A partial increase in circulation rates that included only papers distributed in Des Moines lifted circulation revenue $200,000. After yet another mediocre year in 1962, MacDonald and Kruidenier succeeded in turning the static profit picture around. All advertising rates were increased, circulation rates remained constant, and through careful monitoring, expenses actually declined nearly 1 percent. That resulted in the second-best newspaper operating profit to date and moved the after-tax profit margin up from 4.8 percent to 6.1 percent.[38]

In May 1964, raising the price of the *Sunday Register* was considered, and John Cowles wrote that he was "reluctant" to do so because if "heavier circulation losses occur than estimated and if the Sunday Register circulation falls below ½ million, it will hurt the entire institution." But with MacDonald and Kruidenier both supporting the move, the hike took place in October. Sunday circulation revenue overall was up $138,000. Readership dropped 12,000, or 2.3 percent, by the end of the year, but Sunday circulation still bested the half-million mark by 18,000, and John Cowles thought those numbers were "splendid ... considering the price increase." Regardless of this success, the company was still playing catch-up for the years without price increases. Expenses continued outpacing revenues, however, and the 1964 newspaper operating profit declined 4.9 percent from the previous year.[39]

At the annual stockholders' meeting early the following year, Mike Cowles appeared satisfied that the company's difficulties earlier in the decade were over. He praised MacDonald for solid leadership, told shareholders he was pleased with the firm's performance, and noted his optimism about the future. But there were troubling signs as well, and Cowles "pointed out with concern the general trend toward a narrowing margin of operating profit."[40]

Meanwhile, the R&T building had been updated, and a four-story annex was soon added. In 1961, the 13-story brick tower was modernized by an aluminum-and-glass exterior sheathing at a cost of approximately $305,000. Five years later, plans for a four-story addition along Eighth Street north to Grand Avenue were announced. When completed in 1967, the new wing provided office space for the promotion, syndicate, and commercial photography departments, while the remainder of the structure was taken up by the mail room, loading facilities, and storage of up to 1,500 rolls of newsprint.[41]

For the remainder of the decade, efforts were made to boost revenues. Several additional hikes in circulation rates took place. While the morning *Register*'s circulation actually grew, the *Tribune*'s continued to fall. Readers of the Sunday paper dropped below the half-million mark for the first time since it had achieved this milestone in 1947. At the same time, the company raised advertising rates and added zoned advertising sections. Finally, management lifted its 61-year ban on ads for alcoholic beverages. Beginning in October 1970, beer advertising was accepted in the daily papers but not the *Sunday Register*.[42]

These policies succeeded in raising revenues, but costs went up in tandem. Every year from 1965 through 1970, the R&T enjoyed record revenues. With the exception of 1965 and 1969, however, expenses grew at a faster pace; net profit margins on newspaper operations averaged 6 percent. Company return on investment after taxes, meanwhile, fell from 12.6 percent in 1965 to 10.8 percent in 1969 and 8.5 percent in 1970. Net profits peaked in 1967 at $2.8 million, and then dropped off to $2.25 million in 1969. Members of the Register and Tribune board of directors were well aware of the situation. In the midst of this slide, Ken MacDonald concluded that there "was room for substantial improvement in circulation, advertising, revenue, and operating expenses."[43]

The company's payroll had increased 54 percent from 1961 to 1970. The circulation department led the way, with its payroll rising 72 percent, followed by the news and editorial department at 60 percent and the mechanical department at 52 percent. Overall, however, circulation department expenses rose only 20 percent over the decade, and editorial went up 14 percent, while the mechanical department expenses shot up 44 percent. Given the statewide *Register* distribution, holding the line on the circulation department was difficult. Long taking pride in the R&T's quality journalism, the Cowles family was not likely to demand cuts in the editorial and news department. And this department's 1970 budget, in fact, which stood at 12 percent of total company costs, compared favorably with other large newspapers. That left the mechanical department as a major area where savings might occur.[44]

Technological Improvements

The mechanical department was responsible for printing the newspaper. It comprised the engraving department, the composing room, stereotyping, the press room, and the mail room. In the engraving department, metal plate etchings of photographs were processed. In the composing room, news and advertising copy were keyed into Linotype machines that mechanically laid out lines of type from hot molten lead (the hot-type process). These were then made up into pages. In stereotyping, impressions of the pages were formed onto semicylindrical metal plates. The plates were attached to the presses, and the paper was printed. The finished product went to the mail room, where the papers were counted, bundled, and prepared for distribution.

Newspapers had been put together this way for decades, and the labor-intensive printing operation required skilled workers. Organized into the International Typographical Union, printers were able to garner high wages. If their demands were not met, they could strike and stop publication. In the late 1940s and early 1950s, the invention of the " 'cold-type' process introduced photography into the printing process. Such machines as the Fotosetter, the Linofilm, and the Photon produced words on film and transferred them directly to a printing plate." Much faster and significantly cheaper than old hot-type Linotype machines, photocomposing equipment had the potential to cut production costs drastically. Furthermore, unskilled workers could operate these machines, as opposed to unionized, and more expensive, printers. Where photocomposing equipment was installed, printers' strikes could no longer threaten to close down a newspaper.[45]

Photocomposition was a true technical breakthrough. In 1959, a typical 20,000-circulation daily spent $155,000 (in constant dollars) on production costs. By 1980, after the introduction of the new technology, that paper spent $102,000 to produce over 40 percent more pages. Major newspapers were in the process of converting to photocomposition by the late 1960s, and the R&T was among them. In 1969, renovations needed for the new photocomposing equipment began, and two Photon machines arrived in January 1970. The company first used photocomposition in retail advertising, and then converted the rest of their operation to it in the early 1970s. Conversion to the new system was slow, however, and major savings from photocomposing were thus still several years down the road.[46]

Kruidenier's Impact

Although the potential benefits of this new technology were still in the future, David Kruidenier was interested in making an immediate impact. His desire manifested itself in three ways: his wish to invest treasury funds in a more aggressive manner; his desire to expand the firm through acquisition; and his belief that stockholders should be kept better informed through a newsletter.

By 1969, the R&T had investment assets totaling nearly $13 million. The majority of these investments were managed by four firms: Bankers Trust of New York; Donaldson, Lufkin & Jenrette; J. M. Hartwell Company; and the State Street Fund. For several years, Kruidenier thought about shifting a large portion of the company's treasury account into a business with greater growth possibilities. An opportunity arose late in the decade when land in Scottsdale, Arizona, with development potential went up for sale. Kruidenier, along with chief financial officer Lou Norris and assistant general counsel Hedo Zacherle, went to investigate the property. Seeing tremendous development possibilities for the 2,500 acres, the three men returned to Des Moines in favor of the acquisition. Kruidenier took the proposal to the board. He recommended paying $5 million to $7 million to purchase the land and then spending another $2 million for development. Board members Mike Cowles and Luther Hill were "violently opposed" to the idea, fearing that real estate development "required much more cash ... and took more time to become profitable than amateurs realized." They argued that real estate development required specialized skills that R&T management lacked. John Cowles Jr., who had joined the board in 1960, supported Hill and his uncle in voting down the idea, but noted, "I am personally sympathetic with David's desire to put some of the Treasurer's account funds to work in an operating business, but I would rather have those funds invested in a business we were more familiar with than real estate development."[47]

Blocked in his effort to diversify, Kruidenier expressed an interest in expanding horizontally by purchasing other newspapers. Given the continuing problem of declining circulation in Iowa, top R&T officials agreed that it was one strategy the company should implement. While agreeing to investigate possible expansion, some managers also suggested that distribution costs could be drastically reduced by cutting back on *Register* circulation. Instead of remaining a statewide paper, the *Register* would be reconfigured as a metropolitan one, dropping readers from the peripheral counties where its major advertisers did not have a real market. This strategy, it was argued, would clearly increase profitability. Some other state and regional papers followed this path in the early 1970s, but the *Register*'s long tradition of being an all-Iowa newspaper, combined with the prestige accrued from that status, led the board of directors to drop the idea. That left the path of expansion.[48]

Kruidenier pursued expansion by identifying the Lerner Group, a string of suburban Chicago newspapers, as a possible acquisition target. After discussing the idea with MacDonald, he and Lou Norris went to investigate the property. While Kruidenier felt the Chicago company was a perfect fit, Norris thought there were problems, among them the highly partisan nature of the newspapers' editorial staffs. Whether the general manager missed these signals or the chief financial officer failed to make his opposition clear, Kruidenier returned to Des Moines believing they had agreed on the purchase. Prior to the board meeting that would take up the issue of the acquisition, Norris went to MacDonald and expressed his concerns about the possible purchase. MacDonald agreed that the R&T should not buy the weeklies. At the board meeting, Kruidenier presented the acquisition plan, and Mike Cowles asked Norris his opinion. Norris said he had "reservations" and went on to enumerate them. MacDonald also argued against the purchase largely because the Lerner Group—weeklies in suburban markets—was such a different publishing operation than the R&T. After a lengthy debate, the company decided against the acquisition.[49]

Failing in his quest to expand in the late 1960s, Kruidenier bided his time until another opportunity arose. Meanwhile, he succeeded in pushing through a plan for providing periodic reports to stockholders. One concern was that, in making financial information public, the reports might spur unionization drives, assist unions in salary negotiations, or increase resistance to circulation or advertising rate hikes. Before the plan was discussed by the board, MacDonald surveyed several newspapers that routinely published their financial statements and found that such information did not have an adverse impact. The idea was approved in November 1970, and the first report, issued to all stockholders and the press, came out the following February.[50]

Editorial Positions

Unlike the business side, the newspapers' editorial policy showed a distinct continuity. Guided by Lauren Soth, the editorial page continued its staunch support of civil rights and its skepticism of cold war dogma. With the exception of an endorsement of presidential candidate Richard Nixon in 1960, the Cowles family remained steadfast in its refusal to meddle in or influence its papers' editorial stance. Ever since Soth had taken over the editorial page in 1953, he had instituted a morning conference of all editorial writers to discuss issues and assign topics. Under the previous editor, Forrest Seymour, the department had operated in a laissez-faire fashion; editorial writers wrote on whatever they wished, and Seymour edited their pieces. Sometimes when two writers dealt with the same issue, the editor combined the two pieces. Although the system worked for Seymour, Soth wanted more coordination, which explains the daily editorial conferences. Hill and MacDonald, and then Kruidenier, however, never attended these meetings. Because MacDonald received the galley proofs of the editorials, he had the opportunity to discuss their content with Soth, but that rarely happened.[51]

Clear evidence of the Cowles family's strict belief in staying clear of their papers' editorial decisions came out at a formal dinner party for the retiring Ken MacDonald in January 1977. Top R&T editors and business executives were seated around a long table, with Mike Cowles at its center. In his booming voice, Cowles exclaimed, "There is one thing I've never told anyone. I've never agreed with one word we've written on agricultural policy." Cowles then went on to explain that he had thought Secretary of Agriculture Earl Butz, a frequent target of Soth's editorial attacks, was a great man. MacDonald and Kruidenier were "flabbergasted" at this revelation; no one in Des Moines, Soth included, was apparently aware of Cowles' strong feelings.[52]

Presidential Endorsements

While Cowles completely entrusted the newspapers' editorial positions to his editors, endorsements of major candidates were sometimes a different matter. The *Register*'s support of presidential candidate Richard Nixon in 1960 was a case in point. Nixon was a good friend of John and Mike Cowles, and they wanted the paper to endorse him in 1960. Lauren Soth, however, strongly opposed Nixon and went to discuss the situation with MacDonald. They decided that neither Soth nor his staff would write the editorial. MacDonald, who was lukewarm on Nixon, wrote the *Register*'s endorsement. As editor and chief operating officer, MacDonald felt that Cowles as the principal owner was entitled to see his opinion expressed in the paper. In his mind, the family's interference was so rare that the issue did not justify a confrontation with Cowles or a threat to resign.[53] Thus, two days before the election, a *Register* editorial focused on how each presidential candidate would likely handle foreign policy. MacDonald wrote: "Judging by some of the views he expressed in the campaign, [John] Kennedy would be more prone to take hasty, less-well-thought-out action in a crisis. Nixon impresses us as more likely to think twice before acting. ... We believe he [Nixon] by temperament and experience, can best be entrusted with the conduct of foreign affairs."[54]

The *Register*'s next two presidential endorsements, however, broke with its usual practice of supporting Republicans. In 1964, the paper supported Lyndon Johnson over Barry Goldwater, believing he could "provide the abler leadership for this nation." Four years later, Mike Cowles apparently returned to the sidelines. In an editorial entitled "Difficult Choice for President," the *Register* began by noting the similarities between Nixon and Hubert Humphrey: "If one ignores the campaign oratory and examines the legislative record, the differences on such issues as civil rights, welfare, and foreign aid are more a matter of emphasis than substance." It then continued, finally giving the slight edge to the Democratic candidate, "In the long run, however, there are two paramount issues—finding a peaceful accommodation among hostile forces in the world and uniting the divisive factions in our own country. Because of those issues we think Humphrey has shown a broader human understanding and a keener perception of underlying causes, we favor Humphrey."[55]

Civil Rights

Presidential endorsements aside, the *Register*'s editorial positions were consistent. On the civil rights front, the paper continued backing the cause of African-Americans. In February 1960, Greensboro, North Carolina, became the scene of a nonviolent protest against segregation. Four black college students sat down at Woolworth's "whites only" lunch counter, refusing to move until they were served. Several days after the sit-in began, the *Register* noted that "they resist in a way which must give men of good will pause for thought." It then suggested that the peaceful tactic would work: "The whites will give in some day, much more quickly than they would if the Negroes had demonstrated violently or displayed the bitterness they have every right to feel." The protest soon succeeded, as white leaders realized all the commotion was bad for business. Other young blacks followed their example, and led by the newly formed Student Non-Violent Coordinating Committee (SNCC), the sit-in movement spread across the South.[56]

By 1963, Martin Luther King Jr. decided to step up the pressure of passive resistance by leading a protest march in what he referred to as "the most segregated city in the United States"—Birmingham, Alabama. The peaceful demonstrations began in April but, except for a front-page AP story on King's arrest, the *Register* was relatively quiet on the matter. Instead, the paper looked at the issue of civil rights in Iowa. While blacks amounted to less than 1 percent of the state's population, the *Register* was supporting a bill before Iowa Legislature designed to eliminate discrimination in employment. Such an act, the paper wrote, "would represent a considerable gain." In early May, the Fair Employment Practices Act became law. It forbade discrimination in employment "on the basis of race, religion, color, national origin, or ancestry." On its passage, the *Register* cheered the act as a "human rights milestone," but warned: "The task of eliminating unfair treatment, however, remains to be done. In housing, as well as jobs, Iowa's minority groups are at a serious disadvantage."[57]

Meanwhile, events in Birmingham turned ugly. On May 3, authorities broke up a peaceful protest march of several thousand blacks by attacking them with police dogs and beating them back with clubs and high-pressure fire hoses. These horrendous scenes returned Birmingham to the *Register*'s front page, and the confrontation continued to receive extensive coverage over the next several weeks. Several editorials condemned the action of both the city and state governments, which, the paper noted, "outrage[d] the conscience of the nation." In addition, Frank Miller denounced the brutality and Alabama Governor George Wallace in several front-page cartoons. Especially poignant was his depiction of a Birmingham street scene. The cartoon featured a police officer with a police dog in tow, talking to a firefighter holding his hose at the only other figure pictured, a crawling black man. The caption read: "They just ain't civilized. Next time they'll be using violence."[58]

After several weeks, events in Alabama finally pushed a cautious President John Kennedy to take a stronger stand on civil rights. On June 11, Kennedy announced his plan to sponsor a bill making a national "commitment ... to the proposition that race has no place in American life or law." Eight days later he made good on his pledge, introducing civil rights legislation that granted equal access to public accommodations and employment, created the Equal Employment Opportunity Commission, and made illegal any barriers to the registration of black voters. The *Register* cheered the move: "The best legislation in our opinion would be a clear, simple and direct national law guaranteeing the right of every person to equal treatment in all places that serve the public." Realistically, the paper noted that "compromise [on the bill] may be necessary, but there should be no compromise with the principle that Americans are entitled to equal treatment and entitled to obtain it from their national government."[59]

Three days after the president's speech, the paper made it clear how it expected its congressional delegation to vote: "Iowa's members of Congress should give strong support to the civil rights legislation." But if that direct encouragement was not enough, the *Register* asked its readers for help: "We think Iowans not only have the right but also the obligation to urge their representatives in Congress to reflect the [pro–civil rights] sentiment of this state in voting on civil rights legislation."[60]

A year later, the civil rights bill passed both houses, and the *Register* recorded that "history is being made in Congress this year—slowly, painfully, tardily, but momentously." For the most part, Iowans in Washington, D.C., had voted as the paper advised. Five of the state's seven congressmen supported the legislation, while its two senators canceled each other's vote. When President Lyndon Johnson signed the bill into law, the *Register* wrote: "The Civil Rights Act of 1964 is one more advance, a big one toward the promise of 1776."[61]

Soon, however, events indicated that further federal intervention was necessary. In February 1965, a black activist was killed by sheriff's deputies during a voter registration campaign in Marion, Alabama. King and other black leaders used this tragedy to highlight the plight of black voters. They called for a peaceful, 50-mile march from Selma to the state capital at Montgomery to protest the killing. Their hope was to provoke a violent reaction and again gain national attention, this time for a federal law protecting voting rights. As they expected, Governor George Wallace banned the march, and participants were brutally attacked. Although the *Register* disapproved of "so dangerous (and exhausting) a tactic as a mass march over 50 miles of state highway," it commended King as a "leader of monumental stature and grace."[62]

Like many across the country, Iowans were rightly outraged by the actions of Alabama officials. The state legislature adopted a nonbinding resolution "condemning the denial of civil rights in Alabama." It then discussed joining in a proposed lawsuit being considered by the attorney general of Michigan. The suit would call for decreasing Alabama's representation in Congress "in proportion to the number of people being denied their right to vote." While the *Register* certainly understood the desire to scold the state, it cautioned readers to focus on the real goal: "The important objective, it should be remembered, is not to punish the South or deny it representation, but to obtain for Negroes their lawful right to vote as citizens."[63]

On March 15, Lyndon Johnson went before Congress and spelled out his plan for a federal voting rights law, which the *Register* saw as a "clear and necessary" solution. The paper felt Johnson was "committed wholly on this matter." Furthermore, "he is determined," it noted, "to accomplish equal voting and will brook no compromise." Just five months after the president's call to arms, the Voting Rights Act of 1965 became law. Upon its passage, a *Register* editorial observed, "Nearly 100 years after adoption of the [15th] amendment [giving blacks the right to vote], Congress has declared in unmistakable language that it intends to enforce this fundamental right. America's Negro citizens surely have waited long enough for this historic day."[64]

Just as the newspaper maintained its progressive course on civil rights, so too did its positions on foreign policy remain constant. Never accepting the bipolar, cold war world view, the *Register* continued examining each foreign policy issue on an individual basis and stood against the dangers of impetuous action. The Bay of Pigs, the Cuban Missile Crisis, and the Vietnam War are three cases in point.

Cuba

By the time John Kennedy took office in January 1961, relations between the United States and Cuba had soured. Two years earlier, Fidel Castro took power in Cuba. He soon confiscated American-owned property and nationalized the country's banks and industry. When the dictator signed a trade agreement with the Soviet Union in February 1960, President Eisenhower cut American imports of Cuban sugar and ordered the CIA training of Cuban exiles for a possible invasion of their homeland. Then, in the last weeks of his presidency, Eisenhower broke off diplomatic relations with Castro. The *Register* thought this move was "hasty."[65]

As tensions mounted between the United States and Cuba, the *Register* suggested that any American involvement in ridding the island of Castro was problematic, but appeared likely: "The practicality, the legality, the morality of aiding an attempt to violently overthrow Castro are all in question. Yet Castro has done what President Kennedy and President Eisenhower both said was intolerable: set up a heavily armed Communist satellite dictatorship 90 miles off the coast of Florida."[66]

In April 1961, 1,400 CIA-trained Cuban exiles landed at the Bay of Pigs on the southern coast of Cuba. When the hoped-for general insurrection did not take place, Castro's troops quickly thwarted the invasion attempt. After the failure, a defiant Kennedy told the American people that resisting "communist penetration" was part of our "primary obligations ... to the security of our nation." It appeared that the *Register*'s pre-election concerns of Kennedy acting rashly were justified, and it shuddered at the "grave dangers in the position the President has taken." The editorial then warned against further reckless acts: "The Cuban crisis, however, is no simple matter in which the US can afford to lose its patience and strike out for a quick result on the spot." Several days later, in an editorial entitled "Better Way to Oppose Castro," the paper was relieved that Kennedy had decided to go to the Organization of American States to consider other ways to deal with the Cuban dictator.[67]

The *Register*'s fear of brash presidential action in foreign affairs grew during the Cuban missile crisis. On October 14, 1962, an American U-2 spy plane photographed medium-range (1,100 mile) Soviet missile sites under construction in Cuba. Once informed, the president convened a special committee of advisers to discuss U.S. options. Initially ruling out diplomacy, the team subsequently moved away from use of an air strike to remove the missile bases. When the idea of a full-scale invasion of Cuba was dropped, the president finally decided upon using a naval blockade to stop further arms shipments to the island.[68]

On October 22, Kennedy spoke to the American people about the Soviet missiles in Cuba, announced the blockade, and told Soviet Premier Nikita Khrushchev to "halt and eliminate this clandestine, reckless, and provocative threat to world peace." Over the next few days, 180 U.S. naval vessels patrolled the Caribbean, ready to intercept the 16 Soviet ships heading toward the blockade. Meanwhile, a U.S. invasion force was being readied in Florida, and B-52's loaded with nuclear bombs were kept in the air. As the two cold war adversaries appeared headed toward nuclear war, the *Register* worried about the president's handling of the situation: "While agreeing it was necessary to act, we wish the action might have been taken more calmly. ... A calmer approach to this crisis might have forestalled concern over impulsiveness without lessening the effectiveness of our action."[69]

On October 28, an agreement was finally reached: the blockade was to be lifted and the United States pledged to respect Cuba's territorial integrity in exchange for removal of the missiles. As a secret part of the deal, the United States also agreed to remove its outdated missiles from Turkey. Although Kennedy was hailed at the time for his handling of the situation, critics wondered if quieter, private negotiations, rather than public confrontation, might have averted the crisis altogether. The *Register* had taken this critical position early in the showdown, but it ultimately conceded that such drastic measures "may have been necessary to get the missiles out of Cuba." However, the paper was also convinced that the president's willingness to take the nation to the brink of war was dangerous, and it warned, "As a long-range program, brinkmanship is mad."[70]

Vietnam

While closely watching events in the Caribbean, the *Register* also kept its eye on Southeast Asia. The Kennedy administration was facing immediate problems linked to a continuing civil war in Laos. In May 1961, negotiations to end this fighting began, and the *Register* suggested that while Laos might already be "lost," it was not too late to "save" its neighbors. The Laotian situation "does not mean that the free world should sit quietly by while the Communists continue to gobble up the Indochina peninsula and the rest of Southeast Asia. ... It may be too late to do anything about Laos. It is not too late to do something about protecting the anticommunist countries of Thailand and Viet Nam."[71]

Kennedy apparently agreed with the *Register*. Earlier in January, he had sent funds to beef up the South Vietnamese army, and in May, more American military advisers arrived. Yet, as the communist Vietcong continued making gains in South Vietnam, the *Register* wondered if the United States was providing the best type of assistance: "The question may well be raised whether the free countries of the Far East would be better able to resist communism today if all that military aid money had gone into economic assistance and education." Nonetheless, the Kennedy buildup of American military personnel in South Vietnam continued.[72]

By May 1962, the *Register* estimated there were between 5,000 and 7,000 U.S. military advisers in South Vietnam. The paper worried about what it termed "our dilemma in Indochina." The country's leader, Ngo Dinh Diem, was not only corrupt, he was becoming less and less effective. In the spring of 1963, for instance, the Catholic Diem banned the flying of Buddhist flags and further alienated the South Vietnamese majority. Besides growing problems with Diem, the *Register* recognized the fine line the United States had to walk. If it did too little, South Vietnam would fall to communism, but if it did too much, North Vietnam's allies, China and the Soviet Union, might intervene.[73]

The R&T editorial staff held out hope that the U.S. government could "nudge Diem" toward more sensible policies. That proved impossible, and in November 1963, a CIA-encouraged coup ended with Diem murdered and South Vietnamese generals in charge. The *Register* noted that the United States welcomed the overthrow; it believed the new leaders would "better handle the Viet Cong and establish a stable government." Its hopes were soon dashed, however, when another coup in January 1964 landed General Nguyen Khanh in power. Worse still, the war against the Vietcong continued to go badly. By March, Secretary of Defense Robert McNamara estimated that the Vietcong controlled 40 percent of the countryside. Given these events, the *Register* began questioning the U.S. role in South Vietnam: "So far, at least, the Indochinese people do not seem to want to prevent a Communist takeover badly enough to fight against it. The issue is whether the local governments, especially in South Viet Nam, can develop the support of their own people as an alternative to Communist rule." With this apparent lack of Vietnamese resolve, the paper wondered whether the United States could really "win" the war.[74]

After one North Vietnamese attack on an American destroyer on August 2 and another alleged attack two days later, President Johnson ordered retaliatory air strikes against North Vietnamese targets. Without telling Congress that the U.S. ships were providing intelligence for South Vietnamese commando raids against the North, he asked for authorization to take "all necessary measures to repel armed attack against the forces of the United States and to prevent further aggression." Responding immediately, Congress gave the president a blank check by passing the Tonkin Gulf Resolution on August 7, 1964. The *Register* was skeptical, however. It referred to America's show of force as a "holding action" and just one means of "winning the hearts and minds of men in southeast Asia." On the Tonkin Gulf Resolution and Johnson's quick retaliation, the paper was noncommittal: "There is still room for debate, for new facts and new interpretations and for drawing lessons for the future."[75]

The following March, the American commitment to the war grew with introduction of U.S. ground troops into South Vietnam and the beginning of Operation Rolling Thunder, the continuous bombing of the North. This policy shift did not escape the *Register*'s attention. Since any "experiment to change the course of the war ... is worth undertaking," the paper was initially unwilling to call Johnson's decision to increase the U.S. role wrong. "But," the editorial concluded, "we also believe the dangers of expanding the war are still present and must be considered before any decision to go farther is made." The *Register* could not have been more prescient. When no consideration of changing course was forthcoming, the number of American military personnel in Vietnam rose from 23,000 in 1964 to 184,000 by the end of 1965. Two years later, the figure approached 500,000.[76]

By 1967, the *Register* realized that even with increased involvement, America was no closer to winning the Vietnam War. But, it feared, rigidity had set in at the White House, and "the Johnson Administration has become so committed to a military solution that it cannot change course." The paper therefore backed a group of congressmen led by Senators Frank Church and J. William Fulbright who were calling for peace negotiations. "The appeal [to the North Vietnamese for a negotiated settlement to the war] may not work, but it is worth a try. An honorable peace now would be in everybody's interest." From here, the *Register* remained supportive of a negotiated settlement. In early January 1968, an editorial explained, "The talks might fail, but we can see no reason for not trying." Three weeks later, another piece was more emphatic: "The path to negotiations and peace is diplomatic conciliation, not military coercion."[77]

Neither Washington nor Hanoi could agree to terms for peace talks, and the war went from bad to worse. At the end of January 1968, the North Vietnamese and Vietcong mounted a massive, surprise attack on provincial capitals throughout South Vietnam over Tet, the Vietnamese holiday for the lunar new year. Although the offensive was soon turned around by American and South Vietnamese forces, Vietcong guerrillas had made their way into the U.S. Embassy compound in Saigon before being subdued. The result was a huge political victory for the North. Many Americans now started doubting the government's reports that the United States was winning the war. The *Register* agreed: "The statistics are ... questionable." Even more damning, however, it continued, "But even if accurate, the kill ratio has little to do with whether we're achieving our complex military, political, economic, and social objectives in South Vietnam."[78]

Never fully embracing American military policy in Vietnam, the paper responded harshly to an official U.S. report that the Vietcong's Tet offensive had failed: "The Administration following its military has persistently failed to appreciate the nature of the struggle in Vietnam. It has persistently acted as though this were a conventional war of opposing armies—the enemy supported by irregular guerrillas to be sure—but still mainly a standard military contest." Then, reasoning that the Tet offensive could not have been initially successful unless the insurgents had significant help from many South Vietnamese, the *Register* asked: "Can anyone doubt that the Viet Cong still has strong popular backing in South Vietnam?" As might be expected, this battle of early 1968 only strengthened the paper's desire for a negotiated peace.[79]

As it had in earlier wars, the R&T's reporting on Vietnam consciously sought out the Iowa angle. In 1970, the 59-year-old Gordon Gammack, who had covered both World War II and the Korean conflict for the company, was sent to get a firsthand look at Vietnam. He concentrated on telling the Vietnam story by piecing together the highs and lows of Iowans serving in Southeast Asia. Sometimes, Gammack's desire to recount the travails of Iowa soldiers and the reporter's job of covering the war did not coincide. In February 1970, for instance, Gammack explained to *Tribune* editor Drake Mabry that the accompanying story was devoid of Iowans, but he decided to send it anyway:

> I went up with the 7th Regiment Marines; they are almost completely isolated and are supplied only by helicopter and one daily convoy, out in the real boondocks where the fighting occurs (but mostly at night) and had been led to believe there were plenty of Iowans. There turned out to be just three and not one in our Tribune range [central Iowa]. Yet I think it's a good story on the gut business of pacifying a hostile area. The trouble is that in peaceful areas where men are congregating, we'll have much better luck with the central Iowans and less guts in the copy.[80]

For the most part, however, Gammack's columns remained popular because he provided the Iowa angle to the war. With headlines such as "How Iowans Captured Viet Reds," "Iowans Prowl Skies over Viet," or "D.M. Amputee: Pain, Laughter after Fall," Gammack sent his readers a steady stream of much desired news of their friends or family members serving in Vietnam.[81]

The war continued, but at the R&T a major leadership change took place. By the end of 1970, the 65-year-old MacDonald was ready to lessen his responsibilities. Although he stayed on as editor, he gave up his position as publisher and chief operating officer. The heir apparent was David Kruidenier, Gardner Cowles's grandson who had been running the business affairs of the paper. Some at the paper, however, doubted his business judgment, and Jim Milloy, a close adviser of Mike Cowles, disliked Kruidenier. Cowles, in fact, evidently had his own concerns and told one R&T executive that "he would never let David run the paper because he didn't think he was up to it." Yet, Kruidenier's mother, Florence Cowles Kruidenier, was a sister of Mike Cowles, and she prevailed upon her brother to give her son the top slot in Des Moines.[82]

Kruidenier's Leadership

As publisher, Kruidenier finally filled the shoes his grandfather once wore. He now had the opportunity to make his mark on the family's prized property. With the firm's return on investment slipping and its subpar profit margins, he was taking over the operation at a critical time. Looking back over the 1960s, Kruidenier knew that maintaining costs and boosting revenues would be essential to future success. In addition, he was aware that the company's newspapers were suffering from declining circulation and increasing competition from other Iowa dailies. Under the circumstances, the new chief executive believed the solution to R&T revitalization lay in a strategy of expansion.

Five of the Register and Tribune's 15 Pulitzer Prize winners at the Pulitzer 50th Anniversary Dinner, 1966. From left to right, Frank Miller, Lauren Soth, Clark Mollenhoff, Richard Wilson, and John Robinson. *Courtesy of David Kruidenier.*

Des Moines Sunday Register Transportation Map, 1966. David Kruidenier is pictured on the left. *Courtesy of David Kruidenier.*

CHAPTER 8

Expansion in the '70s: Opportunities and Risks

1971–1980

Now at the Register and Tribune Company helm, David Kruidenier finally had the chance to put his mark on the venerable family newspaper. With two more Pulitzer Prizes during the 1960s, the tradition of journalistic excellence had continued at the *Register,* but business trends were disturbing. Media competition kept increasing; circulation was de-

Jackson Sun employee, holding printing plate, talking to R&T board members, from left to right, Mike Cowles, Michael Gartner, Luther Hill Jr., Ken MacDonald, and David Kruidenier, 1974. *Courtesy of David Kruidenier.*

creasing; and profit margins were declining. Kruidenier, who had lobbied unsuccessfully for horizontal combination in the late 1960s, was free in the 1970s to pursue an aggressive strategy. In fact, the R&T move to acquire other media properties placed it squarely in tune with a major restructuring of the entire newspaper industry. Newspaper chains were expanding in the 1970s, largely by acquiring small and medium-size dailies. But the takeover trend did not preclude big newspapers themselves from being swallowed up by giant concerns. In fact, in the midst of this merger mania, the *Washington Post* guessed "that within two decades, virtually all daily newspapers in America will be owned by perhaps fewer than two dozen major communications conglomerates."[1] The Register was a buyer in this period, but management also feared becoming a takeover target. This concern was quieted by the creation of a voting trust designed to maintain the company's independence.

Because Iowa did not provide a growing market, Kruidenier's goal was to build a company that derived at least half of its revenues from outside the state. To this end, he developed an acquisition plan, put together a new management team headed by Michael Gartner and Gary Gerlach, and over the course of the decade went on a purchasing spree. By the end of 1980, the R&T had grown into a full-fledged media firm comprising four dailies, two weeklies, two television stations, and four radio stations. Expansion, however, rather than solving the company's problems, only exacerbated them in the long run. Inflation and recession, coupled with skyrocketing gasoline and newsprint prices, pushed costs rapidly upward. Meanwhile, because the acquisitions were financed through borrowing, the firm was straddled with huge interest payments.

Some newspapers dealt with the difficulties of the 1970s by purposely cutting distant or unprofitable circulation and investing in the latest computer and printing technology. Register and Tribune management realized that cutting back on circulation could boost profits, but company leaders refused to shed the firm's proud and long-standing tradition of being a statewide newspaper. On the technology issue, R&T leaders continued shifting over to photocomposition, but like most large-circulation papers, it decided to forgo replacing aging letterpress equipment with efficient and expensive offset presses. Instead, management opted for a cheaper interim printing technology.

Although many changes were occurring during the decade, high-quality journalism remained a staple of the *Register.* Michael Gartner, who took over as executive editor in 1974, made the paper even stronger by calling for more aggressive coverage of local business and political issues. This type of investigative reporting often did not endear the paper to Des Moines elites, but the forceful style earned the *Register* its 11th and 12th Pulitzer Prizes.

Meanwhile, leadership of the editorial page passed from Lauren Soth to Gilbert Cranberg. The size of the editorial staff grew, and the editorial page was expanded to a two-page op-ed section. Institutional opinion, however, remained fairly consistent. The paper maintained its progressive stand on civil rights issues, while on international affairs, the *Register* refrained from espousing hard-line cold war positions. Presidential endorsements continued in the independent vein staked out in the 1960s. Also consistent, the Cowles family, now represented by Kruidenier, remained largely committed to staying out of editorial policy decisions. There were, however, several instances in the 1970s when editorial positions, business decisions, and publisher Kruidenier's ideas were not synchronized.

Kruidenier's Turn to Lead

David Kruidenier had waited patiently to head up the family's Des Moines newspaper. During his lengthy apprenticeship, he had once considered getting out of the family business altogether to accept an overseas State Department post that was in the works during the Kennedy administration. He recalled, "I felt blocked here. Ken MacDonald, a very able, competent editor and publisher, was running the company and was going to be in that job until he reached retirement age. It seemed like a long haul for me." When President Kennedy was assassinated, the political appointment did not materialize, and Kruidenier remained at the R&T.[2]

Kruidenier's frustration was compounded when his younger cousin John Cowles Jr. took charge of the family's Minneapolis papers in 1968. A major reason for the long delay was Mike Cowles' apparent reservations about his nephew David's abilities. These concerns, however, had waned by late 1969. Cowles explained to his brother John, "I was more impressed by David Kruidenier than I have ever been before. Ken MacDonald, David, and Lou Norris seem to me to be working harmoniously together as a very competent team. ... I am inclined to think the best thing to do is to name David Kruidenier as president of the R and T [and] ... Lou Norris as publisher." Meanwhile, Kruidenier's mother may have also interceded on her son's behalf, which was later suggested by *Fortune* magazine. As a result of these factors, in January 1971, Kruidenier was named both president and publisher of the company.[3]

Kruidenier's promotion led to another changing of the guard. In 1971, two key executives—Luther Hill Sr. and longtime chief counsel Vincent

Starzinger—retired from the company board. Two years later, 70-year-old Mike Cowles, who had stepped aside as company president in favor of Kruidenier, retired as the R&T chairman of the board. The retirement of these men, who had opposed acquisitions in the 1960s, opened the door for expansion into new markets.[4]

Facing Problems

From the beginning of his tenure as the firm's chief executive officer (CEO), Kruidenier faced the mounting problems that had emerged in the previous decade. Population trends continued to have a negative impact on R&T circulation. Other cities throughout the state were growing in population, and their home papers were becoming more competitive. One way to make the *Register* more attractive in these areas was to provide better coverage at the local level. To that end, the company added a news bureau in Iowa City, its fifth in the state, in the spring of 1971. But over the next few years, circulation in distant areas kept declining; several price increases led to further declines. By 1975, the *Register*'s circulation had fallen by nearly 22,000, or 8.6 percent, the *Tribune*'s readership had tumbled 16,500, or 15 percent, and the *Sunday Register* had lost 50,000 readers since the opening of the decade. These statistics compared unfavorably to national trends; newspaper circulation peaked nationwide at 63.1 million in 1973. After small declines the following two years, national circulation grew, albeit slowly, during the latter half of the decade.[5]

Meanwhile, the cost of producing and distributing newspapers soared. Newsprint, which stood at $152 per ton in 1970, jumped to $260 per ton in 1975. Many newspapers tried to lessen the impact of rising costs and shortages caused by Canadian paper mill strikes by conserving newsprint, decreasing the width of their pages, and reducing the number of columns per page. The *Los Angeles Times,* for instance, decreased its page width by three-fourths of an inch and saved $4.2 million annually. Another strategy used by major companies like the New York Times, Times Mirror, and Washington Post entailed integrating backward. These enterprises assured their supply of newsprint by acquiring newsprint mills or forest land.[6]

The R&T's efforts included several cost-cutting programs. In January 1974, because colored newsprint was more expensive than standard white, the green paper used in the *Tribune* sports section was permanently dropped, while the peach paper of the *Register* sports page was temporarily replaced with regular newsprint. In addition, the company pursued conservation efforts such as the use of recycled newsprint, especially in the comics section, and reductions in the width of their newsprint rolls. The R&T went from a 60-inch to a 58-inch newsprint roll in 1975, resulting in a 3.3 percent savings, and it went to 56 inches the following year. That same year, the *Register* and the *Tribune* were changed from an eight-column to a six-column page format. These measures succeeded in decreasing the company's newsprint consumption from 33,800 metric tons in 1969 to 28,600 metric tons in 1975, but because costs rose so rapidly, newsprint expense rose from $5.5 million to $8.2 million.[7]

Compounding the problems of costly newsprint, the Middle East oil crisis of 1973–1974 hit the company hard. In 1974, gasoline prices rose 80 percent. To distribute its newspapers statewide, R&T vehicles traveled 1.2 million miles annually. Thus, the dramatic increase in fuel prices had a major impact on the company. Transportation costs nearly doubled over a six-year period, rising from $1.44 million in 1970 to $2.74 million in 1976. Because roughly 10,000 subscribers received their *Register* or *Tribune* through the mail, circulation costs were also forced upward following large increases in second-class postal rates. Besides making delivery of its newspaper much more expensive, the energy crunch also affected production. The costs of operating presses, as well as heating and cooling the R&T facility, rose, and, because news ink was a petroleum-based product, its price doubled in 1974. Unfortunately, there were no offsetting increases in advertising revenue.[8]

Labor costs, especially in the production of the newspaper, remained the largest expense of the company. Total payroll rose 44 percent over the first seven years of the decade, but labor costs were beginning to be controlled by the introduction of photocomposition equipment. Conversion was gradual and resulted in both increased productivity and a reduction in paid hours per page. When complete conversion to photocomposing was finally reached in the spring of 1976, the stereotyping department was eliminated and composing hours dropped significantly. While other costs were climbing, the mechanical department's payroll actually fell by $32,000.[9]

Unlike the foregoing areas, the situation for the advertising department initially looked bright. In the fall of 1971, the advertising base in Des Moines improved when Dayton-Hudson announced that its Target stores were taking over two closed Arlans department stores, and a new J. C. Penny store opened. In line with national trends, which showed newspaper advertising revenue growing over the course of the decade, the R&T's ad revenue continued increasing through 1975, largely because rates were adjusted upward. Since the circulation revenue was not growing rapidly, the company became more reliant on advertising revenue. By mid-decade, advertising sales accounted for 58 percent of total newspaper revenue, up 4 percent from 10 years earlier.[10]

In spite of the rapidly escalating expenses, hefty price hikes in both circulation and advertising translated into higher profits through mid-decade. Net profits from Des Moines newspaper operations rose from $1.68 million in 1970 to $2.2 million in 1975, but net profit margins fell from 6.2 percent to 5.8 percent. Compared to the average net profit margins of eight leading newspaper firms, which moved up from 6.9 percent in 1970 and 7.8 percent in 1975, the R&T's performance fell way below industry standards.[11]

Given the realities of the 1970s, Kruidenier was rightfully concerned about the future of his family's newspaper. In fact, in the industry at large, many executives worried about their newspapers' economic viability. Some publishers dealt with the new realities by rethinking their circulation base. In the past, newspaper moguls such as Hearst, Pulitzer, and later Gardner Cowles concentrated on expanding circulation. At the end of the 19th century, when newsprint was falling in price, publishers expanded the size of their newspapers, printed a greater number of copies, and eagerly sought more readers. The problem, as mass communication professor Thomas Leonard explained, was that "all of the economies of scale were not enough to make the huge public drawn to the news profitable on what the reader paid." That is, the paper on which the newspaper was printed was worth more than the product cost. Such a strategy could eventually pay off if a publisher could obtain control of the market. Of course, when one factors in advertising revenue, the picture changes. It was advertising sales that ultimately made the maintenance of large-circulation newspapers possible.[12]

Newspapers therefore catered to two audiences—people hungry for raw news and mass consumers. These groups were often overlapping, but not always. Readers interested in the "news" about products and services frequently sought entertainment rather than enlightenment. Early in the 20th century, advertising trade journals began suggesting potential ways to balance these two audiences. Some readers of newspapers, they noted, were not the typical purchasers of products advertised in them. Phrases such as "cheap circulation" or "worthless circulation" were used to describe readers who were not likely to be free spending. Many experts argued that such readers should be dropped by newspapers. Publishers, however, did not heed such advice; instead they went after every possible reader. It was in this earlier period, of course, that Gardner Cowles proceeded to build a statewide circulation in Iowa, and later his son John emulated this strategy in Minnesota.[13]

Reconsidering Circulation

The rapidly escalating costs of the 1970s led some publishers to reconsider the circulation issue. Not only was the maintenance of a far-flung circulation becoming more and more expensive, but also, Leonard notes, "local retail advertisers, the single most important source of newspaper revenue, lost interest in paying for circulation ... far away." Readers living outside of the metropolitan trading area—which was the basis for advertising rates—were dropped in order to cut delivery and newsprint costs. Hence, some newspapers with large regional or state circulation began cutting back. In Atlanta, the *Journal* and *Constitution* canceled the subscriptions of 50,000 readers in southern Georgia. The *Chicago Tribune* eliminated 25,000 subscribers living outside the metropolitan area. Likewise, John Cowles Jr. felt compelled to trim substantially the mass regional circulation his father had built at the *Minneapolis Star and Tribune*. By 1982, Cowles had reduced circulation by 25 percent from 1973. In taking similar action, *Los Angeles Times* publisher Otis Chandler said simply: "We cut out unprofitable circulation."[14]

Managers at the R&T purposely eliminated some readers. In the fall of 1973, the company discontinued many of its circulation routes outside Iowa. This move decreased Sunday circulation by 4,500. Simultaneously, there was a growing focus on readers in Polk County—in which Des Moines is located—and the surrounding eight counties. In 1976, for instance, the R&T hired Yankelovich, Skelly and Company, a consulting firm, to help develop marketing strategies for boosting sales of the *Register* and the *Tribune* in central Iowa. The following year, a weekly entertainment guide called "The Datebook" was added to the *Tribune*. The guide specifically catered to central Iowa, including the Des Moines area. Overall, these efforts proved successful and reversed the downward circulation trends in central Iowa. With a renewed focus on greater Des Moines, metropolitan circulation held up in the last half of the decade. The metro readership of the morning *Register* and *Sunday Register* actually rose 8.3 percent and 11.5 percent, respectively, while the *Tribune*'s circulation slid by only 2 percent.[15]

A policy of radically slashing the number of readers within Iowa was not pursued, however. Discussions of shrinking the *Register* to a metropolitan paper had first come up in the late 1960s. At that time, corporate officials rejected such a drastic change. When the soaring costs in the 1970s led other newspapers to curtail undesirable readership, the issue was briefly revisited. Even though a 1977 internal memo indicated that managers believed cutting back on R&T circulation would clearly boost immediate profits, they resolved to maintain their presence throughout the state. At a 1975 management retreat, corporate leaders wrote, "It is a goal of the Company that Iowans be able to make informed decisions about their lives. To enable them to do so, the Company will seek to publish and distribute to readers throughout the entire State of Iowa newspapers that are fair, accurate, literate, and complete."[16]

This policy of remaining a statewide institution was aptly symbolized by the Register's Annual Great Bicycle Ride Across Iowa (RAGBRAI) established in 1973. It began as a challenge from copy editor John Karras to columnist Donald Kaul to "ride his bike across Iowa and write a few columns about it." Kaul took up the idea with the proviso that Karras ride with him. They invited "a few friends and anybody else who'd like to go along" and selected a route from Sioux City on the Missouri—the western border of Iowa—to Davenport on the Mississippi—the eastern boundary of the state. Approximately 300 riders joined the R&T journalists in their six-day, 400-mile trek. A 1974 ride was not scheduled until many letters arrived at the paper demanding a repeat performance. In its third year, the ride was officially dubbed RAGBRAI, and the annual event was soon attracting thousands of riders from all parts of the United States and several foreign countries. As an event that takes cyclists across the state and, if only for a week, captures the attention and imagination of people from all corners of the state, RAGBRAI has become a fitting metaphor for the *Register*'s reach throughout all of Iowa.[17]

In spite of maintaining the statewide goal, however, overall circulation at the Des Moines papers continued to tumble. From 1976 to 1980, readership of the morning *Register*, the evening *Tribune*, and the *Sunday Register* fell 6.3 percent, 10.4 percent, and 5.9 percent, respectively. Yet, given consistent rate hikes, circulation revenue grew by 27 percent over the same period. The problem was that such increases proved a double-edged sword. While they boosted revenue, higher prices led to additional losses of readers.[18]

Tradition, pride, and the Cowles family legacy clearly led company managers to stay the course and continue the newspaper's status as a statewide institution. Long recognized as the paper of record for the state, the *Register* was read by the state's politicians, leading business figures, and editors of other Iowa newspapers. Located in the capital city, it had assumed the role of watchdog over the Statehouse. Regarded by a former R&T executive as "the soul of Iowa," the paper was still widely read throughout the state and shaped the way Iowans perceived themselves and their communities. Although business sense dictated otherwise, compromising the paper's influence, power, and commitment throughout all of Iowa by downsizing to a metropolitan market was unacceptable to corporate leaders. Throughout the 1970s, "ego, not economic logic" kept the *Register* true to its masthead motto: "The Newspaper Iowa Depends Upon."[19]

Outside Investments

While the company continued to serve Iowa, its also began looking outside the state for investment possibilities. The president and publisher remained concerned about opportunities in the Iowa market. Kruidenier did not believe this market had great potential; he felt that "the only way for the company to grow was through acquisitions in different geographical locations." His goal, he explained, "was to move the company from a paternalistic family operation to more of a professionally managed communications business."[20] This path of expansion had been trailblazed by many other newspaper firms seeking greater profits through horizontal combination. Gannett, for example, purchased seven papers during the decade, Dow Jones bought five, Lee Newspapers acquired three, Hearst picked up two, and Capital Cities and Times Mirror added one each. Although both large and small dailies were taken over, the latter were generally more appealing because of "the belief that newspapers with circulations of between 50,000 and 100,000 offer optimum profit potential and tend to have fewer labor problems. In addition, such newspapers tend to be the only ones published in their community." Profit margins of 20 percent or more were commonplace in some localities.[21]

Early in his presidency, Kruidenier told the board of directors that there "has been a continuing interest in and investigation of acquisitions desirable for the corporation, and that this activity would continue." Action soon followed. The R&T made an offer for the Harte-Hanks San Antonio newspapers in the spring of 1971. This first attempt at expansion came to naught when Harte-Hanks proved unwilling to sell. But the R&T remained interested in acquisitions, and managers worked over the next several months on developing an acquisition strategy. By the spring of 1972, the plan had gone through several drafts. In essence, the blueprint stated that the company would focus on media properties. Specifically, small- to medium-size dailies with circulation between 15,000 and 125,000 and no local newspaper competition were potential acquisition targets. Their retail regions had to be growing in population and easily accessible by air from Des Moines. Based on the plan, the R&T's research department drew up a list of newspapers that met the various criteria.[22]

Besides developing their own parameters for expansion, the firm also hired an acquisitions expert. In May 1972, John C. Ginn was named to the newly created position of director of corporate development. Ginn's earlier journalism career included stints as editor of the Kingsport, Tennessee, *Times-News* and city editor of the Charlotte, North Carolina, *News.* In his new post, Ginn's sole responsibility was to find and evaluate newspapers suitable for purchase. Soon the Sun Publishing Company of Jackson, Tennessee, was identified. The *Jackson Sun* was an evening and Sunday daily with a circulation of 30,000. The company also owned two local radio stations. The deal was closed in December 1972. The R&T paid $5.75 million plus a brokerage fee of $230,000. In order to gain FCC approval, the R&T agreed to sell the radio stations. The stations were sold the following year to Kirk Broadcasting of Atlanta for $556,000, making the net cost of Sun Publishing $5.2 million. Ginn, who had experience in Kingsport, a Tennessee market similar to Jackson, was subsequently promoted from his development position to president and publisher of the firm's new property, and he moved to Tennessee.[23]

After incurring net losses the first two years, largely because of necessary plant modernization, the *Jackson Sun* proved a profitable addition. Its net profits climbed from $77,400 in 1975 to $444,600 by 1980. Such success whetted top management's appetite for further expansion. To prepare for this growth, the company retained the temporary services of a newspaper consulting firm, and Kruidenier put together a new, young, and aggressive management team. In the summer of 1973, the R&T hired R. Gary Gomm and Associates to develop further and refine the R&T's criteria for future acquisitions.[24]

The following year, Kruidenier hired two key individuals who oversaw the company's rapid expansion in the latter half of the decade. In January 1974, 35-year-old Michael Gartner, then page one editor of the *Wall Street Journal,* was named executive editor of the R&T and added to the firm's board of directors. Born and raised in Des Moines, Gartner had close connections with the *Register* from childhood; his father, Carl Gartner, worked at the R&T for 41 years and retired in 1972 as editor of the Sunday paper's *Picture* magazine. While in high school, Michael Gartner got his start in journalism at the *Register,* working part time in the sports department. Furthermore, his education at Carleton College was underwritten by one of the first R&T scholarships. Gartner was hired with the clear understanding that he would ultimately replace MacDonald as editor. In 1976, he received the promised position. By 1978, he was R&T president and chief operating officer.[25]

Several months after Gartner arrived, Kruidenier hired 33-year-old Gary Gerlach as the firm's assistant general counsel. Gerlach, who also had a master's degree in journalism from Columbia University, had worked as a staff writer for *The National Observer* before going to Harvard Law School. After a brief tenure as a legal assistant to Nicholas Johnson, a member of the Federal Communications Commission, Gerlach joined a Washington, D.C., law firm, where he specialized in communications law. Like Gartner, Gerlach was a native Iowan whose experience with the R&T began years earlier—as a boy, he had a *Register* paper route. Now back in his home state, Gerlach moved rapidly up the managerial ladder. Placed in charge of acquisitions, the young lawyer was named general counsel in 1975.[26]

Labor and Technology Issues

Before the new managers could pursue additional acquisitions, however, several outstanding labor issues and the question of updating the R&T presses required attention. In 1973, the National Labor Relations Board (NLRB) ordered an election to decide whether the company newsroom and editorial staff would be represented by the Newspaper Guild. Although this union had organized such influential papers as the *New York Times* and the *Washington Post* and had nearly 30,000 members nationally, it had not made inroads with the majority of American newspapers. The vote at the R&T was close, but staffers turned down the opportunity to join the Newspaper Guild. Because of several challenged votes, however, the NLRB ordered a new election. Held the following June, Guild representation was again denied, 91 to 89.[27]

Other major labor disputes involved the question of workers displaced by new technologies with lower labor costs. Negotiations with the International Typographical Union were settled in 1975, with an agreement providing early retirement and severance packages for printers whose jobs were eliminated. Similarly, the stereotypers' contract was reconsidered, and offers of early retirement or severance benefits were provided to those affected by the closing of that department. With management acutely aware of rapidly rising costs, R&T officials reached an accord with the pressmen that ended all featherbedding. This new agreement allowed the company to cut fifty overtime shifts per week, most at overtime pay rates, and played a significant role in slowing the growth of payroll. From 1973 through 1975, payroll had risen at a rate of 8 percent annually, while the consumer price index (CPI) moved up at a rate of 8.7 percent. Yet in 1976, payroll edged up only 3 percent, compared to the CPI of 5.8 percent. With these settlements in place, the R&T enjoyed harmonious labor relations through the remainder of the decade.[28]

As corporate leaders worried over labor issues, they were also forced to confront the technological changes in the printing process. In the 1960s and 1970s, the development of the cold type process of photocomposition went hand in hand with offset printing. Instead of the traditional letterpress system, whereby a plate with raised metal type was inked and then pressed against newsprint to make page impressions, offset presses employed photographic images of pages on thin metal plates that were chemically treated so that ink adhered to the correct areas. With the presses running, the plates moved over moisteners, which applied water to the blank sections of the page, and then passed by ink rollers. Ink adhered only to the chemically treated portions. Ernest Hynds picks up the description of the process: "The image is transferred from the plate to a blanket roll and then the web of paper as it passes by the cylinder. The process is referred to as offset because the image is first offset on the blanket roll and then printed rather than being printed directly from the plate."[29]

Offset printing was soon adopted by many small newspapers because it ultimately produced a better quality, less expensive product. Larger newspapers, the R&T among them, had huge investments in letterpress equipment, and they were slow in expending the necessary funds for conversion. Instead, they investigated a number of possible options. While the Register and Tribune was considering offset, it experimented in 1974 with direct printing using plastic plates and the DiLitho system, which was ultimately selected. The equipment was ordered in 1975, and the R&T was completely converted to the DiLitho printing system by April of the following year. The DiLitho process modified existing letterpresses, enabling them to hold offset or lithographic plates. Unlike offset printing, the DiLitho operation rolled the plate images directly onto the passing paper. For the R&T and most other large-circulation dailies, DiLitho, or use of a plastic plate system, offered newspapers a stopgap solution that improved quality but avoided the expense of new presses.[30]

Having maintained labor peace amid cutting costs as well as updating their pressroom, Kruidenier and his new team of managers resumed the search for prospective acquisitions. To investigate potential properties, Gerlach sent two members of his corporate staff, Richard Gilbert and Charles Edwards, the latter a fourth-generation Cowles, throughout the central United States. The first attempt at acquiring additional newspapers failed: in the fall of 1976, the company's bid for the *Macomb Daily Journal* fell short, and the property went to Park Newspapers in New York.[31]

Later that year, the owners of the *Kansas City Star and Times* invited the

R&T to look over their facilities and consider making an offer. Kruidenier authorized Gartner and Gerlach to investigate the firm. Impressed, the two managers returned to Des Moines and argued that with the addition of these newspapers, the Cowles family would have a great newspaper publishing empire running from Kansas City through Des Moines and up to Minneapolis. Such an acquisition, estimated to cost more than $100 million, would have dictated a joint purchase with the Minneapolis Star and Tribune. Seeing the acquisition as expensive and complicated, John Cowles Jr. and David Kruidenier chose not to pursue the Missouri papers. The next year, another expansion effort failed when the owners of the *Daily Journal* of Tupelo, Mississippi, turned down an R&T offer.[32]

Other Media

In 1977, the R&T began branching into the other media areas. Based on a tip from former KRNT manager Bob Dillon, who suggested that television station WQAD-TV in Moline, Illinois, was a good property and soon would be available, the Register and Tribune investigated. Liking what it saw, the company bought the ABC affiliate in September for $9,625,000, and the next month it paid $2,150,000 for radio stations WIBA-AM and FM in Madison, Wisconsin. Acquisition fever continued with yet another purchase: Pinicon Publishing, owner of two weekly newspapers, the *Bulletin-Journal* and the *Conservative* in Independence, Iowa. This purchase, however, was made with the statewide strategy of the *Register* in mind. Located between Waterloo, Cedar Rapids, and Dubuque, the small town of Independence was considered a good location for a satellite printing plant that could provide editions of the *Register* for the eastern portions of the state.[33]

Up to this point, there had been managerial unity on the desirability of expanding the firm, but with the sudden flurry of additions, chief financial officer (CFO) Lou Norris became concerned. Like the *Jackson Sun* purchase, these recent acquisitions had been financed through borrowing. Norris, who had been comfortable with the company's conservative financial past and its large reserves of cash, worried about the amount of debt the R&T was taking on based on the new attitude of top management. The paper, which had virtually no debt in 1971, carried a debt of $7.5 million in 1977. Norris repeatedly warned of the dangers of financing acquisitions in such a dangerous manner. His warnings were not heeded and, in fact, Norris found himself pushed out of the inner circle.[34]

Norris also had misgivings about the rapidity of the firm's expansion. Although he believed that the company had been too conservative in the past and that well-researched acquisitions made good business sense, he thought that the triumvirate of Kruidenier, Gartner, and Gerlach was reckless in its eagerness to buy almost any media property available. Looking back, Norris explained, "They were just extremely gung-ho—this was going to be a big media company. I think they went way too fast and too far."[35]

Continued Expansion

With the CFO's views carrying little weight, the R&T continued down the expansionist path. In 1978, the board of directors approved a proposal to go after the Daily Herald Company, publisher of the *Everett Herald* and the *Western Sun* in Everett, Washington. The two papers were to be jointly acquired with the Minneapolis Star and Tribune Company. Norris was the lone dissenting vote. Although Gartner and Gerlach had a "handshake deal" with the firm's owners and thought they had bought the papers, the *Herald* and *Sun* were ultimately acquired by the Washington Post Company.[36]

Undeterred by the failure of the Daily Herald deal, the R&T soon thereafter made its biggest acquisition of the decade, buying a company that owned both television and radio properties. This acquisition was followed up by yet another newspaper purchase. After completing the Pinicon deal, its smallest acquisition, in March 1978, the R&T pursued its largest target, McCoy Broadcasting of Denver, Colorado. McCoy owned a television station in Honolulu, Hawaii, and four radio stations: two in Portland, Oregon, and two in Denver, Colorado. The Register and Tribune became aware of the company when George Hagar, a McCoy minority stockholder, casually told Michael Gartner that the media concern was about to be put up for sale. Gartner informed Gerlach about the property but explained that because he had a conflict of interest—not only was his father-in-law, Arthur McCoy, the primary owner of the company, but Gartner and his wife, Barbara, owned 1.5 percent of McCoy stock—he could not take the information to the R&T board. Gerlach, however, did, and even after Gartner disclosed his interest in McCoy to his fellow directors, they voted to pursue the media firm. Gartner, meanwhile, abstained from voting on all measures concerning the acquisition of the property. The R&T's original idea called for jointly purchasing McCoy with Minneapolis Star and Tribune. This proposal, however, was ultimately rejected by the Minnesota newspaper company because, as former Star and Tribune publisher Donald R. Dwight remembered, "We thought [the price] was too high." Convinced that McCoy would be a valuable addition, the R&T decided to go after it alone.[37]

While the Register and Tribune was involved in discussions with Arthur

McCoy, a subsidiary of Coca-Cola Bottling of New York offered $27 million for the property. Concerns about Gartner and insider stock transactions were dismissed by Kruidenier and board member John Cowles Jr. because, they reasoned, "the Gartners are going to get the same amount of cash regardless of who is the buyer." Furthermore, they felt the editor's family ties were important: "We would not have a chance at this purchase except for Mike's McCoy connection." Acting quickly to beat out Coca-Cola, the R&T bought McCoy for $27.8 million in July 1978. To pay for the acquisition, the company took out a $30 million loan at a fixed rate of 9⅝ percent. Payment on the 12-year senior notes was to be made in 10 equal annual payments beginning in 1982.[38]

The frenzied pace of expansion continued through the rest of the year as the company eyed another newspaper. The *Waukesha Freeman,* an afternoon daily in suburban Milwaukee with a circulation of 26,000, was the next target. Although Norris again voted against the purchase, he was the only opposition, and the R&T bought the paper for $8.5 million. The firm's debt now totaled $41 million, but Kruidenier and his team were satisfied that the newly diversified R&T could not only handle the enlarged debt but also generate revenues and profits.[39]

Initially, the expanded company performed well. In 1978, the first full year since the purchases of the Moline and Madison television and radio stations, the firm's net profits reached an all-time high of $5.4 million, a 37 percent increase over 1977. Net profit margin, meanwhile, advanced upward to 7.76 percent. The success of the *Jackson Sun* was being matched by the other new media properties. Yet, beginning in 1979, huge interest payments associated with expansion, subpar performance from the new McCoy and Waukesha acquisitions, and mounting expenses at the *Register* and the *Tribune,* in combination, led to a significant downturn.[40]

The large debt needed to fund the acquisitions of 1978 proved to be a serious financial strain. Interest costs, amounting to only $9,000 in 1975, jumped to $3.2 million in 1979 and $4.4 million two years later. At the same time, profits at the recently acquired McCoy properties, now the R&T's Western Sun subsidiary, dropped from $72,000 in 1979 to a loss of $129,000 in 1980. Although net earnings went up at the Portland radio stations, they declined at the television station in Honolulu. The major problems, however, were at the Denver radio stations, which lost $162,000 in 1979 and $313,000 the next year. The *Waukesha Freeman*'s performance was similarly disappointing, with net profits slipping from $175,000 to $54,000 over the same period.[41]

Meanwhile, the company's flagship operation, the Register and Tribune, was struggling to keep up with expenses. Much like circulation revenue, which grew through boosting rates, advertising revenue at the Des Moines papers was growing largely because of rate increases, but also because more space was being devoted to advertising. In 1970, 53.3 percent of the R&T's three papers consisted of editorial content while the remaining 46.7 percent went to advertising. By 1980, these figures had nearly reversed—48.6 percent of the papers was editorial content and 51.4 percent was advertising. Regardless of raising rates and getting more advertising, company revenues, which grew 12 percent from 1978 to 1980, failed to keep pace with mounting expenses, which rose 19 percent. The result was a decline in net earnings of the Des Moines Register and Tribune newspaper operations from $2.87 million to $1.98 million.[42]

Thus, as the new decade opened, the company's situation was deteriorating. Some properties were not performing up to expectations; costs kept climbing; circulation at the *Register* and the *Tribune* was falling; and the firm's debt load was staggering. In fact, by 1981 its operating income of $4.1 million did not cover the interest payments of $4.4 million. The R&T's equity-to-debt ratio stood at an abysmal .67:1, compared to the average ratio of 4.3:1 of industry leaders. These factors pushed the company's net profit margins down to 4.7 percent in 1979 and 1.79 percent in 1980. Such figures were well below the average margins of eight leading newspapers, which stood at 9.7 percent in 1979 and 9.25 percent in 1980.[43]

Voting Trust

Even as the R&T was eagerly buying other media properties, top managers became concerned that the consolidation wave sweeping the industry could make the Des Moines firm a takeover target. Popular periodicals captured the current sensibility by running articles with such titles as "After the Rash of Take-Overs" or "The Big Money Hunt for Independent Newspapers."[44] Although most papers acquired were small- to medium-size dailies, Capital Cities' purchase of the *Kansas City Star* and *Times* in 1977 worried R&T corporate leaders. In response, Kruidenier asked Gartner, Norris, and Hudson to "come up with a value that our company might have in the eyes of a potential unsolicited acquirer." The three managers estimated that the firm might be worth $155 million, or $110 per R&T share. The valuation only escalated fears that the firm was a desirable candidate for takeover. The board of directors began investigating ways to maintain the company's independence.[45]

Harvard Law School professor A. James Casner was retained to study various means of ensuring that the Cowles family and current management would remain in control of the company. By the 1970s, R&T stock was dispersed among nearly 450 shareholders, including more than 70 members of the Cowles family. Besides the possibility of an unfriendly takeover, managers also feared that dissident stockholders might decide to challenge corporate policy. To avoid either of these scenarios, Casner proposed the creation of a voting trust. According to the plan, at least 50.1 percent of voting stock needed to be placed in the trust, which would be controlled by five trustees. At least two trustees were required to be Cowles family members, and one had to be an R&T employee. Only stockholders with 1,000 or more shares of stock—some 90 people, 75 of whom were Cowles family members—were invited to participate in the trust.[46]

In December 1978, the trust was approved by shareholders, and more than 60 percent of the stock was originally pledged to the trust. It was headed by trustees David Kruidenier, R&T chairman and publisher; Morley Cowles Ballantine and John Cowles Jr., Kruidenier's cousins and fellow board members; Michael Gartner, company president and editor; and Luther Hill Jr., another board member. Set up to run for 10 years, the trust did not go into effect as scheduled because of a restraining order resulting from a lawsuit filed by 11 shareholders seeking to block its implementation. Although the order was lifted in January 1979 and the trust went into effect, the plaintiffs, most of whom were descendants of long-deceased R&T business manager Harry Watts Sr., continued their legal action against the company. Their suit made several charges against company management. The major charges involved two alleged incidents of insider trading. The first was Mike Cowles' purchase of 320,000 shares of Cowles Communication stock from the R&T at $2 per share below the prevailing rate on the New York Stock Exchange. The complaint charged that Cowles bought the shares with a down payment of $100,000 and a loan from the R&T at 6 percent for the balance. Critics contrasted this transaction with the 9.62 percent loan, which was 3.62 percent higher, that the company took out in its acquisition of the McCoy properties. Mike Cowles had allegedly gotten a loan at rates below the prevailing market. Second, there was the issue of Gartner's interest in the McCoy firm at the time of its purchase. The litigation dragged on well into the 1980s and would be settled only after the company was sold.[47]

Pulitzer Quality

The suit and other problems notwithstanding, the *Register* maintained its journalistic quality. Many have argued that it became an even better newspaper during the 1970s. Certainly Michael Gartner, whose advent as editor infused new energy into the paper, deserved much of the credit for the improvements. A hands-on manager, Gartner loved being in the newsroom, and he edited many of the news stories himself. Seeing the Iowa Poll as a major asset of the newspaper, he moved the survey from its usual placement on the Sunday editorial page to front-page prominence. With his background at the *Wall Street Journal,* the new editor called for more aggressive reporting and front-page coverage of Iowa businesses. Beginning in 1976, this coverage included an annual report listing the salaries and compensation packages of the top paid executives at publicly held companies in Iowa. According to longtime R&T reporter George Mills, this new investigative approach dismayed some businesspeople who believed "papers should be an extension of the Chamber of Commerce." If this style angered some, it pleased Kruidenier, who felt "the paper was never more interesting than under Gartner."[48]

This hard-hitting approach was being used with great success by R&T Washington Bureau staffer James Risser. In 1975, the 37-year-old reporter discovered widespread corruption in the grain exporting business. Risser's series uncovered "bribery, the misgrading of grain, and short weighting" as well as other abuses. His investigation led to more than 60 indictments and a complete revamping of the grain inspection system within the U.S. Department of Agriculture. These stories incensed many business executives, and one flew to Des Moines and threatened to sue the paper. Upon finding that Risser's charges were accurate, however, the businessman dropped the idea of a lawsuit. For this investigation, Risser won the 1976 Pulitzer Prize for national reporting. Winning this top journalistic honor for the 11th time, the R&T ran a clever, self-promotional advertisement: "In the history of journalism, only one newspaper has won more Pulitzer Prizes for National Reporting than The Des Moines Register. Our congratulations to the New York Times."[49]

Risser, who had been with the *Register* since 1964, was appointed chief of the company's Washington Bureau in August 1976. This added responsibility failed to slow him down. Two years later, Risser was involved in six months of research that eventually led to his second Pulitzer Prize for national reporting in 1979. The seven-part series on environmental damage caused by modern agriculture ran in September 1978. He found that farming methods ruined soil, polluted water, and endangered public health. "Economics and politics," according to Risser, were the obstacles to cleaning up farming practices.[50]

Innovation and Style Changes

During Risser's years as bureau chief, an important innovation occurred at the R&T's Washington operation. The brainchild of Gilbert Cranberg, who succeeded Lauren Soth as editorial page editor in 1975, editorial writers—initially one and soon two—were sent to the Washington Bureau. These staffers were Dick Foster, a specialist on international affairs, and William Symonds, whose expertise was in agricultural economics and policy. Cranberg rightfully reasoned that editorial writers focusing on these important issues were much better placed in the nation's capital, where federal policy on such matters was formulated. In daily contact with Des Moines, the Washington-based editorial writers participated in the daily morning editorial conference via speaker phone.[51]

Besides the additions in Washington, other changes on the editorial page took place under Cranberg. The daily *Register* editorial page expanded to a two-page op-ed format. Cranberg strove to enliven the pages and heighten interest "without trivializing issues." This goal was attained by running editorials from a wide variety of sources. The editor went so far as to use satirical pieces from *MAD* magazine and a spoof of the *Des Moines Register*—called the *Des Moines Rooster*—originally appearing in the University of Iowa's newspaper. The Sunday editorial section was also enlarged to include a "week in review" page as well as book and art reviews.[52]

Editorial Positions

These stylistic changes and the addition of more space, however, did not alter the *Register*'s editorial positions, which continued in the paper's liberal tradition. Domestically, this tradition was reflected by the R&T's support for legalized abortion and the Equal Rights Amendment (ERA), while in international affairs the paper maintained its refusal to accept the hard-line, anticommunist stance toward the Soviet Union. On the endorsement of candidates, the editors in concert with publisher Kruidenier decided whom the paper would support. Kruidenier, however, was "quite reticent about throwing his weight around" regarding either the *Register*'s endorsements or its editorial positions. During the 1970s, the publisher's avoidance of editorial matters was quite clear in a standoff with Younkers Department Stores in 1974 and a senatorial election four years later.

Women's Rights

The *Register*'s long advocacy for civil rights continued during the 1970s and was clearly evident in its strong support of women's rights. The two major issues confronting women were the legalization of abortion and the ERA. In January 1973, while the Supreme Court was considering the abortion issue in the case of *Roe v. Wade,* the *Register* noted that abortion was legal in Iowa only when the mother's life was in danger. Calling such a law "indefensible," the paper explained that the statute required revision, and abortions should be allowed, for instance, if the fetus was determined to have genetic defects. On January 24, the day after the Court legalized abortion, the paper cheered its ruling as "a defense of the individual's freedom of choice at a time when individuals and groups are trying to exploit the state's power so they can impose their moral beliefs on the whole population."[53]

Over the next several years, the *Register* remained committed to a woman's right to choose an abortion. This stance led to the paper's support of the proposal to pay for abortions under Medicaid. In 1978, it backed Governor Robert Ray's position that all women should have equal access to abortions. It explained, "A poor woman should have the same reproductive freedom as does a rich woman. Whether a woman chooses to have an abortion should be a private and a medical decision, not a political one. We commend the governor for standing up for the right of choice for indigent women." Two years later, it repeated this same stance: "A woman should not be deprived of the right [to an abortion] because she accepts welfare payments."[54]

Successful in their quest for legalized abortion, women were also actively pursing an equal rights amendment. When Congress passed the ERA in 1972, the amendment was sent out to be approved by three-fourths of the states by 1979 to become law. Although Iowa ratified the federal ERA in 1973, it had not added an ERA to its own state constitution. In 1978, the state amendment was seriously considered by the Iowa legislature. As the ERA's merits were being debated in the capitol, the *Register* began what became a long campaign for passage. In January 1978, the paper explained, "Without an equal rights guarantee in the constitution, women must depend on legislation which can easily be changed. An ERA provides a moral example for legislators and citizens, and a strong statement to courts interpreting legislation." When the senate version was returned to the house for final approval, the paper urged the lawmakers to support it. Passed in March, the *Register* was guardedly optimistic, for this was only the first hurdle. As the paper noted, "The amendment must be approved again [by the state legislature] in 1979 or 1980 and be ratified by a vote of the people before taking effect."[55]

The following year, ERA was again before the state legislature. Pushed through both houses quickly, ERA was approved the requisite second time in February 1979; it was to be put before voters in November 1980. This time Cranberg and his staff cheered: "We applaud the Iowa House and Senate for the way they brushed aside delaying tactics to complete the legislative action on the Equal Rights Amendment to the Iowa Constitution." After noting that an Iowa ERA was now of greater importance because the federal amendment's passage appeared unlikely, the paper declared, "Such approval would guarantee equality for Iowa men and women regardless of what happens to the federal amendment." The R&T's concern about the federal ERA was certainly correct—although the deadline was extended to 1982, the amendment fell three states short of ratification.[56]

By the fall of 1980, the paper was inundating readers with editorials warning of the scare tactics and disinformation of anti-ERA forces. Realizing that legalized abortion did not have wide support throughout the state, the paper explained that ERA and abortion were two very separate issues and should not be linked. Immediately before the election, the *Register* reminded Iowans that the amendment had been bipartisan and the legislature had approved it the second time by a wide majority—88 to 5 in the House and 44 to 5 in the Senate. It wrote, "The overwhelming vote in the Iowa Legislature reflected the emergence of a consensus—throughout the state, not just on Capitol Hill—that women and men are entitled to the same rights under the law. Now the voters have a chance to nail that principle into the state's Bill of Rights for the protection of future as well as present generations. That is why we favor a yes vote on the Equal Rights Amendment."[57]

Regardless of the *Register*'s persistence, voters turned down a state ERA by a margin of 55 percent to 45 percent. The R&T blamed the defeat on a "fear of change" and singled out the opposition's propaganda, which wrongly suggested that the amendment's passage would give legal sanction to homosexual relationships. The paper tried to rally the troops and work "for re-enactment of the amendment and give the voters of Iowa a second chance." That opportunity came 12 years later, but voters once again turned down the amendment at the polls.[58]

Afghanistan and Olympics

In the international arena, which was still very much dominated by the continuing cold war, the *Register* remained a voice of reasoned moderation. Perhaps this stance was best exemplified by its position on the 1979 Soviet attack on Afghanistan and the ensuing American boycott of the Moscow Olympics. In late December 1979, the Soviet Union invaded Afghanistan to support a client government under attack by Islamic insurgents. Ultimately, the Red Army set up a new regime and stayed to deter Afghan rebels. President Jimmy Carter worried that the Soviet aggression might be the first step toward the Indian Ocean and the oil-rich Persian Gulf, and he responded with a number of measures designed to punish the Soviets. These measures included banning the sale of grain and high technology to Russia, ending cultural exchanges with the Soviets, pulling the Strategic Arms Limitation Talk (SALT) II Treaty from the U.S. Senate, and calling for a boycott of the 1980 Summer Olympic Games in Moscow. Seeing these policies as overblown, the *Register* deplored Carter's reaction.[59]

Specifically, the paper argued that the grain embargo would hurt American farmers more than the Soviet government because the commodity could be readily obtained elsewhere. Curtailing cultural exchanges, the *Register* believed, was the most damaging of all reprisals because such visits to the United States exposed Russian people to American values. On this issue, it noted, "Iron Curtains are a Soviet product. This country should not be erecting them. America should be on the side of openness. It should stand for the fullest and freest exchange of people, ideas, and opinions." Furthermore, the paper was apprehensive about Carter's pulling of the SALT II Treaty and the negative impact this action might have on relations with the Soviets.[60]

On January 24, Carter used the State of the Union address to issue a stern warning: "An attempt by any outside force to gain control of the Persian Gulf region will be regarded as an assault on the vital interests of the United States of America, and such an assault will be repelled by use of any means necessary, including military force." Referred to as the "Carter Doctrine," the president's strong words were well received by most Americans. However, a Gallup Poll taken in February indicated that 60 percent of the public still felt Carter was not tough enough on the Soviets. The *Register*, meanwhile, was dismayed by the increasing "militarized thinking" in Washington and the "vague doctrine that could make any shift in a Persian Gulf government reason to go to war." After noting that Soviet president Leonid Brezhnev had said his country had no intention of invading the Persian Gulf, the paper concluded with its own stern warning: "In a world armed to the teeth with nuclear weapons hard questions must be raised before the United States becomes irretrievably committed to a policy whose major component is the threat of war."[61]

Yet it was Carter's proposed boycott of the Moscow Olympics that really raised the ire of the *Register*. Early in January, when the president suggested that further Soviet aggression might result in an American-led boycott of the 1980 Summer Olympic Games, the R&T editorials argued against the policy because "the athletes would become a propaganda tool." Later that month, the *Register* pointed out the hypocrisy of such a pullout: "If it is proper to signify disapproval of Soviet conduct by boycotting the Olympics, why didn't the United States signify its disapproval of the myriad of daily violations of human rights in the Soviet Union by balking, at the outset, at the award of the Games to Moscow?" Although aware that over 70 percent of Iowans supported the boycott, the paper reminded its readers that politics should not be part of the competition. The Olympics, the *Register* explained, "are not President Brezhnev's and they are not President Carter's. ... They belong to the world's athletes more than they belong to the government of the two superpowers." By April, as the paper kept hammering away at Carter's proposed Olympic pullout, it reported that support for the boycott had slipped to 58 percent of Iowans.[62]

Besides keeping American athletes home, Carter tried organizing an international boycott of the Games. By the end of May, the deadline for announcing attendance at the Games approached, and Carter had failed to line up broad support for the boycott. Although more than 50 nations joined in the boycott, most of Europe, except West Germany, Norway, and Liechtenstein, planned to attend; while 10 of the 14 NATO members disregarded the boycott. Disappointed that the president held to the boycott, the paper was further tormented by its failure: "If there is one thing worse than a misguided effort to organize a boycott, it is failing. Instead of administrating a symbolic rebuff to the Soviets, Carter and the United States have been rebuffed."[63]

Even as the *Register* was chiding President Carter for the boycott, it continued to disapprove of his entire hard-line approach in dealing with the Afghanistan situation. Cranberg's editorial staff believed "that Soviet intervention in Afghanistan was not the first step in an eventual march on the oil fields of Iran or the warm waters of the Arabian Sea." Given this fact, the paper hoped the United States would drop its desire to punish the Soviets and work for "diplomatic solutions" to assure "Afghanistan of the peace and independence it deserved." Two months later, however, the *Register* remained discouraged. While it noted that the Soviets had shown a "willingness to negotiate," the United States refused to talk until the Red Army was pulled out of Afghanistan. Understanding that this was not likely to happen, the paper admonished the administration "to be more zealous than it has been in seeking a negotiated settlement."[64]

Political Endorsements

While the *Register* maintained its call for moderation in relations with the Soviets, the endorsement of presidential candidates continued to reflect its independent stand. In 1964, the paper had broken from its long-standing tradition of supporting Republican candidates. But in the 1972 election, the paper supported Republican incumbent Richard Nixon, even though it had not backed him four years earlier. Although certainly not an avid Nixon supporter, the *Register* applauded the president's dealings in foreign policy, which were marked by such major accomplishments as beginning to normalize relations with China and moving toward nuclear arms control with the Soviet Union. On the domestic front, his experiments in battling inflation had shown a practical rather than an ideological bent. Given his record, the R&T thought a continuation of the Nixon presidency was better than turning the office over to George McGovern. However, the endorsement was less than wholehearted. The paper was especially dismayed with the issue of morality: "We are concerned about the moral climate in Washington. We are disturbed by the Watergate Scandal and the evidence linking it with the White House."[65]

In the 1976 election, the *Register* threw its support behind Jimmy Carter "without enthusiasm." It described his "undistinguished campaign as marked by gaffes and misstatements" and worried about his "lack of experience in foreign and national affairs." Carter was viewed as "an unknown quantity." Incumbent President Gerald Ford, on the other hand, was "a known quantity, but the record he compiled is mediocre." "The country," the paper concluded, "needs better than Ford and [running mate Robert] Dole. On balance, we believe Carter–[and running mate Walter] Mondale would be better."[66] After four years of the Carter presidency, the *Register* was still largely unimpressed, but the belligerent anti-Soviet rhetoric of challenger Ronald Reagan gravely concerned the editors. They opined, "The stakes are high. Reagan's inexperience and his foreign policy outlook trouble us sufficiently that we do not want to run the risk." They concluded, "The realities of this election compel the question, 'Whose finger is on the trigger—Ronald Reagan's or Jimmy Carter's?' To that question, our answer, despite serious misgivings about him on other counts, is Carter's."[67]

Although Kruidenier sat in on endorsement decisions, he sometimes disagreed with what the paper said about a particular candidate. One example involved Iowa's 1978 U.S. Senate race that pitted Democratic incumbent Dick Clark against Republican challenger Roger Jepsen. Prior to the election, the *Register* passionately endorsed the liberal Clark as "a voice of reason" who gave "priority to the welfare and rights of individuals." It was impressed with his record, which included voting for the Panama Canal Treaty, supporting the continuance of government financing of abortions, and leading the fight to reform the grain inspection system—which followed from Risser's Pulitzer Prize–winning series. According to the Iowa Poll, which the R&T ran on the front page prior to the election, Clark led Jepsen by an 11-point margin, 51.4 percent to 40.8 percent. Jepsen, however, stunned the paper by upsetting his rival on election day. Shocked by the outcome and unwilling to concede graciously, the editorial staff drafted a sharp piece that deplored Clark's loss. Cranberg wrote the eye-catching headline: "Best Man Lost." Realizing that the headline was unusual, Cranberg ran it by Michael Gartner. With the editor's approval, the editorial ran two days after the election and said in part, "The defeat of Iowa's Democratic Senator Dick Clark by Republican Roger Jepsen is inexplicable. By all measures Clark should have won—and deserved to win—a second term."[68]

Although the R&T received many complaints about the unorthodox headline and editorial, Cranberg heard nothing about it from any of his superiors at the paper. Then, six months later, the *Des Moines Tribune* ran a series of profiles on prominent people, one of which featured David Kruidenier. It was here, when Cranberg picked up the *Tribune* in May 1979, that he learned his publisher "regretted" the "Best Man Lost" editorial because "it seemed petulant [and] sounded like we were poor losers." The article added that had Kruidenier been in town at the time, he would have "suggested strongly" that the editorial be run differently. Yet, according to Cranberg, the publisher did not see the galley proofs before the paper went to press, and therefore it is unlikely the editorial would have been altered. Even after the *Tribune* article, Kruidenier never confronted Cranberg about the infamous editorial. He had, however, expressed his displeasure to Gartner, who chose not to worry Cranberg about it because "editors are paid to absorb owners' whims." Specifically, Gartner felt that telling the editorial page editor about Kruidenier's reservations might impede his creativity and willingness to experiment.[69]

In Gartner's mind, Kruidenier was a "terrific publisher" because he never interfered with the paper's editorial statements or news stories. He had shown great restraint, for instance, by not requesting to view the proofs of the 1979 *Tribune* profile about him before it went to press. Four years earlier, Kruidenier had followed in the same Cowles tradition of steering clear of editorial positions, and in that particular case, the paper's stance resulted in a loss of advertising revenue.

Consumer Credit

In 1974, the state legislature took up the issue of consumer credit interest rates. Up until the summer of 1973, when the Iowa Supreme Court ruled that the state's usury laws applied to retail charge accounts and limited annual interest to 9 percent, most stores were charging 18 percent interest per year. After the court stepped in, it became clear that a new statute was needed specifically covering consumer credit. As the topic was debated, retailers maintained that the 18 percent rate was a necessary minimum to conduct business. Further, they argued, a ceiling on the amount of interest that could be charged was unnecessary because competition would supposedly keep interest rates in check. The Iowa Consumer League, on the other hand, estimated that a rate of 13.8 percent would cover credit costs and called for limiting the amount of interest that could be charged.

In February 1974, the *Register* came out in favor of establishing an upper limit for interest charges. It stated: "The difficult job of fixing a revolving credit rate ceiling should involve not only a determination of the retailers' costs of offering such credit but also a determination of whether part of that cost may not fairly be considered a general business expense just as other forms of credit expenses are." As the legislators moved toward acceptance of some sort of interest rate ceiling, the paper commended their action and reminded them that "competition is not enough to keep interest rate levels in line." After several revisions and negotiations between the House and Senate versions, the consumer credit law was approved on June 3. The new statute allowed interest rates on retail credit up to 18 percent on amounts under $500 and up to 15 percent on amounts over $500. Although the *Register* was pleased that a limit was established, it saw the new law as "weak" because it had hoped for a lower ceiling.[70]

While the bill was being debated, management at Younkers Department Stores—the major retailer in Des Moines—organized a retailers committee and complained about the paper's editorial position. Kruidenier, MacDonald, and Gartner, who had not been at all involved in the editorials, stood behind their editorial writers and refused to alter the paper's stand. After the consumer credit law passed in early June, Younkers retaliated against the *Register* for its stance on the legislation by canceling all its display advertising. As the R&T's largest advertiser, Younkers cost the company dearly with its boycott of the papers. After nearly two weeks, David Kruidenier met with Younkers CEO Charles Duchen at the Des Moines Club, and the two executives settled their differences.[71]

Younkers advertising gradually returned to the paper toward the end of June, and by the fall the department store's advertising was moving up toward preboycott levels. The R&T clearly missed Younkers, however, and its display advertising linage declined from 1973 figures. Company advertising director Lyle Lynn estimated that the newspaper lost $50,000 as a result of Younkers' brief absence.[72]

When the dispute was settled, the paper welcomed Younkers back in an editorial and commented on the standoff. While it noted that all advertisers certainly had the right to pull their advertising at any time, it hoped "advertising decisions regarding this newspaper would be made on the pragmatic basis of whether our columns attract potential customers." It then explained the significance of separating the editorial and business side of the paper:

> Modifying editorial policy to retain advertising would be only one step removed from selling advertising in the news and editorial columns. This would destroy the confidence of the reader and, in the long run, of the advertiser, too. Because if we modify our policy for one advertiser, we ultimately must modify our policy for all advertisers. And, in the end, we would not be publishing a newspaper, we would be printing a shopper's guide.[73]

Downtown Development

Managers at Younkers were not alone in their concern about the *Register*'s clout. In the late 1970s, trucking magnate John Ruan and his supporters were angered at what they saw as Kruidenier's use of the paper for his own political ends. Earlier in the decade, as part of a downtown Des Moines renewal project, Ruan proposed the construction of a new high-rise hotel. Many civic leaders, David Kruidenier among them, were in agreement that such an addition was needed in the revitalization effort. Kruidenier, in fact, was a leading booster of the downtown area, and he successfully led the $9.5 million fund-raising drive to build the new Civic Center. The facility, which included a 2,750-seat indoor theater and an outdoor plaza, was to be the cultural anchor of the new downtown, and it was completed in the spring of 1979. As construction was underway, Kruidenier and other Civic Center supporters called for the building of a city parking ramp immediately north of the Second and Locust streets theater location. Ruan, meanwhile, looked to erect a 30-story hotel several blocks west at Seventh and Locust streets.[74]

Although the R&T sold land for the Ruan project and invested $500,000 in the undertaking, Kruidenier opposed the plan because he thought the lot was too small. His preference was to locate the hotel closer to the Civic Center. Another part of the conflict between the two businessmen involved the proposed construction of two new public parking ramps for both the hotel and the Civic Center. Kruidenier, who had already obtained approval for construction of a $2.4 million city parking structure near the Civic Center, objected to the $8 million parking garage to service Ruan's hotel. Both the *Register* and the *Tribune* came out editorially against building two downtown public parking ramps. More specifically, the *Tribune* wrote in March

1978 that the Ruan-proposed hotel was "misplaced" and its suggested garage "too costly." Kruidenier agreed with the editorial, but he had no hand in writing it. Editor Cranberg and his staff arrived at their position independently of their publisher. This claim was not believed by many, however, including John Ruan and Des Moines Mayor Richard Olson.[75]

Mayor Olson and Robert Sterling, president of the Ruan Corporation, blamed Kruidenier and the paper for causing the controversy surrounding the hotel project. Sterling noted that "comments by Kruidenier and the newspaper appeared to be 'a deliberate attempt to sabotage the whole (hotel) project.'" Other critics were more pointed. City Councilman Russell LaVine charged Kruidenier with "using the newspapers to carry out a 'personal vendetta' against John Ruan, and, out of spite, running editorials questioning aspects of the hotel ... and the city parking garage." Many, in fact, saw this confrontation between Kruidenier and Ruan as something linked to another completely different issue—the long-standing battle between the R&T and Ruan over larger trucks on Iowa roads.[76]

Despite the paper's editorials, the Ruan hotel project went forward, and the 416-room, 31-story Marriott Hotel opened for business in January 1981. Meanwhile, the parking garage dispute had been settled. As the city broke ground for a parking ramp that would serve the Civic Center at Fourth Street and Grand Avenue, Equitable of Iowa offered to finance and build a parking facility at Seventh and Locust streets. Approved by the city council, the parking structure was combined with retail space that became known as the Locust Street Mall.[77]

Taking Stock

The conclusion of the hotel controversy coincided with the anniversary of David Kruidenier's first 10 years as leader of the family's Des Moines newspaper. Over the decade, the CEO had succeeded in expanding the company beyond Iowa. Taking stock in the spring of 1980, Kruidenier was pleased to tell the board of directors that, through the strategy of diversification, the company was well on its way to meeting his goal of bringing in half its revenues from operations outside Iowa. In 1971, all the R&T's operating revenue had been earned in Iowa; by 1980, 32 percent of the firm's operating revenue came from its newspaper and broadcasting holdings outside the state.

Expansion did boost profits, but not as dramatically as anticipated because of the large bite of interest payments. Net operating profit rose from $1.88 million in 1971 to $3.78 million in 1979. In 1980, however, increased interest expense lowered operating profits to $2.64 million. Servicing the large debt amassed to allow for the acquisition strategy would remain a difficult problem, and the Des Moines papers' declining circulation—especially that of the *Tribune*—had not been addressed satisfactorily.[78]

Although now a diversified media company, the R&T's future prospects were not as bright as Kruidenier had hoped, and he began looking for solutions. One possibility, which had been discussed informally for several years, was to merge the Register and Tribune Company with the Cowles family's other major midwestern enterprise, the Minneapolis Star and Tribune Company. Combining the two firms, some believed, would create greater economies; it might also create a favorable market for a public offering of company stock. This proposed consolidation of Cowles properties would be pursued in the early 1980s.

CHAPTER 9

Failed Solutions: The Cowles Tradition Ends

1981–1985

By the early 1980s, it was clear to all concerned that the expansion of the 1970s, rather than bettering the Register and Tribune Company's position as intended, had actually made the company's situation worse. Generally speaking, acquisition was not necessarily a bad strategy; other publishers had employed it with solid results. Dow Jones, Gannett, and Lee Enterprises, for instance, continued buying newspapers in the 1970s, and their pretax operating margins rose from

John Cowles Jr., left, president of the Minneapolis Star and Tribune Company, and cousin David Kruidenier, chairman and publisher of the R&T, 1981. *Courtesy of David Kruidenier.*

1976 to 1981. The R&T's margins, meanwhile, fell.[1] In 1982, hampered by large interest payments and poor performances from new holdings such as the *Waukesha Freeman* and the McCoy broadcasting properties, the R&T experienced its first overall loss since Gardner Cowles had purchased the paper 80 years earlier. Given this situation, CEO David Kruidenier thought the solution to the R&T's financial woes might be merging with the Cowles family's other major newspaper property, the Minneapolis Star and Tribune Company (S&T). Increased size would make takeover less likely, and greater economies, it was hoped, could lead to higher margins.

When Kruidenier and Minneapolis CEO John Cowles Jr. could not agree to terms, the merger was shelved, and the R&T continued dealing with its problems alone. Doing so entailed selling off some of its recently acquired holdings, and like others in the industry, it ceased publication of its afternoon paper, the *Tribune*. In addition, greater attention was devoted to strategic planning. Meanwhile, two events occurred that would have lasting consequences for the firm. First, Kay Graham of the *Washington Post* offered to buy the Des Moines company. Second, minority stockholder Shawn Kalkstein undertook a detailed analysis of the firm's financial status. After expressing his concerns to fellow shareholders at the 1982 annual meeting, Kalkstein began a series of highly critical letters to stockholders, arguing that the R&T should be sold.

In early 1983, John Cowles Jr. was ousted as chairman of the board of directors of the Minneapolis Star and Tribune Company, now called Cowles Media Company (CMC). He was replaced by his cousin, David Kruidenier. As chairman of the board of both Cowles companies, Kruidenier again thought about the possibility of merging the two properties. In the midst of strategic planning the following year, Kruidenier told key R&T executives of his interest in reopening merger talks with CMC. Such an idea worried *Register* executives Michael Gartner and Gary Gerlach, and they began considering other possibilities. Ultimately, these executives, in combination with two other Iowa investors and the Dow Jones organization, decided to try to buy the company. They pitched their offer in November 1984, and after it was publicly announced, Kruidenier received two additional bids. Events moved rapidly from that point on. A First Boston valuation suggested that the Register and Tribune was worth far more than any offer on the table, but by that time, a majority of family members wished to sell out. By the spring of 1985, the company had been broken up and sold, with Gannett getting the prized *Register*. Shareholders benefited greatly from the sale; R&T shares, which had traded for between $15 and $30 per share, were paid at roughly $280 per share when the dissolution was completed. How the managers and owners arrived at the decision to sell out is the main focus of this chapter.

Exploring a Merger

In October 1980, the boards of both the Des Moines and the Minneapolis companies met jointly at the Pheasant Run Resort in St. Charles, Illinois, to discuss common issues, problems, and the possibility of merging the properties. Although no immediate action toward combining the companies took place, it was agreed that talks should continue, and another joint meeting was scheduled for the following fall. By August, however, discussions of a merger grew serious, and on August 24, Cowles invited Kruidenier and fellow board member Luther Hill Jr. to Minneapolis to meet with Star and Tribune executives Otto Silha and David Cox as well as John Jamison of Goldman Sachs to consider the implications of a merger. Apparently liking what they heard, the R&T board of directors met two weeks later and on September 9 approved a merger in principle. Kruidenier announced that the merger would assure the continuation of "strong, quality, independent journalism in Iowa." Ken MacDonald, however, disagreed. He feared that the Minneapolis headquarters of the merged company would ultimately lower editorial quality in Des Moines, and he alone voted against the resolution.[2]

To prepare for the merger, the R&T and S&T each established merger committees. The former's consisted of Kruidenier and outside directors John Chrystal, a banker; James Heskett, a Harvard Business School professor; and Burke Marshall, a Yale University law professor. The latter was represented by Cowles and board members Winthrop Knowlton, chairman of the board of Harper and Row, and Kingsley Murphy Jr., heir to the family that sold the Minneapolis Tribune to the Cowleses in 1941. Each company also retained its own investment banking firm—the S&T hired Goldman Sachs and the R&T retained First Boston Corporation—to do valuations of the firms' various holdings. According to First Boston managing director Nick Paumgarten, his firm was "to come up with relative valuations in [the proposed] exchange of the two companies' shares for one another." The investment banking firms visited both the Register and Star and Tribune plants during the end of October to interview executives and look over company facilities.[3]

Over the course of the next three months, the details were ironed out through various meetings in Des Moines, Minneapolis, and New York City. The investment banking firms' valuations of the two newspapers were relatively close in terms of exchange ratios and indicated that the Minneapolis company was approximately three times larger than that of Des Moines: First Boston put the R&T's worth at between $96 million and $117 million, while it valued the S&T's at between $251 million and $304 million. Goldman Sachs, meanwhile, estimated the R&T at between $60 million and $80 million and the S&T at between $175 million and $195 million. By the end of 1981, it was agreed that Cowles would serve as chairman and CEO, Kruidenier would be president, and top management positions would be equally distributed between R&T and S&T personnel.[4]

There were several reasons for wanting the merger. Together the media companies would have annual revenues of $330 million and rank 12th in newspaper circulation. Plans called for the new firm to trade its stock publicly. *Business Week* noted that "going public would set the merged company back on the acquisition trail and bolster its balance sheet. ... 'Being able to swap stock rather than paying cash would be one more tool in making acquisitions, said David Kruidenier.'" In addition, "the markets the two companies have maintained in their closely held stocks have been pegged at only a modest premium over book value, making them potentially susceptible to a takeover offer from the outside. Combined the companies would be harder to acquire." At a more basic level, it was thought that costs could be reduced through greater economies of scale. Yet, sticking points remained. Cowles and Kruidenier were very close to agreeing on exchange ratios, but one to two percentage points continued to separate them. In addition, questions on managerial compatibility persisted, and the more aggressive style of Des Moines managers—especially Michael Gartner, who was apparently slotted to serve as editorial head of both papers and had not endeared himself to Minneapolis executives—was problematic.[5]

By late January 1982, however, Kruidenier decided the merger was not a good idea. Although he and Cowles never quite agreed on stock exchange ratios, that difference most likely could have been resolved. From Kruidenier's perspective, the problem was one of clashing personalities. He and Cowles had had what could be characterized as a "competitive relationship," and the Des Moines CEO worried about working with his cousin. More broadly, there were conflicts between the managements of the two firms. Besides the Michael Gartner problem, S&T publisher Donald Dwight refused to report to Kruidenier in the proposed combined company. On Friday, February 5, the Des Moines merger committee agreed with Kruidenier's concerns and voted unanimously against the merger. Later that day, Kruidenier telephoned John Cowles to break off negotiations. Cowles was "greatly disappointed," because he had assumed that the differences were going to be worked out. Although the talks were suspended, Kruidenier still held out hope that such a combination might come to pass in the future. He firmly denied that the "failure of the merger with the Minneapolis company means that the Des

Moines company is for sale to another party." The idea of the merger indicated to many in the industry that the R&T was trying to strengthen its financial position, and a few firms decided to test the waters to see if the R&T board was interested in selling out. Less than two weeks after the merger was called off, the R&T was shaken by a visit from Kay Graham, chairman of the *Washington Post.*[6]

Washington Post Bid

Soon after Kruidenier announced the end of merger talks with the S&T, he received inquiries from Capital Cities, Times Mirror, and media mogul Rupert Murdoch, all expressing interest in buying the Register and Tribune. Another newspaper went to even greater lengths. Graham called Kruidenier several times, saying she wished to come to Des Moines for a visit. He finally agreed to see her on February 16. Management at the *Post* had been following the R&T-S&T merger, and when talks broke off, they thought the R&T might be ripe for purchase. After a quick study of the property, an offer was prepared, and Graham flew to Iowa. Kruidenier met her private plane at the airport and took her to his house for lunch. In the midst of conversation about the failed merger, Graham suggested the Washington Post Company could take the place of Minneapolis. She then described how both companies shared the same goals and mentioned $50 a share as a price the Post Company would be willing to pay. As Graham described in her notes of the meeting, Kruidenier "vigorously said he was not interested ... in a sale" of the R&T and noted that the figure of $50 per share was "way low." She still felt she should leave a written offer, and when she pulled it out, Kruidenier "jumped ten feet and said he didn't want to take it."[7]

Kruidenier refused to accept the envelope that apparently contained the offer. Unsuccessful in her overture, Graham made the best of the situation. On her way to the airport, she suggested they get to know each other better, and maybe in the future Kruidenier would reconsider selling. As quickly as possible, the R&T CEO informed members of the board of her visit and the Post offer. The directors he immediately contacted supported his action. Two days later, Kruidenier wrote the entire board describing his meeting with Graham. Trying to quiet the publicity and set the record straight, Kruidenier told a *Tribune* reporter that the Washington Post offer was completely unsolicited. He added that he did "not expect a bidding contest among the larger newspaper companies, and he repeated that the company is not for sale."[8]

Stockholder Dissent

These events, combined with the R&T's worsening financial situation, led to a lively annual stockholder meeting in March, 1982. After Gartner reported on the current conditions of the company, Kruidenier rose and made a lengthy presentation assuring stockholders that the company's poor performance was tied to the depressed Iowa economy, but he was optimistic about the future. After describing the termination of merger talks with Minneapolis and the Washington Post's offer, he explained that the firm's debt, 83 percent of which was "long term at attractive interest rates, 9 5/8 percent or less," was not a problem. The dividend, Kruidenier promised the audience, would remain at 40 cents per share per quarter. On a less positive note, the CEO informed shareholders that the moratorium on the company's general policy of buying all R&T shares offered to the company, which had been established during the merger discussions, would remain in effect. The continued suspension of the R&T's stock buyback policy was necessary because several large estates had recently sold their stock to the company; such purchases were draining the firm of valuable cash that could have been used for other purposes. To handle R&T stock transactions, the company began investigating plans to establish a limited public market for its stock.[9]

Kruidenier was then faced with an unusual situation: for the first time at an R&T annual meeting, there was visible stockholder dissent. First, the CEO addressed a number of questions that Frank Watts—a shareholder, a descendant of a former company business manager, and a plaintiff in the case against the R&T—had circulated to shareholders. Most of Watts's questions dealt with issues of the company's debt load, the dividend, and how the proposed new market for the firm's stock would work. Then, because he wanted to know the real value of his Register and Tribune stock, Watts asked about the terms of the Washington Post offer. Kruidenier sidestepped the question by saying that Graham had only made an inquiry "since I did not receive a purchase offer," and he made no further comment about it. The issue of stock's market value did not drop here, however. Later in the meeting, during the question-and-answer period, Frank Watts's brother, Des Moines attorney Harry Watts, asked about the stock's value, but this time he referred to the valuations done by the investment bankers during the recent merger talks. Kruidenier insisted that the bankers only offered "exchange ratios" and did not provide estimates of what the firm was worth. Harry Watts persisted but never had his question answered.[10]

Besides questions from the Watts brothers, management also faced a public challenge from Shawn Kalkstein, the husband of Karen Jurs, a great-granddaughter of Gardner Cowles Sr. Kalkstein met Jurs while working at *Look* magazine, and they married in 1963. He later studied business and finance at New York University and then devoted his full-time attention to managing his family's portfolio, which included 9,228 shares of R&T stock. Kalkstein first became concerned about the financial condition of the R&T when he and Karen were asked to join the voting trust in 1978. When investigating the idea, Kalkstein talked to R&T CFO Lou Norris, who also served as a trustee of Karen's trust fund. The Kalksteins ultimately decided against joining the trust, and Shawn began paying closer attention to the R&T annual reports. Over the next few years, he grew more and more apprehensive about the firm's poor performance, and through conversations with Norris, he learned that other shareholders had similar reservations.[11]

In 1981, Kalkstein and his wife wanted to sell their shares in the R&T, but because of the moratorium, the company was not buying back any stock. In order to get a list of R&T stockholders in hopes of finding someone to buy the shares, Kalkstein traveled to the 1982 annual meeting. He also intended to alert his fellow shareholders of the company's troubles by giving a brief speech at the proceedings. Prior to leaving his Connecticut home for the Iowa meeting, Kalkstein received a telephone call from Jonathan Jordan, an accountant and fourth-generation Cowles, who was also worried about the newspaper. The two met in the R&T building the day before the annual meeting, and Jordan gave Kalkstein audited financial statements of the Register and Tribune. The documents seemed to confirm his idea that the media firm was in decline.[12] After their discussion, Kalkstein returned to the Des Moines YMCA where he was staying and, borrowing a Royal typewriter from the night clerk, he sat in the lounge to rework his speech. He completed the final draft early the following morning at Lou Norris's home. Later that day at the annual meeting, Kalkstein waited until the end of the question-and-answer period and raised his hand. Recognized by Kruidenier, he rose and delivered his speech.[13]

After providing a brief autobiography, Kalkstein told the stockholders he was gravely concerned about the company's declining earnings and its profit margins, which, he said, were by far the lowest in the industry. He was troubled about the R&T's huge debt load and worried that dividends could not continue at present rates. According to Kalkstein, these factors meant that stock prices would likely decline in the public market that was being discussed. He concluded that the only way for shareholders to get the real value out of the company was to call for the firm to put its assets up for outside bids. That way, R&T stock would almost certainly be worth substantially more than the $31 a share currently pegged by the firm's board of directors.[14]

For those not at the annual meeting, Kalkstein sent out a written transcript of his speech and promised a "more detailed report" soon.[15] Bothered by such action, the 79-year-old Mike Cowles, who still kept an attentive eye on the company, wrote his 83-year-old brother John, "It has upset me that Shawn Kalkstein has circulated to all of the Register and Tribune shareholders a copy of his remarks at the R&T stockholders meeting. I want to be sure that none of my children nor grandchildren will support him in any way." He closed saying, "I have confidence in the present management of the R&T and I would be very unhappy to see the property sold."[16]

Yet for Mike Cowles, the situation went from bad to worse. As promised, Kalkstein followed his March letter to shareholders with a four-page typewritten critique of R&T management. When Cowles tried to lessen the impact of these letters with his own message to family members questioning Kalkstein's qualifications to do such analyses, Kalkstein responded with five additional letters during the remainder of 1982. These lengthy reports examined various facets of the R&T, comparing, for instance, its earnings, profit margins, and debt load to those of other newspapers. Making ample use of bar graphs and charts, Kalkstein's account painted a grim picture of a mismanaged company performing well below industry standards. The letters then turned to such issues as the voting trust and possible options for the future—remaining independent, merging with the Minneapolis papers, or the option that Kalkstein thought best, selling out to another media firm. Following an eight-month hiatus, Kalkstein began a second series of letters in August 1983. They continued, albeit much more sporadically, until the final installment in December 1984, when the company was put up for sale.[17]

Just as Kalkstein's letters were beginning to stir the waters, Jonathan Jordan also expressed his fears in a letter to shareholders. This time, Kruidenier responded with a memo to his family in which he cleared up "a number of errors" contained in Jordan's communication. Regardless, it seemed that by early 1982, the genie was out of the bottle. Management was struggling to put the company back on course, but it was being closely watched by a growing number of skeptical stockholders as well as other communications firms interested in acquiring the R&T and its properties.[18]

Good-bye to *Tribune*

Following this contentious annual meeting, management returned its focus to restoring the company's financial situation. By 1980, circulation for the evening *Tribune* stood at 80,700, a decline of nearly 50 percent from its 1946 peak of 155,300. Several times management tried to revamp it as the paper for central Iowa, but this plan failed to stem the tide of an ever-shrinking number of readers. The R&T was not alone in its struggle to maintain its evening offering. Publishers of similar papers across the country were battling a changing culture that included competition from television and a growing number of two-income families. With people leading busier lives, fewer had the time to read a second newspaper in the evening hours. These trends, combined with rising expenses in newspaper production and distribution, led to a rapid decline in evening newspapers. They were either changed to morning publications, merged with morning papers, or ceased publication altogether.[19]

In 1981, management created a special committee to investigate various strategies for its *Register* and *Tribune*. The group was headed by Gary Gerlach and included Robert Hudson, editor Drake Mabry, CFO Jim Kiser, who had replaced Lou Norris upon his retirement earlier in 1981, and director Jim Heskett. After conducting advertising, circulation, and readership studies, the committee presented its recommendations in May 1982. Its major proposal called for merging the evening *Tribune* with the morning *Register*. Layoffs and the printing of zoned editions of the resulting paper were also suggested. Kruidenier and Gartner approved the decision, and the following month the board unanimously ratified the plan. Many of the *Tribune*'s features, such as its cartoons and its "Datebook" entertainment guide as well as some of its columnists, were to join the pages of the *Register*. In addition, it was promised that "news space in local editions of The Register will be increased roughly by one-third from the space available in the Tribune." Obviously a key motivating factor in consolidating the company's two papers was cutting costs, and much of this savings would result from the dismissal of 187 R&T employees no longer needed.[20]

On Saturday, September 25, 1982, the final edition of the *Tribune* bid its readers good-bye with the banner headline, "So long! It's been good to know you." In its last editorial, the *Tribune* rightfully explained that its combining with the morning *Register* was part of a nationwide trend: "We're the 10th company to merge papers this year and the 32nd since 1978." In fact, many of the nation's major evening papers collapsed in this period. In addition to the *Tribune*, newspapers closing down between 1980 and 1982 included the *Washington Star*, *Chicago Daily News*, *Philadelphia Bulletin*, *Cleveland Press*, *Minneapolis Star*, *Atlanta Journal*, *Portland Journal*, *Buffalo Evening News*, and *Tampa Times*.[21]

Selling Off Holdings

Folding the *Tribune* was not the only effort to improve the firm's balance sheet. In late 1981, company officials began discussing the possibility of selling off some of its properties as a means of raising cash to lower its debt load. In July 1982, a deal was cut selling the R&T's two struggling Denver-area radio stations, KLAK-AM and KPPL-FM, to Malrite Communications of Cleveland. The transaction was completed in early 1983, transferring the stations to the Ohio corporation for $6 million in cash and a $2 million payment for a noncompetition agreement. Even as the details of the radio stations' sale were being worked out, the R&T sold the *Waukesha Freeman* to Thomson Newspapers for $9.75 million. Once both deals were consummated, the company used a large portion of the proceeds to decrease its debt load by 30 percent, from $42 million to $29 million.[22]

While selling off some holdings, the firm also moved to solidify its newspaper position in greater Des Moines by buying a twice-weekly newspaper in Indianola, a small town 12 miles south of the capital city. In March 1980, the R&T had signed an option to buy the Record and Herald Company. Management exercised the option in February 1982, paying nearly $1 million for the Indianola business. The purchase was predicated on the belief that the city of Des Moines was moving south, and the R&T wanted to avoid competition in this critical market.[23]

Although these steps improved the company's position in the long run, their benefits were not immediately apparent. In 1982, the Register and Tribune lost $816,000; it was the company's first loss since Gardner Cowles Sr. bought a controlling interest in the paper 79 years earlier. Such a dismal performance seemed to give credence to Kalkstein's charge that the situation at the R&T had become "precarious."[24]

Family Feud and Funeral

If red ink did not capture the attention of three generations of Cowleses, an apparent family feud in early 1983 did. On January 25, directors of Cowles Media Company (CMC), formerly the S&T, met at the O'Hare Hilton in Chicago in order to avoid media attention. There, they asked John Cowles Jr. to step down as the firm's president and publisher. Instead, Cowles proposed that the firm be sold. Cowles's suggestion had little support, and he was voted out by the board. He was replaced by his cousin and R&T chairman, David Kruidenier. Concern over Minneapolis had been growing as company profits tumbled from $7.66 million in 1980 to $747,000 in 1982. The removal of Cowles, however, was prompted by two of his most recent unilateral decisions: in September 1982, Cowles had ordered the closing of the firm's *Buffalo Courier Express,* and in November, he had fired Minneapolis publisher Donald Dwight. Both these actions were taken without notifying the board. Those on the CMC board who opposed Cowles included his sister, Morley Cowles Ballantine, cousins Kruidenier and Lois Cowles Harrison, and Luther Hill Jr. Those who also served concurrently as directors of the R&T were Ballantine, Cowles, Kruidenier, and Hill.[25]

One former R&T executive believed the move was a "power play "on Kruidenier's part because, he believed, "it always stuck in Dave's craw" that the younger Cowles headed the Minneapolis company several years before David had attained the top job in Des Moines. Not surprisingly, Kruidenier denied the charge and said he was selected to lead CMC for three reasons: his "familiarity with the Minneapolis operations and its business community; a financial incentive from the Register and Tribune's block of Cowles Media stock; and strong leadership in Des Moines will allow him to take time off." Some, however, questioned these statements, arguing that the "Des Moines company ... is no model of success." They worried "about Kruidenier's ability to improve on Cowles' performance since he will still be running the Des Moines operation and will commute between the two cities." Others felt Kruidenier's advent as CEO of Cowles Media signaled its eventual merger with the R&T.[26]

Several months prior to the deposing of John Cowles Jr., the "limited public market" for R&T stock that had been mentioned at the 1982 annual meeting was established. In essence, with the company no longer buying back its stock at the established price of $31 per share, brokers from either Paine, Webber, Jackson & Curtis or Piper, Jaffray & Hopwood acted as middlemen, matching up those wishing to sell R&T stock with those interested in purchasing shares. The market opened in August 1982. Register and Tribune voting stock was soon trading at about $26 per share, while nonvoting stock fell to $15 before rebounding to about $20 per share. For the remainder of 1982, nearly 110,000 shares changed hands before trading trailed off. Two major sellers—Nancy Cowles, widow of Russell Cowles, the older brother of John Sr. and Mike, and the Russell Cowles estate—and two major buyers—Grinnell College's Endowment Fund and Fred Eychaner, owner of a commercial printing business in Chicago—accounted for a good portion of the stock transactions. Here again, dissident shareholder Kalkstein had been correct. Before the public market for the R&T stock opened, he predicted, "My guess is the stock would come out offered at $31 by sellers who still think the R&T is worth it—and there may be a *few* buyers in the mid-20s. The stock could mill around in that range on very low volume."[27]

The bad news continued unabated for the Cowles family. On February 25, 1983, John Cowles Sr. died. Deeply saddened by his passing, company board members in the minutes of their March meeting eulogized Cowles for his "immeasurable contribution." They wrote, in part:

> John Cowles was actively involved in the operations of the Des Moines Register and Tribune Company for 55 years. For most of that time he was an officer, director and major stockholder. His titles ranged from reporter to chairman of the board, indicating the scope of his contribution to all phases of the newspaper's development from editorial philosophy to marketing policy. With his father, Gardner Cowles, and his brother Mike (Gardner Jr.), he guided this company through its crucial formative years and committed it to a goal of editorial excellence underpinned by financial security.[28]

At that same meeting the board considered the dividend, and just as Kalkstein, Jordan, and others had feared, the directors felt it necessary to cut the payout. It was slashed 37.5 percent from 40 cents to 25 cents per share for the fourth quarter 1982 and remained at this level through 1984. Yet while the dividend's downward adjustment was being discussed, the R&T was actually in the midst of a rebound. Over the course of the 1983, circulation of the daily *Register* rose over 17 percent from 203,000 to 239,000, while the *Sunday Register*'s readers increased 2.5 percent. Retail advertising linage was up 38.8 percent, and overall advertising revenues rose 4.7 percent. Although operating revenues actually declined from $90.7 million to $88.5 million, operating expenses fell by $5.4 million, greatly aided by reducing personnel from 1,117 to 817. All of this added up to a net profit of $5.26 million. This figure, however, factored in a $3 million net gain of the sale of the firm's two radio stations and a newspaper. If that is subtracted out, the company's profit margin for 1983 was 2.6 percent, well below the 9.5 percent average recorded by the eight newspaper firms followed by *Standard and Poor's.* Although pleased with the turnaround, Gary Gerlach, publisher as of late 1982, noted: "Our margins are still much too low compared to industry standards and we are working hard to improve them." Worse still, he worried about the "heavy capital investment" that would soon be needed to replace the company's dated letterpresses.[29]

Amid the earnings turnaround, the R&T received national recognition. In April 1984, *Time* magazine included the *Register* on its list of top 10 dailies in the United States. Correctly citing the *Register* as one of Iowa's "most powerful and respected institutions," *Time* noted that the paper circulated throughout the entire state and "relentlessly stresses the local angle in news events." Praise was lavished on the paper for having the "nation's best reporting of agribusiness" and a "strongly worded editorial page." It concluded, "The *Register* is perhaps not an automatic choice for the top 10, but as a monopoly newspaper it has resisted the temptation to laziness. ... And perhaps the best measure: it is trusted deeply by the people who read it every day."[30]

Strategic Planning

Meanwhile, the firm's strategic planning process was focusing on the long-term needs and goals of the company. Under the auspices of Robert Hudson, the Register and Tribune began strategic planning in 1980 by borrowing much of the system used at the Meredith Corporation, a Des Moines publishing firm best known for its *Better Homes and Gardens* magazine. The R&T established a three-year planning horizon that was updated annually. The plan was revised each year, beginning with a situation analysis, which included information gleaned from interviews with the company's top managers. Therefore, 1984 would be the year during which the R&T developed its strategic plan for 1985 through 1987.[31]

Before the planning process could begin, Hudson thought it necessary to know whether a merger with the Minneapolis paper was going to be pursued. At the request of the R&T board, director Jim Heskett wrote the CMC board to see if its members were interested in reopening merger talks. At its August 23 board meeting, the directors of Cowles Media—except Ballantine, Cowles, Hill, and Kruidenier, who also sat on the R&T board and therefore abstained from the vote—decided against "reopening merger talks at this time." Merger, however, appeared like "a good possible course" to Kruidenier, and given his "dual role as CEO of both companies," the move seemed sensible. Over the next year, he grew even "more enthusiastic about the possibility of a merger" but remained "concerned about the lack of earnings in both companies and the need for further restructuring to improve the earnings before any consideration should be given."[32]

Six months later, in February 1984, Hudson began interviewing company officers and managers "in preparation of the situation analysis section of the 1985–1987 Strategic Plan." To assure frankness, the interviews were kept confidential. Discussion topics covered a wide variety of issues ranging from communication, financial performance, and human and technological needs to the owners' objectives and assumptions for the future. When Kruidenier was interviewed in April, he told Hudson that "we must do something. ... Merger [with CMC] is inevitable, but timing is important." Although most corporate officials thought that was where the company was headed, the CEO had not actually made the merger a corporate goal. This lack of direction frustrated many R&T managers who, with the exception of Kruidenier, "unanimously wished to remain an independent company."[33]

Besides this divergence of opinion between the chief executive officer and senior company officials, the shareholders—largely Cowles family members—were split over what to do as well. One group, including the Kruideniers, the Ballantines, Luther Hill Jr., and R&T's employee stockholders, were willing to make sacrifices for the long-term good of the paper. Another branch of the family more closely tied to Minneapolis was largely indifferent to the fortunes of the R&T and desired what was best for Cowles Media. The third group of Cowles descendants was distant from the newspaper business altogether and were primarily interested in maximizing the value of their shares, which in due course came to mean selling out.[34]

By the middle of May 1984, the first draft of the situation analysis was distributed to the company's planning group. Meetings were then to be held in June, when subcommittees were to work on specific segments of the strategic plan, which was to be presented to the board on July 25. After reviewing the preliminary analysis, Kruidenier chose a luncheon meeting that included Gartner, Hudson, and Kiser to explain that he was interested in merging the R&T with Minneapolis and would be pursuing such a course in the next six to nine months. Kruidenier's revelation at the meeting, and the months of uncertainty about the firm's future that preceded it, concerned Gartner and Gerlach. Neither favored combining with Minneapolis, but both were convinced that remaining independent was becoming less likely. When interviewed for the situation analysis, Gartner told Hudson he opposed the R&T merger with CMC and suggested several alternatives. Instead, he considered employee ownership, sale to another local company—Meredith, for instance—or selling to a leading media firm such as Dow Jones, Times Mirror, the New York Times, the Washington Post, or Knight-Ridder.[35]

Insecure about their futures and now wrongly believing that Kruidenier had been conducting merger talks without their knowledge, Gartner and Gerlach lost faith in their CEO. Worried about their positions if the merger did indeed go through, the two executives decided to discuss their situation with attorney David Belin.[36] Although it is clear that Kruidenier favored combining the two Cowles companies, the CMC board had voted against renewing merger talks in August 1983, and there is no evidence that Kruidenier was actively pursing such a plan until August 1984, when the

CMC board discussed the possibility. Regardless, the two R&T officials met with Belin on July 9. They originally initiated the meeting to have Belin draft employment contracts for them, which they then planned to present to Kruidenier. During the meeting, Gartner and Gerlach told the attorney of their frustrations, their concerns about their future, and what they perceived as Kruidenier's lack of leadership.[37]

When Kruidenier received Gartner's and Gerlach's employment contracts, he refused to sign the documents, because the R&T had never used them and no one else in the company possessed one. Now further alienated from the CEO, Gartner and Gerlach received a call from Belin, who suggested the three talk again on July 16. At this afternoon meeting, Belin proposed a solution to the executives' woes. He asked: "Why don't we buy the company?" Caught off guard by the bold idea, Gartner and Gerlach needed time to think about it. Two weeks later, after returning from a seminar in Aspen, Colorado, Belin met again with the two managers on August 3; they were now ready to work on a buyout plan. Given the movement toward merger, Gerlach hoped the three could present the R&T board with a "concrete, countervailing proposal" that members could compare to the consolidation with Minneapolis.[38]

That summer, in fact, executives in Minneapolis again raised the issue of merging with the R&T. In a July CMC board meeting, director Winthrop Knowlton proposed putting together some kind of leveraged buyout of Cowles Media. This plan would allow those shareholders who wished to sell their stock a way out. The suggestion did not receive serious consideration, and as John Cowles observed in his notes of the meeting, the proposal "doesn't solve D[es] Moines R&T [problems]." The next month CMC president David Cox invited John Cowles over to his office to discuss the company's future. Here, Cox said that the unresolved relationship between Cowles Media and the Register and Tribune was a problem when considering strategic planning. He wanted to expand the Minneapolis company, and a merger with the R&T was a means to accomplishing such a goal. Since early 1983, Cowles had favored selling Cowles Media, but he told Cox that since the rest of the Minneapolis voting trust—Kruidenier, Hill, Ballantine, and Lois Cowles Harrison—opposed the idea, he would not oppose a merger with the R&T.[39]

In September, Cox and Cowles met again for further discussion about combining with Des Moines. Cowles now felt that, if the consolidation of the two firms could be made "on the right basis," he would actively support it and "speak in favor of the merger" at various shareholder briefing sessions. The question of what to do with Michael Gartner in the combined company, however, was a problem. Gartner was not popular with CMC's executives, and it was unclear if he would fit into the new managerial mix. Later that month, Kruidenier met with Cowles and Cox and the merger discussions continued. Their focus was the composition of the proposed company's board of directors, and the issue of what to do with Gartner was rehashed. One possible scenario called for replacing Gartner with Gerlach on the Des Moines Voting Trust. Gerlach would then represent the R&T operation on the merged firm's board of directors.[40]

As merger talks were proceeding, Gartner, Gerlach, and Belin were laying the groundwork for their plan to acquire the R&T. After narrowing the field of potential partners to Dow Jones and Knight-Ridder, the two newspaper executives first pitched their idea to Dow Jones because both had worked for that company before coming to Des Moines. Gartner called Robert Potter, Dow Jones general counsel, on October 9 and explained his group's proposal. Potter expressed interest, and Gartner sent him a descriptive letter and a memorandum laying out the venture. The Des Moines contingent, referred to in the document as "TBTG"—an acronym for "the bow tie guys" because Gartner, Gerlach, and Belin favored such neckwear—argued that their idea was "in the best interests of the shareholders compared with other alternatives they will be presented." The merger with Minneapolis, they noted, was not supported by R&T management and, because of the poor relationship between Kruidenier and Cowles, "the place will fall apart" if such a consolidation were consummated. Instead, TBTG called for acquiring the company for between \$100 and \$150 per share, or \$112 to \$168 million. Following the acquisition, the company's non-*Register* properties were to be sold off, which, as estimated by TBTG, would more than cover the purchase price.[41]

After reviewing the material, Potter passed on the offer to Warren Phillips, chairman of the board of Dow Jones. Over the course of the month, Gartner and Gerlach met with Phillips several times, and Dow Jones agreed to the joint venture. Under its terms, Dow Jones would have 50 percent of the voting stock in the resulting company, while the Iowa group would control the remaining 50 percent. Gartner and Gerlach were to serve as chief executive and chief operating officer, respectively. As the details were being worked out, Belin added his friend and well-connected banker Richard Levitt to TBTG group.[42]

Meanwhile, merger talks between Kruidenier and Cowles were moving forward until October, when the long-standing Watts case intervened. Earlier in April, the six-year Watts lawsuit was tentatively settled. In exchange for dropping the suit, the twenty Watts descendants would be paid \$1.45 million for their 25,000 shares of R&T stock. Although company officials stated that about \$700,000 of the figure went to legal expenses, resulting in an approximate payment of $30 per share, others saw the settlement as a $58 per share payoff, or nearly three times what R&T shares were worth on the market. A month later, shareholders Fred Eychaner, Jonathan Jordan, and Shawn Kalkstein objected to the settlement because as a derivative suit, "its settlement must benefit all stockholders, not simply the Watts group." The main aspect that upset Kalkstein was a provision that forbade further litigation on issues covered in the Watts suit. In September, the settlement was finalized, but the following month, Kalkstein and the others filed a formal appeal. Ultimately, however, the appeal came to naught, and it appeared that the long-running litigation was finally over.[43]

On October 18, Kruidenier called Cowles, and they discussed the impact of the appeal on the proposed merger. Although CMC general counsel William Busch Jr. thought it had little chance of success, he advised shelving the merger until the appeal was resolved. There was apparently a consensus among members of the CMC board of directors about putting consolidation talks on hold, but, according to Cowles, Cox was worried that delaying the merger could mean the R&T might be bought by someone else. This was a concern because of the Register and Tribune's 14 percent stake in Cowles Media. The issue of whether to go forward with merger discussions, however, was soon rendered meaningless by the early-November TBTG–Dow Jones offer to buy the R&T.[44]

Gartner-Gerlach Group's Offer

David Belin and Richard Levitt had scheduled an appointment with David Kruidenier for Friday afternoon, November 2. When the two arrived at the ninth-floor office in the R&T building, Kruidenier assumed they were soliciting a donation for charity. Instead, he was "completely surprised" when Belin and Levitt informed him that they were representing a group of Iowa investors—including R&T executives Gartner and Gerlach—that, in conjunction with Dow Jones, wished to buy the R&T for $112 million, or $100 per share. The offer carried a November 20 deadline. Shocked that he had been "stabbed in the back" by his two top lieutenants, Kruidenier wondered why the offer had not been presented by Gartner and Gerlach in person. Gartner and Gerlach, however, thought the offer would carry "greater weight and credibility" if it came from the likes of Belin and Levitt, two prominent figures in the close-knit Des Moines business community. Yet, according to Denny Allen, head of the Cowles Syndicate and a good friend of both Kruidenier and Gartner, the failure to present the offer to their boss in person "was a horrible miscalculation."[45]

Devastated after the meeting, Kruidenier collected himself and called director Luther Hill Jr. to tell him of the offer and discuss options. With a scheduled board meeting on Monday, November 5, immediate action was necessary. The two decided to call a special dinner meeting of the voting trust on Sunday at Kruidenier's house to consider the offer and options. As a trustee, Gartner attended the meeting. He was invited to explain the proposal and then, because of the obvious conflict of interest, asked to excuse himself from the remainder of the gathering. Once Gartner was gone, the remaining trustees—Ballantine, Cowles, Hill, and Kruidenier—all expressed shock at the offer and the way in which it had been presented. They voted unanimously against selling the company. The following morning, they met at 10 a.m. and formally voted not to accept the offer.[46]

After the voting trust, the R&T board of directors held their scheduled Monday meeting. Kruidenier announced the Dow Jones offer, and Gartner and Gerlach formally presented the proposal. Gerlach, in particular, emphasized that the "joint venture arrangement would provide for local control of the operations of The Des Moines Register." Robert Potter of Dow Jones then joined the meeting and tried to ease fears about his company's motives. "Dow Jones," he explained, "had no desire to become involved in a hostile takeover attempt, and was interested in preserving a high-quality newspaper operation in Des Moines." Following a question-and-answer period, Gartner, Gerlach, and Potter left the meeting. Discussion ensued in their absence, and Richard Covey, attorney for the R&T voting trust, noted that because company stock was being traded, the board had an obligation to announce the Dow Jones offer publicly. It was then agreed that "no offer could be adequately considered without counsel from an investment banker." At that point, Gartner and Gerlach were invited to rejoin the meeting, and the directors—with Gartner and Gerlach abstaining—unanimously passed resolutions to take the Dow Jones offer "under serious consideration" and to retain First Boston, one of the nation's leading investment banking firms, to offer advice and do an appraisal of the R&T.[47]

With the First Boston study to be completed by December 7, Kruidenier scheduled special voting trust and board of directors meetings for Monday, December 10, to decide on a course of action. Meanwhile, he insisted that the company's board was not seeking a buyer.[48]

Several days later, on Friday, November 9, Kruidenier announced that he was placing both Michael Gartner and Gary Gerlach on "a paid leave of absence until this matter [the Dow Jones offer] is resolved. This temporary action will avoid any potential conflicts of interest." To ensure the "routine operations of the Company's business," he named Richard Gilbert, an R&T

vice president and head of the broadcast properties, as acting chief operating officer. Then, on Gilbert's recommendation, Kruidenier appointed his nephew Charles Edwards, a fourth-generation Cowles and the company's marketing director, as acting publisher.[49]

On Saturday, Kruidenier asked Gartner and Gerlach up to his office for an explanation of their actions. The two executives responded that their decision was a difficult one, but they felt compelled to do whatever was necessary to maintain editorial control in Iowa. Concern over the possible merger with Minneapolis, they explained, drove them to put together the Dow Jones deal. Kruidenier remained convinced he had been "blindsided" by their action, and the following day, in a speech to the twenty-year club of Register and Tribune employees, he said, "I very much regret this offer was made, and I particularly regret the manner in which it was made." Beyond that, Kruidenier clearly felt threatened; his two top managers were trying to buy the paper out from under him. Gartner responded with a conciliatory statement saying that he and Gerlach "share the same goals and principles that we learned from David [Kruidenier]. If the manner of our approach was wrong, we apologize publicly for that."[50]

Although Gartner and Gerlach were sincere in believing their action was in the best interest of the stockholders, the newspaper, and the readers, they apparently failed to consider the possible consequences if Kruidenier and the board did not embrace their offer. Their explanations to the contrary, company managers and staffers were stunned by the two executives' buyout plan. The collective mood seemed best captured by *Register* feature writer Valerie Monson, who referred to the move as "a palace revolt." In a December column, James Gannon, the paper's editor, wrote of the Gartner and Gerlach proposal, "This is sort of like having your two older brothers and a large bank trying to buy your Mom and Dad's house even though your parents don't want to move. You want to run to the basement and hide."[51]

Prior to removing Gartner and Gerlach, Kruidenier flew to Minneapolis for a CMC board meeting to discuss the Dow Jones offer. He still considered a merger with Cowles Media a viable option, and over the next four weeks, he made several additional trips to Minneapolis. On various occasions he met with Cowles, Cox, and Parkinson as well as other executives and members of CMC's board. As late as December 5, in fact, Kruidenier and Cowles discussed a possible CMC offer for the R&T that, combining cash and stock, could have totaled $175 per share, or roughly $195 million. Nothing came of this idea, however, and soon after announcing the Dow Jones offer, events seemed to spin out of control.

Other Bidders

With the R&T board's decision to hire an investment banking firm and go public with the Gartner and Gerlach group's $112 million offer, Dow Jones chairman Warren Phillips wrote his fellow directors, "I am not optimistic that we will get this company now that discussions are no longer private." Just as he feared, news of the bid led others to submit offers for the R&T. Within a week, Ingersoll Publications, which owned 25 dailies and 50 weeklies in 14 states, offered $150 million. Ralph Ingersoll II, however, would only say publicly that his offer exceeded $123 million. Three weeks later, Ackerley Communications—owner of 11,000 billboards in the Pacific Northwest, Florida, and Massachusetts, several television stations, and the National Basketball Association's Seattle Supersonics—made an overture. Headed by Des Moines native Barry Ackerley, the media company offered $156 million for the R&T.[52]

Besides formal offers, several additional media firms expressed interest in the Register and Tribune. These included the (Chicago) Tribune Company, Gannett, Ogden Newspapers, Palmer Communications, and the Washington Post. In general, executives of these firms had telephone conversations with Kruidenier that were followed up with confirmation letters. Al Neuharth and the Gannett chain, however, chose a different tact. Neuharth was immediately interested in the Register and Tribune, but because he did not know Kruidenier well, he sought someone close to the R&T chairman to serve as an emissary. Soon after the Dow Jones offer was announced, Gannett retained the services of Otto Silha, the retired chairman of Cowles Media. Silha had convinced Neuharth that he was a good friend of Kruidenier and the Cowles family. Neuharth thought a hand-delivered letter from Silha to Kruidenier would give Gannett an inside track in acquiring the company. If Gannett was successful in buying the *Register*, Silha was to receive a consultant's fee based on a percentage of the sale price.[53]

On November 20, Kruidenier received a telephone call from Silha, who told him he had a proposal regarding the R&T that he was sure Kruidenier would find interesting. Kruidenier, who had long distrusted Silha and sensed that he wanted to discuss an offer for the company, refused to set up a meeting with the retired Cowles Media executive. Minutes later, however, Silha called again and confessed that he was actually downstairs in the R&T building. He asked to come up to Kruidenier's office to discuss what he termed "a special proposal." Kruidenier declined to see him, and on his way out, Silha left an envelope for Kruidenier at the cashier's cage. When he later had the letter sent up to the ninth floor, the CEO saw that his suspicions had been correct: Silha had delivered an inquiry from Al Neuharth and Gannett.[54]

Neuharth began his letter by identifying his midwestern roots and expressing long admiration for both the R&T and Cowles Media. He mentioned, for example, that as a boy, he had been a *Minneapolis Tribune* carrier in Alpena, South Dakota. Following the brief biography, Neuharth suggested that if a sale of the Register and Tribune became inevitable, Gannett wanted "to be the first outsiders you invite in to talk about a possible association." The advantages of selling to Gannett included the chain's vast financial resources, its "long rather than short view of any acquisition," and its understanding of newspapers of similar size and location. In addition, if Gannett bought the R&T, Neuharth offered Kruidenier "a key role at the policy-making and/or operational level for you if you wish and arrangements and assurances of future attractive and rewarding roles for key associates."[55]

Given his continued statements that the company was not for sale, Kruidenier was outraged by the Gannett inquiry and especially incensed at the manner in which it was delivered. He responded by calling Neuharth. The chairman of Gannett immediately apologized and explained that he had mistakenly believed Silha was a close friend of Kruidenier's. News of the letter soon circulated throughout the R&T newsroom, where it became known as "the bribe letter." Neuharth later said he deserved a "dunce cap" for trying such a strategy to gain an inside track with the R&T.[56]

Meanwhile, R&T stock, which in late October had been trading for between $33 and $36 per share, jumped to $92 to $95 a share after news of the first offer and moved up over $100 per share in the ensuing weeks. Interested in just what the company was worth, Fred Eychaner, now the largest individual shareholder of the R&T with 6 percent of the voting stock, hired media analyst Paul Kagan to estimate the firm's value. In early December, Eychaner released Kagan's evaluation to the public; he appraised the R&T at $226 million, or $202 per share, if the firm's properties were sold off separately. This figure was much greater than any offer the company had received to date, and rumors that Eychaner might be putting together a joint venture to buy the R&T temporarily pushed company stock prices up to the $120 level. The Chicago businessman soon ended this speculation by announcing that he would not make an offer because Kruidenier refused to disclose the details of the earlier bids.[57]

With soaring stock prices and several purchase offers for the R&T, Kruidenier began receiving inquiries from family members wondering about the firm's financial status. Given the situation, the CEO began "polling members of the third and fourth generation as well as retired employee shareholders, in order to learn their views concerning the future course for the company."[58] Kalkstein's letters and the big-dollar offers for the R&T were leading a growing number of stockholders to believe that selling the company was the best alternative. In late November, Nancy Edwards Schned, sister of the acting publisher of the paper, felt that a majority of the family was prepared to sell: "I think most everyone is fairly well adjusted to that idea now." Some members of the family, including Schned's cousin, Gardner "Pat" Cowles III, believed the "lack of interest by the fourth generation in the Register and Tribune Company is a classic example of what happens to nearly all family businesses." But Elizabeth Ballantine, another great-grandchild of Gardner Cowles, suggested that her generation's lack of interest in the newspaper business was largely the fault of her mother's generation. She explained: "They [the third generation] made it an uphill battle just to get a job at the papers." In fact, when Ballantine inquired about a job at the *Minneapolis Star and Tribune,* her uncle, John Cowles Jr., told her there was no position available. Instead, he sent her a copy of *Editor and Publisher* to foster her job search. "The real mistake," Ballantine felt, "was that no one in the fourth generation was groomed to take over the newspaper."[59]

Decision to Sell

The weeks of speculation concerning the company's fate were nearly over. With First Boston's valuation completed, Kruidenier invited members of the voting trust, Dick Covey, the trust's attorney, and First Boston's Nick Paumgarten to his house on December 9 to discuss the situation. Paumgarten told the trustees that in his firm's estimation, the R&T was worth between $162 million and $200 million. These figures did not include the company's CMC stock, which could contribute an additional $46 million to $56 million. At 9 a.m. December 10, the trustees met at the R&T building. Kruidenier reported the results of his survey of key family figures. He had spoken to 14 of 16 members of his third generation, and all but four favored selling the R&T. An even higher percentage of the fourth generation called for a sale. Upon this news and in light of First Boston's report, the trustees voted to petition the board of directors to put the company up for sale.[60]

The board of directors met that afternoon at the Hotel Fort Des Moines. Kruidenier reported that the majority of the family wished to sell the R&T and that the voting trustees unanimously resolved "to go forward with the sale of the Company." Given this situation, he told the board the sale of the firm was likely and that, based on the study, First Boston recommended rejecting all offers to date. With "great regret," Luther Hill Jr. made the motion to put the company up for sale. First Boston was to assist in the solicitation and evaluation of bids. All directors, except Gartner and Gerlach, voted in favor of the measure. Then, because Gartner and Gerlach were participants with Dow Jones in an offer for the R&T, they were asked to leave the room so the First Boston report could be discussed.[61]

After going over details of the valuation, First Boston's Nick Paumgarten explained the schedule for the "prompt and orderly sale" of the firm and its subsidiaries. The process to sell the papers was to take six weeks. Prospective buyers would be invited to visit the R&T in the first weeks of 1985 before submitting bids, which were due to First Boston on January 25. The board would vote on the deal at its meeting six days later. The bidding for the radio properties was scheduled to take place in February. The meeting closed with Kruidenier discussing the list of companies that had expressed interest. It totaled roughly 40 firms and included most of the nation's media chains.[62]

Kruidenier was visibly "shaken" at a press conference that evening to announce the board's decision. He explained that he had not wanted to sell, but he could not find enough support among family members to prevent an ownership change. "Many of them have never lived in Iowa. I suspect many of them have never been to Des Moines. I expect many of them want to cash in. ... I'm sorry about it."[63]

Over the course of the next week, large three-ring notebooks filled "three inches thick of information" about the R&T were prepared for distribution to a select group of the companies who had expressed interest in buying the newspaper. Because Kruidenier said the shareholders only wished to sell "to a high-quality newspaper company which would respect and maintain the journalistic standards of *The Des Moines Register*," the list of firms receiving financial information was, according to First Boston's Jeffrey Epstein, "quite small." These binders, dubbed "blue books" because of their color, were sent to 12 firms including the Chicago Tribune, Cox Enterprises, Dow Jones, Gannett, Hearst, the New York Times, and the Washington Post. Those not privy to this material included Heritage Communications, a Des Moines-based cable television company, and Lee Enterprises. A larger number of media businesses received material on a specific property such as KHON or WQAD.[64]

During the second and third weeks of January, representatives from the major media firms that had received the informational packet—except Dow Jones, which did not put in another bid, wishing instead to deal with the Register privately—visited the R&T facility and met with key Register personnel. Gannett, by its own design, was the last interested party to tour the

Des Moines company. With all the bids submitted by January 25, First Boston immediately overnight-mailed the offers to R&T general counsel Barbara Mack. The attorney spread the offers out on her living room floor, and when she saw Gannett's bid, she whispered to herself, "It's over." Several days later, the R&T board met with First Boston representatives to discuss the sale. It soon became clear why Mack was so struck by Gannett's $165 million offer for the *Register* and the weeklies in Independence and Indianola, Iowa. According to one board member, "jaws dropped" when the Gannett offer was put on the table. This bid was $30 million greater than Hearst's $135 million offer. The remaining bids were significantly lower: the Washington Post came in at $110 million, followed by Lee Enterprises at $105 million, and the Chicago Tribune—which factored in that it would need to add new presses—at $90 million.[65]

With Gartner and Gerlach abstaining, the board recommended that shareholders approve the sale of the family's flagship to Gannett. Very few at the time knew that, besides the huge amount Neuharth paid for the *Register*, he also paid Silha a consulting fee of nearly $1.1 million. Although Silha's brief work as an emissary failed miserably, his agreement with Neuharth said only that if Gannett acquired the Des Moines newspaper, he would receive a percentage of the sale price. Neuharth later described his blunder: "We paid him [Silha] more than a million dollars to deliver a single letter. ... A 25-cent stamp could have done the job equally well. Better, actually, I doubt Kruidenier hated the mailman as he did Silha." Meanwhile, the future of two other R&T properties was also determined: Gannett came away with the *Jackson Sun* for $40.3 million, and the New York Times bought WQAD-TV for $25.25 million. Two firms were still vying for KHON-TV, and no bids were submitted for the 430,536 shares of CMC stock. A special committee consisting of Chrystal, Heskett, and Marshall was therefore established to work with First Boston and facilitate the sale of the R&T's 14 percent stake in Cowles Media.[66]

Kruidenier and Al Neuharth, chairman of Gannett, announced the blockbuster deal at a packed press conference. Neuharth was elated about the acquisition of the "prestige paper" and explained that the high price Gannett paid was not for "the brick or the mortar" but the *Register* staff and "reputation." He later assured listeners that he had no plans to alter the editorial product or the paper's design. Likewise, he promised to maintain the statewide distribution. When Kruidenier spoke, he stated that he "had gotten over the sadness of the sale." A reporter asked him, "What do you think your grandfather would say about the sale?" Kruidenier responded with a twinkle in his eye, "Well, he'd probably say I turned out to be a pretty good businessman."[67]

All seemed surprised at the amount Gannett had paid. Jeff Epstein of First Boston called it "an extraordinary price," and one that would set the standard for large family-owned dailies. Fourth-generation Cowles family member Charlie Edwards, who would stay on as *Register* publisher, joked, "If my [great] grandfather had known these papers could make this much money, he never would have died." Michael Gartner, meanwhile, could only mutter, "incredible." By paying $205 million for the *Register,* the *Jackson Sun,* and two weeklies, Gannett shelled out nearly double what Gartner, Gerlach, and Dow Jones had offered for the entire company.[68]

Agreement on the whopping price paid for the *Register* did not translate into unanimity on what the sale meant. Referring to the deal as "terribly sad," Elizabeth Ballantine, who had opposed the sale, noted, "We were educated to think of the newspaper as a family trust." Once a reporter for the R&T, Ballantine remained bitter about the sale: "I wouldn't want to do business with a lot of my cousins. Some don't know the difference between a newspaper and a real-estate company." A majority of the Cowleses, however, came to the position of Shawn Kalkstein, who said, "Everyone has had to weigh family ties against economic reality, and most put more weight on the latter." Neuharth later described what happened with the Register and Tribune by writing: "Money is thicker than blood."[69]

As the shock of the initial Gannett purchase wore off, the rest of the R&T properties were sold. Burnham Broadcasting of Chicago purchased KHON-TV for $47.5 million. The two Portland, Oregon, radio stations—KSGO and KGON-FM—went to Ackerley Communications for $6.75 million, while the two Madison, Wisconsin, stations—WIBA and WIBA-FM—were acquired by New York–based Price Communications for $5.6 million. Gannett, meanwhile, paid $56 million, or $130 a share, for the R&T's 14 percent interest in Cowles Media. Taken together, the dissolution of the R&T grossed $346 million prior to the deduction of fees and payment of debt. When the company books were closed early the following year, shareholders received approximately $280 per share, nearly three times what TBTG–Dow Jones had offered and roughly 10 times the amount at which R&T shares had traded in October 1984.[70]

At least two dozen Cowles heirs received more than $1 million for their Register and Tribune stock. Some family members received much greater amounts. David Kruidenier and his wife, Elizabeth, for example, together held over 38,000 shares worth approximately $10.6 million. Gartner and Gerlach, meanwhile, came away from the sale with nearly $4 million and $2.9 million, respectively. Institutions fared well also. Grinnell College's $500,000 investment in R&T stock, purchased at $15 to $20 a share in 1982 and 1983, brought the school more than $8.7 million.[71]

Handing Over the Reins

A special stockholders meeting was called for July 1 to approve the company's liquidation and transfer of the *Register* to Gannett. Staffers and readers alike wondered what the changeover would mean. Many, like veteran reporter Larry Fruhling, were not optimistic. "It's been a great place to work," he noted, but "it has nowhere to go but down." David Schoenbaum, a University of Iowa history professor and frequent contributor to the *Register*'s op-ed page, worried, "This newspaper is an institution like no other institution in the state or most states. If it doesn't define our conscience, at least it defines our consciousness. There is nothing to replace it if it goes away." As the date of new ownership approached, Kruidenier used an internal memo to placate fears of R&T employees. After acknowledging the difficulties of the past few months and thanking his "colleagues" for their "support and dedicated effort," the CEO said he was "confident about The Register's future under Gannett ownership." He continued, "Gannett paid a very large premium for The Register's reputation and I am sure will do everything it can to protect it. Furthermore, Gannett has ample resources to make whatever capital investments may be needed in the future. The Register organization is in excellent shape as the paper is changing hands. The Pulitzer Prize tradition is thriving and we are continuing to produce first rate newspapers."[72]

At the July 1 meeting, the liquidation plan was officially approved by 88 percent of the voting shares. As the votes were being tallied, Kruidenier addressed the Register and Tribune shareholders for the last time. He spoke of the 82-year "grand partnership" that his family and the newspaper shared with Iowa. The Cowles grandson explained, "The history of the state and The Register are intertwined. Together, both have changed and matured, each dependent on the other, inseparable, as Iowa's rugged pioneer individualism has been replaced by the increasingly complex national and international problems of the late 20th century." At that point, Kruidenier voiced what many had long thought about the venerable Cowles newspaper: "I believe the state of Iowa is a better place because of The Register—more progressive, more aware and supportive of civil rights—more internationalist."[73]

The first sign of the changing of the guard was the presence of Al Neuharth at the July meeting. He rose to speak following the remarks of the outgoing CEO. Neuharth praised the Cowles family and promised "all of our Gannett resources to try to help make The Register an even better newspaper." Although he said he expected the company's poor earnings to improve, he assured the audience that no deadline had been set to boost profits. Neuharth stressed that the Gannett policy of local autonomy would mean that Gilbert, Edwards, and editor James Gannon would make the decisions affecting the company.[74]

The following day, Gannett put out its first issue of the *Register*, but as editor James Gannon had noted, readers would see little that was different. In fact, except for the editorial page masthead, which referred to the *Register* as a Gannett newspaper, nothing else had changed. In the lead editorial entitled "A New Beginning," the paper pledged to remain "a statewide marketplace for information, ideas and opinion." Regardless of the new ownership, editors stated their intention to continue the *Register*'s tradition of serving as "the voice of Iowa's highest values—individual freedom, clean and open government, common sense and compassion in public policy, and international understanding and cooperation."[75]

Symbolic of the closing of the Cowles era in Iowa was the death of family patriarch Mike Cowles, who died of cancer on July 8, just one week after Gannett took over the *Register*. Fittingly, perhaps, Cowles had been born 82 years earlier, in 1903, the year his father bought the *Register*. His life, therefore, spanned the family's ownership of the Register and Tribune. Of Cowles' legacy the paper wrote, "In an age when instant opinion polls, global jet travel, and satellite-beamed television are taken for granted, it's hard to appreciate what an innovator Gardner 'Mike' Cowles was for publishing more photographs in his newspapers, for using airplanes to gather news, and for engaging a young Iowan named George Gallup to try the new science of opinion research." President Ronald Reagan recalled Cowles as a "well-respected journalist who always exemplified the best of his profession. He was tough but fair and had a keen sense of the role of the newspaper in the community. He helped make *The Des Moines Register* the great paper it is today." Several days earlier, Al Neuharth revealed that Mike Cowles "was one of my idols when I was a kid in South Dakota wanting to be a journalist."[76]

End of an Era

The Register and Tribune's dissolution had been brought about by a number of factors. By the early 1970s, rapidly rising costs and declining circulation led to questions about the viability of remaining a statewide newspaper. Factors that made the *Register* financially successful as an all-Iowa institution had changed. Current studies suggested that cutting back circulation and giving greater attention to metropolitan Des Moines would increase profits. But top management was unwilling to break its commitment to all Iowans. Charlie Edwards later explained that these "decisions to maintain the statewide presence were often based on an emotional attachment to that role rather than financial realities."[77] Given this situation, Kruidenier's move to expand into other media markets outside of Iowa made good economic sense and was in line with the strategy of many other newspapers. Early acquisitions, such as the *Jackson Sun,* were carefully planned and proved profitable. Some of the later additions, however, such as the McCoy radio and television properties, were acquired hastily with little research or forethought. Although these subsidiaries were ultimately sold for significantly more than their purchase price, their poor performance and the large debt taken on to acquire them led to a downward spiral the R&T could not escape. In the wake of sharply falling profits, Shawn Kalkstein's letters alerted stockholders to recurring problems and gradually undermined faith in management. Meanwhile, Kruidenier's continuing interest in merging the R&T with Cowles Media led Gartner and Gerlach to seek another alternative, and they put together the Dow Jones offer that ultimately broke the ice.

Somewhat naive, Gartner and Gerlach did not foresee the situation their offer created. The company, as those in the industry explained, was "put into play," and the door had been opened for others interested in the media property. Kruidenier immediately received many inquiries about the R&T's status, and two unsolicited bids came in; both were significantly higher than that of Dow Jones. A growing number of Cowles family members, many of whom had little connection to the R&T, wanted to cash in their stock and sell the company. After conducting an informal survey, Kruidenier was aware of this mounting sentiment, and the voting trust felt it had no option but to put the firm on the auction block.

With the sale, the R&T was one of several important newspaper companies acquired by larger media corporations. Others swallowed up in the mid-1980s included: the *Baltimore Sun* and *Evening Sun* by Times Mirror; the *Boston Herald* by Rupert Murdoch; the *Columbia State* (South Carolina) and *Columbia Record* by Knight Ridder; the *Houston Chronicle* by Hearst Newspapers; and the *Detroit News,* the *Louisville Courier-Journal,* and the *Arkansas Gazette* by Gannett. This consolidation of the industry led many to fear that the bottom line would dictate a decline in the quality of journalism. Added to these concerns, readers of the *Register* wondered if their paper would remain a statewide institution in both news coverage and distribution. Whether Gannett ownership was committed to maintaining a newspaper worthy of the motto "The Newspaper Iowa Depends Upon" was a question on almost everyone's mind.

This question would be answered over the next few years under a new *Register* management team headed up by Edwards, Gilbert, and Gannon. Gone were the three former top executives. David Kruidenier chose not to take a position in the new organization because, he said, "of possible conflicts arising from Gannett's interest in Cowles Media Co." Still very involved in Cowles Media, Kruidenier soon stepped down as CEO in favor of cousin John Cowles Jr. but stayed on as the company's chairman of the board. In addition, Kruidenier headed up the Register and Tribune Liquidation Corporation that oversaw the dissolution of the company's various properties. Gartner and Gerlach, likewise, were not part of Gannett's *Register*, although they continued on the company's payroll until January 1986. Together the two bought the *Daily Tribune*, a newspaper with a circulation of roughly 10,000 located in Ames, 30 miles north of Des Moines. While Gerlach ran the company and expanded it by acquiring smaller newspapers along the way, Gartner took a job with Gannett and soon was serving as editor of its *Louisville Courier-Journal*. Gartner moved on to head NBC News until 1993, when he was forced to resign over the *Dateline* TV newsmagazine's staging of a fiery crash of a General Motors pickup truck. He returned to Ames to edit the *Daily Tribune* and won a Pulitzer Prize for editorial writing in 1997.[78]

Gannett Chairman Al Neuharth, front left, with David Kruidenier and *Des Moines Register* staff after announcement of sale, 1985. *Reprinted with permission from The Des Moines Register.*

Charlie Edwards, Register and Tribune publisher from 1984 to 1996. *Reprinted with permission from The Des Moines Register.*

Ground-breaking ceremony for the Register and Tribune's new printing facility, April 1998. From left to right, Austin Ryan, R&T vice president for production; Gary Watson, president of Gannett's newspaper division; Iowa Governor Terry Branstad; Barbara Henry, R&T president and publisher; Mike Coleman, Gannett south regional group president; and Des Moines Mayor Preston Daniels. *Copyright 1998, reprinted with permission from The Des Moines Register.*

EPILOGUE
GANNETT'S NEWSPAPER

Gannett's acquisition of the *Register* produced mixed feelings among the newspaper's staff. *Register* political reporter David Yepsen noted in February 1985, "There's a concern about Gannett. A lot of people don't think they are the world's best newspaper chain." Others, Yepsen explained, thought there was little to fear. "Why would Gannett," he said they reasoned, "spend this kind of money to buy a prestige paper just to screw it up?"[1] But herein was the new owner's essential challenge. The communications giant had been drawn to the *Register* because it was a respected, award-winning daily. To buy the newspaper, CEO Al Neuharth outbid his closest competition by an astounding $30 million. Moreover, the $165 million Gannett paid staggered most media analysts, especially given the R&T's dismal financial performance. Compared to Gannett's industry-leading operating profit margins, which approached 30 percent annually, the R&T's margins had not risen above 6 percent since 1980 and had hit a low of 1.6 percent in 1982.[2] While the new parent company wanted to maintain the *Register*'s reputation for journalistic excellence, it expected to recoup its investment and raise the new subsidiary's profit levels to company standards. Neuharth optimistically told his new staff, "Most newspapers have better profits by putting out better news products. You can do both."[3]

By the time Neuharth had set his sights on Des Moines, Gannett had a well-oiled profit formula employed at all its holdings. Local management teams were often retained, but they received operating guides that, according to media analyst James Squires, "included a list of the best-earning comparable properties within Gannett, a number of which earned between 30 and 40 percent or higher." Profit goals based on these figures went out from Gannett headquarters to local publishers with specific quotas for each three-month period. Great autonomy was generally allowed as long as profit standards were met. This policy seemingly gave local publishers tremendous leeway, but in reality, emphasis was placed on "minimizing costs and raising advertising and circulation prices to the limit."[4]

True to form, Gannett played a "rather benign" role during its first years of holding the *Register,* and significant changes were not immediately apparent. Dynasty founder Gardner Cowles's great-grandson, Charlie Edwards, stayed on as president and publisher, and other top managers remained in place. Likewise, many time-honored features of the paper endured. The *Register*'s trademark editorial cartoon stayed on the front page; the Washington Bureau continued covering the Iowa delegation and farm legislation from the nation's capital; the Iowa Poll still gauged Iowans' thinking on important issues; the Sunday sports section was set apart by its peach-colored paper; news stories persistently stressed the Iowa angle; and the news and editorial staff remained largely in place. Meanwhile, earnings rose, and it appeared that Neuharth's statement about better profits meaning better journalism was not far off the mark. In fact, during Gannett's first six years of ownership, the *Register* won its 14th and 15th Pulitzer Prizes. Staffer David Peterson received the 1987 award for his heart-wrenching photographs of the human suffering during the farm crisis, and in 1991, the Pulitzer for public service went to reporter Jane Schorer for her story on the rape and recovery of Nancy Ziegenmeyer.

Refocused Circulation

The profit demands Gannett placed on the *Register,* however, almost cost the paper its Pulitzer in 1987. Late in the previous year, editor Jim Gannon suggested the paper run a series of Peterson's pictures of the desperate farm situation. Edwards was impressed with the photographs, but he knew the special section would cost an additional $30,000 in newsprint and cut into the earnings goal he was expected to meet. In the midst of a poor fourth quarter, the publisher was certain that running the photos would anger Gannett management. Finally exclaiming, "To hell with it. Let's do it," Edwards decided to publish the photo spread. As expected, Edwards was reprimanded by Gannett officials, and he pledged to make up the costs over the next three months.[5] Following the condemnation, Edwards thought he might be fired. Months later, however, he was vindicated when the photos won the Pulitzer. Soon afterward, Brian Donnelly, head of Gannett's large newspaper division, called Edwards and jokingly said that "he now knew the precise cost of winning a Pulitzer."[6]

While R&T executives struggled to meet profit expectations, the *Register*'s circulation continued its downward slide. When Gannett bought the paper in 1985, daily circulation stood at 255,000, while Sunday's was 385,000. By early 1991, those figures had declined to 209,000 and 343,000, a drop of 18 percent and 11 percent, respectively. Company management had been battling this problem for nearly forty years, and in the early 1980s, when the paper was still owned by the Cowles family, the pullback from statewide presence slowly began. This withdrawal was exemplified by the closing of the *Register's* state news bureaus in Dubuque and Sioux City, on Iowa's eastern and western borders, respectively. But it was Edwards who took the most dramatic step. In 1990, the *Register* publicly repudiated its statewide mission and declared central Iowa its primary audience. Then in early 1991, the company stopped carrier delivery of its morning daily to 21 western and northeastern counties. The paper was still available to some of these readers by same-day mail. Later that year, the R&T shut down its Davenport news bureau in southeastern Iowa and, in a telling move, relocated that bureau's reporter to Des Moines.[7]

In a letter to the R&T staff, Edwards explained the move to focus on central Iowa and warned that additional cuts might be necessary if the expected drop in circulation continued. Managing editor David Westphal noted, "We're coming to grips with the fact that we're a different state now." The problems the company confronted were not new and had been around for decades. Such difficulties included the state's eroding rural population, shrinking advertising revenues from distant counties, and huge increases in distribution costs. These were the issues that led to a rethinking of company strategies, and Edwards was careful to take full responsibility for the central-Iowa focus. He recalled, "I made those decisions. ... It wasn't dictated by a Gannett person. It was more appropriate for me to make that decision because of my tie to the past. It was easier for me to pull off." In 1991, however, referring to the cutbacks and resulting savings, Edwards said that Gannett had "the right to have a reasonable return on the $165 million they've spent." While the decision to abandon its statewide circulation was not mandated by Gannett, it is clear that R&T executives were responding to profit imperatives from corporate headquarters.[8]

Reaction to the new strategy was often negative. Editor Geneva Overholser considered resigning, but after Edwards convinced her of the soundness of the policy, she chose to stay. Meanwhile, the views of many readers in outlying areas were expressed by a Sioux City woman in her letter to the editor: "If the *Register* really is going to concentrate more on central Iowa local news, it will not be the great newspaper I looked forward to every day anyway, and I can probably live without it very well." The policy clearly ruffled feathers and failed to curb the overall circulation decline, but readership in the targeted metropolitan area inched upward. From 1989 to

1994, the Sunday *Register* circulation in greater Des Moines rose by 5 percent, while the daily enjoyed an increase of 5.25 percent.[9]

On the one hand, these circulation trends suggested that focusing resources on central Iowa was yielding desired results. Therefore, coverage of the capital city and surrounding areas was stepped up, and efforts were made to buy weeklies in greater Des Moines. After failing to acquire a newspaper in Adel, a small town 25 miles west of the downtown area, the firm successfully purchased the weekly newspaper in the eastern suburb of Altoona in 1994. On the other hand, the dwindling number of statewide readers meant that further retrenchment was necessary. In December 1994, the R&T curtailed home delivery to Sioux City as well as 12 other western Iowa towns. Edwards justified the "painful decision" by saying that "it just doesn't work out financially" to distribute the paper to areas "when you have very thin circulation as we do, in the southwest corner and the far west part of the state." The future of the paper, according the publisher, was central Iowa, "particularly Des Moines and its booming suburbs." With this area accounting for roughly two-thirds of its total circulation, Edwards's thinking was understandable.[10]

But readers and staffers alike were troubled by the changes. Former "Iowa Boy" columnist Chuck Offenburger, a native Iowan, said he had "stars in my eyes" when he joined the R&T in 1972 because of the *Register*'s state and national reputation. Upset by the move away from the Iowa-wide distribution, Offenburger devoted a column to the topic and opened the piece by writing, "The big boss [Edwards] at The Des Moines Register broke my heart Tuesday [the day the circulation cutbacks were announced]." He referred to the action as "a major break of faith with Iowa by Register management." David Hurd, former CEO of the Des Moines-based Principal Financial Group, explained that he had liked the *Register*'s statewide coverage: "It made it a larger thing, with a larger mission." Hurd's perspective reflected a broader view. For many Iowans, the *Register*'s luster had begun to wear off.[11]

Changes in Leadership

Two months after the R&T ended home delivery to parts of western Iowa, editor Overholser and managing editor David Westphal surprised Edwards and the news staff by resigning. Overholser explained that she was "worn down" and "found it very draining" when she had to defend corporate policies she personally opposed. Edwards was "depressed and upset" over the resignations but understood. On Overholser's decision to leave, he said,

"I'm not surprised she's tired. She has been pivotal in implementing the strategy focusing the newspaper increasingly on central Iowa and Des Moines. It's been a challenging transition for all of us." Although both editors claimed they were not leaving because of Gannett's ownership, Overholser had grown increasingly exasperated over the mounting "profit demands" in the newspaper industry.[12]

Overholser had been worried about Gannett's influence at the R&T for several years. In her 1990 acceptance speech for being named "Gannett Editor of the Year," she shocked corporate executives by questioning the company's emphasis on profits. The following year, when the R&T instituted its first round of circulation cuts, Overholser considered quitting. At that point, she asked herself, "Do I want to stay here and preside over the dismantling of a great newspaper?" After a discussion with Edwards, Overholser towed the company line until early 1995. When she and her managing editor finally did resign, the story was picked up nationally. According to *New York Times* columnist William Glaberson, the resignations were representative of the "debate in American journalism about whether corporate pressure for profits is stripping the quality from many American newspapers. ... Geneva Overholser and her managing editor, David Westphal, have quickly become public symbols of a battle between news professionals and business executives that is raging behind closed doors at many of the country's newspapers."[13]

Incensed by Glaberson's piece, Gannett CEO John Curley, who had replaced Neuharth in 1989, issued a sharp response about the resignations at the *Register.* After referring to the *New York Times* as one of the "self-anointed ... guardians of truth," Curley argued that while the R&T profits had declined "from a modest base" since 1989, the news staff had increased by 15 people, and the daily news hole—the portion of the paper set aside for news as opposed to advertising—was up 12 percent. In fact, Curley's statistics suggested some significant improvements at the *Register* under Gannett. Two weeks after he resigned, Westphal admitted that the *Register* had become "a lot better paper," and "there's more of it." The larger paper was devoting more space to news. Specifically, the Sunday *Register* carried more farm coverage, and the central Iowa editions included new sections on cars and careers. Meanwhile, the daily boasted an enlarged Metro section and a new real estate supplement on Friday. Edwards, in fact, noted that despite criticism to the contrary, Gannett had "not run his newspaper as a cash cow." Edwards did not comment on profits, however, and Overholser challenged Curley's statement that R&T profits had been "modest" since 1989.[14]

With the dramatic resignations, the *Register* was thrust into the middle of a national discussion over the direction of journalism, but the changes taking place at the Des Moines paper were hardly unique. Many prominent newspapers, whether or not they had been absorbed by chains, were in the midst of scaling back "unprofitable" circulation. Similarly, the demand for higher profits was being felt nationwide. New policies at Times Mirror, for instance, were illustrative. In 1995, former Wharton Business School professor and General Mills executive Mark Willes was named publisher of the *Los Angeles Times* and CEO of Times Mirror. Soon after the appointment, Willes announced that he "expected to double operating profit margins and 'grow our earnings per share by 50 percent in 1996.' " To accomplish these goals, he drastically cut costs. These cuts included killing New York City's *Newsday,* the evening edition of the *Baltimore Sun,* and the national edition of the *Los Angeles Times,* as well as laying off 2,000 employees. In the midst of these moves, columnist Glaberson worried that Willes "may represent, more clearly than anyone else, the vast changes sweeping the newspaper industry." Wall Street, however, smiled upon such an austerity program, and during Willes's first two and a half years at the company, Times Mirror stock doubled in value, moving from $23 to $55 per share.[15]

While *Register* readers cared little about national trends in the industry, they worried about their changing newspaper. Their frustration was expressed in several letters to the editor. One wrote that the paper was "losing circulation and revenue because it is absolutely out of touch with the average person in the state." Another felt that the current problems at the R&T resulted from the "rationale of trying to save money on every corner, the insidious inside pressures, and bean-counting excellence." And a central Iowa man called for a return to the paper's long-standing all-state mission. He summed up his thoughts by playing on the *Register*'s motto. "Iowa," he wrote the editor, "does need to depend on you."[16]

In September 1995, Edwards sought to allay these and other concerns with an open letter to readers and advertisers. Placed in the Sunday *Register,* the message acknowledged the challenges the paper had faced in the recent years. Edwards affirmed the *Register*'s increasing focus on central Iowa, but he assured readers, "Our commitment to you is that we will continue to make a high-quality news product available to anyone in the state who wants it." That paper, however, might reach the reader by "home delivery, single copy sales, the U.S. mail or emerging technologies." Second, he pledged that the *Register* would "listen to your [the readers'] views about the newspaper and consider those views as we edit your newspaper." And finally, he assured advertisers "that we will work as partners to increase your success in the marketplace."[17]

Despite this statement from the publisher, many remained skeptical. Retrenchment was a fact, and Offenburger explained that people whose morning delivery had been terminated were "angrier than hell about it. ... I think it is a terrible blow to the state. This [the *Register*] is one of the most important social institutions in this state; it is part of the glue that holds us together."[18] Veteran *Register* staffer Jim Flansburg agreed and especially bemoaned the breakdown of the statewide community: "I think it's really a sad thing, and I think I can already see some sectional divisions building. It's kind of like upstate New York versus the city or downstate Illinois versus Chicago. That's new for Iowa."[19]

It was soon apparent that even the 49-year-old Edwards had serious doubts about the paper's direction. Six months after issuing the open letter, Gardner Cowles' great-grandson "stunned" the newsroom by resigning. After having spent 26 years at the newspaper and the last 12 as publisher, Edwards said he was "ready to try something else." But the abruptness of his resignation, coupled with his lack of another job, led some to speculate that the publisher had been forced out by Gannett. Edwards later explained, "It was time to move on and they didn't beg me to stay." Although this move ended the Cowles family's last connection to the *Register*, Edwards saw the event as "more symbolic that it is substantive. ... We've been a Gannett newspaper for 11 years." The reality of Gannett's ownership of the R&T was clear to former publisher Ken MacDonald. When asked to evaluate Edwards's leadership, MacDonald observed, "Charlie tried very hard to continue the general policies and programs of the Cowles family. I don't think he was entirely successful in that, but I don't think it was his fault because he was operating under Gannett direction."[20]

Edwards downplayed the importance of his departure, but others saw it as troubling. Art Neu, a former lieutenant governor of Iowa, said, "It has always been comforting to know they had somebody there [in the office of R&T publisher] with Iowa roots." Possibly more significant were the comments of Geneva Overholser. During her years at the R&T, she was generally recognized as the leading opposition to the *Register*'s retrenchment policy and "bottom-line" journalism. When she heard the news that her former boss was stepping down, Overholser revealed that it had been Edwards who served as the real "buffer" between Gannett and the *Register*.[21]

Forty-three-year-old Barbara Henry replaced Edwards as the company's publisher. All of Henry's 22 years in the newspaper business were with Gannett, and she had most recently served as the president and publisher of the group's *Great Falls* (Montana) *Tribune*. The new chief executive felt that following the long Cowles tradition was "a huge responsibility," and she referred to the *Register* as "an excellent newspaper." Henry acknowledged that the paper's statewide heritage would not be ignored, but she stressed that the central-Iowa focus was working and would continue.[22]

Staff Exodus

Changes at the top, however, were not the only ones. From the time Overholser quit in 1995 through 1997, there was a significant exodus from the R&T. Over 30 staffers, including a large number of veterans, retired or resigned and sought work elsewhere. Among those who left were reporters Ken Fuson and Larry Fruhling and columnist James Flansburg. Fuson resigned after a 15-year *Register* career to take a position with the *Baltimore Sun*. Growing up in Granger, a small town northwest of Des Moines, he dreamed of working for the celebrated *Register*, and when he joined the paper in 1981, he "felt like a kid picking up a bat for the 1927 Yankees." Fuson loved writing for Iowans, and during his years at the R&T, he became the only Gannett employee to receive the company's excellence in reporting award three times. Ultimately, Fuson felt, "I could have stayed at the paper even with the reduced circulation if I believed we were serving Iowans. What I believe they care about is Rosslyn, Virginia [Gannett headquarters], and how much money they put on the armored truck and send to them."[23]

Fruhling's story was similar. The longtime R&T reporter had difficulty accepting the idea that the paper no longer set the state's agenda. For Fruhling, the *Register*'s pullback from the all-Iowa strategy, coupled with its declining readership and influence, was "like watching an old friend die." Unwilling to watch the paper "pissing away its franchise," Fruhling took early retirement in 1997. He moved to Bellevue, a small town 25 miles south of Dubuque on the Mississippi River, and began a career as a freelance journalist.[24]

The absence of two highly regarded veteran writers such as Fuson and Fruhling was clearly noticed. But to former R&T president Michael Gartner, their departure was part of a bigger problem that was transforming the very nature of the paper. For years, the R&T had been run and staffed by Iowans. That was one of the reasons both Gartner and Gary Gerlach were hired by the company in the 1970s. According to Gartner, this link between the newspaper staff and its region was important. He believed that knowledge of Iowa's "history, traditions, heritage, and characteristics" gave native-born editors and reporters a distinct advantage in covering events throughout the state. Furthermore, coverage of day-to-day life was possible only when journalists knew, for instance, "who was whose brother-in-law, who was married to whose step-mother, [and] who spent five years in jail." With longtime reporters leaving and managers being brought in from the outside, Gartner thought the *Register* was losing its unique ability to reflect the Iowa experience.[25]

In a 1997 lecture at the University of Kentucky, Gartner explained that the changes at the R&T were part of a national phenomenon involving large media groups, especially Gannett. Although Gannett sent "wonderful managers" and "solid news people" to its various papers, the assignments were generally brief. "Chains keep transferring middle and upper level managers, and reporters keep jumping from one place to another," Gartner observed. "No one stays anywhere long enough to understand his or her town, let alone to develop an affection for it." This transient journalism concerned Gartner, and he emphatically told his audience, "You simply cannot cover a town if you don't know it, understand it, and, probably love it.'"[26]

Edwards agreed. "When editors and publishers are less and less community based and more corporate-based, more corporate-focused, you lose the connection [between the community and the newspaper]." The former publisher believed such a situation existed at the *Register,* leading "the paper to miss things. It doesn't have a sense of history, and it doesn't have a sense of place that it once had." Edwards worried that this turn of events could "erode the [paper's] franchise," but he readily acknowledged that the newspaper was a very successful business.[27]

This was one of the reasons that the retirement of Jim Flansburg had such an impact. A native Iowan, Flansburg's knowledge and understanding of the state informed his coverage of public affairs in both Des Moines and Iowa. After 40 years as an R&T reporter, editor, editorial page editor, and columnist, the journalist called it quits in January 1997. Within months, however, Michael Gartner convinced Flansburg to return to the business, and the 65-year-old journalist began a periodic column entitled "Letter from Des Moines" for Gartner's Ames, Iowa, newspaper, the *Daily Tribune.*[28]

During his last years at the R&T, Flansburg had expressed some concerns about the paper's pullback from its statewide mission, but these sporadic remarks were nothing compared to the salvo he launched in a June 1997 *Daily Tribune* column. He wrote, "The decline and fall of the Des Moines Register is the most significant Iowa news story in the last decade of the 20th century. ... The story's significant because the Register—its fierce coverage of the news, its unyielding presentation of opinion and commentary—had been the unifying force in Iowa for at least 125 years." Without the paper's ability to bind Iowans together, he believed, the state was bound to join the ranks of others "torn by regional factions." While the columnist acknowledged the company's growing profitability, he saw the *Register* as "a business success and a social tragedy. And a journalism failure. It gave up doing the one thing it knew how to do, covering the state, for the very thing it didn't know how to do, cover the city and its suburbs."[29]

The Flansburg piece received wide attention as the national discussion on the direction of newspapers continued. Not surprisingly, R&T management had a very different view. Editor Dennis Ryerson explained that Flansburg failed to look at the realities facing the industry, and he added that the *Register* was among a number of newspapers that withdrew from their once expansive markets. Henry, meanwhile, argued that if the paper had not redirected its focus on central Iowa, the expansion of the R&T news staff would not have been possible. "If we were honest with ourselves, if we tried to be the paper this was in 1950 or 1970 or even 1980, then there wouldn't be 205 people in the newsroom." Indeed, this increase in news staff, up 25 people since the Cowleses owned the property, meant the paper could undertake more in-depth, multipart stories. In 1997, for instance, the *Register* ran several major series, including reports on "gambling, Sudanese refugee resettlement, taxation, school desegregation, groundwater, teen driving, and sentencing for child killers."[30]

New Look, New Equipment

Although Flansburg had stirred debate about the *Register*, publisher Henry and her management team stayed the current course of focusing on metropolitan Des Moines. Meanwhile, in an effort to attract new readers, the R&T adopted a new look. Much like other chain-owned papers, the *Register* had established reader advisory groups to identify what its customers wanted in the newspaper. Based on their opinions, the paper was redesigned in the late 1990s. With a " 'newsier,' livelier tone," the *Register* devoted even greater attention to central Iowa. Changes, for instance, included zoned "Around Town" local news sections, more frequent "special sections" dealing with a variety of topics ranging from voting in Iowa to holiday fashion, and a weekly "Work and Money" supplement that offered stories on careers, personal finance, technology, and local business. A new "Living Here" feature provided "residents and visitors interesting and useful information about life in the Des Moines area." It was counterbalanced by "Iowa Closeup," which gave readers a daily thumbnail sketch of towns around the state and seemed to be an acknowledgment of the paper's former statewide tradition.[31]

Financially, the strategy was highly successful. According to journalist Mark Lisheron, the 1997 *Register* was "among the most profitable papers in a [Gannett] chain that has enjoyed margins of between 20 and 30 percent in the last three years."[32] As profits rose, Gannett devoted additional resources to the R&T. The firm's newsroom was completely revamped to accommodate a new computer system that transferred page production from the composing room to the newsroom. In a much more publicized move, the corporate parent showed its commitment to central Iowa with its plans to construct a $51 million production plant designed to house new, state-of-the-art offset presses. At the ground-breaking ceremony in April 1998, Gary Watson, president of Gannett's newspaper division, noted the long-time need for such an upgrade: "We recognized [when we purchased the paper in 1985] that for all the many strengths as Iowa's leading newspaper, The Register had an Achilles' heel. That was and is the aging press equipment."[33]

When the project was announced in the spring of 1997, publisher Barbara Henry described its significance. She began by noting the "valuable and enduring" relationship the newspaper had had with its readers. Then she explained:

> By making this large investment, The Register and our parent company, Gannett, are declaring that we intend to continue this relationship with you. We are declaring our strong commitment to this community. We are declaring our continued commitment to service and quality. We are declaring our strong belief in the very bright future of all newspapers, and the exceptionally bright future of The Register. ... The metro Des Moines area is growing steadily and that trend will continue. The Des Moines Register plans to grow with our town. This investment will ensure it.[34]

With these few words, Henry gave an indication of the present and future course of the *Register.* Any lingering questions about what Gannett ownership meant for the paper could be put to rest.

Gannett's *Register* was clearly a different newspaper than it had been under Cowles ownership. Yet Henry argued that the paper's transformation was necessary. She explained, "We can't grow this newspaper if we draw a line in the sand and say there won't be any more change. The only thing that won't change is the need for change." Editor Ryerson had similar sentiments: "We have to change, like all businesses, to better serve our readers."[35]

A Constant of Change

Change, in fact, had been a constant in the 150-year history of the Register and Tribune. Over the years, the company passed through several major permutations, and generally, management enjoyed success by adopting new ideas and embracing change. The paper began as a tiny Democratic weekly in Fort Des Moines. After struggling and failing, the paper was reestablished under a new name, ultimately becoming the independent *Des Moines Leader* in the 1890s. Meanwhile, the city's Whig paper grew into the Republican *Iowa State Register* in 1860. The Clarkson family purchased the paper a decade later and soon turned it into the dominant voice of the Iowa Republican Party. But the family did much more than make the paper a platform for the GOP. Like other publishers of the late 19th century, the Clarksons enlarged the *Register* by introducing a variety of sections designed to attract new readers. Simultaneously, they expanded the paper's circulation base by increasing their coverage of the entire state. The strategy paid off, and the number of readers tripled. Besides bringing in additional revenue, a larger readership meant more advertising dollars as well because businesses could now reach more potential customers.

Yet, the *Register* fell on hard times in the 1890s. In poor health, Richard Clarkson could no longer run the paper, and his brother Ret put the property up for sale. He was concerned that the *Register* be placed in the hands of a person who would continue to support his business wing of the Republican Party. When a deal was finally cut, Ret thought he had succeeded. The paper, now merged with the *Leader,* was editorially controlled by the politically friendly George Roberts. Much to Ret's chagrin, however, Roberts and his partner Samuel Strauss held the paper only 18 months. It was purchased in 1903 by Gardner Cowles. Under Cowles and editor Harvey Ingham, the paper became an advocate of a more progressive agenda.

Cowles and Ingham transformed the partisan Republican paper into a highly visible, statewide institution. Cowles concentrated on the business side, carefully watched costs, and employed the extensive railroad system and later trucks to deliver his paper throughout the state. Ingham gave the paper broader appeal by moving toward a more independent editorial position and, whenever possible, presented the Iowa angle to national and international stories. Their innovative approach brought growth and success.

John and Mike Cowles followed in their father's footsteps, applying new ideas and technologies. They took the R&T into radio, utilized more photographs with news stories, bought an airplane to carry reporters and photographers around the state, and introduced a state opinion poll. Under their guidance, circulation increased, profits rose, and, after receiving several Pulitzer Prizes, the paper gained national prominence.

By the company's centennial anniversary in 1949, the Register and Tribune had established itself as Iowa's newspaper. Half of all the state's households received at least one of the company's dailies. Through its papers, the R&T reported and reflected the Iowa experience, and because of its extensive reach, it shaped and influenced what it meant to be an Iowan.

During the postwar years, the Cowles brothers became preoccupied with their other endeavors, and active management of the R&T fell to Luther Hill and Ken MacDonald. They stayed the course that brought success and built on the all-Iowa strategy. Unfortunately, the 1950s and 1960s ushered in a period of rapid social and economic change. The new trends hurt newspapers generally and the R&T particularly. Strategies that had once proved highly profitable no longer guaranteed prosperity. With fewer people subscribing to both a morning and evening paper, rising costs, and a shrinking rural newspaper market, circulation began a long period of decline and profit margins fell. Even though maintaining its statewide presence was increasingly expensive, the Cowles family and top managers refused to drop what they saw as their commitment to readers across all of Iowa.

In continuing its all-Iowa tradition, the paper, according to Gilbert Cranberg, former editorial page editor, "created a big sense of statewide community."[36] Guided by Cowles ownership, the *Register* became an accessible forum of ideas in which all Iowans could participate. From this position, the paper informed, instructed, and enlightened its readers. One former R&T manager referred to the *Register* as "a bastion against smallness" because of its strong, progressive editorial stance. Over the years, for example, the editorial page demanded civil rights for African-Americans, clean government, and equality for women. In world affairs, the *Register* shunned isolationism and provincialism in favor of internationalism, and at the height of cold war hysteria, it counseled moderation. The paper played such a significant role in the state that Michael Gartner called the *Register* "the soul of Iowa."[37]

In an effort to maintain this statewide institution and raise dwindling company profits, new CEO David Kruidenier and his managers Gartner and Gary Gerlach expanded the firm by acquiring other media properties. Ultimately, however, the strategy failed, and the R&T was put on the auction block. Gannett purchased the *Register.* Guided by new profit imperatives, first Charlie Edwards and then Barbara Henry moved to cut costs, and once again, the paper went through a period of change.

Undoubtedly, Gannett poured large amounts of capital into its Des Moines operation, and the R&T was certainly not a cash cow being bled dry by its corporate parent. Such important investments included a new computer system, larger news staff, and new presses. While Gannett spent millions on the *Register,* however, it also found that cuts were necessary. Driven to increase profits and not constrained by the heritage and traditions that bound the Cowleses, Gannett managers reinvented the paper. But as Barbara Henry had suggested, the paper remained committed to its readers and community. The difference was that Gannett's *Register* redefined its readership and region. Statewide coverage and circulation, longtime hallmarks of the *Register,* were unceremoniously dropped in favor of the much smaller marketing area of central Iowa. Reporting on Des Moines and its suburbs was expanded, and local news often took precedence over national or international stories. No longer dedicated to shaping Iowa opinion or explaining the world to its far-flung readership throughout the state, the *Register* settled into being a Des Moines newspaper.

Most of the problems faced by the R&T since World War II confounded other American newspapers as well. Similarly, Gannett's solutions in the 1980s and 1990s were hardly novel; many big newspapers cut distant circulation, trimmed expenses, and increased local coverage. What was unique about the *Register*'s situation was the drastic and rapid nature of its transformation. In a little over a decade, Gannett had taken a nationally regarded, but financially struggling, paper with extraordinary statewide reach, downsized and refocused it, and created a financially successful metropolitan paper. A year before Gannett bought the paper, the *Register* was included on *Time* magazine's list of top 10 dailies. The magazine saw the paper as "enormously influential in the state" and noted that it had "targeted its resources to achieve national impact." By the mid-1990s, however, the majority of R&T resources were earmarked for central Iowa, and the paper's impact and importance were local by design. The newspaper Iowans had come to depend upon for reflecting their daily life, for statewide news, for national and international news told from their perspective, for setting the state's agenda or serving as its watchdog was no more. Once "of and for Iowa," the *Register* under Gannett became the paper of and for Des Moines and its suburbs.[38]

A NOTE ON SOURCES

Much of this book is based on manuscript collections, some of which are privately held. Unfortunately, there is no known collection of Gardner Cowles Sr.'s papers, although some of his letters and records may be found in the papers of Gardner Cowles Jr. and John Cowles and in material held by David Kruidenier. Other important components of my research consisted of interviews and correspondence with key people in the Register and Tribune Company's history.

Manuscript Collections

Clarkson, James S. Papers. State Historical Society of Iowa, Des Moines.
Cowles, Gardner Jr. Papers. Drake University, Des Moines, Iowa.
Cowles, John. Papers. Drake University, Des Moines, Iowa.
Cummins, Albert B. Papers. State Historical Society of Iowa, Des Moines.
Dolliver, Jonathan. Papers. State Historical Society of Iowa, Iowa City.
Granger, Barlow. Papers. State Historical Society of Iowa, Des Moines.
Harlan, Edgar. Papers. State Historical Society of Iowa, Des Moines.
Hudson, J. Robert. Papers. Private collection, West Des Moines, Iowa.
Ingham, Harvey. Papers. State Historical Society of Iowa, Des Moines.
Kalkstein. Shawn. Papers. Private collection, Stamford, Connecticut.
Kruidenier, David. Papers. Private collection, Des Moines, Iowa.
Neuharth, Al. Papers. Private collection, Cocoa Beach, Florida.
Perkins, George D. Papers. State Historical Society of Iowa, Des Moines.
Roberts, Glenn. Papers. Private collection, Des Moines, Iowa.
Watts, Harry. Papers. Private collection, Des Moines, Iowa.

Interviews and Correspondence with Author

Ballantine, Elizabeth. Interview by author. Des Moines, Iowa, September 18, 1993.
Ballantine, Morley. Interview by author. Des Moines, Iowa, October 10, 1992.
Cranberg, Gilbert. Interview by author. Des Moines, Iowa, July 18, 1996.
Edwards, Charles. Interviews by author. Des Moines, Iowa, September 23, 1993, and June 25, 1998.
Foster, Mary LeCron. Interview by author. Des Moines, Iowa, July 30, 1994.
Gartner, Michael. Interview by author. Des Moines, Iowa, June 11, 1997.
Gerlach, Gary. Interview by author. Ames, Iowa, June 30, 1993. Telephone conversation, August 11, 1997.
Gilbert, Richard. Interview by author. Des Moines, Iowa, September 14, 1992.
Hill, Luther L. Jr. Interview by author. Des Moines, Iowa, February 4, 1993.

Hudson, Robert J. Interview by author. West Des Moines, Iowa, September 15, 1992.
Kalkstein, Shawn. Interviews by author. West Des Moines, Iowa, August 4, 1993, and July 30, 1997. Telephone conversation with author, July 21, 1997.
Kruidenier, David. Interviews by author. Des Moines, Iowa, July 20, 1992, and July 22, 1997. Telephone conversation with author, June 16, 1997.
Lynn, Lyle. Interview by author. Des Moines, Iowa, August 11, 1993.
MacDonald, Kenneth. Interviews by author. Des Moines, Iowa, July 14, 1992, and June 17, 1995. Telephone conversations with author, June 26 and July 30, 1996.
Mack, Barbara. Telephone conversation with author, August 5, 1997.
Neuharth, Al. Letters to author, 15 and 29 August, 1997.
Norris, Louis. Interview by author. Des Moines, Iowa, January 26, 1993. Telephone conversation with author, June 25, 1996.
Roberts, Glenn. Interview by author. Des Moines, Iowa, June 8, 1993.
Rosenberg, Norman. Letter to author, August 26, 1996.
Silha, Otto. Telephone conversation with author, August 8, 1997.
Soth, Lauren. Interview by author. West Des Moines, Iowa, October 20, 1992.
Watts, Harry. Interview by author. Des Moines, Iowa, March 9, 1993.
Zacherle, Hedo. Interview by author. Des Moines, Iowa, June 28, 1996.

NOTES

Notes to Chapter 1

1. The newspapers' distribution per Iowa household comes from Register and Tribune Company, *The Des Moines Register and Tribune* (Des Moines: Register and Tribune Company, 1952), 22. The daily and Sunday *Register* were sold widely throughout the state, while the evening *Tribune* circulated more regionally in and around central Iowa.

2. Works that examine nationally prominent newspapers include, for example: Jack Hart, *The Information Empire: The Rise of the Los Angeles Times and the Times Mirror Corporation* (Washington, D.C.: University Press of America, 1981); Chalmers Roberts, *In the Shadow of Power: The Story of the Washington Post* (Cabin John, Md.: Seven Locks Press, 1989); Jerry Rosenberg, *Inside the Wall Street Journal* (New York: Macmillan, 1982); and Gay Talese, *The Kingdom and the Power* (New York: New American Library, 1969). Histories of smaller newspapers include: David Chander, *The Binghams of Louisville* (New York: Crown, 1987); Jack Clairborne, *The Charlotte Observer: Its Time and Place, 1869–1986* (Chapel Hill: University of North Carolina Press, 1986); and John Harris, *The Blade of Toledo: The First 150 Years* (Toledo, Ohio: Blade, 1985). Surprisingly little has been written on the *Des Moines Register.* The only attempts are the interesting, but largely anecdotal, works of George Mills, "The Des Moines Register," *Palimpsest* 30 (September 1949): 273–304; and *Harvey Ingham and Gardner Cowles, Sr.: Things Don't Just Happen* (Ames: Iowa State University Press, 1977).

3. Lyle Lynn, interview by author, Des Moines, Iowa, August 11, 1993.

4. William Furlong, "The Cowles Empire Expands," *Saturday Review,* May 11, 1968, 71–72.

5. The quotation is taken from Jim Flansburg's column in the (Ames, Iowa) *Daily Tribune,* June 27, 1997.

6. *Daily Iowa State Register,* June 15, 1870.

7. The idea that markets and new technologies played major roles in the rise of big business in the 19th and early 20th centuries has been stressed by Al Chandler and his students of business history. See, for instance, Alfred Chandler, *The Visible Hand: The Managerial Revolution in American Business* (Cambridge: Harvard University Press, 1977) and *Scale and Scope: The Dynamics of Industrial Enterprise* (Cambridge: Harvard University Press, 1990). Over the last few years, some scholars have begun to call for new ways of approaching journalism history, and the concepts of business historians are beginning to enjoy wider use among those examining the newspaper industry. See David Nord, "A Plea for Journalism History," *Journalism History* 15 (spring 1988): 8–15; and Carol Smith and Carolyn Stewart Dyer, "Taking Stock, Placing Orders: A Historiographic Essay on the Business History of the Newspaper," *Journalism Monographs* 132 (April 1992): 1–56.

8. See typescript "The Des Moines Register and Tribune" (April 13, 1949), John Cowles Papers, Drake University, Des Moines, Iowa.

9. Shawn Kalkstein was married to a fourth-generation Cowles family member, Karen Jurs, a great-grandaughter of Gardner Cowles Sr. See Shawn Kalkstein, interviews by author, West Des Moines, Iowa, August 4, 1993, and July 30, 1997; Shawn Kalkstein, Letters to Shareholders, 1982–1984, in possession of author; and Minutes of Des Moines Register and Tribune Board of Directors' Meetings, 1980–1984, David Kruidenier Papers, private collection, Des Moines, Iowa.

10. See Des Moines Register and Tribune Company, "Proposed Plan of Complete Liquidation of Company," July 1, 1985, Kruidenier Papers.

11. See Gary Gerlach, interview by author, Ames, Iowa, June 30, 1993. For the notion that the paper set state agenda, see Elizabeth Ballantine, interview by author, Des Moines, Iowa, September 18, 1993.

12. Jean Folkerts, "From the Heartland," in Philip Cook , Douglas Gomery, and Lawrence Lichty, eds., *The Future of News: Television—Newspapers—Wireservices—Newsmagazines* (Washington, D.C.: Woodrow Wilson Center Press, 1992), 134–35.

13. Charles Edwards, interview by author, Des Moines, Iowa, September 23, 1993.

14. See Sig Gissler, "What Happens When Gannett Takes Over," *Columbia Journalism Review* 36 (November–December 1997): 42–47; Ira Lacher, "The Register Regroups," *Columbia Journalism Review* 30 (May–June 1991): 16; Mark Lisheron, "The Retrenching Register," *American Journalism Review* 19 (November 1997): 28–35; *Los Angeles Times,* February 9, 1996; and Al Neuharth, *Confessions of an S.O.B.* (New York: Doubleday, 1989), 202.

15. See the *Des Moines Register,* March 26, April 14, and June 14, 1996; and Gissler, "When Gannett Takes Over," 42.

16. *Daily Tribune,* June 27, 1997.

17. Furlong, "Cowles Empire Expands," 71.

18. David Kruidenier, interview by author, Des Moines, Iowa, July 20, 1992.

Notes to Chapter 2

1. Robert Wiebe, *The Search for Order* (New York: Hill and Wang, 1967).

2. Menahem Blondheim, *News over the Wires: The Telegraph and the Flow of Public Information in America, 1844–1897* (Cambridge: Harvard University Press, 1994), 13.

3. Allan G. Bogue, *From Prairie to Corn Belt: Farming on the Illinois and Iowa Prairies in the Nineteenth Century* (Chicago and London: University of Chicago Press, 1963), 9–13; Leland Sage, *A History of Iowa* (Ames: Iowa State University Press, 1974), 52–92; Katherine M. Young, "Notes on the History of Iowa Newspapers, 1836–1870," *University of Iowa Extension Bulletin* (1924): 37–38.

4. Dorothy Schwieder, *Iowa: The Middle Land* (Ames: Iowa State University Press, 1996), 3–20; George Mills, "The Des Moines Register," *Palimpsest* 30 (September 1949): 274.

5. Michael Schudson, *Discovering the News: A Social History of American Newspapers* (New York: Basic Books, 1978), 13.

6. See Michael Emery and Edwin Emery, *The Press and America: An Interpretative History of the Mass Media,* 6th ed. (Englewood Cliffs, N.J.: Prentice Hall, 1988), 112–43; Alfred M. Lee, *The Daily Newspaper in America: The Evolution of a Social Instrument* (New York: Macmillan, 1947), 97–132; and Schudson, *Discovering the News,* 14–60. See also James Crouthamel, *Bennett's New York Herald and the Rise of the Popular Press* (Syracuse, N.Y.: Syracuse University Press, 1989) and Richard Kluger, *The Paper: The Life and Death of the New York Herald Tribune* (New York: Vintage, 1986), 28–39.

7. Lee, *Daily Newspaper in America,* 716. On manuscript newspapers in early Iowa, see Roy Alden Atwood, "Handwritten Newspapers on the Iowa Frontier, 1844–1854," *Journalism History* 7 (summer 1980): 56–59, 66–67.

8. For background on the Republican Party in Iowa, see Robert Cook, *Baptism of Fire: The Republican Party in Iowa, 1838–1878* (Ames: Iowa State University Press, 1994). For information on the party nationally, see Eric Foner, *Free Soil, Free Labor, Free Men: The Ideology of the Republican Party Before the Civil War* (New York: Oxford University Press, 1970), and *Politics and Ideology in the Age of the Civil War* (New York: Oxford University Press, 1980). The term *Radical Republican* was understood at the time to mean those in the party who prior to the Civil War took an uncompromising position on the evil of slavery and during Reconstruction demanded that full civil and political rights be accorded to African-Americans.

9. Granger and Bates were both among the earliest land agents in central Iowa. See Robert Swierenga, *Pioneer and Profits: Land Speculation on the Iowa Frontier* (Ames: Iowa State University Press, 1968). Origins of the paper and the locating of the press are discussed in Curtis Bates to Barlow Granger, April 29, May 23, 1849, vol. 1, Barlow Granger Papers, State Historical Society of Iowa, Des Moines. As to the price paid for the press, Bates explained to Granger that a Mr. Crum would accept either $150 in cash or a $125 land warrant and $95 cash. No existing correspondence explains which offer was taken. See Curtis Bates to Barlow Granger, June 5, 1849, vol. 1, Granger Papers.

10. *Iowa Star,* July 26, 1849. As tradition has it, Granger originally intended to call the paper the *Fort Des Moines Star,* but because he lacked enough large type to spell that out, he settled on the *Iowa Star.* On Granger, the *Iowa Star,* and early journalism in Iowa, see Johnson Brigham, *Des Moines: The Pioneer of Municipal Progress and Reform of the Middle West, Together with the History of Polk County, Iowa,* vol. 1 (Chicago: S. J. Clarke Publishing Co., 1911), 66–70; Young, "History of Iowa Newspapers," 85; David C. Mott, "Early Iowa Newspapers: A Contribution of the Newspapers Established in Iowa before the Civil War," *Annals of Iowa* 16 (January 1928): 206; Register and Tribune Company, *The Story of the Des Moines Register and Des Moines Tribune* (Des Moines: Des Moines Register and Tribune Company, 1940).

11. Brigham, *Des Moines,* 68; *Iowa Star,* February 1, 1850.

12. See Curtis Bates to Barlow Granger, November 3, 15, December 22, 1849, and January 3, 1850, vol. 1, Granger Papers.

13. *Iowa Star,* January 7, 1850, quoted in Brigham, *Des Moines,* 68. See also *Iowa State Register,* June 29, 1902.

14. *Iowa Star,* November 23, 1849; Granger was responding to a prospectus of the *Fort Des Moines Gazette.* Edited by Lampson P. Sherman (half brother of Des Moines pioneer developer Hoyt Sherman), the Gazette was published from January 14, 1850, to February 6, 1851.

15. *Iowa Star,* February 22, 1850.

16. Johnson originally left the paper in November to serve as a delegate at a state railroad convention. See the *Iowa Star,* November 28, 1850. A. Y. Hull's initial editorial appeared in the *Iowa Star,* September 4, 1851.

17. See, for example, the *Iowa Star,* September 11, 1851; March 1, 1850; and June 7, 1850. On the issue of expansion, the thinking of Bates (and two editors who worked for him) was in line with many midwestern editors who believed Cuba would naturally become part of the United States. See Frederick Merk, *Manifest Destiny and Mission in American History: A Reinterpretation* (New York: Alfred A. Knopf, 1963).

18. Young, "History of Iowa Newspapers," 85.

19. See the *Iowa Star,* January 19 and August 17, 1854. See also Register and Tribune Co., 4.

20. See Brigham, *Des Moines,* 81; *Iowa State Journal,* February 27 and August 22, 1857.

21. After selling the *Journal,* Hutchins purchased the *Dubuque Herald.* He went on to found the *St. Louis Daily Times* in 1866 and the *Washington Post* in 1877. See Brigham, *Des Moines,* 550–51; and Benjamin F. Gue, *History of Iowa: From the Earliest Times to the*

Beginning of the Twentieth Century, vol. 4 (New York: Century History Company, 1903) 206–7.

22. Register and Tribune Co., 2; Mott, "Early Iowa Newspapers," 297.

23. See Gue, *History of Iowa,* vol. 4, 259; and Edward Younger, *John A. Kasson: Politics and Diplomacy from Lincoln to McKinley* (Iowa City: State Historical Society of Iowa, 1955), 91, 97.

24. For more information on John Brown's time in Iowa, see James Conor, "The Antislave Movement in Iowa," *Annals of Iowa* 40 (fall 1970): 462–63, 465, 467–71; Benjamin F. Gue, "John Brown and His Iowa Friends," *Midland Monthly* 7 (March 1897): 273–76; Stephen Oates, *To Purge This Land with Blood: A Biography of John Brown* (New York and London: Harper and Row, 1970), 210, 221–23, 242–43, 265; and Charles E. Payne, *Josiah Bushnell Grinnell* (Iowa City: State Historical Society of Iowa, 1938), 108.

25. As quoted in Mills, "Des Moines Register," 296.

26. Background on Des Moines and its population figures are taken from Orin Dahl, *Des Moines: Capital City* (Tulsa, Okla.: Continental Heritage, 1978), 32–34, 79; for information on the moving of the capital, the state constitution of 1857, and the rise of the Republican Party, see Sage, *History of Iowa,* 116–49.

27. Teesdale explained changing the name of his paper in the *Daily Iowa State Register,* January 10, 1860. The phrase "Official Paper of the State" appeared on the very first issue of the daily *Iowa State Register,* January 9, 1860.

28. See, for example, various issues of the daily *Iowa State Register,* January 9–April 3, 1860.

29. See *Biographical Directory of the United States Congress, 1774–1989* (Washington, D.C.: United States Government Printing Office, 1989), 1607; Brigham, *Des Moines,* 553; and Young, "History of Iowa Newspapers," 87–88.

30. Information on Palmer may be found in *Biographical Directory,* 1607; Brigham, *Des Moines,* 553; and Young, "History of Iowa Newspapers," 87–88. See also Cook, *Baptism of Fire,* 140–41, 144, 149, 161, 190, 194; Gue, *History of Iowa,* vol. 4, 207; Leland Sage, *William Boyd Allison: A Study in Practical Politics* (Iowa City: State Historical Society of Iowa, 1956), 46, 94–95, 99–100; and *Register and Leader,* December 4, 1907.

31. Frank M. Mills, *The Mills Family and Its Collateral Branches, with Autobiographical Reminiscences* (Sioux Falls, S.D.: [n.p.], 1911), 70.

32. Daily *Iowa State Register,* January 19, 1862.

33. Daily *Iowa State Register,* February 12, 1865, as quoted in Cook, *Baptism of Fire,* 155.

34. See daily *Iowa State Register,* February 2, June 4, 13, 15, 1865; Robert Dykstra, *Bright Radical Star: Black Freedom and White Supremacy on the Hawkeye Frontier* (Cambridge: Harvard University Press, 1993), 200–206; and Hubert Wubben, "The Uncertain Trumpet: Iowa Republicans and Black Suffrage, 1860–1868," *Annals of Iowa* 47 (summer 1984): 416–17.

35. See daily *Iowa State Register,* December 6, 1866.

36. Following two terms in Congress (1869–1873), Palmer moved to Chicago, bought into the *Inter-Ocean,* and served as its editor in chief. He later was the postmaster of Chicago and then served as Public Printer of the United States from 1889 to 1894.

37. Mills, *Mills Family,* 44–45, 156–58, 162–75. For additional information on Mills, see also Mills, *Early Days in a College Town and Wabash College in the Early Days and Now with Biographical Reminiscences* (Sioux Falls, S.D.: Sessions Printing, 1924.

38. Dykstra, *Bright Radical Star,* 224.

39. Ibid., 240. See *Iowa State Daily Register,* November 4 and 7, 1868.

40. See Mills, *Mills Family,* 71, 97; and J. M. Dixon's obituary, *Iowa State Register,* January 9, 1883. In 1867, James Clarkson had purchased a stagecoach ticket for Den-

ver, and it was only the promotion to city editor that kept him in Iowa.

41. Mills, *Mills Family,* 75.

42. See Ibid., 75–76; *Daily State Register,* January 15 and 17, 1868; *Des Moines City Directory and Business Guide, 1866* (Des Moines, Iowa: Mills and Company, 1866), 30, 115; *Des Moines City Directory and Business Guide, 1869* (Des Moines, Iowa: Mills and Company, 1869), xxi.

43. For more on the coming of the telegraph to Iowa, see Robert L. Thompson, *Wiring a Continent: The History of the Telegraph Industry in the United States, 1832–1866* (Princeton, N.J.: Princeton University Press, 1947), 22–27, 131–32. 281–97, 363, 368–69; and Ben H. Wilson, "Telegraph Pioneering," *Palimpsest* 6 (November 1925):373–93. The quotation is from "The Telegraph Reaches Iowa," unmarked clipping, n.d., Iowa Clipping File 2, Communications—Telegraph in Iowa, State Historical Society of Iowa, Des Moines [hereafter cited as SHSI]. See also *Iowa State Daily Register,* January 14, 1862.

44. Blondheim, *News over the Wires,* 56. Besides Blondheim, other important sources on the telegraph and news services are Victor Rosewater, *History of Cooperative News-Gathering in the United States* (New York: D. Appleton and Company, 1930); and Richard A. Schwarzlose, *The Nation's Newsbrokers,* vol. 1, *The Formative Years: From Pretelegraph to 1865*, vol. 2, *The Rush to Institution, from 1865 to 1920* (Evanston, Ill.: Northwestern University Press, 1989, 1990).

45. *Iowa State Daily Register,* January 14, 1862.

46. With the outbreak of the Civil War in 1861, the federal government wanted a telegraph line completely in Union territory, and with the uncertainty of Missouri, a telegraph line was strung across Iowa, building west from Cedar Rapids and east from Council Bluffs. Because Des Moines was included in this line, it gained a telegraph connection four years before it was reached by a railroad. See "How the Telegraph Came into Iowa," unmarked clipping, June 29, 1938, SHSI. On Des Moines and the railroads, see Barbara B. Long, *Des Moines and Polk County: Flag on the Prairie* (Northridge, Calif.: Windsor Publications, 1988), 24–27.

47. The original members of the Northwestern Associated Press were, in Illinois, the *Alton Democrat* and *Telegraph,* the *Bloomington Pantagraph,* the *Freeport Journal,* the *Galesburg Register,* the *Jacksonville Journal,* the *Peoria Taeglicher Demokrat* and *Transcript,* the *Quincy Herald* and *Whig,* the *Rock Island Argus* and *Union,* the *Illinois State Journal,* and the *Illinois State Register;* in Iowa, the *Burlington Gazette* and *Hawkeye,* the *Council Bluffs Nonpariel,* the *Davenport Democrat* and *Gazette,* the Des Moines daily *Iowa State Register* and *Statesman,* the *Dubuque Herald* and *Times,* the *Keokuk Constitution* and *Gate City,* and the *Muscatine Courier* and *Journal;* in Nebraska, the *Omaha Herald* and *Republican,* and the *Nebraska City Press.* See Schwarzlose, *Nation's Newsbrokers,* vol. 2, 23–24, 38; Lee, *Daily Newspaper in America,* 509; and Rosewater, *History of Cooperative News-Gathering,* 199.

48. Schwarzlose, *Nation's Newsbrokers,* vol. 2, 34.

49. Ibid., 51; Blondheim, *News over the Wires,* 150–51; Lee, *Daily Newspaper in America,* 508–509; Susan R. Brooker-Gross, "News Wire Services in the Nineteenth-Century United States," *Journal of Historical Geography* 7 (1981): 171–72.

50. Blondheim, *News over the Wires,* 170; Lee, *Daily Newspaper in America,* 509.

51. See advertisement, daily *Iowa State Register,* September 15, 1867.

52. See Mott, "Early Newspapers," 207; and *Iowa Statesman,* November 23, 1868, January 6, June 15 and 16, 1869, August 1, November 9, 1870.

Notes to Chapter 3

1. *Iowa State Register,* December 7, 1871.

2. Information on the Clarkson family comes from Leland Sage, "The Clarksons of Indiana and Iowa," *Indiana Magazine of History* 50 (December 1954): 429–46; and

Edward Stiles, *Recollections and Sketches of Notable Lawyers and Public Men in Early Iowa* (Des Moines, Iowa: Homestead Publishers, 1916), 504–8.

3. Both Richard and Ret learned the printer's trade at their father's newspaper. For Ret's reminiscences, see James S. Clarkson to the President of Typographical Union No. 118 Des Moines, April 30, 1907, and James Clarkson to Lowell Chamberlain, December 15, 1908 (the quotation is taken from the latter), James S. Clarkson Papers, Volume Two, SHSI, Des Moines. See also James S. Clarkson to Edgar Harlan, October 1, 1912, Edgar Harlan Papers, SHSI, Des Moines.

4. Richard Clarkson had worked for the *Register* in the printing department in 1860 before going off to fight in the Civil War. See *Iowa State Register,* January 9, 1883.

5. See biographical entries on all three Clarksons in Benjamin F. Gue, *History of Iowa: From the Earliest Times to the Beginning of the Twentieth Century,* vol. 4 (New York: Century History Company, 1903) 53–55.

6. Clarkson's story appeared in the *Chicago Tribune,* November 19, 1869. It was reprinted in the *Iowa State Register,* December 1, 1869. See also Mildred Throne, *Cyrus Clay Carpenter and Iowa Politics, 1854–1898* (Iowa City: State Historical Society of Iowa, 1974), 100.

7. See F. M. Mills to Edgar Harlan, February 3, 1921, Harlan Papers; Frank M. Mills, *The Mills Family and Its Collateral Branches, with Autobiographical Reminiscences* (Sioux Falls, S.D.: [n.p.], 1911), 71–74; "Source Material of Iowa History: James S. Clarkson's Letter on Allison's 1872 Election," *Iowa Journal of History* 57 (January 1959): 78; *Iowa State Register,* November 12, 1870; and Cyrenus Cole, *I Remember, I Remember: A Book of Recollections* (Iowa City: State Historical Society of Iowa, 1936), 138–39.

8. See *Iowa State Register,* November 22, 1870. Although this lengthy statement was an unsigned piece on the editorial page, it was most likely the writing of Ret Clarkson, already the editor for Mills and Company, who was to be the editor when he and his family took over on December 6. The terms *Radical and progressive* must be understood in the context of the times. Ret had been a Radical Republican in that he supported (and continued to support throughout his editorship) political and civil rights for African-Americans. On most other matters, however, he and his wing of the Republican Party were conservative. On Ret's commitment to civil rights, see Robert Dykstra, *Bright Radical Star: Black Freedom and White Supremacy on the Hawkeye Frontier* (Cambridge: Harvard University Press, 1993), 233–34, 334 n.36.

9. Gerald Baldasty, *The Commercialization of News in the Nineteenth Century* (Madison: University of Wisconsin Press, 1992), 30, 35.

10. See *Bushnell's Resident and Business Directory of Des Moines, 1871* (Des Moines, Iowa: Jos. P. Bushnell, 1871), 23.

11. Ret Clarkson (Mum) to Cyrus Carpenter, April 22, 1871, as quoted in Throne, *Cyrus Clay Carpenter,* 110–11.

12. See James S. Leonardo, "From Military Express to Free Delivery: The Postal History of Des Moines, Iowa, 1843–1873," (master's thesis, Drake University, 1984), 220–21, 259–60; and Leland Sage, *William Boyd Allison: A Study in Practical Politics* (Iowa City: State Historical Society of Iowa, 1956), 105–7. Clarkson held the Des Moines postmastership from 1871 to 1879.

13. *Iowa State Register,* October 3, 1871.

14. See F. M. Mills to Edgar Harlan, October 1, 1912, Harlan Papers. The defeated Harlan privately claimed that Ret borrowed $25,000 from Allen and received the remaining $5,000 needed from William Allison; see James Harlan to Azro B. F. Hildreth, February 7, 1872, quoted in Sage, *William Boyd Allison,* 115. There is no evidence that supports Harlan's claim of Allison's payment. Another view holds that Ret received the necessary $30,000 from political boss Jacob Rich; see George Mills, "The Des Moines Register," *Palimpsest* 30 (September 1949): 283.

15. See Dan Elbert Clark, *History of the Senatorial Elections in Iowa* (Iowa City: State

Historical Society of Iowa, 1912), 152–67; Robert Cook, *Baptism of Fire: The Republican Party in Iowa, 1838–1878* (Ames: Iowa State University Press, 1994), 194–95; and Sage, *William Boyd Allison,* 105–18. Sage correctly argues that although Ret liked to remember that the *Register* led the fight for Allison, it did not support him until mid-December. With the election held in the General Assembly in January, it is most likely the paper did not have a decisive influence in this election. See Sage, *William Boyd Allison,* 353 n. 22.

16. See F. M. Mills to Edgar Harlan, February 3, 1921, Harlan Papers; and Sage, *William Boyd Allison,* 115.

17. Palmer to Dodge, January 18, 1872, as quoted in Sage, *William Boyd Allison,* 354 n. 40.

18. Cook, *Baptism of Fire,* 196.

19. David Paul Nord, "The Business Values of American Newspapers: The 19th Century Watershed in Chicago," *Journalism Quarterly* 61 (summer 1984): 272.

20. See Leland Sage, *A History of Iowa* (Ames: Iowa State University Press, 1974), 188–89. For more on the Grange in Iowa, see Myrtle Beinhauer, "Development of the Grange in Iowa, 1868–1930," *Annals of Iowa* 34 (April 1959): 597–618; Solon J. Buck, *The Granger Movement: A Study of Agricultural Organization and Its Political, Economic, and Social Manifestations, 1870–1880* (Cambridge: Harvard University Press, 1913); Cook, *Baptism of Fire,* 203–26; Jeffrey Ostler, *Prairie Populism: The Fate of Agrarian Radicalism in Kansas, Nebraska, and Iowa, 1880–1892* (Lawrence: University of Kansas Press, 1993), 37–53; Mildred Throne, "The Anti-Monopoly Party in Iowa, 1873–1874," *Iowa Journal of History* 52 (October 1954): 289–326; and Mildred Throne, "The Grange in Iowa, 1865–1875," *Iowa Journal of History* 47 (October 1949): 289–324.

21. *Iowa State (Weekly) Register,* January 11, 1871.

22. *Iowa State (Weekly) Register,* March 6, 1874, as quoted in Throne, "Grange in Iowa," 308.

23. *Iowa State Register,* February 6, 1873.

24. *Iowa State (Weekly) Register,* April 25, 1873.

25. *Iowa State Register,* August 14 and 15, 1873.

26. *Iowa State Register,* October 30, 1873.

27. George H. Miller (*Railroads and the Granger Laws* [Madison: University of Wisconsin Press, 1971], 102–14) argues that merchants along the Mississippi fought for railroad legislation, hoping that lower rates would expand their business. Cook (*Baptism of Fire,* 203–26) and Ostler (*Prairie Populism,* 37–39) contend, I believe correctly, that the agrarian antimonopoly movement created the climate necessary for regulatory legislation to pass. Oddly, Miller does not mention the Clarksons or the *Register*, although both the family and the newspaper appeared to play an important role in its passage and later its repeal.

28. See Cook, *Baptism of Fire,* 224–25.

29. *Iowa State Register,* January 9 and 27, 1876, as quoted in Mildred Throne, "Repeal of the Iowa Granger Law, 1878," *Iowa Journal of History* 51 (April 1953): 109.

30. Nine years later, the Supreme Court reversed itself in *Wabash Railway v. Illinois,* disallowing states from regulating railroads that traveled beyond their borders. It argued that only Congress had the authority to oversee interstate commerce. This ruling led to the 1887 passage of the Interstate Commerce Act and the creation of the Interstate Commerce Commission (ICC). The first federal regulatory agency, the ICC was authorized to insure that railroad rates were "reasonable and just," but it could not set these rates or enforce its decisions. Real power did not come to the commission until additional legislation was passed during the Progressive era.

Ret had favored federal oversight of the railroads since 1876, and the *Register* praised the creation of the ICC, writing on January 27, 1887, for instance: "There is every reason to justify the people in believing that both Congress and Legislatures were never more disposed than they are now to protecting the public interests as justice and equity shall demand."

31. *Iowa State (Weekly) Register,* February 15, 1878. Ret Clarkson had argued the need for federal regulation as early as 1876; see *Iowa State Register,* May 12, 1876.

32. Throne, *Cyrus Clay Carpenter,* 224.

33. Thomas R. Ross, *Jonathan Prentice Dolliver: A Study in Political Integrity and Independence* (Iowa City: State Historical Society of Iowa, 1958), 65.

34. Judith Gildner, "An Organizational History of the Iowa Farmers' Alliance, 1881–1890," (master's thesis, Drake University, 1972), 1–30.

35. *Iowa State Register,* January 13, 1881.

36. *Iowa State Register,* May 25, 1881. Coker had started his campaign against Washburn and Moen in "Farm, Orchard and Garden," *Iowa State Register,* March 19, 1879.

37. See FPA company's advertisement in the *Iowa State Register,* February 25, 1885.

38. Gildner, "Iowa Farmers' Alliance," 37–42. See also Gue, *History of Iowa,* vol. 3, 103–7; and Herman C. Nixon, "The Populist Movement in Iowa," *Iowa Journal of History and Politics* 24 (January 1926): 17–18.

39. Ostler, *Prairie Populism,* 49.

40. *Iowa State Register,* November 2, 1887, as quoted in Ostler, *Prairie Populism,* 63.

41. *Iowa State Register,* January 25 and 26, 1888.

42. Gildner, "Iowa Farmers' Alliance," 86–90; Nixon, "Populist Movement in Iowa," 34–38; Ostler, *Prairie Populism,* 63–68; and Sage, *History of Iowa,* 204–8.

43. *Iowa State Register,* July 22, 1891, as quoted in Ostler, *Prairie Populism,* 166.

44. *Iowa State (Weekly) Register,* June 10, 1892, as quoted in Walter E. Nydegger, "The Election of 1892 in Iowa," *Iowa Journal of History and Politics* 25 (July 1927): 426.

45. Nydegger, "Election of 1892," 436–37.

46. *Iowa State Register,* November 6, 1896, as quoted in Nixon, "Populist Movement in Iowa," 99–100.

47. Ostler (*Prairie Populism*) argues convincingly that Populism failed in Iowa because of the existence of a competitive two-party system that offered voters real choices and responded to their demands.

48. Samuel P. Hays, "History as Human Behavior," *Iowa Journal of History* 58 (July 1960): 193–206.

49. See Ballard C. Campbell, "Did Democracy Work? Prohibition in Late-Nineteenth-Century Iowa: A Test Case," *Journal of Interdisciplinary History* 8 (summer 1977): 87–88; Dan E. Clark, "The History of Liquor Legislation in Iowa, 1846–1861," *Iowa Journal of History and Politics* 6 (January 1908): 55–87; Dan E. Clark, "The History of Liquor Legislation in Iowa, 1861–1878," *Iowa Journal of History and Politics* 6 (July 1908): 339–74; Dan E. Clark, "The History of Liquor Legislation in Iowa, 1878–1908," *Iowa Journal of History and Politics* 6 (October 1908): 503–608; and Diana Pounds, "Booze, Ballots, and Wild Women: Coverage of Suffrage and Temperance by Three Iowa Newspapers, 1870–1875," (master's thesis, Iowa State University, 1990), 83–86.

50. On "pray ins," see, for example, *Iowa State Register,* January 24 and March 4 and 7, 1874, as quoted in Pounds, "Booze, Ballots, and Wild Women," 87, 89. On the social costs of drinking, see, for example, *Iowa State Register,* February 22, 1874, and June 13, 1882.

51. *Iowa State Register,* February 27, 1877. This distillery was built, and in 1882 when a prohibition amendment was being discussed, the *Register* made it clear that although it supported the amendment, it would not endorse it if the manufacture of alcohol for export were included. A resolution was added to the amendment excluding manufacture for export. See *Iowa State Register,* February 21, 1882; and Clark, "Liquor Legislation, 1878–1908," 517–18.

52. *Iowa State Register,* March 9, 1877. For the Republican platform and the *Register*'s endorsement of it, see *Iowa State Register,* June 28,1877.

53. *Iowa State Register,* April 3, 1884.
54. Campbell, "Did Democracy Work?" 95.
55. *Iowa State (Weekly) Register,* April 1,1892, as quoted in Clark, "Liquor Legislation, 1878–1908," 591.
56. *Iowa State (Weekly) Register,* March 31, 1893, as quoted in Clark, "Liquor Legislation, 1878–1908," 592.
57. For discussion of this position in the Republican platform, see *Iowa State Register,* August 14–18, 1893.
58. *Iowa State Register,* March 15, 1894.
59. The simplest explanation of the Mulct Law can be found in Campbell, "Did Democracy Work?" 90.
60. *Iowa State Register,* March 30, 1894.
61. Campbell, "Did Democracy Work?" 113.
62. Cook, *Baptism of Fire,* 244.
63. On women's suffrage in Iowa, see Louise R. Noun, *Strong-Minded Women: The Emergence of the Woman-Suffrage Movement in Iowa* (Ames: Iowa State University Press, 1969); and Glenda Riley, *Frontierswomen: The Iowa Experience* (Ames: Iowa State University Press, 1981), 135–36, 152–53, 157–70.
64. Pounds, "Booze, Ballots, and Wild Women," 59, n. 59, 68.
65. See *Iowa State Register,* February 25, March 2, 1877, June 29, 1882, and February 8, 1885.
66. *Iowa State Register,* March 13, 1877.
67. The title of this section changed over time, but from the mid-1870s on, a women's column was a regular offering of the paper.
68. See *Iowa State Register,* March 2, 1877, February 8, 1885, December 14, 1882, and July 6, 1882.
69. Geo. P. Rowell and Co., *American Newspaper Directory, 1873* (New York: Geo. P. Rowell and Co., 1873), 77. According to this directory, the the *Register's* daily circulation was 2,100, making it the largest daily in Iowa.
70. Michael Schudson notes that "the ratio of editorial material to advertising in American newspapers changed from about 70-30 to 50-50 or lower" by the 1880s. See Michael Schudson, *Discovering the News: A Social History of American Newspapers* (New York: Basic Books, 1978), 93.
71. Alfred M. Lee, *The Daily Newspaper in America: The Evolution of a Social Instrument* (New York: Macmillan, 1947), 748.
72. On this general trend, see Frank L. Mott, *American Journalism, A History: 1690–1960,* 3d ed.(New York: Macmillan, 1962), 478–88.
73. Baldasty, *Commercialization of News,* 121.
74. Lee, *Daily Newspaper in America,* 749.
75. Baldasty, *Commercialization of News,* 95. Baldasty describes county weeklies and small dailies as using this technique to obtain local and regional news. The *Register* used this method to obtain stories from all over the state.
76. See Mills, "Des Moines Register," 287; and *Iowa State Register,* May 5, 1880,
77. Mills, "Des Moines Register," 287–88.
78. For the complete list of towns where the *Register* was available, see *Iowa State Register,* February 5, 1885.
79. See Rowell and Co., *American Newspaper Directory, 1873, 77*; and N. W. Ayer and Son, *American Newspaper Annual, 1890* (Philadelphia: N. W. Ayer and Son, 1890), 206, 197–230. According to N. W. Ayer and Son, the *Register* remained the state's largest daily.
80. As quoted in the *Iowa State Register,* January 9, 1883. For comparison purposes, another growing midwestern paper,the *St. Louis Post-Dispatch* (with a circulation of 22,000 in 1882), which had been bought and put together by Joseph Pulitzer in the mid-

1870s, was posting annual net profits of $45,000 by the early 1880s. See Michael Emery and Edwin Emery, *The Press and America: An Interpretative History of the Mass Media,* 6th ed.(Englewood Cliffs, N.J.: Prentice Hall, 1988), 204; and Julian S. Rammelkamp, *Pulitzer's Post-Dispatch, 1878–1883* (Princeton, N.J.: Princeton University Press, 1967).

81. *Algona Republican,* December 17, 1884.

82. See Baldasty, *Commercialization of News,* esp. 36–80. For changes in society, business, and the economy, see Alfred Chandler, *The Visible Hand: The Managerial Revolution in American Business* (Cambridge: Harvard University Press, 1977); Robert Wiebe, *The Search for Order* (New York: Hill and Wang, 1967);.and Olivier Zunz, *Making America Corporate, 1870–1920* (Chicago: University of Chicago Press, 1990).

83. See Michael E. McGerr, *The Decline of Party Politics: The American North, 1865–1928* (New York and Oxford: Oxford University Press, 1986), 14; Harry W. Baehr Jr., *The New York Tribune Since the Civil War* (New York: Octagon Books, 1972), 98–125; Donald W. Curl, *Murat Halstead and the Cincinnati Commercial* (Boca Raton: University Presses of Florida, 1980), 57–74; and Mott, *American Journalism,* 411–12.

84. Quoted in George Mills, *Harvey Ingham and Gardner Cowles, Sr.: Things Don't Just Happen* (Ames: Iowa State University Press, 1977), 27.

85. Circulation of the four Des Moines dailies in 1902 was as follows:

Paper	Daily Circulation
Capital	17,419
Iowa State Register	7,588
Leader	20,441
News	30,187

See N. W. Ayer and Son, *American Newspaper Annual, 1902* (Philadelphia: N. W. Ayer and Son, 1902), 248–49.

Richard Clarkson's health was clearly in decline. He was increasingly hard of hearing and suffered from diabetes. See James Clarkson to Jonathan Dolliver, December 28, 1901, and March 26 and June 7, 1902, Jonathan Dolliver Papers, SHSI, Iowa City, and Sage, "Clarksons of Indiana and Iowa," 439, 445.

86. James Clarkson to Jonathan Dolliver, November 12, 1901, Dolliver Papers.

87. Roberts recalled his dream of owning the *Register,* the newspaper competition in Des Moines, and the move to merge with the *Leader* in George Roberts to Gardner Cowles, June 17, 1927, Ingham Scrapbook, Harvey Ingham Papers, SHSI, Des Moines.

88. Two groups expressed interest in purchasing the *Register.* The first was led by railroad attorney and Iowa political boss Joseph W. Blythe and former Iowa governor Leslie Shaw, while the second was headed by Iowa governor and future U.S. senator Albert B. Cummins and newspaperman Abraham Funk. Both groups were intent on gaining a U.S. senate seat, and Ret wanted to keep the paper in the Dolliver camp. The situation is described in Ross, *Jonathan Prentice Dolliver,* 328 n. 38. On the negotiations, see James Clarkson to Jonathan Dolliver, December 12, 24, 28, 30, 1901; January 3, March 13, 26, April 3, 21, 26, May 1, 19, June 2, 7, 1902; George Roberts to Dolliver, May 11, 1902; Dolliver to Clarkson, April 12, 1902, Dolliver Papers; and George Roberts to George Perkins, April 9, 1902, George D. Perkins Papers, SHSI, Des Moines.

89. The details of the sale of the *Register,* the merger with the *Leader,* and the politics of the new paper can be found in Minutes of the Board of Directors Meetings, Register and Tribune Company, 1902–1933, vol. 1, 1–8, part of a collection privately held by David Kruidenier, Des Moines, Iowa.

Notes to Chapter 4

1. Since 1960, a large number of works have examined the relationship of the rise of big business and the importance of managerial expertise to its development. See for

example, Alfred D. Chandler Jr., *Strategy and Structure: Chapters in the History of the Industrial Enterprise* (Cambridge: M.I.T. Press, 1962), *The Visible Hand: The Managerial Revolution in American Business* (Cambridge: Belknap Press of Harvard University Press, 1977), and *Scale and Scope: The Dynamics of Industrial Capitalism* (Cambridge: Harvard University Press, 1990); Daniel Nelson, *Managers and Workers: Origins of the New Factory System in the United States, 1880–1920* (Madison: University of Wisconsin Press, 1975); and JoAnne Yates, *Control Through Communication: The Rise of System in American Management* (Baltimore and London: Johns Hopkins University Press, 1989). For the importance of sound managerial practices in smaller operations, see Mansel G. Blackford, *A History of Small Business in America* (New York: Twanye Publishers, 1991). On newspaper management, see, for instance, W. Parkman Rankin, *The Practice of Newspaper Management* (New York: Praeger, 1985); Frank W. Rucker and Herbert L. Williams, *Newspaper Organization and Management* (Ames: Iowa State University Press, 1974); Jon G. Udell, *The Economics of the American Newspaper* (New York: Hasting House, 1978); and Jim Willis, *Surviving in the Newspaper Business* (New York: Praeger, 1988).

2. See Frank W. Rucker, *Newspaper Circulation: What, Where and How* (Ames: Iowa State University Press, 1958), 1.

3. George Mills, *Harvey Ingham and Gardner Cowles, Sr.: Things Don't Just Happen* (Ames: Iowa State University Press, 1977), 35.

4. Alfred M. Lee, *The Daily Newspaper in America: The Evolution of a Social Instrument* (New York: Macmillan, 1947), 749.

5. Gardner Cowles, *Mike Looks Back: The Memoirs of Gardner Cowles, Founder of Look Magazine* (New York: Gardner Cowles, 1985), 11. Professor of journalism W. Parkman Rankin made a very similar statement some eighty years after Cowles's quip on the importance of circulation: "No matter how excellent the editorial product of the newspaper may be, its advertising revenue will be nonexistent if the newspaper is not sold and read," see Rankin, *Practice of Newspaper Management,* 11.

6. See Special Report, Register and Tribune Company, 1925–1952, 123–25, held by David Kruidenier. For comparison purposes, the following are 1919 circulation figures from several dailies around the region and country. Data are from N. W. Ayer and Son, *American Newspaper Annual and Directory* (Philadelphia: N. W. Ayer and Son, 1919).

Paper	Circulation	Population of City
Des Moines Register (and Tribune)	119,257	106,000
Kansas City Star (and Times)	354,614	282,000
Minneapolis Tribune	129,990	375,000
New York Times	339,238	5,047,000
St. Louis Post-Dispatch	148,084	735,000

7. George E. Roberts to George D. Perkins, June 24, 1902, George D. Perkins Papers, SHSI, Des Moines.

8. Thomas A. Way to Albert B. Cummins, July 6, 1903 and Albert B. Cummins to Thomas A. Way, July 14, 1903, Albert B. Cummins Papers, SHSI, Des Moines. Cummins and Way had apparently already discussed the possibility of purchasing a portion of the *Register* by investing $50,000, but Roberts needed to be assured that the paper would not be used to injure Dolliver in any way. See also George E. Roberts to Gardner Cowles, June 17, 1927, Harvey Ingham Scrapbook, Harvey Ingham Papers, SHSI, Des Moines.

9. Harvey Ingham to William C. Dewel, January 10, 1940, Ingham Papers; and Minutes of Special Stockholders' Meeting, October 5, 1903, in Minutes of Board of Directors Meetings, Register and Tribune Company, 1902–1933, 14. Although the stock had a par value of $100 per share, the price had been pegged at $45.83 per share. After Strauss sold, the company's stock was held in the following proportions.

Stockholder	Shares
George Roberts	1,790
Samuel Strauss	645
Moses Strauss	10
Harvey Ingham	545
M. D. O'Connell	10
	3,000

See also undated (ca. October 1903) press release written by George Roberts, Ingham Papers.

10. See undated (ca. October 1903) press release written by George Roberts, Ingham Papers; and Memorandum of Agreement, October 31, 1903, Harvey Ingham Papers. The three men were to acquire 1,500 shares (500 shares each) at $45.83 per share, or $68,745.

11. On Ingham's situation at the paper under Funk, Meredith, and Smith, see William H. Ingham to Harvey Ingham Jr., (n.d.); undated (ca. October 1903) press release written by George Roberts, Ingham Papers. Quotation comes from Harvey Ingham to Gardner Cowles, November 3,1903, Ingham Papers.

12. Announcement (of agreement) published in *Register and Leader,* November 7, 1903, Ingham Papers. See also Minutes of Annual Stockholders' Meeting, January 19, 1904, in Minutes of Board of Directors Meetings, Register and Tribune Company, 1902–1933, 22, and *Des Moines Register and Leader,* January 21, 1904. Cowles purchased 1,500 shares at the $45.83 per share price. Stock distribution after his purchase was as follows:

Stockholder	Shares
Gardner Cowles	1,500
Harvey Ingham	545
Samuel Strauss	500
George Roberts	455
	3,000

13. Quoted in Mills, *Harvey Ingham and Gardner Cowles, Sr.,* 16.

14. Cowles was too good a businessman to be duped by the inflated circulation figures. He was brought into the deal by his good friend Harvey Ingham, and it is most likely the editor apprised Cowles of the company's true financial situation. In addition, circulation figures were readily available from A. W. Ayer and Son, which as of 1902 had listed the *Register* as a distant fourth in Des Moines daily newspaper circulation (see note 84 to chapter 3).

15. Gardner Cowles to Harvey Ingham, June 23, 1939, Ingham Scrapbook, Ingham Papers.

16. *Des Moines Capital,* November 7, 1903.

17. Quoted in Cowles, *Mike Looks Back,* 9.

18. *Algona Republican,* July 16, 1884.

19. Cowles was also quite interested in politics and served two terms in the Iowa General Assembly, from 1899 to 1903. For more biographical information on Gardner Cowles, see Associated Press Biographical Service, "Sketch 3084, Gardner Cowles" (November 15, 1943); Cowles, *Mike Looks Back,* 7–10; Edgar Harlan, *A Narrative History of the People of Iowa,* vol. 4 (Chicago and New York: American Historical Society, 1931), 9; Mills, *Harvey Ingham and Gardner Cowles, Sr.,* 1–16; and Benjamin F. Reed, *History of Kossuth County, Iowa,* vol. 1 (Chicago: S. J. Clarke Publishing, 1913), 341–42, 353, 354, 441.

20. Cowles, *Mike Looks Back,* 10; *Gardner Cowles, 1861–1946* (Des Moines, Iowa: Des

Moines Register and Tribune Company, 1946), 12; Mills, *Harvey Ingham and Gardner Cowles, Sr.,* 17; Minutes of Special Stockholders' Meeting February 16, March 9, 16, June 16, 1904, in Minutes of Board of Directors Meetings, Register and Tribune Company, 1902–1933, 24–26; *Des Moines Register and Leader,* January 21, 1904; unpublished internal typescript history of Des Moines Register and Tribune (n.d.), in possession of author; and "Iowa Formula," *Time,* July 1, 1935, 26.

21. Quotation comes from *Washington Post* obituary of Gardner Cowles, quoted in *Gardner Cowles, 1861-1946*, 79–80. See also *The Story of the Des Moines Register and Des Moines Tribune* (Des Moines: Des Moines Register and Tribune Company, 1940), 6; and "Iowa Formula," 26.

22. Cowles's poring over Iowa maps, memorizing railroad timetables, and learning rail routes out of Des Moines is widely reported. See, for example, Cowles, *Mike Looks Back,* 11; Mills, *Harvey Ingham and Gardner Cowles, Sr.,* 30–31; "The Cowles Boys," *Newsweek,* July 4, 1949, 52; and interview with David Kruidenier, July 20, 1992. Cordingley, who had been working for an Algona grain company, was originally hired as a *Register and Leader* bookkeeper in 1904. Two years later, Cowles named Cordingley circulation manager.

23. See pamphlet "Ten Successful Agents Tell How to Sell the Sunday REGISTER AND LEADER," (1908); pamphlet "Instructions and Terms to News Dealers and Newsboys" (ca. 1907); and advertisement (1908), Harry T. Watts Scrapbook, in Harry Watts Papers, held by Harry Watts, Des Moines.

24. See Gerald Baldasty, *The Commercialization of News in the Nineteenth Century* (Madison: University of Wisconsin Press, 1992), 134–37; Lee, *Daily Newspaper in America,* 284–85; and Frank L. Mott, *American Journalism, A History: 1690–1960,* 3d ed. (New York: Macmillan, 1962), 597–98.

25. See Register and Leader promotional flier, 1906; Register and Leader to subscriber, 1908; "Cartoons by J. N. 'Ding' Darling" advertisement, *Des Moines Register and Leader* (ca. 1908); "Gibson Girl" advertisement, *Des Moines Register and Leader,* June 16, 1906; "Teddy Bear" advertisement, *Des Moines Register and Leader* (ca. 1907); and Gardner Cowles to Subscriber, December 24, 1906, January 29, 1907, all in Watts Scrapbook, Watts Papers.

26. See, for example, advertisement for Sunday edition, *Des Moines Register and Leader,* July, 21, 1906; advertisement for Sunday *Register and Leader,* May 1906, advertisement poster for women's page; advertisement for baseball coverage, *Des Moines Register and Leader,* April 7, 18, 1907; posters regarding baseball coverage; Register and Leader to potential subscriber, 1907; all in Watts Scrapbook, Watts Papers.

27. For examples of promotional letters, see Register and Leader to Subscriber, 1908; Register and Leader to Sir, January 12, 1907; and Register and Leader to Sir, February 1908; all in Watts Scrapbook, Watts Papers. Such campaigns were apparently successful, as the same technique was used to build up *Tribune* circulation after Cowles acquired the afternoon paper in 1908. See John Cowles to John Marston, February 18, 1941, John Cowles Papers, Drake University, Des Moines, Iowa.

28. See Register and Leader promotional flier, 1907; and A. J. Knight to Register and Leader, December 9, 1907; Watts Scrapbook, Watts Papers.

29. For a discussion of newspapers serving the two markets of readers and advertisers, see Udell, *Economics of the American Newspaper* , 42–47.

30. Quoted in William Leach, *Land of Desire: Merchants, Power,and the Rise of a New American Culture* (New York: Vintage Books, 1993), 43.

31. See *Register and Leader* Daily Advertising Report, August 31, 1908, Watts Scrapbook, Watts Papers.

32. "Where the Register and Leader Circulates" pamphlet, June 1908, Watts Scrapbook, Watts Papers. On the issue of sources of circulation, see Rucker, *Newspaper Circulation,* 8–23.

33. Mills, *Harvey Ingham and Gardner Cowles, Sr.,* 34, 36; and *Register and Leader* advertisement in *Printers'Ink,* 1908, in Watts Scrapbook, Watts Papers.

Paper	1905 Column Inches of Advertising	1907 Column Inches of Advertising
Register and Leader	244,985	294,001
Capital	237,172	268,130
News	256,604	251,263

34. See John Cowles to John Marston, February 18, 1941, John Cowles Papers. Although Cowles was a leader in dropping liquor advertising, as the movement for prohibition grew, other papers followed suit. The *New York Times,* for example, stopped taking liquor ads January 1, 1911. These decisions not to accept alcohol advertising were made in the context of muckraking crusade of truth in advertising. Cowles and many others were refusing to print ads for medicines of questionable value, especially after *Collier's* magazine in 1905 and 1906 ran Samuel H. Adams's series of articles exposing the false claims of various patent medicines and so-called physicians. See Lee, *Daily Newspaper in America,* 327–32; and Mott, *American Journalism,* 575–76. Cowles's ban on liquor advertising was a long-standing one. The policy continued long after he died in 1946. Beer advertising reappeared in the Cowles Des Moines papers in 1970; hard liquor in 1971.

35. Cowles sold the *Iowa State Register and Farmer* to the Iowa Farmer Publishing Company in December 1906. See Minutes of Stockholders' Meeting, December 12, 1906, in Minutes of Board of Directors Meetings, Register and Tribune Company, 1902–1933, 29. On consolidations going on at the time, see Frank L. Mott, *The News in America* (Cambridge: Harvard University Press, 1952), 188–93.

36. *Des Moines Register and Leader,* November 14, 1908.

37. See *Des Moines Register and Leader,* November 13, 29, 1908; Cowles, *Mike Looks Back,* 13; "Proposed Booklet for Employees, 1938," 3, John Cowles Papers; and Mills, *Harvey Ingham and Gardner Cowles, Sr.,* 36–37.

38. See Special Report, Register and Tribune Company, 1925–1952, 123. From 1906 to 1912, company dividends rose from $4,500 to $27,223. See also "Proposed Booklet for Employees, 1938," 3; and Mills, *Harvey Ingham and Gardner Cowles, Sr.,* 37–38. A comparison of advertising linage follows:

Paper	1912 Column Inches of Advertising
Register and Leader	365,372
Capital	338,803
Tribune	316,023
News	260,898

39. See Minutes of Board of Directors Special Session, June 14, 1909, Minutes of Board of Directors Meetings, Register and Tribune Company, 1902–1933, 36; Johnson Brigham, *Des Moines: The Pioneer of Municipal Progress and Reform of the Middle West, Together with the History of Polk County, Iowa,* vol. 1 (Chicago: S. J. Clarke Publishing Co., 1911), 556; and *Des Moines Register and Leader,* November 26, 29, 1908. On new printing press technology, see, Lee, *Daily Newspaper in America,* 125–26; and Mott, *American Journalism,* 600–601.

40. *Editor and Publisher,* March 2, 1935, 31. For more on the importance of prompt delivery service, see Rankin, *Practice of Newspaper Management,* 18–19.

41. See George S. May, "The Good Roads Movement in Iowa," *Palimpsest* 46 (February 1965): 66. The term *improved road* was used broadly at the time and meant surfaced with gravel, stone, or some other material. Of Iowa's improved roads in 1904, the vast

majority were surfaced with gravel.

42. Ibid., 96–110. For the *Register*'s support of Meredith and opposition to Harding, see *Des Moines Register,* October 1–November 6, 1916. A broader perspective on the Good Roads Movement and the creation of the highway system in general is provided in Bruce Seely, *Building the American Highway: Engineers as Policy Makers* (Philadelphia: Temple University Press, 1987). Another issue that affected who the *Register* endorsed was the candidates' stand on Prohibition. In a strange reversal of usual party positions, the Republican Harding opposed Prohibition, while the Democrat Meredith supported it. This gave the "dry" *Register* an additional reason to break with its tradition of supporting Republicans and throw its support behind Meredith. See Leland Sage, *A History of Iowa* (Ames: Iowa State University Press, 1974), 249–50.

43. On World War I and its impact on the newspaper industry, see Mott, *American Journalism,* 615–34; and Michael Emery and Edwin Emery, *The Press and America: An Interpretative History of the Mass Media,* 6th ed. (Englewood Cliffs, N.J.: Prentice Hall, 1988), 334. Net earnings come from Special Report, Register and Tribune Company, 1925–1952, 123; and circulation figures are from typescript "The Des Moines Register and Tribune," (April 13, 1949), John Cowles Papers. See also Minutes of Special Stockholders Meeting, November 22, 1915, Minutes of Board of Directors Meetings, Register and Tribune Company, 1902–1933, 42. At the outset of World War I, a subscription to the *Register and Leader* cost $4 a year for the daily, $2 a year for the Sunday paper, and $6 per year for the combined daily and Sunday. By August 1917, the fee for the Sunday paper had risen to $3 per year. Six months later, in February 1918, the fee had risen to $5 a year for the daily alone and $8 a year for the daily and Sunday *Register.*

44. See *Des Moines Register and Leader,* February 22–25, 1915; *Des Moines Register,* October 21, 1917; and Special Report, Register and Tribune Company, 1940–1963, 150, held by David Kruidenier. The building at Fourth Street and Court Avenue was refurbished, and the space was leased until the facility was sold in December 1942.

45. *Des Moines Register,* February 16, 1922.

46. Emery and Emery, *Press in America,* 333–35.

47. See Agreement between Register and Tribune Company and the Des Moines News Company, October 28, 1924, Kruidenier Papers; *Des Moines Register,* November 9, 1924; and "Iowa Formula," 26.

48. "The Des Moines Register and Tribune" (April 13, 1949).

49. The portrait that emerges of Gardner Cowles comes from interviews with various people—for example, Morley Ballantine, October 10, 1992; David Kruidenier, July 20, 1992; and Kenneth MacDonald, July 14, 1992. Also informative are *Gardner Cowles: 1861–1946,* 7–14; Mills, *Harvey Ingham and Gardner Cowles, Sr.*; and John Cowles to John Marston, February 18, 1941, John Cowles Papers. For an example of daily reports sent to a vacationing Cowles, see the telegrams of Harry T. Watts to Gardner Cowles, February 1916, and Gardner Cowles to Harry Watts, February 13, 1916, Watts Scrapbook, Watts Papers.

50. See interviews in note 49; Mills, *Harvey Ingham and Gardner Cowles, Sr.;* and "Proposed Booklet for Employees, 1938," 2.

51. Statement about Cowles reading "every line" comes from the recollections of John Cowles to John Marston, February 18, 1941, John Cowles Papers.

52. Cowles, *Mike Looks Back,* 10. For more on the relationship between Cowles and Ingham, see recollections of Cowles to Marston, Cowles Papers.

53. *Des Moines Register and Leader,* July 2, 1902.

54. Emery and Emery, *Press in America,* 194. By stressing independence and accuracy, Ingham's blueprint for the *Register* sounded remarkably similar to Adolph Ochs's 1896 announcement of policy for his newly purchased *New York Times*: "It will be my earnest aim that the New York Times give the news, all the news, in concise and attractive form, in language that is parliamentary in good society, and give it early if not earlier, than it

can be learned through any other reliable medium, [and] to give the news impartially, without fear or favor, regardless of any party, sect, or interest involved. ..." See Michael Schudson, *Discovering the News: A Social History of American Newspapers* (New York: Basic Books, 1978), 110.

55. See 1905 promotional flier, Watts Scrapbook, Watts Papers. Historian Michael McGerr includes the *Des Moines Register* in a list of Republican newspapers that were representative of "watered-down partisanship" from the 1890s to the 1920s. Other papers he includes are the *Minneapolis Journal,* the *Minneapolis Tribune,* and the *New York Herald Tribune.* The *Register* appeared to belong on this list, although certainly not until after 1903, when Cowles and Ingham were running the paper. See Michael E. McGerr, *The Decline of Party Politics: The American North, 1865–1928* (New York and Oxford: Oxford University Press, 1986), 292–93.

56. *Des Moines Register and Leader,* August 2, 6, 1906.

57. On the Don Berry story, see undated typescript, Ingham Papers; and Mills, *Harvey Ingham and Gardner Cowles, Sr.,* 54. For the story of the purchase of the *Tribune,* see *Des Moines Register and Leader,* November 29, 1908.

58. Max McElwain, *Profiles in Communication: The Hall of Fame of the University of Iowa School of Journalism and Mass Communication* (Iowa City: Iowa Center for Communication Study, 1991), 12.

59. Newspaper magnate E. W. Scripps, for example, believed product differentiation was the most cost-effective way to battle competitors. He instructed one of his editors: "Would it not be better to follow the line of the least resistance and instead of competing with your contemporaries in the field which they occupy, simply devote yourself largely to dealing with subjects of interest which your contemporaries neglect or treat only incidentally? Let the public or the larger portion of the public, depend upon the old papers for the things which they furnish well, while being compelled to patronize your paper in order to find interesting subjects which have scant or no attention from other papers." See Gerald Baldasty, "Managing a Newspaper Chain: The Scripps Concern and the Newspaper Enterprise Association, 1902–1910" (paper presented at the Economic and Business History Society Conference, Santa Fe, New Mexico, April 28–30, 1994), 11. On the use of product differentiation, see Michael E. Porter, *Competitive Strategy: Techniques for Analyzing Industries and Competitors* (New York: Free Press, 1980), 37–38, 41, 46.

60. Leighton Housh, "First Person Pronoun" (SHSI, Des Moines, Iowa, 1981, typescript), 55.

61. See *Des Moines Register and Leader,* November 29, 1908; and various ads, 1906–1908, Watts Scrapbook, Watts Papers.

62. *Des Moines Register and Leader,* January 5, 1906.

63. On farm coverage, see *Des Moines Register,* November 26, 1921. For the editorial comparing Belgium to Iowa, see *Des Moines Register and Leader,* August 11, 1914.

64. For the *Des Moines Register and Leader*'s announcement of its new comic strip section, see *Register and Leader,* September 17, 1904. The comic section first appeared on Sunday, September 18, 1904.

65. On the introduction of comic strips, see Emery and Emery, *Press and America,* 231–34, 331–33; and Mott, *American Journalism,* 584–87. Ingham's editorial appeared in the *Des Moines Register and Leader,* September 17, 1904. For more on comic strips, see Coulton Waugh, *The Comics* (New York: Macmillan, 1947); and Jerry Robinson, *The Comics: An Illustrated History of Comic Strip Art* (New York; Putnam, 1974).

66. Mott, *American Journalism,* 483.

67. The nickname Ding was an abbreviated form of Darling. Darling's father and brother had used that nickname earlier. Darling signed his artwork "D'ing" as a contraction for his last name. See David L. Lendt, *Ding: The Life of Jay Norwood Darling* (Ames: Iowa State University Press, 1979), 13.

68. Advertising copy sent to other newspaper and journals, December 4, 1906, Watts Scrapbook, Watts Papers.

69. Lendt, *Ding,* 23.

70. Ibid., 24–29.

71. Mills, *Harvey Ingham and Gardner Cowles, Sr.,* 18–19.

72. Lendt, *Ding,* 31.

73. Richard Kluger, *The Paper: The Life and Death of the New York Herald Tribune* (New York: Vintage, 1986), 353.

74. The four-panel cartoon originally appeared in the *Register* May 6, 1923. Darling was the second cartoonist to be awarded a Pulitzer. The first went to Rollin Kirby of the *New York World* in 1922, and no award was given in 1923. See Lendt, *Ding,* 38. A number of Ding's cartoons are reproduced in Jay Darling, *Ding's Half Century* (New York: Duell, Sloan and Pearce, 1962) and John M Henry, "A Treasury of Ding," *Palimpsest* 53 (March 1972): 81–118. Darling received a second Pulitzer in 1943 for a cartoon of the previous year entitled, "What a Place for a Waste Paper Salvage Campaign." It featured a drawing of the U.S. Capitol buried under piles of government reports and press releases.

75. Lendt, *Ding,* 32.

76. Early in Darling's *Register* career, management realized that Darling could be valuable in attracting subscribers. Advertisements frequently made use of Darling's name and work. One, for instance, noted that only the *Register* carried Ding Darling's cartoons, while another offered new subscribers a book featuring the best of Darling's political cartoons. Much later, at the time of Darling's retirement in 1949, John and Mike Cowles recognized the significance of the cartoonist's contribution. They decided to continue paying Darling's salary for the rest of his life. John Cowles explained to Darling: "You contributed enormously to the upbuilding of the Register and Tribune. ... Your help and loyalty to my father throughout the years, wholly in addition to the many kindnesses that you have shown Mike and me, is something that we won't forget." See John Cowles to Jay N. Darling, November 1, 1949, John Cowles Papers, Drake University. For information on the use of Ding Darling cartoons in early advertising, see "Cartoons by J. N. 'Ding' Darling" advertisement, *Des Moines Register and Leader* (ca. 1908); and Register and Leader advertising copy sent to other journals and newspapers (ca. 1909), Watts Scrapbook, Watts Papers.

77. Mills, *Harvey Ingham and Gardner Cowles, Sr.,* 70–71. See also *Des Moines Sunday Register,* March 30, 1919.

78. On Cobb, see John L. Heaton, *Cobb of "The World"* (New York: Dutton, 1924); on White, see William Allen White, *The Autobiography of William Allen White* (New York: Macmillan, 1946) and John McKee, *William Allen White: Maverick on Main Street* (Westport, Conn.: Greenwood Press, 1975); on Scripps, see Oliver H. Knight, ed. *I Protest: The Selected Disquisitions of E. W. Scripps* (Madison: University of Wisconsin Press, 1966); and on Hearst, see Roy E. Littlefield III, *William Randolph Hearst: His Role in American Progressivism* (Lanham, Md.: University Press of America, 1980). and on reform-oriented editors, see Jonathan Daniels, *They Will Be Heard: America's Crusading Newspaper Editors* (New York: McGraw Hill, 1965).

79. On corruption of cities and the Progressives' move to reform them, see Lincoln Steffens, *The Shame of the Cities* (New York: McClure, Phillips and Son, 1904); Samuel P. Hays, "The Politics of Reform in Municipal Government in the Progressive Era," *Pacific Northwest Quarterly* 55 (October 1964): 157–69; Martin J. Schiesl, *The Politics of Efficiency: Municipal Administration and Reform in America, 1880–1920* (Berkeley: University of California Press, 1977); and Michael H. Ebner and Eugene M. Tobin, eds., *The Age of Urban Reform: New Perspectives on the Progressive Era* (Port Washington, New York: Kennikat Press, 1977).

80. Mills, *Harvey Ingham and Gardner Cowles, Sr.,* 28.

81. Bradley R. Rice, *Progressive Cities: The Commission Government Movement in America, 1901–1920* (Austin: University of Texas Press, 1977), 34.

82. Ibid., 35.

83. See *Des Moines Register and Leader,* November 18, 1905, January 16, 21, March 18, 1906; and Rice, *Progressive Cities,* 36.

84. *Des Moines Register and Leader,* February 2, 1907.

85. Rice, *Progressive Cities,* 36; and *Des Moines Register and Leader,* March 10–30, 1907.

86. Quoted in Mills, *Harvey Ingham and Gardner Cowles, Sr.,* 29. Des Moines kept the commission government until it opted for a mayor–city manager system in 1949. For a more detailed explanation, see Rice, *Progressive Cities.*

87. Quoted in McElwain, *Profiles in Communication,* 13.

88. *Des Moines Register and Leader,* August 20,31, 1912.

89. Jack Lufkin, "The Founding and Early Years of the National Association for the Advancement of Colored People in Des Moines, 1915–1930," *Annals of Iowa* 45 (fall 1980): 447.

90. *Des Moines Register,* November 8, 1922, as quoted in Kay Johnson, "The Ku Klux Klan in Iowa: A Study in Intolerance" (master's thesis, University of Iowa, 1967), 123.

91. *Des Moines Tribune,* March 1, 1923.

92. See Johnson, "The Ku Klux Klan in Iowa," 128.

93. *Des Moines Register,* April 1, 1924, as quoted in Ibid., 130.

94. Mills, *Harvey Ingham and Gardner Cowles, Sr.,* 49.

95. McElwain, *Profiles in Communication,* 13.

96. Lufkin, "Founding and Early Years of NAACP," 448.

97. Louise Noun points out a possible reason for Ingham's steadfast support for women's suffrage. His mother, Caroline Ingham, was one of the founders of the second women's suffrage association in Iowa, the Equal Rights Association founded in 1869. See Louise R. Noun, *Strong-Minded Women: The Emergence of the Woman-Suffrage Movement in Iowa* (Ames: Iowa State University Press, 1969), 120.

98. *Des Moines Register and Leader,* October 11, 1913, as quoted in Noun, *Strong-Minded Women,* 250.

99. *Des Moines Register and Leader Woman's Suffrage Edition,* May 12, 1915.

100. *Des Moines Register and Leader,* May 12, 1915.

101. *Des Moines Register,* March 9, 1920.

102. *Des Moines Register,* July 6, 1920. Women obtained the right to vote when Tennessee, the 36th state to ratify the 19th Amendment, gave it the necessary three-quarters majority on August 18, 1920.

103. See *Des Moines Register and Leader,* August 14, 19, 1914, May 10, 1915; and *Des Moines Register,* February 2, 1917.

104. See *Des Moines Register,* March 1, 19, 23, and April 7, 1917.

105. For a discussion of the idea of an isolationist Midwest and a survey of 30 midwestern newspapers that suggests the area was not isolationist, see Warren F. Kuehl, "Midwestern Newspapers and Isolationist Sentiment," *Diplomatic History* 3 (1979): 283–306. Kuehl surveyed editorials in the 1920s from 30 newspapers at the center of the Midwest (eastern Iowa, northern Illinois, and southern Wisconsin). His findings were as follows:

13 papers were strongly internationalist or internationalist
9 papers were middle-of-the-road
8 papers were isolationist or strongly isolationist

The *Des Moines Register,* which would have fallen into the strongly internationalist category, was not part of the study. According to Kuehl, the midwestern papers supporting internationalism included the *Beloit Daily News,* the *Davenport Daily Times,* the *Davenport Democrat,* the *Dubuque Telegraph-Herald,* the *Freeport Journal-Standard,* the *La Crosse*

Tribune and Leader-Press, the *Milwaukee Catholic Citizen,* the *Monroe Evening Times,* the *Racine Times-Call,* the *Rock Island Argus,* the *Stroughton Courier-Hub,* the *Sterling Daily Gazette,* and the *Wisconsin State Journal.*

106. *Des Moines Register,* January 11, November 11, 19, 20, December 4, 10, 26, 1918.

107. See John A. Aman, "View of Three Iowa Newspapers on the League of Nations 1919–1920," *Iowa Journal of History and Politics* 39 (July 1941): 236–37.

108. *Des Moines Register,* June 3, 1919.

109. *Des Moines Register,* November 6, 1919.

110. *Des Moines Register,* March 21, 1920, as quoted in Aman, "View of Three Iowa Newspapers," 283.

111. Thomas G. Paterson, J. Garry Clifford, and Kenneth J. Hagan, *American Foreign Policy: A History/Since 1900* (Lexington, Mass.: D. C. Heath and Company, 1991), 289.

112. See *Des Moines Register,* March 11, May 4, 1920. In the 1920 presidential election, the *Register* endorsed no candidate. This stance was repeated the next election, when the paper found the incumbent Calvin Coolidge, the Democrat John Davis, and the Progressive Robert LaFollette equally qualified and merely encouraged its readers to vote.

113. *Des Moines Register,* November 14, 1921. The tonnage ratio for capital ships was set at 5:5:3:1.75:1.75 for Britain, the United States, Japan, France, and Italy, respectively.

114. *Des Moines Register,* February 12, 1922.

115. *Des Moines Register,* August 14, 1924.

Notes to Chapter 5

1. See "The Des Moines Register and Tribune" (John Cowles Papers, Drake University, Des Moines, Iowa, April 13, 1949, typescript); and Special Report, Register and Tribune Company, 1925–1952 (David Kruidenier Papers, private collection held by David Kruidenier, Des Moines, Iowa), 14–15, 61.

2. Quoted in George Mills, *Harvey Ingham and Gardner Cowles, Sr.: Things Don't Just Happen* (Ames: Iowa State University Press, 1977), 85.

3. "Iowa Formula," *Time,* July 1, 1935, 29.

4. Gardner Cowles and wife Florence Call Cowles had six children, in descending order of age: Russell Cowles, who spent several years in the *Register*'s advertising department before leaving to pursue a successful career in painting; Helen Cowles LeCron, who edited the *Register*'s Sunday book section for a number of years; Bertha Cowles Quarton, whose husband, Sumner Quarton, once managed the Cowles radio station in Cedar Rapids; Florence Cowles Kruidenier, whose son David Kruidenier went on to be president and publisher of the R&T; and John and Mike Cowles, who took the R&T reins from their father.

5. "Iowa Formula," 26.

6. Ibid.; Biography of John Cowles, John Cowles Papers; Gardner Cowles, *Mike Looks Back: The Memoirs of Gardner Cowles, Founder of Look Magazine* (New York: Gardner Cowles, 1985), 23; *Editor and Publisher,* February 6, 1943, 32; Mills, *Harvey Ingham and Gardner Cowles, Sr.,* 89–90; and *New York Herald-Tribune,* April 16, 1961.

7. Cowles, *Mike Looks Back,* 7.

8. Ibid., 21.

9. See *Des Moines Register,* April 12, 1973, July 10, 1985, and Mills, *Harvey Ingham and Gardner Cowles, Sr.,* 103.

10. Quotation is taken from Cowles, *Mike Looks Back,* 41.

11. *New York Herald-Tribune,* April 16, 1961. See also Cowles, *Mike Looks Back,* 23; David Kruidenier, interview by author, July 20, 1992, Des Moines, Iowa; Kenneth MacDonald, interview by author, July 14, 1992, Des Moines, Iowa.

12. See Kruidenier, interview, July 20,1992; Morley Ballantine, interview by author,

October 10, 1992, Des Moines, Iowa; and Don Gussow, *Divorce Corporate Style* (New York: Ballantine Books, 1972), 294–95.

13. On Cowles's service on the RFC, see *Des Moines Tribune,* April 27, 1933.

14. See *Current Biography 1947* sketch on William Waymack, Iowa Journalists Clipping file, SHSI, Des Moines; *Des Moines Register,* November 6, 1960; *New Republic,* November 11, 1946, 621. When Ingham stepped aside as editor of the editorial page in favor of Waymack in 1931, he sold his R&T stock (3,375 shares) back to the company for $787,500. See Minutes of Special Stockholders' Meeting, June 1, 1931, in Minutes of Board of Directors Meetings, Register and Tribune Company, 1902–1933.

15. "The Des Moines Register and Tribune," employee publication, 1952, 3.

16. In 1937, for example, the Register and Tribune won "outstanding advertisement of the year" in the Des Moines Advertising Club's contest for its "The Three Commandments" advertisement. See Proposed Employee Pamphlet, 1938, John Cowles Papers.

17. Charles Whited, *Knight: A Publisher in a Tumultuous Century* (New York: E. P. Dutton, 1988), 119.

18. Ibid., and Raymond Moscowitz, *Stuffy: The Life of Basil "Stuffy" Walters* (Ames: Iowa State University Press, 1982), 33–51.

19. The nickname "Sec" came from Taylor's years serving as the secretary of the Wichita Western Association baseball franchise. Taylor was a highly regarded sports journalist, and he received many honors throughout his career. One of the most notable was having the Des Moines baseball park renamed Sec Taylor Stadium on September 1, 1959. For more on Taylor, see *Des Moines Tribune,* February 26, 1965; *Des Moines Register,* February 28, 1965; Leighton Housh, "First Person Pronoun" (SHSI, Des Moines, Iowa, 1981, typescript), 51–52. For early sports coverage, see Frank L. Mott, *American Journalism, A History: 1690–1960,* 3d ed. (New York: Macmillan, 1962), 443, 578–79.

20. Alfred M. Lee, *The Daily Newspaper in America: The Evolution of a Social Instrument* (New York: Macmillan, 1947), 463.

21. See *Des Moines Register,* September 27, 1925, February 28, April 11, 14, 1926; Cowles, *Mike Looks Back,* 43; and Mills, *Harvey Ingham and Gardner Cowles, Sr.,* 127–28.

22. Story about Cowles hiring Russell conditionally comes from Mills, *Harvey Ingham and Gardner Cowles, Sr.,* 125.

23. See *Des Moines Register,* January 20, 1926, January 1, 1936; Michael Emery and Edwin Emery, *The Press and America: An Interpretative History of the Mass Media,* 6th ed. (Englewood Cliffs, N.J.: Prentice Hall, 1988), 365; and William B. Ward, *Reporting Agriculture through Newspapers, Magazines, Radio, Television* (Ithaca, N.Y.: Comstock Publishing Associates, 1959), 29.

24. See *Des Moines Register,* March 31 and April 8, 1926.

25. For more on the purchase, see Agreement of Sale between the Register and Tribune Company and the Des Moines Capital Company, February 12, 1927, Kruidenier Papers; and *Des Moines Register,* February 13, 1927.

26. Emery and Emery, *Press and America,* 693 n.26.

27. Frank L. Mott, *The News in America* (Cambridge: Harvard University Press, 1952), 189; and Mills, *Harvey Ingham and Gardner Cowles, Sr.,* 77.

28. Advertising revenue rose from $2.1 million to $3.2 million. For circulation figures, advertising revenue, and net income, see Special Report, Register and Tribune Company, 1925–1952, 14–15, 61. Dividends had consistently been paid since 1906.

Year	R&T Dividends Paid
1925	$240,000
1926	$240,000
1927	$330,000
1928	$360,000

29. *Des Moines Register,* January 1, 1936.
30. As quoted in Susan J. Douglas, *Inventing American Broadcasting, 1899–1922* (Baltimore: Johns Hopkins University Press, 1987), 303.
31. See Erik Barnouw, *A Tower of Babel: A History of Broadcasting in the United States,* vol. 1 (New York; Oxford University Press, 1966), 33–34, 61–64, 98–99. The eleven newspapers owning radio stations by May 1922 were the *Detroit News,* WWJ; the *Chicago Daily News,* WGU; the *Rochester Times Union,* WHQ; the *Atlanta Journal,* WSB; the *St. Louis Post Dispatch,* KSD; the *Des Moines Register and Tribune,* WGF; the *Fort Worth Record,* WPA; the *Spokane Chronicle,* KOE; the *Los Angeles Examiner,* KWH; the *New Orleans Times Picayune,* WAAB; and the *Richmond Times Dispatch,* WBAZ. For more on newspaper's early involvement in radio, see Paul H. Wagner, "The Evolution of Newspaper Interest in Radio," *Journalism Quarterly* 23 (June 1946): 182–88.
32. See *Des Moines Tribune,* March 10 and 11, 1922; *Des Moines Register,* March 11, 1922; R&T employee magazine *The Spirit,* May 1972, 2–5; and Register and Tribune Newspaper Radio Clipping File.
33. See Barnouw, *Tower of Babel,* 104–14; and Proposed Employee Pamphlet, 1938, John Cowles Collection.
34. *Des Moines Tribune,* March 30, 1931.
35. See *Des Moines Register,* November 2, 5, and 6, 1932; "Register and Tribune Milestones" (David Kruidenier Papers, n.d., typescript); and Special Report, Register and Tribune Company, 1925–1952, 122. Iowa Broadcasting's net losses for its first three years of operation were as follows:

Year	Net Losses
1931	-$51,719
1932	-$49,281
1933	-$30,971

36. Des Moines already had KSO, the R&T's affiliate of NBC's blue network, and WHO, a radio station carrying the programs of NBC's red network. KRNT was affiliated with CBS. The FCC forced NBC to sell its blue network, which was purchased by Edward Noble and renamed the American Broadcasting Company (ABC) in 1945. On the radio networks, see Emery and Emery, *Press and America,* 315–16. See also Minutes of Special Meeting of the Board of Directors of The Register and Tribune Company, October 29, 1934, Kruidenier Papers.
37. See *Des Moines Register,* March 17, 1935; Luther L. Hill Jr., interview by author, February 4, 1993, Des Moines, Iowa; Luther Hill, interview by George Benneyan, transcript, September 17, 1959, Gardner Cowles Jr. Papers, Drake University, Des Moines, Iowa; Minutes of Meeting of the Stockholders of the Des Moines Register and Tribune Company, January 7, 1971; *Spirit,* May 1972, 5. Lister Hill served in Congress from 1923 to 1938 and in the Senate from 1938–1969. For more on Lister Hill, see Virginia Van der Veer Hamilton, *Lister Hill: Statesman from the South* (Chapel Hill: University of North Carolina Press, 1987).
38. Special Report, Register and Tribune Company, 1925–1952, 88, 122, 124. Iowa Broadcasting's net income follows:

Year	Net Income
1934	$10,917
1935	-$29,281
1936	$132,332
1937	$93,244
1938	$38,862
1939	$125,416

39. On Gallup, see Becky Wilson Hawbaker, "George Gallup, Iowa, and the Origin of the Gallup Poll," *Palimpsest* 74 (fall 1993) 98–113; and Max McElwain, *Profiles in Communication: The Hall of Fame of the University of Iowa School of Journalism and Mass Communication* (Iowa City: Iowa Center for Communication Study, 1991), 1–5.

40. Moscowitz, *Stuffy*, 40–43.

41. See Cowles, *Mike Looks Back*, 44; Hawbaker, "George Gallup," 106; Robert Desmond, *Windows on the World: The Information Process in a Changing World, 1900–1920* (Iowa City: University of Iowa Press, 1980), 527–28; and Special Report, Register and Tribune Company, 1925–1952, 61. In 1931, Gallup left Drake for Northwestern University. The following year, he was hired by advertising agency Young and Rubicam, and in 1935 he set up his American Institute of Public Opinion. From there, his career as a professional public opinion pollster took off.

42. *Des Moines Register*, January 4, 1930.

43. Moscowitz, *Stuffy*, 51–52.

44. Ibid. For some of the first machine-gun pictures, see *Des Moines Register*, September 29, 1935.

45. See *Des Moines Register*, March 30, 1994; William W. Waymack, "Good News," *Palimpsest* 11 (September 1930): 398–403; and Cowles, *Mike Looks Back*, 43–44.

46. *Des Moines Register*, January 1, 1935, January 1, 1936; Mott, *American Journalism*, 682; and Proposed Employee Pamphlet, 1938, John Cowles Papers.

47. See "Register and Tribune," John Cowles Papers; *Des Moines Register*, October 19, 1935; Lee, *Daily Newspaper in America*, 594–95; Special Report, Register and Tribune, 1925–1952, 17, 75; and Herbert Strentz, "John Cowles Sr." (1994, typescript), 2.

48. Moscowitz, *Stuffy*, p. 50.

49. Circulation for the Sunday *Register* dropped from 217,418 in March 1932 to 208,122 one year later. Circulation figures are from "Register and Tribune," John Cowles Papers.

50. *Des Moines Register*, September 19, 1933.

51. *Des Moines Register*, January 19, 1981.

52. McElwain, *Profiles in Communication*, 43–49.

53. Ibid. Circulation figures are from "Register and Tribune," John Cowles Papers. Circulation rose from 208,122 in March 1933 to 235,645 by March 1934. See also Special Report, Register and Tribune, 1925–1952, 26.

54. See Dorothy Schwieder, *Iowa: The Middle Land* (Ames: Iowa State University Press, 1996),256, 266.

55. See Ibid., and *Des Moines Tribune*, April 26, 1929.

56. Frank W. Rucker, *Newspaper Circulation: What, Where and How* (Ames: Iowa State University Press, 1958), 46–47.

57. On the origin of the farm division and the weekly pay system, see interview with J. Robert Hudson, September 15, 1992. See also Special Report, Register and Tribune, 1925–1952, 125. Although circulation figures by division are not available until 1936, circulation of the farm service division from 1936 to 1940 doubled, moving up from 15,510 to 30,705.

58. See MacDonald, interviews, July 14, 1992, June 17, 1995; and J. Robert Hudson, interview by author, September 15, 1992, West Des Moines, Iowa. Iowa Film Delivery Service was founded in 1932. See *Polk's Des Moines City Directory, 1933* (Des Moines: R. L. Polk and Company, 1932), 423.

59. Rucker, *Newspaper Circulation*, 79–109; and *Des Moines Register*, May 24, 1919.

60. See, for instance, the *Des Moines Register*, June 11 and 12, 1934. See also Special Report, Register and Tribune, 1925–1952, 125.

61. Emery and Emery, *Press and America*, 347.

62. See Mott, *American Journalism*, 675-676; Leland Sage, *A History of Iowa* (Ames: Iowa State University Press, 1974), 310–11; and Special Report, Register and Tribune,

1925–1952, 61. From 1930 to 1940, Iowa's population grew from 2.47 million to 2.54 million.

	Circulation		
Year	Daily Register	Tribune	Sunday Register
1930	127,447	117,929	212,072
1939	172,366	144,810	368,487

63. In 1933, for example, even in the midst of advertising cutbacks, advertising revenue still made up 61 percent of newspaper revenue nationally. That year, advertising revenue accounted for 54 percent of R&T revenue. See Lee, *Daily Newspaper in America,* 749; and Special Report, Register and Tribune, 1925–1952, 18.

64. Schwieder, *Iowa: The Middle Land,* 272.

65. Salaries for 1934 were reported in the *Des Moines Register,* January 8, 1936. The top salary in Iowa that year was $52,000. Register and Tribune Company dividends were as follows:

Year	Total Dividend	Dividend Per Share	Percent of Dividends to Profits
1925	$240,000	$4.80	49.6
1926	240,000	4.80	49.0
1927	330,000	6.00	50.7
1928	360,000	6.00	39.2
1929	420,000	7.00	37.1
1930	420,000	7.00	41.2
1931	420,000	7.00	54.0
1932	300,000	5.00	63.8
1933	553,888	9.50	82.0
1934	659,920	11.00	90.2
1935	720,000	12.00	80.4
1936	900,000	15.00	80.8
1937	900,000	15.00	82.6
1938	600,000	10.00	72.5
1939	720,000	12.00	77.2

Although these dividends were sometimes paid in company shares and not cash, they still provided the brothers a sizable amount of money. In 1931, for instance, John Cowles held 2,900 shares of R&T stock, while Mike owned 3,000. See Minutes of Special Meeting of the Stockholders of the Register and Tribune Company, June 1, 1931.

66. See Paul P. Posel, "The End of Newspaper Competition in Minneapolis, 1935–1941," (master's thesis, University of Minnesota, 1964), 17–18, 106; and James A. Alcott, *A History of Cowles Media* (Minneapolis Cowles Media Company, 1998), 10–11.

67. For more on the purchase of the *Star* and the reorganization that took place soon thereafter, see Agreement between John Cowles and the owners of the Minneapolis Daily Star Company, June 12, 1935; Contract between John Cowles and the Register and Tribune Company, August 1, 1935; and Contract between John Cowles and Gardner Cowles Jr., September 2, 1935, all in Kruidenier Papers. See also James A. Alcott, *A History of Cowles Media,* 9–10.

68. "Cowles Boys," 53.

69. See Cowles, *Mike Looks Back,* 24; J. Edward Gerald notes of interview with John Cowles, October 16, 1961, John Cowles Papers; and Gardner Cowles to John and Mike Cowles, June 15, 1937, Kruidenier Papers.

70. See all sources in note 69; Posel, "End of Competition," 106–16; and Moscowitz, *Stuffy,* 54–71.

71. Posel, "End of Competition," 81–91, 131; and Moscowitz, *Stuffy,* 54–71.

72. See Posel, "End of Competition," 106. The *Star*'s circulation of 150,100 compared favorably to the *Journal*'s at 135,300 and the *Tribune*'s at 148,100.

73. The Register and Tribune agreed to purchase 73,200 Star shares (at $10.70 per share) from John and Mike Cowles. Very little money initially changed hands, however. At the signing of the contract, the R&T paid John and Mike $22,807.60, or roughly $.31 per share, leaving a balance of $760,432.40. A 5 percent interest charge was to be added semiannually to all Register advances to the Star. The unpaid balance was then to be paid only "at the end of any fiscal year when the Star has had ... enough net earnings after all taxes so that the Register and Tribune's share of those earnings, based upon its proportionate stock interest in the Star ... has been sufficient to make up any previously unearned accumulation. At 5 percent compounded semiannually upon the Register and Tribune total investment. ... At the end of any such fiscal year, the Register and Tribune shall pay the Cowles group [John and Mike] an amount equal to two-thirds of the excess net earnings." By November 12, 1940, the R&T paid the remaining money owed John and Mike. See Contract between John Cowles and Gardner Cowles Jr., and the Register and Tribune Company, August 23, 1938; Minutes of Special Meeting of the Board of Directors, Register and Tribune Company, August 23, 1938; and Contract between John Cowles and Gardner Cowles Jr., and the Register and Tribune Company, November 12, 1940, all in Kruidenier Papers. For information on the R&T's divestiture of its Minneapolis common stock, see Minutes of Register and Tribune Board of Directors Meetings, November 12, 1940, December 26, 1940, and March 17, 1941.

74. See Contract of Sale between the Minneapolis Star Company and the Journal Printing Company, July 31, 1939, Kruidenier Papers.

75. See Contract of Sale between the Minneapolis Star Journal Company and the Minnesota Tribune Company, April 29, 1941, Kruidenier Papers.

76. "The Prudent Publishers," *Fortune,* August 1950, 87.

77. *Editor and Publisher,* February 13, 1943, 7, as quoted in Posel, "End of Competition" 126–27.

78. Net earnings are taken from Alcott, *History of Cowles Media,* 236. Carl Koester, R&T business manager, remembered that the first month after the merger, the new company made a profit of $92,000. See Carl Koester memorandum to Gardner (Mike) Cowles, May 10, 1979, Harry Watts Papers, held by Harry Watts, Des Moines, Iowa.

79. As quoted in Mott, *News in America,* 192.

80. Ernest C. Hynds, *American Newspapers in the 1980s* (New York: Hastings House, 1980), 313–14.

81. See Luther Hill, interview, 3–4; and Opal Wilson, interview by George Benneyan, transcript, September 17, 1959, 23–24, Gardner Cowles Jr. Papers.

82. Hill, interview, 12–13; Wilson, interview, 17–18.

83. On the origins of both *Look* and *Life,* see James L. Baughman, *Henry R. Luce and the Rise of the American News Media* (Boston: Twayne Publishers, 1987), 82–102; and John W. Tebbel and Mary Ellen Zuckerman, *The Magazine in America* (New York: Oxford University Press, 1991), 227–39.

84. See Cowles, *Mike Looks Back,* 60; Hill, interview, 5–6.

85. Baughman, *Henry R. Luce,* 93; Cowles, *Mike Looks Back,* 62–63; Minutes of the Annual Meeting of the Stockholders of the Register and Tribune Company, January 4, 1937, January 18, 1938; and Cowles Communications, Inc., *Records of the Look Years* (New York: Cowles Communications, Inc., 1973), 74–80.

86. Cowles, *Mike Looks Back,* 62–63; and Cowles Communications, *Look Years,* 29, 74–80.

87. *Des Moines Register,* August 24, 1929.

88. As quoted in Earle D. Ross, *Iowa Agriculture: An Historical Survey* (Iowa City: State Historical Society of Iowa, 1951), 153.

89. *Des Moines Register,* January 27, 1927. On earlier, temporary efforts to deal with the farm problem, see Ross, *Iowa Agriculture,* 148–56.

90. Hoover called for the veto because the legislation lacked any attempt to control production. See explanation of the McNary-Haugen bill in W. Elliot Brownlee, *Dynamics of Ascent: A History of the American Economy* (Chicago: Dorsey Press, 1988), 396–98. For the *Register*'s reaction to the second veto, see *Des Moines Register,* February 26 and 27, 1927. Wallace quotation comes from *Des Moines Register,* May 24, 1928, as quoted in Mary C. Wichman, "Responses of Iowa Farm Organizations to the New Deal's Agricultural Adjustment Act" (master's thesis, Catholic University of America, July 1968), 9.

91. *Des Moines Register,* January 11, 1930.

92. Mills, *Harvey Ingham and Gardner Cowles, Sr.,* 147.

93. *Des Moines Register* as quoted in Mills, *Harvey Ingham and Gardner Cowles, Sr.,* 148.

94. On Miles Reno and the Farmers Holiday Association, see Sage, *History of Iowa,* 273–74, 277–78, 281–82; John Stover, *Corn Belt Rebellion: The Farmers Holiday Association* (Urbana: University of Illinois Press, 1965); and Roland White, *Miles Reno: Farmers' Union Pioneer* (Iowa City, Iowa: Athens Press, 1940). On Hoover's speech, see *Des Moines Register,* October 5, 1932.

95. *Des Moines Register,* January 11, 1930, November 8, 1932.

96. On Hoover's foreign policy, see Alexander DeConde, *Herbert Hoover's Latin American Policy* (Stanford, Calif.: Stanford University Press, 1951); Robert H. Ferrell, *American Foreign Policy in the Great Depression* (New Haven, Conn.: Yale University Press, 1957); and Armin Rappaport, *Henry L. Stimson and Japan* (Chicago: University of Chicago Press, 1963).

97. On the *Register*'s endorsement of Hoover in the election of 1932, see *Des Moines Register,* November 2, 7, and 11, 1932. For the lack of editorial support for FDR in the 1932 election, see Betty H. Winfield, *FDR and the News Media* (New York: Columbia University Press, 1994), 127. For the *Register*'s early support of President Roosevelt, see, for instance, *Des Moines Register,* March 9, 1933.

98. *Des Moines Register,* March 18, 1933.

99. See *Des Moines Register,* May 11 and 13, 1933.

100. *Des Moines Register,* May 16, 1933.

101. *Omaha World-Herald,* May 19, 1933, and *Kansas City Star,* May 23, 1933, as quoted in James B. Beddow, "Midwestern Editorial Response to the New Deal, 1932–1940," *South Dakota History* 4 (winter 1973): 4–5.

102. See *Des Moines Register,* June 6, 1933; April 8, 1934; and May 28, 1935.

103. *Omaha World-Herald,* May 28, 1935, and *Kansas City Star,* May 28, 1935, as quoted in Beddow, "Midwestern Editorial Response," 4–5.

104. *Des Moines Register,* April 24, 1934.

105. *Des Moines Register,* January 7, 1936.

106. See, for instance, *Des Moines Register,* November 3, 1936.

107. Winfield, *FDR and the News Media,* 127–29.

108. Phrase is taken from Robert Divine et al., *America Past and Present* (New York: Harper Collins, 1995), 823.

109. *Des Moines Register,* January 30, 1935.

110. *Des Moines Register,* October 3, 1935.

111. *Des Moines Register,* October 5, 1935.

112. The Neutrality Act of 1936 added a ban on loans to belligerents, and the following year, another piece of legislation added that all trade with belligerents, exclusive of munitions, be conducted on a cash-and-carry basis. For more on FDR and the coming

of World War II, see Robert Dallek, *Franklin D. Roosevelt and American Foreign Policy* (New York: Oxford University Press, 1979).

113. *Des Moines Register,* October 7 and 8, 1937.

114. *Des Moines Register,* September 3, 1939.

115. *Des Moines Register,* October 24, November 3, 1939.

Notes to Chapter 6

1. William N. Burkhardt to Forrest Geneva, May 15, 1940, John Cowles Papers, Drake University, Des Moines, Iowa.

2. "Twenty-four Year Report, Register and Tribune Company, 1940–1963" (David Kruidenier Papers, held by David Kruidenier, Des Moines, Iowa), 77; "The Des Moines Register and Tribune" (John Cowles Papers, April 13, 1949, typescript). The nine other cities that had Sunday newspaper circulations larger than Des Moines were New York, Chicago, Philadelphia, Boston, Los Angeles, San Francisco, Minneapolis, Pittsburgh, and Detroit. See also William Peterson, *The Story of Iowa,* vol. 2 (New York: Lewis Historical Publishing, 1952), 657. For a comparison of city size, see *Statistical Abstract of the United States, 1952* (Washington, D.C.: United States Government Printing Office), 18–21.

3. "Twenty-four Year Report," 25.

4. "The Cowles Boys," *Newsweek,* July 4, 1949, 53.

5. Herbert Strentz, "Compatriots: Wendell Willkie, the Press, the Cowles Brothers, An Introductory survey, including Willkie's 'One World' trip with Publisher Gardner (Mike) Cowles" (paper presented at meeting of the Newspaper Division of the Association for the Education in Journalism and Mass Communication, Portland, Ore., July 1988), 12–17.

6. "John Cowles," *Current Biography 1954* (New York: H. W. Wilson, 1954), 214; John Cowles, interview by J. Edward Gerald, May 21, 1963, John Cowles Papers.

7. Strentz, "Compatriots," 29–33. See also Wendell L. Willkie, *One World* (New York: Simon and Schuster, 1943).

8. On the OWI in general, see Allan M. Winkler, *The Politics of Propaganda: The Office of War Information, 1942–1945* (New Haven, Conn.: Yale University Press, 1978). On the president's personal appeal to Mike to take the job, see Cowles Communications, Inc., *Records of the Look Years* (New York: Cowles Communications, Inc., 1973), 30.

9. John Cowles to Russell Cowles, December 16, 1942, John Cowles Papers.

10. See John Cowles to Mother and Dad [Gardner and Florence Cowles], October 12, 1942, John Cowles Papers.

11. See John Cowles to Mother and Dad, December 12, 1942, John Cowles Papers; and "John Cowles," 214.

12. Mike Cowles expressed concern about the increasing tax burden at the annual stockholders meeting in 1944. See Minutes of the Annual Register and Tribune Stockholders Meeting, January 18, 1944.

13. John Cowles to Dad, September 23, 1942, John Cowles Papers. For circulation figures, taxes paid, and newsprint costs, see "Twenty-four Year Report."

14. One day in 1943, for instance, space limitations forced the *New York Times* to delete 51 columns of advertising. Two years later, the *New Orleans Item* was so squeezed for space, it carried no advertising for a week. See Frank L. Mott, *American Journalism, A History: 1690–1960,* 3d ed. (New York: Macmillan, 1962), 783; and Richard Kluger, *The Paper: The Life and Death of the New York Herald Tribune* (New York: Vintage, 1986),357–58.

15. See Minutes of the Annual Register and Tribune Stockholders Meeting, January 18, 1944.

16. The following is a space and content analysis of the morning *Register,* the evening *Tribune,* and the *Sunday Register.*

Year	Register			Tribune			Sunday Register		
		Percent of Content			Percent of Content			Percent of Content	
	Pages	Adv.+	News	Pages	Adv.	News	Pages*	Adv.	News
1940	5,846	29.21	70.79	6,602	37.07	62.93	2,556	29.27	70.73
1941	5,832	29.94	70.06	6,580	36.78	63.22	2,484	28.88	71.12
1942	5,330	31.44	68.56	6,086	36.13	63.87	2,326	28.97	71.03
1943	5,190	36.85	63.15	5,924	40.13	59.87	2,288	35.04	64.96
1944	4,648	38.83	61.17	5,312	41.78	58.22	1,972	40.56	59.44
1945	4,722	36.01	63.99	5,138	41.06	58.94	1,988	40.27	59.73

*Does not include Sunday color comic or magazine sections; + = Advertising.
Source: "Twenty-four Year Report."

Combined advertising linage for the war years follows:

Year	Total Advertising Linage	Increase or Decrease from Previous Year
1940	13,126,895	
1941	12,982,888	-144,007
1942	12,062,077	-920,811
1943	13,530,934	+1,468,857
1944	13,122,670	-408,264
1945	12,733,197	-389,473

Source: "Twenty-four Year Report," 49, 116–21.

17. Gardner [Mike] Cowles to John Cowles, March 2, 1942, John Cowles Papers.
18. Circulation rates varied depending on where and how the paper was delivered. Weekly rates for the war years follow by category:

	City Circulation	Carrier Outside of Des Moines			Farm Service		
	Morn., Eve., Sun.	Morn.	Eve.	Sun.	Morn.	Eve.	Sun.
1940	$.30	$.20	$.20	$.10	$.13	$.13	$.13
1941	NA	NA	NA	NA	$.15	$.15	$.13
1942	$.35	NA	NA	NA	NA	NA	NA
1943	$.40	$.20	$.20	$.12	$.17	$.17	$.15
1944	NA	$.23	$.20	$.12	NA	NA	NA

Source: "Twenty-four Year Report," 81.

19. Malcolm W. Browne, reviews of *Reporting World War II,* 2 vols. (no credited author) and *Typewriter Battalion,* by Jack Stenbuck, ed., *New York Times Book Review,* August 27, 1995, 22.
20. For more on Ernie Pyle, see Lee G. Miller, *The Story of Ernie Pyle* (New York: Viking, 1950); and three works by the correspondent himself: Ernie Pyle, *Brave Men* (New York: Henry Holt, 1944); *Here is Your War* (New York: Henry Holt, 1943); and *Last Chapter* (New York: Henry Holt, 1946).
21. *Des Moines Register,* October 8, 1943.
22. Andrea Clardy, ed., *Gordon Gammack: Columns from Three Wars* (Ames: Iowa State University Press, 1979), 3. See any number of Gammack's war columns in either the

Register or the *Tribune.*

23. See John Cowles memorandum, December 15, 1949, and "Des Moines Register and Tribune," John Cowles Papers.

24. John Cowles memorandum, December 15, 1949. In dollar amounts, the portions each Cowles company contributed to cover the costs of Eastern Enterprises in 1949 were:

Minneapolis Papers	$ 58,000
R&T	44,000
Look	40,000
Radio Stations	
(WOL, WCOP, WNAX, and KRNT, $500 each)	2,000
Total Expenses of Eastern Enterprises (1949)	$ 144,000

25. Glenn Roberts, interview by author, Des Moines, Iowa, June 8, 1993.

26. John Cowles to Mom and Dad, December 17, 1943, as quoted in *Des Moines Register,* December 19, 1993. John Cowles obviously felt public opinion surveys were important; in 1944 , he introduced a poll in the Minneapolis paper modeled after the Iowa Poll.

27. For the creation of the Iowa Poll, see Glenn Roberts, "The Iowa Poll: Des Moines Register and Tribune" (1947, typescript), 24–26, and Roberts, interview. The advisory committee consisted of a diverse group including a banker, two bishops (one Catholic and one Methodist), a rabbi, a college president, a *Register* editor, a farm leader, a labor union leader, a president of a manufacturing company, a public school superintendent, and a brigadier general. After the poll was up and running, the advisory committee was disbanded.

28. *Des Moines Register,* December 19, 1943.

29. For a listing of general subjects covered by the Iowa Poll from 1943 to 1947, see Roberts, "Iowa Poll," appendix.

30. As quoted in Roberts, "Iowa Poll," 10.

31. Ibid., 4–5.

32. Ibid., 7.

33. MacDonald is quoted in the *Des Moines Register,* December 19, 1993.

34. James L. Baughman, *The Republic of Mass Culture* (Baltimore: Johns Hopkins University Press, 1992), 16.

35. Harvey J. Levin, *Broadcast Regulation and Joint Ownership of Media* (New York: New York University Press, 1960), 42–43.

36. Special Report, Register and Tribune Company, 1925–1952, 79, 122.

37. See "Dynasty in Radio," *Business Week,* November 4, 1944, 81–83.

38. On the sale of KSO, see J. B. Faegre to Gardner Cowles Jr., May 2, 1944; John Cowles to Mike Cowles, May 2, 1944; John Cowles to Iowa-Des Moines National Bank, May 2, 1944; all in John Cowles Papers; Minutes of a Special Meeting of the Board of Directors of the Register and Tribune Company, May 3, 1944, Kruidenier Papers; and *Des Moines Register,* May 4, 1944.

39. See " 'Bulletin' Buys WPEN; Cowles in New York," *Broadcasting,* May 22, 1944, 7; and Minutes of Special Meeting of the Board of Directors of the Register and Tribune Company, May 5, 1944.

40. See "Comdr. Craven to Join Cowles' Station," *Broadcasting,* May 22, 1944, 7.

41. See Minutes of a Special Meeting of the Board of Directors of the Register and Tribune Company, May 29, 1944; and *Broadcasting,* June 5, 1944, John Cowles Papers. Bulova was required to sell his company's interest in WCOP because his general manager was the licensee of another Boston radio station, and the FCC regulation covers management as well as ownership in the same markets.

42. This issue is discussed in a Mike Cowles memo sent to John Cowles, Jim Milloy, and T. A. M. Craven, May 10, 1944, John Cowles Papers.

43. Ibid.

44. T. A. M. Craven to Mike Cowles, John Cowles, and Jim Milloy, May 15, 1944, John Cowles Papers.

45. For more on the station trade, see Minutes of a Special Meeting of the Board of Directors of the Register and Tribune Company, July 6, 1944; and T.A.M. Craven to Gardner Cowles Jr., September 29, 1944, John Cowles Papers. For station expansion and capital outlays, see Minutes of a Special Meeting of the Board of Directors of the Register and Tribune Company, May 28, 1945; Minutes of a Special Meeting of the Board of Directors of Cowles Broadcasting Company, December 2, 1947; John Cowles Papers; and "Twenty-four Year Report," 101.

46. The decisions to sell WHOM and drop plans for a regional East Coast network are discussed in John Cowles memo, April 7, 1945; and Jack Harding to Vincent Starzinger, November 8, 1946, John Cowles Papers. Cowles Broadcasting sold the station to Generoso Pope and family for $450,000. It had purchased the station two years earlier for $350,000 plus an additional $64,000 to take over station debts. Considering the expenditures for improvements already made at the station, CBC did not make any profit on the sale of WHOM.

47. Gardner Cowles to Luther Hill, Vincent Starzinger, Arthur Gormley, and Carl Koester, November 1, 1946, John Cowles Papers.

48. See Cowles Broadcasting Company, Profit and Loss Statements, 1947 to 1950, John Cowles Papers.

49. Gardner Cowles Jr. to Smith Davis, March 29, 1948, John Cowles Papers.

50. On the selling of WOL, see Luther Hill to Gardner Cowles Jr., December 7, 1949, and January 26, 1950; and Carl Koester to Gardner Cowles Jr., May 20, 1950, John Cowles Papers. For the sale of WCOP, see Carl Koester memo regarding the disposition of WCOP, July 18, 1951; Luther Hill to Gardner Cowles Jr. and John Cowles, October 20, 1951, John Cowles Papers. In 1944, Cowles Broadcasting paid $275,000 for WCOP, and John and Mike Cowles paid in an additional $14,000 for stock. The station was sold for $200,000 on December 22, 1951.

51. Minutes of a Special Meeting of the Board of Directors of Cowles Broadcasting Company, December 2, 1947, John Cowles Papers.

52. Minutes of Annual Stockholders Meeting, Register and Tribune Company, January 29, 1947.

53. Waymack had been pulling double duty as both editor of the paper and editor of the editorial pages. When he resigned, the position of editor was not immediately filled. The functions of the editor were fulfilled by MacDonald in the newly created position of executive editor. In 1953, MacDonald was finally given the title of editor. See "Twenty-four Year Report," 159; and MacDonald, interview by author, Des Moines, Iowa, July 14, 1992.

54. On Mike Cowles' move to New York, see "Look Homeward," *Newsweek,* December 9, 1946, 71–72, and "Look, No Fringe," *Time,* December 9, 1946, 47. On the R&T's growing financial stake in CMI, see "Twenty-four Year Report," 102. In 1953, Mike Cowles bought back $914,515 worth of CMI stock from the R&T and decreased the newspaper's investment to $571,767. At the same time, he sold $1,200,000 of Minneapolis Star and Tribune stock to the R&T, which increased the company's holdings of Minneapolis Star and Tribune stock to $1,575,000. On these transactions, see Minutes of the Annual Meeting of the Stockholders of the Register and Tribune Company, January 3, 1949; and Minutes of a Special Meeting of the Board of Directors of the Register and Tribune Company, April 29, 1953. By 1957, the R&T interest in CMI decreased to only $84,549; see "Twenty-four Year Report," 102.

55. On Mike Cowles' frequent trips and phone calls to Des Moines, see his Office

Diaries, 1947–1959, Gardner Cowles Jr. Papers, Drake University, Des Moines, Iowa. Much like MacDonald and the position of executive editor, Hill was named to the newly created position of general manager (GM), but he was, in essence, filling the job of publisher. After serving as GM for three years, Hill was named R&T publisher in 1950.

56. See *Des Moines Tribune,* March 1, 1946; Minutes of the Annual Stockholders of the Register and Tribune Meeting, January 29, 1947. Hickenlooper's comments are part of a collection of tributes, eulogies, and editorials regarding Gardner Cowles Sr. They are gathered together in *Gardner Cowles, 1861–1946* (Des Moines, Iowa: Des Moines Register and Tribune Company, 1946).

57. *Des Moines Register,* November, 2, 1946.

58. See Minutes of a Special Meeting of the Board of Directors of the Register and Tribune Company, November 4, 1946.

59. Waymack's tribute was in the *Des Moines Register,* August 22, 1949; the farewell editorial appeared the following day.

60. Max McElwain, *Profiles in Communication: The Hall of Fame of the University of Iowa School of Journalism and Mass Communication* (Iowa City: Iowa Center for Communication Study, 1991), 57. See also MacDonald, interview, July 14, 1992.

61. Quotation is from McElwain, *Profiles in Communication,* 43. For a listing of *Register* Pulitzer Prizes, see "History of the Des Moines Register Past Publishers and Presidents" (Register and Tribune Company, Des Moines, Iowa, n.d., typescript; in possession of author).

62. *Des Moines Register,* February 10, 1955.

63. As quoted in Harold Lee, *Roswell Garst: A Biography* (Ames: Iowa State University Press, 1984), 179.

64. As part of the American delegation to tour Russian farms, Soth sent dispatches home, which were printed in the *Register.* See, for instance, *Des Moines Register,* August 14, 16, 1955.

65. For more on the exchange, see Lee, *Roswell Garst,* 174–185, and Lauren Soth, interview by author, West Des Moines, Iowa, October 20, 1992. The quotation is from Luther Hill to John Cowles, July 19, 1955, John Cowles Papers. For contemporary accounts of the Russians' visit to Iowa, see "Soviets Eye Iowa's Ears," *Life,* August 1, 1955, 30–32; "Covering the 'Red Farmers' ... Our Lush Midland Mightily Impresses Them," *Newsweek,* August 1, 1955, 26–27; and "What the Russians Saw and What They Learned," *U.S. News and World Report,* July 29, 1955, 38–42. Khrushchev's Iowa visit is recounted in the *Des Moines Register,* February 5, 1995.

66. Quotation is taken from *Des Moines Register,* May 31, 1970; see also *Des Moines Register,* July 10, 1977. Mollenhoff's prize-winning reporting ran in the *Register* in September 1957. For a sketch on Mollenhoff, see John C. Behrens, *The Typewriter Guerrillas: Closeups of 20 Top Investigative Reporters* (Chicago: Nelson Hall, 1977), 155–66.

67. See Ernie Schwartz to John Cowles, September 16, 1954; A. T. Gormley to John Cowles, September 30, 1954, and accompanying circulation maps, March 1954, John Cowles Papers.

68. John Cowles to Luther Hill, January 25, 1957, John Cowles Papers; and circulation figures in "Twenty-four Year Report," 77–78.

Circulation, 1950–1959

Year	Register	Tribune	Sunday Register
1950	228,300	152,400	546,300
1951	231,900	151,000	553,000
1952	226,900	145,900	529,800
1953	227,800	144,800	539,000
1954	229,000	141,800	535,300
1955	226,200	137,300	528,200
1956	226,300	137,100	525,000

Circulation, 1950–1959 continued			
Year	Register	Tribune	Sunday Register
1957	220,400	128,700	517,200
1958	223,700	130,400	522,900
1959	228,600	129,700	526,200

69. Baughman, *Republic of Mass Culture,* 59.

70. See "Twenty-four Year Report," 25–28, 31–32, 37. William Dwight's statement was originally published in *Editor and Publisher,* April 26, 1958, 13, and is quoted from Elizabeth MacIver Neiva, "Chain Building: The Consolidation of the American Newspaper Industry, 1953–1980," *Business History Review* 70 (spring 1996): 19.

71. John Cowles' many letters to Luther Hill and Mike Cowles's frequent visits to Des Moines strongly suggest that the brothers were still trying to run the operation in Des Moines. Mike's office diaries offer evidence that he was in Des Moines at least monthly through most of the decade. See Gardner Cowles Jr. office diaries, Gardner Cowles Jr. Papers.

72. Minutes of the Annual Stockholders Meeting of the Register and Tribune Company, January 9, 1953. Net profits for the period were as follows:

Year	Total Net Profit	Net Advertising/ Circulation Revenue	Newspaper Operating Profit (After Taxes)	Profit Margin on Newspaper Operations (Percent)
1946	$1,143,587	$ 8,845,855	$ 890,259	10.1
1947	1,035,991	10,947,141	1,143,061	10.4
1948	1,589,555	12,559,028	1,108,377	8.8
1949	1,416,983	13,184,472	1,046,412	7.9
1950	1,450,168	14,005,325	994,792	7.1
1951	1,274,700	14,670,702	803,950	5.5
1952	1,049,522	15,371,717	710,312	4.6
1953	1,172,739	16,040,673	1,067,235	6.7
1954	1,162,888	15,861,379	680,449	4.3
1955	1,356,611	16,892,819	99,243	5.9

Source: "Twenty-four Year Report," 26–27.

73. Baughman, *Republic of Mass Culture,* 60.

74. Minutes of a Special Meeting of the Board of Directors of Cowles Broadcasting Company, December 2, 1947; John Cowles Papers.

75. KVTV went on the air in July 1953. This station, along with radio property WNAX (Yankton, South Dakota) were sold to Peoples Broadcasting Company, a subsidiary of Nationwide Mutual Insurance, in December 1957 for $3 million. Cowles Broadcasting wished to use the money to update and expand its holdings in Des Moines and the Huntington, West Virginia, property, WHTN-AM-FM-TV, it purchased in August 1956. Cowles Broadcasting owned 60 percent of KRNT-TV; the remaining 40 percent was owned by Murphy Broadcasting. In 1959, CBC acquired the Murphy share of KRNT-TV. On KVTV and its sale, see Luther Hill to John Cowles, October 3, 1957; Luther Hill to Mike Cowles, January 7, 1958, John Cowles Papers; and *Broadcasting,* November 4, 1957. See also "Twenty-four Year Report," 150.

76. Quotation on FCC policy is from Levin, *Broadcast Regulation,* 173. For the spin-off of CBC, see, Vincent Starzinger to Mike Cowles, October 10, 1955, John Cowles Papers; Minutes of a Special Meeting of the Board of Directors of The Register and Tribune Company, October 31, 1955; and Minutes of a Special Meeting of the Stockholders of The Register and Tribune Company, December 12, 1955.

77. Mott, *American Journalism,* 824.

78. See "Twenty-four Year Report," 13.

79. Leo Bogart, *Preserving the Press: How Daily Newspapers Mobilized to Keep Their Readers* (New York: Columbia University Press, 1991), 26.

80. The five shoppers consisted of:

> *South Des Moines Shopper,* converted from a newspaper to a shopper in 1956, served south Des Moines and the small towns of Norwalk and Cumming (both immediately south of Des Moines).
>
> *Week End Shopper,* begun in 1956, was distributed in the northwest section of the city.
>
> *Westside Shopper,* started in 1957, circulated in the western sections of the city.
>
> *Highland Park Shopper,* founded in 1954, served northern parts of the city.
>
> *Lee Town Shopper,* created in 1958, covered eastern Des Moines.

See "Twenty-four Year Report," 12.

81. See Special Report, R&T, 1925–1952, 15; and "Twenty-four Year Report," 26.

82. John Cowles to Luther Hill, January 25, 1957, John Cowles Papers.

83. On the idea that Hill should retire, see Mike Cowles to John Cowles, February 14, 1957, John Cowles Papers. Unfortunately, there is nothing more specific in the Cowles papers regarding the brothers' feelings about Hill and his performance. The John Cowles Papers do, however, contain hundreds of letters from John Cowles to Luther Hill expressing concerns about various costs and rising expenses. See, for instance, John Cowles to Luther Hill, September 22, 1950; June 18, December 3, 1952; January 25, October 21, 1957, John Cowles Papers. For information on Kruidenier starting at R&T and being promoted, see "Twenty-four Year Report," 158–59; and Kruidenier, interview, July 20, 1992.

84. On Kruidenier, see Kruidenier, interview, July 20, 1992. For comment on Kruidenier's work, see Luther Hill to Mike Cowles, February 18, 1957, John Cowles Papers.

85. See Remarks at Des Moines Register and Tribune Company Stockholders' Meeting, January 25, 1958, John Cowles Papers.

86. Register and Tribune financial performance for 1956–1959 was as follows:

Year	Total Net Profit	Net Advertising/ Circulation Revenue	Newspaper Operating Profit (After Taxes)	Profit Margin on Newspaper Operations (Percent)
1956	$1,084,055	$17,173,825	$ 640,159	3.7
1957	1,340,988	17,644,267	951,194	5.4
1958	1,356,722	17,910,988	1,005,674	5.6
1959	1,666,202	18,936,402	1,207,445	6.4

On the consolidation of the newspaper industry and the growing number of chains, see Leo Bogart, *Press and Public: Who Reads What, When, Where, and Why in American Newspapers* (Hillsdale, N.J.: Lawrence Erlbaum Associates, 1989), 356; and Mott, *American Journalism,* 813–17.

87. John Cowles to Luther Hill, November 4, 1957, John Cowles Papers.

88. John Cowles memo to Mike Cowles and Luther Hill, November 2, 1959, John Cowles Papers.

89. See William L. O'Neill, *American High: The Years of Confidence, 1945–1960* (New York: Free Press, 1986), 94; and *Des Moines Register,* February 4, 1948.

90. This first editorial in a series of studies of the status of civil rights appeared in the

Des Moines Register, August 15, 1948. Succeeding pieces appeared on March 27, April 11, April 28, and September 25, 1949.

91. See *Des Moines Register,* October 8, 1948. The following year, one of the defendants brought a $10,000 civil damage suit against Katz because she had been denied service at the fountain. An all-white jury agreed with her argument but awarded her only $1. See *Des Moines Register,* October 12, 15, 1949.

92. On Truman and the Fair Deal, see Alonzo L. Hamby, *Beyond the New Deal: Harry S. Truman and American Liberalism* (New York: Columbia University Press, 1973), and *Man of the People: A Life of Harry S. Truman* (New York: Oxford University Press, 1995); and David G. McCullough, *Truman* (New York: Simon and Schuster, 1992). On Truman and civil rights, see William C. Berman, *The Politics of Civil Rights in the Truman Administration* (Columbus: Ohio State University Press, 1970) and Donald R. McCoy and Richard T. Ruetten, *Quest and Response: Minority Rights and the Truman Administration* (Lawrence: University Press of Kansas, 1973). For the *Register*'s response, see *Des Moines Register,* January 6, 1949, and January 7, 1951.

93. *Des Moines Register,* May 18, 1954. For more on *Brown* v. *Board of Education,* see Richard Kluger, *Simple Justice: The History of Brown v. Board of Education: Black America's Struggle for Equality* (New York: Alfred A. Knopf, 1976).

94. See Harvard Sitkoff, *The Struggle for Black Equality* (New York: Hill and Wang, 1993), 23; and *Des Moines Register,* June 1, 1955.

95. *Des Moines Register,* August 16, 1955.

96. On Virginia's plans for evading the integration ruling, see *Des Moines Register,* January 9–10, 1956.

97. See *Des Moines Register,* March 10, 13, 1956. On massive resistance see, for instance, Numan V. Bartley, *The Rise of Massive Resistance* (Baton Rouge: Louisiana State University Press, 1970).

98. More on the boycott can be found in Jo Ann Gibson Robinson, *The Montgomery Bus Boycott and the Women Who Started It* (Knoxville: University of Tennessee Press, 1987). Two biographies of Martin Luther King Jr. should also be consulted: David Garrow, *Bearing the Cross: Martin Luther King, Jr., and the Southern Christian Leadership Conference* (New York: William Morrow, 1986) and Stephen Oates, *Let the Trumpet Sound: The Life of Martin Luther King, Jr.* (New York: Harper and Row, 1982).

99. See *Des Moines Register,* November 15, December 23, 1956.

100. *Des Moines Register,* September 11, 1957. The Civil Rights Act of 1957 to which the *Register* referred was relatively weak, although it did establish a permanent Commission on Civil Rights and authorized the Justice Department to seek injunctions against those interfering with another's right to vote. For more on the Little Rock situation, see Tony A. Freyer, *The Little Rock Crisis: A Constitutional Interpretation* (Westport, Conn.: Greenwood Press, 1984).

101. *Des Moines Register,* September 24–25, 1957. For more on Eisenhower's handling of the civil rights issue, see Robert F. Burk, *The Eisenhower Administration and Black Civil Rights* (Knoxville: University of Tennessee Press, 1984).

102. *Des Moines Register,* September 29, 1957.

103. See *Des Moines Register,* April 3, 13, 1947. Good overviews of the cold war include: H. W. Brands, *The Devil We Knew: Americans and the Cold War* (New York: Oxford University Press, 1993); John L. Gaddis, *Strategies for Containment: A Critical Appraisal of Postwar American National Security Policy* (New York: Oxford University Press, 1982); and Walter LaFeber, *America, Russia, and the Cold War, 1945–1992* (New York: McGraw Hill, 1993).

104. *Des Moines Register,* June 29, 1948, August 1, 1949.

105. See *Des Moines Register,* July 1, 22, 1949, February 1, 1950.

106. For more on the Korean War, see Bruce Cumings, *The Origins of the Korean War,* 2 vols. (Princeton, N.J.: Princeton University Press, 1981 and 1990); Bruce Cumings,

ed., *Child of Conflict: The Korean-American Relationship, 1943–1953* (Seattle: University of Washington Press, 1983); Burton Kaufman, *The Korean War: Challenges in Crisis, Credibility and Command* (Philadelphia: Temple University Press, 1986); and William Stueck, *The Korean War: An International History* (Princeton, N.J.: Princeton University Press, 1995). For the *Register*'s support of American intervention into Korea, see *Des Moines Register,* July 6–10, 16–17, 21, 1950.

107. Examples of stories of Iowans serving in Korea were abundant and appeared in both the *Register* and the *Tribune.* For a sampling of his dispatches, see Clardy, *Gordon Gammack.*

108. See *Des Moines Register,* July 16, 1950, and January 9, 1951.

109. See *Des Moines Register,* April 10, 15, 1951.

110. *Des Moines Register,* February 1, 1950.

111. *Des Moines Register,* May 10, 15, 1954.

112. On the *Register*'s stand on Dulles and its opposition to U.S. action in Lebanon, see *Time,* December 8, 1958, 57–58. Statement about Dulles's "fervent anticommunism" is quoted from Townsend Hoopes, *The Devil and John Foster Dulles* (Boston: Little, Brown, 1973), 505. For more on Eisenhower and his handling of the cold war, see Stephen Ambrose, *Eisenhower: The President* (New York: Simon and Schuster, 1984); H. W. Brands, *Eisenhower's Generation and American Foreign Policy* (New York: Columbia University Press, 1988); and Robert Divine, *Eisenhower and the Cold War* (New York: Oxford University Press, 1981).

113. *Des Moines Register,* April 5, 1947.

114. *Des Moines Register,* July 26,1949.

115. See *Des Moines Register,* February 14, 1950; and Edwin R. Bayley, *Joe McCarthy and the Press* (Madison: University of Wisconsin Press, 1981), 51. Bayley provides an examination of how a number of newspapers initially viewed McCarthy and they covered the senator's activities. For more on McCarthy and McCarthyism, see David Caute, *The Great Fear: The Anti-Communist Purge under Truman and Eisenhower* (New York: Simon and Schuster, 1978); Richard Fried, *Nightmare in Red: The McCarthy Era in Perspective* (New York: Oxford University Press, 1990); and David Oshinsky, *A Conspiracy So Immense: The World of Joe McCarthy* (New York: Free Press, 1983).

116. See *Des Moines Register,* July 19, October 27, 1950.

117. See *Des Moines Register,* May 9, June 27, July 16, 1954; and *Des Moines Tribune,* May 7, June 18, 1954.

118. Minutes of the Adjourned Meeting of the Stockholders of Des Moines Register and Tribune Company, February 5, 1960.

119. Although he retired as publisher, Luther Hill remained a vice president for several more years and stayed on the company's board of directors until he completely retired in January 1971. He was succeeded on the R&T board by his son, attorney Luther L. Hill Jr.

Notes to Chapter 7

1. David Kruidenier to John Cowles, November 10, 1961, John Cowles Papers, Drake University, Des Moines, Iowa.

2. MacDonald was finally named publisher in 1966 and held the title until 1971.

3. John Cowles to Mike Cowles, June 11, 1960, John Cowles Papers.

4. Quotation comes from George Mills, *Harvey Ingham and Gardner Cowles, Sr.: Things Don't Just Happen* (Ames:Iowa State University Press, 1977), 162.

5. For Zacherle's statement on MacDonald, see Hedo Zacherle interview by author, Des Moines, Iowa, June 28, 1996. For additional information on MacDonald, see Lyle Lynn interview by author, Des Moines, Iowa, August 11, 1993; Ken MacDonald interview by author, Des Moines, Iowa, July 14, 1992; and Louis Norris interview by author,

Des Moines, Iowa, January 26, 1993.

6. On David Kruidenier, see Lynn, interview; Norris, interview; and Thomas Moore, "Trouble and Strife in the Cowles Empire," *Fortune,* April 4, 1983, 158.

7. Minutes of the board of directors' meetings are, in general, brief and provide little detail. On the informality of these meetings, see Luther Hill Jr., interview by author, Des Moines, Iowa, February 4, 1993; Norris, interview; and Zacherle, interview.

8. Ben Bagdikian, *The Media Monopoly* (Boston: Beacon Press, 1992), 195–96.

9. James N. Rosse, Bruce M. Owen, and James Dertouzos, *Trends in the Daily Newspaper Industry, 1923–1973,* Studies in Industrial Economics, no. 57 (Stanford, Calif.: Department of Economics, Stanford University, 1975), 30.

10. See James L. Baughman, *The Republic of Mass Culture* (Baltimore: Johns Hopkins University Press, 1992), 120, 187–88; and J. Robert Hudson, interview by author, West Des Moines, Iowa, September 15, 1992.

11. James N. Rosse, *Economic Limits of Press Responsibility,* Studies in Industrial Economics, no. 56 (Stanford, Calif.: Department of Economics, Stanford University, 1975). Quotation is taken from Benjamin M. Compaine, ed., *Who Owns the Media: Concentration of Ownership in the Mass Communications Industry* (New York: Harmony Books, 1979), 37. See also Stephen Lacy and Todd Simon, *The Economics and Regulation of United States Newspapers* (Norwood, N.J.: Ablex Publishing, 1993), 112–15. Rosse's umbrella model originally suggested four layers of competition: the metropolitan daily, newspapers in satellite cities, local or suburban dailies, and weeklies or shoppers. Lacy and Simon have now updated the hypothesis to include, in addition to the four original layers, national dailies such as *USA Today* or the national edition of the *New York Times* and group-owned nondaily papers.

12. Circulation for the six city dailies and the *Register* and *Tribune* were as follows:

Publication	**1960**	**1964**	**1969**
Omaha World-Herald (morning/evening combined)	250,330	253,394	245,540
Sioux City Journal (all day)	72,395	73,326	72,624
Cedar Rapids Gazette (evening)	65,554	68,027	74,445
Davenport Times-Democrat	54,355	54,471	60,138*
Dubuque Telegram-Herald (evening)	39,200	40,449	41,213
Waterloo Courier (evening)	50,690	52,129	54,229
Register and Tribune (combined)	352,623	352,437	360,940

*Davenport had the morning *Democrat* and the evening *Times* in 1961. By 1964 they had combined the two into the all-day *Times-Democrat.*

Source: *Editor & Publisher International Year Book,* 1961, 1965, 1970.

13. See Leland Sage, *A History of Iowa* (Ames: Iowa State University Press, 1974), 310–14. For a comment on these population trends and growing urban competition, see Minutes of Meeting of the Stockholders of Des Moines Register and Tribune Company, February 14, 1969. The *Register* and *Tribune*'s rural circulation was derived by combining figures from the company's country mail and farm service divisions.See Register and Tribune Company Annual Reports, 1960 and 1971.

14. See Register and Tribune Company Annual Reports, 1960 and 1970. On the general problems for afternoon newspapers nationwide, see Ernest C. Hynds, *American Newspapers in the 1980s* (New York: Hastings House, 1980), 95–96.

15. Advertising manager Lyle Lynn described how 70 percent market coverage was the advertisers' target figure; see Lynn, interview. The following chart shows comparative metro circulation in relationship to Audit Bureau of Circulations (ABC) Occupied Housing Unit figures. Metropolitan coverage was computed by dividing area circulation by the ABC occupied housing unit figure.

Year	ABC Occupied Housing Units	Register Metro Circulation	Percent of Metro Coverage	Tribune Metro Circulation	Percent of Metro Coverage
1964	80,738	43,909	54	65,355	81.4
1969	82,825	47,335	57	66,775	80.6

Source: *Editor and Publisher International Yearbook,* 1965, 120; *Editor and Publisher International Yearbook,* 1970, 118; Register and Tribune Company Annual Report, 1970, 22–23.

16. The following chart shows a comparative view of advertising revenue and net profits of the *Register,* the *Tribune,* and the *Sunday Register.*

	Register	Tribune	Sunday Register
1960			
Net Advertising Revenue	$ 3,294,992	$3,258,525	$ 4,173,652
Net Profit	187,751	238,484	555,117
1965			
Advertising Revenue	2,664,098	4,183,315	4,697,483
Net Profit	−120,132	667,741	922,578
1970			
Advertising Revenue	3,172,706	5,588,506	6,229,387
Net Profit	−363,743	766,257	1,281,789

Source:Register and Tribune Company Annual Reports, 1960, 62; 1965, 58; and 1970, 66.

17. Register and Tribune Company Annual Reports, 1969, 3; 1970, 22.

18. See *Des Moines Register,* March 5, 1967; and Register and Tribune Company Annual Reports, 1967, 6; 1968, 7.

19. See "Twenty-four Year Report, Register and Tribune Company, 1940–1963" (David Kruidenier Papers, held by David Kruidenier, Des Moines, Iowa), 152.

20. On zoned advertising, see Lacy and Simon, *Economics and Regulation of Newspapers,* 44–45. For creation of zoned advertising sections in the *Sunday Register,* see Register and Tribune Company Annual Reports, 1964–1967. Retail advertising linage figures for the *Sunday Register* follow:

1964	Introduction of Eastern Zone Advertising	2,286,574
1965		2,476,712
1966	Introduction of Western and Central Zoned Advertising	2,431,666
1967	Zoned Advertising Rates Lowered	2,625,179
1968		2,907,715
1969		2,875,341
1970		3,075,374

Source: Register and Tribune Annual Report, 1970, 20–21.

21. John Cowles Jr. to John Cowles, December 6, 1969, John Cowles Papers.

22. Bagdikian, *Media Monopoly,* 129. On MacDonald and his interest in state and local coverage, see MacDonald, interview; and Lauren Soth, interview by author, West Des Moines, Iowa, October 20, 1992.

23. See Annual Reports of the Register and Tribune Company, 1960, 87; 1970, 109. For a statement about cutbacks and the *Washington Post* as an exception, see William Greider, *Who Will Tell the People: The Betrayal of American Democracy* (New York: Simon and Schuster, 1992), 293. The quotation about the Cowleses is taken from James D. Squires, *Read All about It: The Corporate Takeover of America's Newspapers* (New York: Times Books, 1994), 128.

24. For quotation and synopsis of the changes in the presentation of news, see Baughman, *Republic of Mass Culture,* 124–26.

25. See Register and Tribune Annual Reports, 1963–1966, and Lynn, interview. National advertising had been declining in newspapers nationwide since it peaked in 1950. Such advertisers sought better coverage for their products through the medium of television. See Jim Willis, *Surviving the Newspaper Business: Newspaper Management in Turbulent Times* (New York: Praeger Publishers, 1988), 84.

26. For MacDonald's views, see Mills, *Harvey Ingham and Gardner Cowles, Sr.,* 165. Otis Chandler is quoted in Jon G. Udell, *The Economics of the American Newspaper* (New York: Hastings House, 1978), 66.

27. The fifteen leading dailies ranked ahead of the *Des Moines Register* according to the *Saturday Review* 1961 poll of journalism educators were *New York Times, Christian Science Monitor, Wall Street Journal, St. Louis Post-Despatch, Milwaukee Journal, Washington Post, New York Herald-Tribune, Louisville Courier-Journal, Chicago Tribune, Chicago Daily News, Baltimore Sun, Atlanta Constitution* and *Minneapolis Tribune* (tie), and *Kansas City Star* and *Los Angeles Times* (tie). See John Tebbel, "Rating the American Newspaper—Part I," *Saturday Review,* May 13, 1961, 59, 60–62.

28. *Des Moines Register,* May 7, 1963. The cartoon identified by the Pulitzer committee as an example of Miller's work originally appeared in the *Des Moines Register,* January 15, 1962.

29. *Des Moines Register,* February 18, 1983. See also MacDonald, interview.

30. *Des Moines Register,* February 27, 1983.

31. Max McElwain, *Profiles in Communication: The Hall of Fame of the University of Iowa School of Journalism and Mass Communication* (Iowa City: Iowa Center for Communication Study, 1991), 58.

32. *Des Moines Register,* May 7, 1968.

33. See Hynds, *Newspapers in the 1980s,* 84–85; Michael Emery and Edwin Emery, *The Press and America: An Interpretative History of the Mass Media,* 6th ed. (Englewood Cliffs, N.J.: Prentice Hall, 1988), 621–23; and *Editor and Publisher,* April 16, 1966, 11, 47.

34. On Zacherle's start as the R&T's labor negotiator, see John Cowles to Mike Cowles, June 11, 1960, John Cowles Papers. For the R&T's peaceful labor relations, see Zacherle, interview.

35. See Register and Tribune Annual Report, 1970, 8; and Udell, *Economics of American Newspaper,* 73.

36. See Register and Tribune Annual Report, 1960, p. T-2, T-14.

37. Leo Bogart, *Press and Public: Who Reads What, When, Where, and Why in American Newspapers* (Hillsdale, N.J.: Lawrence Erlbaum Associates, 1989), 59–60; and Udell, *Economics of American Newspaper,* 26.

38. See Register and Tribune Annual Reports, 1961, pp. T-1-T-9; 1962, pp. T-1-2; 1963, pp. T-1-T-10.

39. See John Cowles to David Kruidenier, May 29, 1964; Ken MacDonald to John and Mike Cowles, August 8, 1964; and John Cowles to David Kruidenier, January 9,

1965, John Cowles Papers; and Register and Tribune Annual Report, 1964, 1.

40. Minutes of Meeting of Stockholders of Des Moines Register and Tribune Company, January 8, 1965.

41. Register and Tribune Annual Reports, 1966, 5–6; 1967, 3.

42. There were circulation rate increases in 1966, 1967, 1968, and 1969, and advertising rate increases in 1966, 1967, and 1970. On the acceptance of beer advertising, see Minutes of a Special Meeting of the Board of Directors of Des Moines Register and Tribune Company, November 6, 1970, and Register and Tribune Annual Report, 1970, 6. Circulation Figures for the papers from 1960 to 1970 were as follows:

Year	Register	Tribune	Sunday Register
1960	231,082	129,046	524,553
1961	234,242	127,596	525,331
1962	230,685	125,761	525,435
1963	234,470	125,450	530,040
1964	236,993	122,757	518,046
1965	242,065	122,353	520,096
1966	244,769	119,466	518,546
1967	249,836	117,779	522,395
1968	254,868	114,589	527,184
1969	251,878	109,584	491,378
1970	251,341	110,253	484,156

43. Register and Tribune Annual Reports, 1965–1970. See also Ken MacDonald comments, Minutes of Meeting of the Stockholders of Des Moines Register and Tribune Company, January 23, 1968. Net profits fell even further in 1970, but this decline was largely because of a bad year for company investments in the stock market. It lost over $600,000 on the sale of stock. Furthermore, that year, Cowles Communications, Incorporated (CCI)—the company formed by the merger of Cowles Magazines and Cowles Broadcasting in 1961—suspended dividend payments. Because of the R&T's CCI holdings, that resulted in a decrease of $126,000 in R&T investment income.

44. See Register and Tribune Annual Reports, 1969, 15–16; 1970, 18–19, 48–49, 52–53; and Udell, *Economics of American Newspaper,* 122.

45. Quotation is taken from Emery and Emery, *Press and America,* 643. See also Elizabeth MacIver Neiva, "Chain Building: The Consolidation of the American Newspaper Industry, 1953–1980," *Business History Review* 70 (spring 1996): 22; and Udell, *Economics of Newspaper,* 94–96.

46. Neiva, "Chain Building," 15; and Register and Tribune Annual Reports, 1969, 3, 7; 1970, 3.

47. John Cowles Jr. to John Cowles, December 6, 1969, John Cowles Papers; Zacherle, interview.

48. See MacDonald, interview. On the issue of consciously cutting certain segments of circulation, see William B. Blakenburg, "Newspaper Ownership and Control of Circulation to Increase Profits," *Journalism Quarterly* 59 (autumn 1982): 390–98; and Squires, *Read All about It,* 90–91.

49. Norris, interview; Louis Norris, telephone conversation, June 25, 1996; Kenneth MacDonald, telephone conversation, July 30, 1996.

50. See Memorandum of Meeting of Board of Directors of Des Moines Register and Tribune, July 24, 1970, John Cowles Papers; Kenneth MacDonald to Gardner Cowles, John Cowles, John Cowles Jr., Luther Hill, Lou Norris, Hedo Zacherle, and Vincent Starzinger, October 30, 1970, John Cowles Papers; Minutes of Special Meeting of the Board of Directors of Des Moines Register and Tribune Company, November 6, 1970; and Register and Tribune Company Annual Report, 1971, 8.

51. Gilbert Cranberg, interview by author, Des Moines, Iowa, July 18, 1996; Soth, interview.

52. The incident was recalled by Gilbert Cranberg; see Cranberg, interview.

53. Soth, interview; MacDonald, telephone conversation. For the paper's endorsement of Nixon, see *Des Moines Register,* November 6, 1960.

54. *Des Moines Register,* November 6, 1960.

55. See *Des Moines Register,* October 11, 1964, and October 27, 1968.

56. *Des Moines Register,* February 13, 1960. For the impact of the Civil Rights movement on Greensboro, see William Chafe, *Civilities and Civil Rights: Greensboro, North Carolina, and the Black Struggle for Freedom* (New York: Oxford University Press, 1980).

57. On King's arrest, see *Des Moines Register,* April 13, 1963. On the Iowa Fair Employment Practices Act, see *Des Moines Register,* April 18, May 3, 5, 1963.

58. See *Des Moines Register,* May 14–June 15, 1963.

59. See Irwin Unger and Debi Unger, *America in the 1960s* (St. James, New York: Brandywine Press, 1988), 104. See also *Des Moines Register,* June 12, 20, 1963.

60. *Des Moines Register,* June 14, 1963.

61. *Des Moines Register,* June 22, 1964. In Iowa's congressional delegation, Democrat Neal Smith and Republicans Fred Schwengel, James Bromwell, Charles Hoeven, and John Kyl supported the bill, and Republicans H. R. Gross and Ben Jensen opposed it. On the Senate side, Republican Bourke Hickenlooper opposed the measure, while Republican Jack Miller supported it. See *Des Moines Register,* June 20, July 3, 4, 1964.

62. *Des Moines Register,* March 11, 1965. For an account of Selma, see David Garrow, *Protest at Selma: Martin Luther King, Jr., and the Voting Rights Act* (New Haven, Conn.: Yale University Press, 1978).

63. *Des Moines Register,* March 12, 1965.

64. *Des Moines Register,* March 13–16, 1965. The editorial on Johnson's call for a voting rights act is from *Des Moines Register,* March 17, 1965. See also *Des Moines Register,* August 8, 1965.

65. *Des Moines Register,* January 8, 1961.

66. *Des Moines Register,* April 12, 1961.

67. See *Des Moines Register,* April 22 and 28, 1961. For more on the Bay of Pigs episode, see Peter Wyden, *Bay of Pigs: The Untold Story* (New York: Simon and Schuster, 1979); Richard E. Welsh, *Response to Revolution: The United States and the Cuban Revolution, 1959–1961* (Chapel Hill: University of North Carolina Press, 1985); and Trumbull Higgins, *The Perfect Failure: Kennedy, Eisenhower, and the CIA at the Bay of Pigs* (New York: W. W. Norton, 1987).

68. For an analysis of the Cuban missile crisis, see Graham Allison, *Essence of Decision: Explaining the Cuban Missile Crisis* (Boston: Little, Brown, 1971); David Detzer, *The Brink: Cuban Missile Crisis, 1962* (New York: Crowell, 1979); Raymond Garthoff, *Reflections on the Cuban Missile Crisis,* rev. ed. (Washington, D.C.: Brookings Institution, 1989); and Mark J. White, *The Cuban Missile Crisis* (New York: Macmillan, 1996). For the view of a participant, see Robert Kennedy, *Thirteen Days: A Memoir of the Cuban Missile Crisis* (New York: W. W. Norton, 1969).

69. See Thomas G. Paterson, J. Garry Clifford, and Kenneth J. Hagan, *American Foreign Policy: A History/Since 1900* (Lexington, Mass.: D. C. Heath and Company, 1991), 544, and *Des Moines Register,* October 23–24, 1962.

70. *Des Moines Register,* October 30, 1962.

71. *Des Moines Register,* May 3, 1961.

72. *Des Moines Register,* May 26, 1961. For more on the Vietnam War, see George Herring, *America's Longest War: The United States and Vietnam, 1950–1976* (New York: Knopf, 1986); Michael Hunt, *Lyndon Johnson's War: America's Cold War Crusade in Vietnam, 1945–1968* (New York: Hill and Wang, 1996); Edwin Moise, *Tonkin Gulf and the Escalation of the Vietnam War* (Chapel Hill: University of North Carolina Press, 1996);

and Robert McNamara, *In Retrospect: The Tragedy and Lessons of Vietnam* (New York: Times Books, 1995).

73. *Des Moines Register*, May 21, 1962; June 11–15, 1963.

74. *Des Moines Register*, October 8, November 4–5, 1963, June 2, 18, 1964; and Paterson, Clifford, and Hagan, *American Foreign Policy*, 556.

75. *Des Moines Register*, August 4, 6, 8–11, 1964.

76. *Des Moines Register*, March 9, 1965.

77. *Des Moines Register*, May 3, 19, 1967; January 7, 27, 1968.

78. *Des Moines Register*, February 9, 1968.

79. *Des Moines Register*, February 5, 1968.

80. Gammack's letter to Mabry is quoted from Andrea Clardy, ed., *Gordon Gammack: Columns from Three Wars* (Ames: Iowa State University Press, 1979), 86–87.

81. See, for example, *Des Moines Tribune*, February 16, March 2, May 4, 1970.

82. Moore, "Trouble in Cowles Empire," 158.

Notes to Chapter 8

1. Quoted in Anthony Smith, *Goodbye Gutenberg: The Newspaper Revolution of the 1980's* (New York: Oxford University Press, 1980), 51.

2. *Des Moines Tribune*, May 9, 1979. According to journalist Thomas Moore, Jim Milloy, a close adviser to Mike Cowles, told *Register* reporter Clark Mollenhoff to "prevail upon his Kennedy connections to have Kruidenier named ambassador to a minor country to get him out of the U.S." See Thomas Moore, "Trouble and Strife in the Cowles Empire," *Fortune*, April 4, 1983, 158.

3. See Moore, "Trouble in Cowles Empire," 158; Mike Cowles to John Cowles, September 2, 1969, John Cowles Papers, Drake University, Des Moines, Iowa; and *Des Moines Register*, January 8, 1971.

4. Minutes of Meeting of the Stockholders of the Des Moines Register and Tribune Company, January 7, 1971; and Minutes of the Meeting of the Board of Directors of the Des Moines Register and Tribune Company, April 11, 1973. When Luther Hill Sr. retired from the R&T board in 1971, the vacancy was filled by his son, Luther Hill Jr., executive vice president and general counsel of the Equitable of Iowa Insurance Company of Iowa.

5. Minutes of Meeting of the Board of Directors of the Des Moines Register and Tribune Company, April 22, June 28, October 5, 1971, and July 19,1972. See also Register and Tribune Annual Report, 1971. See Ernest C. Hynds, *American Newspapers in the 1980s* (New York: Hastings House, 1980), 135. Circulation figures for 1970 through 1975 were as follows:

Year	Register	Tribune	Sunday Register
1970	251,341	110,253	484,156
1971	244,653	107,703	484,742
1972	243,891	106,940	483,827
1973	248,775	106,459	484,775
1974	238,608	99,650	461,662
1975	229,650	93,714	433,781

6. For conservation measures taken by various newspapers, see *Standard and Poor's Industry Surveys*, vol. 1 (New York: Standard and Poor's Corporation, 1978), C75; Conrad Fink, *Strategic Newspaper Management* (Carbondale: Southern Illinois University Press, 1988), 295; Hynds, *American Newspapers in the 1980s*, 137; Jon G. Udell, *The Economics of the American Newspaper* (New York: Hastings House, 1978), 124; and Jim Willis, *Surviving the Newspaper Business: Newspaper Management in Turbulent Times* (New York:

Praeger Publishers, 1988), 116–17.

7. See Register and Tribune Annual Reports, 1971–1976, 1980; and Minutes of Meeting of Board of Directors of the Des Moines Register and Tribune Company, April 23, 1975. The *Register* dropped the peach-colored paper from its sports section in 1973 but returned to its use later that year.

8. See Fink, *Strategic Newspaper Management,* 178; and William J. Thorn and Mary Pat Pfeil, *Newspaper Circulation: Marketing the News* (New York: Longman, 1987), 73; and Register and Tribune Annual Reports, 1971–1976.

9. Des Moines Register and Tribune Annual Reports, 1974, 1977, 1980.

10. Register and Tribune Annual Reports, 1971–1975; Minutes of Meeting of the Board of Directors of the Des Moines Register and Tribune Company, October 30, 1972, and January 23, 1973. Register and Tribune revenues from advertising and circulation were as follows:

Year	Advertising Revenue ($)	Circulation Revenue ($)
1970	14,990,559	12,037,642
1971	16,006,299	12,340,033
1972	17,924,762	12,421,474
1973	19,287,677	12,567,355
1974	21,445,030	13,805,355
1975	22,361,002	15,561,698

Source: Register and Tribune Annual Report, 1976.

11. The newspaper firms included in the comparison are Dow Jones, Gannett, Harte-Hanks, Knight-Ridder, Lee Enterprises, New York Times, Times Mirror, and Washington Post. For profit margin data, see *Standard and Poor's Industry Surveys,* vol. 1 (New York: Standard and Poor's, 1979), C86; and Register and Tribune Annual Reports, 1970–1975.

12. Thomas C. Leonard, *News For All: America's Coming-of-Age with the Press* (New York: Oxford University Press, 1995), 162–64.

13. Ibid., 166–67.

14. Ibid., 174. Chandler quoted in Fink, *Strategic Newspaper Management,* 175–76. See also William Blankenburg, "Newspaper Ownership and Control of Circulation to Increase Profit," *Journalism Quarterly* 59 (autumn 1982): 392; and James D. Squires, *Read All about It: The Corporate Takeover of America's Newspapers* (New York: Times Books, 1994), 90–91.

15. Register and Tribune Annual Reports, 1973, 1977, and 1980; Minutes of a Meeting of the Executive Committee of the Board of Directors of the Des Moines Register and Tribune Company, July 28, 1976. Metropolitan circulation of the three papers was as follows:

Year	Register	Tribune	Sunday Register
1976	44,945	63,392	85,142
1977	45,032	62,425	86,020
1978	44,373	60,862	86,848
1979	45,639	60,896	89,179
1980	48,667	62,142	94,329

16. The statement that cutting circulation would increase profits was made in a confidential memo from Michael Gartner, Lou Norris, and J. Robert Hudson to David Kruidenier, June 9, 1977, Harry Watts Papers, private collection held by Harry Watts, Des Moines, Iowa. On the corporate decision to remain a statewide newspaper, see Register and Tribune Board of Directors Meeting, July 24, 1975, John Cowles Papers.

17. On the original RAGBRAI, see *Des Moines Register,* July 22, 1973; and Dora Jane Hamblin, "Everybody Puffs to Keokuk," *Smithsonian* 12 (July 1981): 100–105.

18. See Register and Tribune Annual Reports, 1976–1980. Circulation and circulation revenue figures follow:

Year	Circulation Figures			Circulation
	Register	Tribune	Sunday Register	Revenue
1976	228,793	92,919	428,664	$15,317,000
1977	226,112	90,979	431,799	$15,450,000
1978	215,879	86,037	406,828	$16,870,000
1979	209,775	83,440	394,819	$17,265,000
1980	214,334	83,252	403,520	$19,525,000

19. The issue of a newspaper's influence is discussed briefly in Thorn and Pfeil, *Newspaper Circulation,* 27–28. Michael Gartner referred to the paper as the "soul of Iowa." See Michael Gartner, interview by author, Des Moines, Iowa, June 11, 1997. The phrase "ego, not economic logic" is borrowed from Leonard, *News for All,* 163.

20. Moore, "Trouble in Cowles Empire," 158.

21. See David Kruidenier, interview by author, Des Moines, Iowa, July 20, 1992; Benjamin M. Compaine, ed., *Who Owns the Media: Concentration of Ownership in the Mass Communications Industry* (New York: Harmony Books, 1979), 30–31; and *Standard and Poor's Industry Survey,* vol. 1 (New York: Standard and Poor's Corporation, 1982), C70. Final quotation of the paragraph is from *Standard and Poor's.*

22. See Minutes of Special Meeting of the Board of Directors of Des Moines Register and Tribune Company, April 22, June 28, 1971. For acquisition plan, see Newspaper Search Analysis, March 15, 1972; Acquisition Policy of Register and Tribune Company, April 11, 1972; Newspaper Search Analysis, 1972; and Acquisition Policy of The Des Moines Register and Tribune Company, revised, July 30, 1973. As cited in Newspaper Search Analysis (1972), a preliminary list of newspapers that met the R&T's criteria for acquisition included smaller newspapers such as the *Mesa Tribune* in Arizona, the *Fullerton News-Tribune* in California, the *Manchester Herald* in Connecticut, and the *Belleville News-Democrat* in Illinois. Larger newspapers included the *Fresno Bee* in California, the *Clearwater Sun* in Florida, and the *Bloomington Pantagraph* in Illinois.

23. See *Des Moines Tribune,* November 3, 1972; Minutes of Meeting of the Board of Directors of Des Moines Register and Tribune Company, April 11, July 19, October 30, 1972, January 23, November 6, 1973; Register and Tribune Annual Reports, 1972–1973; Kruidenier, interview; and Louis Norris, interview by author, Des Moines, Iowa, January 26, 1993.

24. See Register and Tribune Annual Reports, 1975, 1980; R. Gary Gomm material, John Cowles Papers; and Minutes of Meeting of the Board of Directors of the Register and Tribune Company, July 24, 1974.

25. Gartner, interview. See also *Des Moines Register,* March 3, 1993, April 17, 1994; and *Spirit,* March-April 1978, 6–7.

26. Gary Gerlach, interview by author, Ames, Iowa, June 30, 1993.

27. On the Guild, see Michael Emery and Edwin Emery, *The Press and America: An Interpretative History of the Mass Media,* 6th ed. (Englewood Cliffs, N.J.: Prentice Hall, 1988), 576–77; and Willis, *Surviving the Newspaper Business,* 137–39. For the R&T Guild elections, see Register and Tribune Annual Reports, 1973–1974; and Minutes of Meeting of the Board of Directors of the Register and Tribune Company, November 6, 1973 and July 24, 1976.

28. See Register and Tribune Annual Reports, 1975–1976; Minutes of Meeting of the Board of Directors of the Des Moines Register and Tribune Company, January 20,

1975; and Norman Rosenberg to author, August 26, 1996. The issue of manning levels did prove troublesome for other newspapers and led to strikes such as the one against New York's three metropolitan dailies in 1978. See Hynds, *American Newspapers in the 1980s,* 164–65; and Smith, *Goodbye Gutenberg,* 230–31. Consumer Price Index figures are taken from *Statistical Abstracts of the United States 1996* (Washington, D.C.: U.S. Department of Commerce, 1996), 484.

29. Hynds, *American Newspapers in the 1980s,* 266–68; and Smith, *Goodbye Gutenberg,* 90–93.

30. Clearly, the R&T was among its large-circulation peers in not converting to offset. As of 1978, only 28 percent of the country's dailies were still using letterpresses, but they accounted for more than 60 percent of the nation's total circulation. See Hynds, *American Newspapers in the 1980s,* 265–66. On the Register's decision to use DiLitho, see Norman Rosenberg to author, August 26, 1996; Register and Tribune Annual Reports, 1974–1976; Minutes of Meeting of the Executive Committee of the Board of Directors of the Des Moines Register and Tribune Company, September 26, 1975; *Des Moines Tribune,* April 5, 1976; and *Des Moines Register,* April 6, 1976.

31. Charles Edwards, interview by author, Des Moines, Iowa, September 23, 1993; Gerlach, interview; and Richard Gilbert, interview by author, Ded Moines, Iowa, September 14, 1992; and Minutes of a Meeting of the Executive Committee of the Board of Directors of the Des Moines Register and Tribune Company, November 17, 1976.

32. See Gartner, interview; and Minutes of the Meeting of Board of Directors of the Des Moines Register and Tribune Company, May 11, 1977.

33. Gartner, interview; and Edwards, interview, September 23, 1993; Gerlach, interview; Gilbert, interview; Kruidenier, interview, July 20, 1992, and telephone conversation with author, June 16, 1997. See also Minutes of a Meeting of the Executive Committee of the Board of Directors of the Des Moines Register and Tribune Company, February 1, April 7, May 13, September 6, 1977; Minutes of the Meeting of the Board of Directors of the Des Moines Register and Tribune Company, May 11, August 2, November 2, 1977; and Register and Tribune Annual Report, 1977.

34. See Register and Tribune Annual Report, 1977; and Norris, interview.

35. Norris, interview; *Washington Post,* March 20, 1983. The *Post* quoted an anonymous person described as an "executive of the Register and Tribune who has since left the company." Through the interview with Norris, it became clear that he was the person quoted in the *Post.*

36. For information on the attempted acquisition of the Daily Herald Company, see Minutes of a Meeting of the Executive Committee of the Board of Directors of the Des Moines Register and Tribune Company, January 5, 1978; and Gartner, interview.

37. See *Washington Post,* March 20, 1983; Gartner, interview.

38. See Gilbert, interview; memo to David Kruidenier and others from John Cowles, May 6, 1978, John Cowles Papers; Minutes of a Meeting of the Executive Committee of the Board of Directors of the Des Moines Register and Tribune Company, May 10, June 14, 1978; Register and Tribune Annual Report, 1978. Quotations are taken from John Cowles memo. According to the *Washington Post* of March 20, 1983, the Gartners made an estimated $500,000 on the R&T acquisition of McCoy Broadcasting. For details of the $30 million loan, see Minutes of Meeting of the Board of Directors of the Des Moines Register and Tribune Company, November 1, 1978, and March 13, 1979.

39. See Minutes of Meeting of the Executive Committee of the Board of Directors of the Des Moines Register and Tribune Company, August 9, 1978; and Minutes of a Meeting of the Board of Directors of the Register and Tribune Company, August 14, November 1, December 6, 1978.

40. Register and Tribune Annual Report, 1978.

41. Register and Tribune Annual Reports, 1979–1980.

42. Register and Tribune Annual Reports, 1970–1980.

43. See Register and Tribune Annual Reports, 1975–1981; and *Standard and Poor's Industry Survey,* vol. 2 (New York: Standard and Poor's Corporation, 1984), M105. R&T net profit margins have been adjusted for several extraordinary stock exchanges with various family members. See Shawn Kalkstein, "Letter to Fellow Shareholders," July 14, 1982, Shawn Kalkstein Papers, private collection held by Shawn Kalkstein, Stamford, Connecticut.

44. "After the Rash of Take-Overs New Worries about 'Press Lords,'" *U.S. News and World Report,* January 24, 1977, 54–56; and "The Big Money Hunt for Independent Newspapers," *Business Week,* February 21, 1977, 56–62.

45. See Michael Gartner, Lou Norris, and J. Robert Hudson to David Kruidenier, June 9, 1977; and Minutes of the Meeting of the Board of Directors of the Des Moines Register and Tribune Company, November 2, 1977. The estimate in June 1977 was made before the Madison, Wisconsin, McCoy, or Waukesha acquisitions.

46. Connected to the creation of the voting trust was a recapitalization plan that involved a "reverse stock split." For every eight shares of R&T stock held, the shareholder received one share of voting common stock and seven shares of nonvoting common stock, each with a par value of $10. This reorganization resulted in the former 2,000,000 shares of company stock being converted to 250,000 shares of voting stock and 1,750,000 shares of nonvoting stock. On the recapitalization plan and the establishment of the voting trust, see Minutes of a Meeting of the Board of Directors of the Des Moines Register and Tribune Company, August 14, November 1, December 7, 1978; Minutes of a Special Meeting of the Stockholders of the Des Moines Register and Tribune Company, December 7, 1978; Study of Des Moines Register and Tribune Company, Eighth Town Meeting, August 22, 1978, Summary Minutes.

47. Under Iowa law, such trusts were limited to a twenty-year duration. The R&T decided to limit its trust to ten years because the MS&T was simultaneously considering a trust, and as a Delaware corporation, its trust would be limited to ten years. Since many R&T shareholders also held stock in Minneapolis, it was thought to be less confusing if the Des Moines trust had the same ten-year existence as the MS&T's. It turned out, however, that the MS&T dropped the idea of a voting trust until establishing one a couple of years later. On the Watts case, see *Des Moines Tribune,* December 7, 1978; *Wall Street Journal,* January 23, 1979; Frank S. Watts to Stockholders of the Register and Tribune Co., Inc., March 8, 1979, Watts Papers; and Harry Watts, interview, Des Moines, Iowa, March 9, 1993.

48. See Cranberg, interview; Gartner, interview; Kruidenier, interview, July 20, 1992; and Glenn Roberts, interview, Des Moines, Iowa, June 8, 1993. See also George Mills, *Harvey Ingham and Gardner Cowles, Sr.: Things Don't Just Happen* (Ames: Iowa State University Press, 1977), 164. For an example of the annual salary survey, see *Des Moines Register,* September 10, 1978.

49. See *Des Moines Register,* May 4, 5, 1976; and Mills, *Harvey Ingham and Gardner Cowles, Sr.,* 163.

50. *Des Moines Register,* April 17, 1979.

51. Cranberg, interview.

52. Ibid.

53. *Des Moines Register,* January 11, 24, 1973.

54. *Des Moines Register,* February 17, 1978 and February 21, 1980.

55. *Des Moines Register,* January 15, March 21, 23, 31, 1978.

56. *Des Moines Register,* January 25, February 7, 9, 1979.

57. See, for example, editorials in the *Des Moines Register,* September 14, 25, October 14, 17, 25, and November 3, 1980.

58. *Des Moines Register,* November 5, 6, 1980.

59. On the invasion of Afghanistan, see M. Hasssan Kakar, *Afghanistan: The Soviet Invasion and the Afghan Response* (Berkeley and Los Angeles: University of California Press, 1995); and Nancy P. and Richard S. Newell, *The Struggle for Afghanistan* (Ithaca, N.Y.: Cornell University Press, 1981). On Jimmy Carter's foreign policy, see Charles O. Jones, *The Trusteeship Presidency: Jimmy Carter and the United States Congress* (Baton Rouge: Louisiana State University Press, 1988); Jerel Rosati, *The Carter Administration's Quest for Global Community: Beliefs and Their Impact on Behavior* (Columbia: University of South Carolina Press, 1987); and Gaddis Smith, *Morality, Reason, and Power: American Diplomacy in the Carter Years* (New York: Hill and Wang, 1986).

60. *Des Moines Register,* January 6, 17, 23, 1980.

61. *Des Moines Register,* January 25, February 10, 1980. See also Kenneth E. Morris, *Jimmy Carter: American Moralist* (Athens: University of Georgia Press, 1996), 274.

62. *Des Moines Register,* January 8, 20, 29; February 22; March 14, 19, 25; April 7, 12, 1980.

63. *Des Moines Register,* May 29, 1980.

64. *Des Moines Register,* March 2, 5; May 21, 1980

65. *Des Moines Register,* October 29, 1972.

66. *Des Moines Register,* October 24, 1976.

67. *Des Moines Register,* November 2, 1980.

68. On the Clark-Jepsen race, see *Des Moines Register,* October 29, November 5, 8, 1978; and Cranberg, interview. The "Best Man Lost" editorial ran in the *Des Moines Register,* November 9, 1978.

69. See Cranberg, interview; Gartner, interview; and David Kruidenier, telephone conversation with author, June 16, 1997. See also *Des Moines Tribune,* May 9, 1979.

70. On the consumer credit legislation, see *Des Moines Register,* February 19, March 5, 11, 13, 14, 22, May 1, 3, 4, 6, June 5, 1974.

71. See Cranberg, interview; Lyle Lynn, interview by author, Des Moines, Iowa, August 11, 1993; Kruidenier, telephone conversation, June 16, 1997; Kenneth MacDonald, telephone conversation with author, June 26, 1996; and Register and Tribune Annual Report, 1974.

72. Des Moines Register Annual Report, 1977; and Minutes of the Meeting of the Board of Directors of the Des Moines Register and Tribune Company, July 24, 1974.

73. *Des Moines Register,* June 22, 1974.

74. See *Des Moines Register,* November 11, 1975; March 19, 24, October 10, 27, 1978; and June 11, 1979. See also Minutes of a Meeting of the Board of Directors of the Register and Tribune Company, April 23, October 15, 1975. The R&T pledged $250,000 to the Civic Center fund-raising drive.

75. Minutes of a Meeting of the Executive Committee of the Board of Directors of the Des Moines Register and Tribune Company, February 23, 1978; Kruidenier, telephone conversation, June 16, 1997; Cranberg, interview; Gartner, interview; *Des Moines Tribune,* March 23, 1978; *Des Moines Register,* March 24, 1978.

76.Sterling quotation from *Des Moines Register,* March 24, 1978. LaVine quotation from *Des Moines Tribune,* May 9, 1979.

77. *Des Moines Register,* July 20, 1979; December 7, 1980; and *Des Moines Tribune,* January 22, 1981.

78. Register and Tribune Company Annual Reports, 1971, 1980.

Notes to Chapter 9

1. The pretax operating margins (net sales and operating revenues less cost of goods sold and operating expenses divided by operating revenues) were as follows:

Year	Operating Income (as percent of revenues) Dow Jones	Gannett	Lee Enterprises	R&T
1976	25.7	26.2	26.4	10.8
1977	25.9	28.9	26.2	12.9
1978	25.5	28.8	28.1	12.0
1979	22.6	30.0	29.8	9.6
1980	21.0	29.5	30.1	6.1
1981	25.8	30.2	30.0	4.6

Source: *Standard and Poor's Industry Survey,* 1982, 1984, and Register and Tribune Annual Reports, 1976–1981.

2. See Action of the Executive Committee of the Board of Directors of the Des Moines Register and Tribune Company, August 3, 1981; Minutes of a Special Meeting of the Board of Directors of the Des Moines Register and Tribune Company, August 8, September 9, 1981; *Des Moines Register,* September 11, 1981; deposition of David Kruidenier, January 28, 1996, 52–56; and deposition of John Cowles Jr., February 5, 1986, 5–8. Both depositions were taken in regard to *Harry T. Watts, et. al. vs. R & T Liquidation, Inc.,* Harry Watts Papers, private collection held by Harry Watts, Des Moines, Iowa.

3. Deposition of Nick Biddle Paumgarten, June 14, 1985, 7, taken in regard to *Frank S. Watts, et. al., vs. Des Moines Register and Tribune Co., et al.,* Watts Papers. On the visit of the investment bankers to Des Moines and the schedule of meetings to consider the merger, see Gary Gerlach to David Kruidenier et al., October 9, 1981, Watts Papers.

4. Depositions of Cowles and Kruidenier, as well as The First Boston Corporation, Range of Liquidation Values (n.d.) and Goldman Sachs Register and Tribune Valuation analysis and Star and Tribune Valuation Analysis (n.d.), Watts Papers. See also Minutes of a Meeting of the Board of Directors of the Des Moines Register and Tribune Company, September 9, 1981; and "Cowles Consolidates to Survive," *Business Week,* December 7, 1981, 100.

5. Depositions of Cowles and Kruidenier; "A Washington Post Bid to Buy into Cowles," *Business Week,* March 8, 1982, 33; *Des Moines Tribune,* August 11, 1981; Thomas Moore, "Trouble and Strife in Cowles Empire," *Fortune,* April 4, 1983, 160.

6. Deposition of John Cowles, 23–25; David Kruidenier, interviews by author, Des Moines, Iowa, July 20, 1992, and July 22, 1997; Minutes of a Meeting of the Board of Directors of the Des Moines Register and Tribune Company, March 18, 1982; *Des Moines Register,* February 7, 1982; *Washington Post,* March 20, 1983.

7. Kay Graham's notes on meeting with David Kruidenier, Des Moines Register and Tribune, February 16, 1982; Kay Graham to David Kruidenier, February 15, 1982; deposition of David Kruidenier, 110–44, Watts Papers; and Kruidenier, interview, July 22, 1997. See also *Des Moines Register,* February 26, 1982, and *Washington Post,* March 1, 1982.

8. See Graham's notes on meeting; deposition of David Kruidenier, 140–41; David Kruidenier to the Board of Directors, February 18, 1982, Watts Papers; and *Des Moines Tribune,* February 26, 1982.

9. See Annual Stockholders' Meeting Des Moines Register and Tribune Company, March 18, 1982: Remarks by David Kruidenier, John Cowles Papers, Drake University, Des Moines, Iowa. The price of R&T stock had been pegged by the company's board at $31 per share.

10. See ibid., and Partial Transcript of the Annual Meeting of the Des Moines Register and Tribune Company, held on March 18, 1982, Watts Papers.

11. Shawn Kalkstein, interviews by author, West Des Moines, Iowa, August 4, 1993, and July 30, 1997.

12. Earlier Shawn Kalkstein had asked Lou Norris for names of the others who were

worried about R&T management. Although Norris did not give Kalkstein the names, he did, on Kalkstein's authorization, pass on Kalkstein's name to Jonathan Jordan, which led to Jordan contacting Kalkstein and their eventual meeting.

13. Kalkstein, interviews.

14. See Shawn Kalkstein to Fellow Cowles Family Members and Fellow Shareholders in the Des Moines R&T Co., March 25, 1982, 2, Shawn Kalkstein Papers, private collection held by Shawn Kalkstein, Stamford, Connecticut.

15. This Kalkstein letter, and all those in the first series, were sent to all R&T stockholders who held 1,000 or more shares.

16. Mike Cowles to John Cowles, April 1, 1982, John Cowles Papers.

17. All told, there were seven Kalkstein letters in the first series coming out roughly monthly from March through November 1982. The second series picked up in August 1983, with six letters sent out for the remainder of that year and two in 1984. Fred Eychaner, the Chicago businessman who purchased several thousand shares of R&T stock when the limited public market opened in August 1982, provided Kalkstein with financial assistance to defray the cost of producing the second series of letters. See Kalkstein, interview, July 30, 1997. For a reference to Mike Cowles letter and Kalkstein's response, see Shawn Kalkstein to Fellow Cowles Members and Fellow Stockholders of the Des Moines R&T Co., June 25, 1982, 8, Kalkstein Papers.

18. See David Kruidenier to Cousins and Other Members of the Cowles Family, May 11, 1982, John Cowles Papers.

19. *Tribune* circulation figures come from "Twenty-four Year Report, Register and Tribune Company, 1940–1963" (David Kruidenier Papers, held by David Kruidenier, Des Moines, Iowa), 77; and *Editor and Publisher International Yearbook* (New York: Editor and Publisher, 1981), I-97. For more on the decline of the evening newspaper in general, see Leo Bogart, *Preserving the Press: How Daily Newspapers Mobilized to Keep Their Readers* (New York: Columbia University Press, 1991), 40–44; Leo Bogart, *Press and Public: Who Reads What, When, Where, and Why in American Newspapers* (Hillsdale, N.J.: Lawrence Erlbaum Associates, 1989), 21, 30; Ernest C. Hynds, *American Newspapers in the 1980s* (New York: Hastings House, 1980), 95–96; and J. Thorn and Mary Pat Pfeil, *Newspaper Circulation: Marketing the News* (New York: Longman, 1987), 65–79.

20. Gary Gerlach, interview by author, Ames, Iowa, June 30, 1993; Minutes of a Meeting of the Board of Directors of the Des Moines Register and Tribune Company, March 18, June 21, 1982; Register and Tribune Annual Report, 1982; and *Des Moines Tribune,* September 25, 1982.

21. *Des Moines Tribune,* September 25, 1982; Thorn and Pfeil, *Newspaper Circulation,* 67.

22. The Denver-area radio stations had originally been purchased for $4.5 million as part of the McCoy deal, while the R&T paid $8.5 million for the *Waukesha Freeman.* On the sale of these properties, see the *Milwaukee Journal,* February 2, 1983; Minutes of a Meeting of the Board of Directors of the Des Moines Register and Tribune Company, December 9, 1981; June 21, September 15, 1982; January 25, March 28, 1983; and Register and Tribune Annual Reports, 1982, 1983.

23. Michael Gartner, interview by author, Des Moines, Iowa, June 11, 1997; Kenneth MacDonald, interview by author, Des Moines, Iowa, July 14, 1992; David Kruidenier to Lewis Kimer, January 24, 1980, Kruidenier Papers; Minutes of a Meeting of the Board of Directors of the Register and Tribune Company, March 12, 1980; and Register and Tribune Annual Report, 1982.

24. See Shawn Kalkstein to Fellow Cowles Members and Fellow Stockholders in the Des Moines R&T Co., June 25, 1982, 8, Kalkstein Papers; and Register and Tribune Annual Report, 1982.

25. Kruidenier, interview, July 22, 1997; *New York Times,* February 10, 1983; *St. Paul*

Pioneer Press/Dispatch, February 7, 1983; James A. Alcott, *A History of Cowles Media* (Minneapolis: Cowles Media Company, 1998), 121–22, 236.

26. *Washington Post,* March 20, 1983; *St. Paul Pioneer Press/Dispatch,* February 7, 1983; Kruidenier, interview, July 22, 1997.

27. David Kruidenier to Shareholder, August 23, 1982; Minutes of a Meeting of the Board of Directors of the Register and Tribune Company, June 21, 1982, and January 25, 1983; Des Moines Register and Tribune Company, Stock Transactions, 1982–1984, Kruidenier Papers. See also Shawn Kalkstein to Fellow Cowles Family Members and Fellow Stockholders in the Des Moines R&T Co., August 9, 1982, 23–27, and December 8, 1983, 67–73, Kalkstein Papers; and Shawn Kalkstein, telephone conversation with author, July 21, 1997.

28. Minutes of the Annual Meeting of the Board of Directors of the Des Moines Register and Tribune Company, March 28, 1983. For more on the death of John Cowles, see *Des Moines Register,* February 26, 1983; *Minneapolis Star and Tribune,* February 26, 1983; and *New York Times,* February 26, 1983.

29. Minutes of the Annual Meeting of the Board of Directors of the Des Moines Register and Tribune Company, March 28, 1983; *Editor and Publisher,* May 12, 1984, 31–32; Register and Tribune Annual Report, 1983; and *Standard and Poor's Industry Surveys,* vol. 2 (New York: Standard and Poor's Corporation, 1984), M 105.

30. See "The Ten Best U.S. Dailies," *Time,* April 30, 1984, 58–63. The magazine's ten best dailies were, in alphabetical order: *Boston Globe, Chicago Tribune, Des Moines Register, Los Angeles Times, Miami Herald, New York Times, Philadelphia Inquirer, St. Petersburg Times, Wall Street Journal,* and *Washington Post.*

31. Robert Hudson, interview by author, West Des Moines, Iowa, September 15, 1992; Gartner, interview; Minutes of a Meeting of the Board of Directors of the Register and Tribune Company, September 4, 1980.

32. See James Heskett to Board of Directors, Cowles Media Company, August 15, 1983; deposition of John Cowles Jr., 95–98; deposition of David Kruidenier, 172–74, Watts Papers; and Minutes of a Regular Meeting of the Board of Directors of the Des Moines Register and Tribune Company, October 19, 1983.

33. See Handwritten Notes by J. R. Hudson of interviews of company officers and managers, March–May, 1984, Watts Papers. Those interviewed in the spring of 1984 were David Kruidenier, Michael Gartner, Gary Gerlach, Richard Gilbert, James Gannon, James Kiser, Glenn Roberts, Barbara Mack, Michael Giudicessi, Ronald Peterson, James Worthington, John Chrystal, and Joseph Thornton. See Hudson's notes of Kruidenier interview, April 17, 1984, Watts Papers; and J. Robert Hudson's remarks to Register and Tribune Board of Directors, July 25, 1984, J. Robert Hudson Papers, private collection held by J. Robert Hudson, West Des Moines, Iowa.

34. Gerlach, interview.

35. See J. Robert Hudson notes of luncheon meeting, May 31, 1984; deposition of David Kruidenier, January 28, 1996, 175–76; and deposition of Joseph R. Hudson, January 29, 1986, pp. 29-35, 54, 96, taken in regard to *Harry T. Watts, et. al. vs. R & T Liquidation, Inc., et. al.*; deposition of Michael Gartner, May 15, 1985, 33, 45, taken in regard to *Frank S. Watts, et. al., vs. Des Moines Register and Tribune Company, et al.*; and deposition of Michael Gartner, January 27, 1986, 26–27, 74, taken in regard to *Harry T. Watts, et. al, vs. R&T Liquidation, Inc., et. al.,* Watts Papers.

36. If the R&T had merged with CMC, it appears that Gartner's employment position would have been more precarious than Gerlach's. David Cox, the president of CMC, was apparently slated to be the combined company's president, and Gartner was not well liked by CMC management. See deposition of John Cowles, February 5, 1986, 114–16; deposition of David Cox, February 4, 1986, 41; and deposition of Luther Hill Jr., April 10, 1986, 28–30, in regard to *Harry T. Watts, et. al., vs. R&T Liquidation, Inc.,* Watts Papers.

37. The initiation of merger discussion is described in deposition of John Cowles, February 6, 1986, 104–31; deposition of David Cox, February 4, 1986, 52–54, in regard to *Harry T. Watts, et. al., vs. R&T Liquidation, Inc., et. al.*; and deposition of David Kruidenier, January 28, 1986, 184–97. On Gartner and Gerlach's meeting with Belin, see Gartner, interview; Gerlach, interview; and deposition of David Belin, May 15, 1985, 25–26, taken in regard to *Frank S. Watts, et. al. vs. Des Moines Register and Tribune Company, et. al.*, Watts Papers.

38. See Gartner, interview; Gerlach, interview; and deposition of David Belin.

39. Deposition of John Cowles, February 5, 1986, 110–18; and John Cowles handwritten notes of meetings, July 31, August 28, 1984, Watts Papers.

40. Deposition of John Cowles, February 5, 1986, 122–27; and John Cowles handwritten notes of meetings, September 11, 19, 1984, Watts Papers.

41. See Gartner, interview; deposition of Robert S. Potter, December 4, 1985, 10–11, taken in regard to *Harry T. Watts, et. al., against R&T Liquidation, Inc., et al.*; Mike Gartner to Bob Potter, October 9, 1984; and Memo to File: TBTG-DJCO Joint Venture Acquisition, October 5, 1984, Watts Papers. TBTG estimated that the purchase price would likely be $125 per share, or $140 million. According to the Memo to File document, Gartner and Gerlach estimated the value of the company's various properties as follows:

Jackson Sun	$ 30,000,000
Wisconsin and Oregon Radio Stations	12,000,000
Quad-Cities Television	18,000,000
CMC stock (approx. value)	32,000,000
Honolulu Television	60,000,000
	$152,000,000

This would pay for the acquisition of the newspaper and leave an excess of $12 million, which was to be used to pay off company debt.

42. See Gartner interview; deposition of Robert S. Potter, 10–11; Michael Gartner and Gary Gerlach to David Kruidenier, November 29, 1984; and Affidavit of Warren H. Phillips, March 1986, taken in regard to *Harry T. Watts, et. al., vs. R&T Liquidation, Inc., et. al.*, Watts Papers.

43. See Kalkstein, interviews; Watts, interview; Barbara Mack to Gary Gerlach et. al., September 11, 1984, Kruidenier Papers; *Editor and Publisher*, June 2, 1984, 18–19; *Editor and Publisher*, September 28, 1985, 14; *Editor and Publisher*, November 17, 1984, 9, 16; and *Des Moines Register*, September 11, 1984. In September 1985, several months after the sale of the company, the Watts family filed a new lawsuit charging that R&T executives had concealed the true value of the company. The suit asked that the original settlement be overturned, charged that R&T managers violated a federal antiracketeering statute, and asked for $17 million. When the lawsuit was settled the following year, the R&T Liquidation, Inc., the corporate successor of the old Register and Tribune Company, agreed to pay the Watts family $3.75 million, or $150 per share. While this figure was roughly 2.5 times larger than the original settlement, it fell far short of the nearly $280 per share R&T stockholders received when the company was finally broken up and sold.

44. See deposition of William Busch Jr., February 4, 1986, 22–36, taken in regard to *Harry Watts, et. al. vs. R&T Liquidation, Inc., et. al.*; deposition of John Cowles, 128–32; deposition of David Kruidenier, 194–209; and John Cowles handwritten notes, October 18, 1984, Watts Papers.

45. Kruidenier, interviews; Gary Gerlach, telephone conversation, August 11, 1997; "Dow Jones Group of Investors Offer to Buy Des Moines Register and Tribune," *Broadcasting*, November 12, 1984, 70, 72; *Editor and Publisher*, November 10, 1984, 11;

Cheryl Arvidson, "The Price That Broke the Register: Gannett's Bid and the Family Fallout," *Washington Journalism Review,* April 1985, 22.

46. Morley Ballantine, interview by author, Des Moines, Iowa, October 19, 1992; Gartner, interview; Luther Hill Jr., interview by author, Des Moines, Iowa, February 4, 1993; Kruidenier, interviews.

47. See Morley Ballantine, interview; Hill, interview; Hudson, interview; Kruidenier, interviews; Minutes of a Regular Meeting of the Board of Directors of the Register and Tribune Company, November 5, 1984; *New York Times,* November 6, 1984.

48. Barbara Mack to David Kruidenier, November 9, 1984, Kruidenier Papers; Kruidenier, interview, July 22, 1997.

49. David Kruidenier to All Register and Tribune Company Directors, November 9, 1984, and David Kruidenier to the Shareholders, November 9, 1984, Kruidenier Papers. See also Charles Edwards, interview by author, Des Moines, Iowa, September 29, 1993; and Richard Gilbert, interview by author, Des Moines, Iowa, September 14, 1992.

50. Gartner, interview; Gerlach, interview; Kruidenier, interviews. See also *Editor and Publisher,* November 17, 1984, 9, 16; and *New York Times,* November 13, 1984.

51. Arvidson, "Price That Broke the Register," 23; and *Des Moines Register,* December 9, 1984.

52. Warren Phillips to Board of Directors, Dow Jones & Company, Inc., November 6, 1984; John Cowles handwritten notes, November 13, 1984, Watts Papers; Kruidenier, interview, July 22, 1997; *Editor and Publisher,* December 1, 1984, 14; *Editor and Publisher,* December 8, 1984, 15. For the Ingersoll bid, see Christopher J. H. M. Shaw to David Kruidenier, November 9, 1984, Kruidenier Papers. On the Ackerley offer, see Barry Ackerley to David Kruidenier, November 29, 1984, Kruidenier Papers.

53. See William Ryan to David Kruidenier, November 14, 1984; Stanton Cook to David Kruidenier, November 14, 1984; G. Odgen Nutting to David Kruidenier, November 15, 1984; and Kay Graham to David Kruidenier, November 26, 1984, Kruidenier Papers. On Gannett's hiring of Silha, see *Advertising Age,* November 15, 1984, 34; *Editor and Publisher,* November 24, 1984, 12; and Al Neuharth, *Confessions of an S.O.B.* (New York: Doubleday, 1989), 201.

54. Kruidenier, interviews; Neuharth, *Confessions,* 201.

55. Al Neuharth to David Kruidenier, November 20, 1984, Al Neuharth Papers, private collection held by Al Neuharth, Cocoa Beach, Florida.

56. Kruidenier, interviews; Neuharth, *Confessions,* 201; "The Media Bulls are Running," *Newsweek,* February 11, 1985, 53.

57. Fred Eychaner to Barbara Mack, November 29, 1984; *Des Moines Register,* November 24, 1984; *Editor and Publisher,* November 17, 1984, 9; *Editor and Publisher,* November 24, 1984, 12; *Editor and Publisher,* December 8, 1984, 15.

58. Kruidenier, interview, July 22, 1997; Des Moines Register and Tribune News Release, December 10, 1984.

59. *Des Moines Register,* December 2, 1984; Elizabeth Ballantine, interview by author, Des Moines, Iowa, September 18, 1993.

60. *Des Moines Register,* December 2, 1984; Deposition of John Cowles, 147–49; Barbara Mack's handwritten notes of Register and Tribune Board of Directors Meeting, December 10, 1984, Kruidenier Papers; Kruidenier, interviews. Cowles family members who did not support the sale included Kruidenier, Morley Ballantine, and Lois Cowles Harrison.

61. Minutes of a Special Meeting of the Board of Directors of the Des Moines Register and Tribune Company, December 10, 1984.

62. Hill interview; Kruidenier interviews; Barbara Mack, telephone conversation with author, August 5, 1997; Barbara Mack's handwritten notes of Register and Tribune Board of Directors Meeting, December 10, 1984; Jeffrey Epstein to Leroy Paul, Janu-

ary 21, 1985; Des Moines Register and Tribune News Release, December 10, 1984, Kruidenier Papers.

63. *Wall Street Journal,* December 11, 1984.

64. See *Des Moines Register,* December 18, 20, 1984; Lloyd Schermer to David Kruidenier, January 14, 1985; Barbara Mack to David Kruidenier, January 15, 1985, Kruidenier Papers; Kruidenier interview, July 20, 1992; and Arvidson, "Price That Broke the Register," 25–26.

65. See David Kruidenier to ALL REGISTER AND TRIBUNE COMPANY EMPLOYEES, January 7, 1985; Dick Gilbert to Charlie Edwards, et. al., January 8, 11, 1985; handwritten notes (n.a.) of Register and Tribune Board of Directors Meeting, January 31, 1985; Frank A. Bennack Jr., to Jeffrey Epstein, January 25, 1985, Kruidenier Papers; Gerlach, interview; Kruidenier, interview, July 20, 1992; Mack, telephone conversation; and "Media Bulls are Running," 53.

66. Minutes of a Meeting of the Board of Directors of the Des Moines Register and Tribune Company, January 31, 1985; Neuharth, *Confessions,* 201.

67. *Advertising Age,* February 4, 1985, 2–3; *Editor and Publisher,* February 9, 1985, 12–13; and "Media Bulls are Running," 53.

68. "Media Bulls are Running," 53; and James D. Squires, *Read All about It: The Corporate Takeover of America's Newspapers* (New York: Times Books, 1993), 128.

69. "Behind the Demise of Family Newspapers," *U.S. News and World Report,* February 11, 1985, 59–60; Neuharth, *Confessions,* 194.

70. See Minutes of a Meeting of the Board of Directors of the Des Moines Register and Tribune Company, February 28, March 25, April 30, July 1, 1985; Barbara Mack to David Kruidenier, April 30, 1985; and Book put together for the Des Moines Register and Tribune Company, Special Shareholders Meeting, July 1, 1985, Kruidenier Papers.

71. Arvidson, "Price That Broke the Register," 26; *Des Moines Register,* June 30, 1985; Des Moines Register and Tribune Stock Transactions 1982–1984, Kruidenier Papers; and Des Moines Register and Tribune Stock Purchases by In-House Directors, 1-1-69-1-1-79, Watts Papers. Much of Gartner and Gerlach's R&T stock was purchased with company loans at attractive below-market interest rates. Kruidenier also participated in this stock purchase program for company directors and executives.

72. See "Media Bulls are Running," 53; Arvidson, "Price That Broke the Register," 21; and David Kruidenier to All My Colleagues at The Des Moines Register, June 28, 1985, Kruidenier Papers. The continuing Pulitzer Prize tradition Kruidenier mentioned was a reference to R&T staffer Tom Knudson winning the paper's thirteenth Pulitzer. His series on agriculture took the prize in the national reporting category.

73. *Des Moines Register,* July 2, 1985.

74. See Minutes of a Special Meeting of the Shareholders of the Des Moines Register and Tribune Company, July 1, 1985; Minutes of Meeting of the Board of Directors of the Des Moines Register and Tribune Company, July 1, 1985; and *Des Moines Register,* July 2, 1985.

75. *Des Moines Register,* July 2, 1985.

76. *Des Moines Register,* July 9, 10, 1985.

77. Mark Lisheron, "The Retrenching Register," *American Journalism Review* 19 (November 1997): 31.

78. See Kruidenier, interview, July 20, 1992; Gerlach, interview; and Gartner, interview; and *Des Moines Register,* June 30, 1985, March 3, 1993, and April 17, 1994. In 1999, Gartner and Gerlach left the Iowa newspaper industry and went into the baseball business. That spring, the two joined Des Moines attorney Michael Giudicessi to purchase the Iowa Cubs, the Chicago Cubs' Triple A affiliate. Later that year, partly because of the death of their partner, David Belin, Gartner and Gerlach sold the *Tribune* and their other Iowa newspapers to the Omaha World-Herald Company. In October, Gartner bought out Gerlach's share of the Iowa Cubs.

Notes to Epilogue

1. *Editor and Publisher,* February 9, 1985, 13.

2. See Register and Tribune Company Annual Reports, 1980–1984, and *Standard and Poor's Industry Survey* (New York: Standard and Poor's Corporation, 1982, 1984).

3. *Des Moines Register,* July 2, 1985.

4. James D. Squires, *Read All about It: The Corporate Takeover of America's Newspapers* (New York: Times Books, 1994), 126. For a discussion of Gannett's system of operation, see Ben H. Bagdikian, *The Media Monopoly* (Boston: Beacon Press, 1992), 72–82.

5. The story is recounted in both Sig Gissler, "What Happens When Gannett Takes Over," *Columbia Journalism Review* 36 (November–December 1997): 47; and Mark Lisheron, "The Retrenching Register," *American Journalism Review* 19 (November 1997): 35.

6. Charlie Edwards, interview by author, Des Moines, Iowa, June 25, 1998.

7. See *Des Moines Register,* October 12, 1994, and February 26, 1995.

8. See Ira Lacher, "The Register Regroups," *Columbia Journalism Review* 30 (May–June 1991): 16; and *Des Moines Register,* March 26, 1996.

9. Lacher, "Register Regroups," 16; *Des Moines Register,* February 26, 1995. From 1989 to 1994, the Sunday circulation moved up from 103,050 to 108,466, while the daily numbers increased from 78,262 to 82,607.

10. Edwards, interview, June 25, 1998. See also *Des Moines Register,* October 12, 1994, and February 26, 1995.

11. *Des Moines Register,* October 12–13, 1994, and February 26, 1995; *Los Angeles Times,* February 9, 1996.

12. *Des Moines Register,* February 14, 16, 19, 1995.

13. Gilbert Cranberg, "A Swan Song in Des Moines," *Columbia Journalism Review* 34 (May 1995): 19–20; Gissler, "When Gannett Takes Over," 46–47; Lacher, "Register Regroups," 35; *Des Moines Register,* February 17, 1995.

14. Curley's comments were reprinted in *Des Moines Register,* February 17, 1995. See also *Des Moines Register,* February 18, 23, 26, 1995. The story of Overholser and Westphal, however, did not end there. In April, the *Register* reported that Overholser had accepted a position as ombudsman of the *Washington Post.* Two months later, Overholser and her Des Moines schoolteacher husband filed for divorce. Meanwhile, it was noted that Westphal had also landed a job in the nation's capital as the assistant Washington bureau chief for the McClatchy Newspapers. Then in September, the stated reasons for Overholser's and Westphal's resignations came under scrutiny when real estate records in Washington, D.C., revealed that the two former *Register* editors jointly purchased a house in the northwest section of the city. Simultaneously, the story of a romance between the two surfaced. This unfolding story was covered in the *Des Moines Register,* April 4, June 9, September 26, and October 3, 1995. See also Alicia Shepard, "An Editor Finds Her Personal Life on Page One," *American Journalism Review* 17 (November 1995): 14–15; and Mark Fitzgerald, "Editor's Life Made Public," *Editor and Publisher,* October 14, 1995, 9–10.

15. Ken Auletta, "Demolition Man," *New Yorker,* November 17, 1997, 41; *New York Times,* July 24, 1995.

16. *Des Moines Register,* February 26, 1995.

17. *Des Moines Register,* September 24, 1995.

18. *Los Angeles Times,* February 9, 1996. Offenburger remained disturbed by the *Register*'s pullback from its statewide distribution. After many disagreements with management, Offenburger decided he had had enough when his "Iowa Boy" column was relocated without consulting him first. He resigned from the paper in July 1998. See *Des Moines Register,* July 7, 1998.

19. *Los Angeles Times,* February 9, 1996. See also Michael Gartner, interview by author, Des Moines, Iowa, June 11, 1997. Gartner expressed similar ideas about the unifying

role of the paper and the mounting sectional divisions after the *Register*'s retreat from its statewide presence.

20. See *Des Moines Register,* March 26, April 11, 1996; Gissler, "When Gannett Takes Over," 44; and Edwards, interview, June 25, 1998. In 1997, the year after Edwards' departure from the R&T ended the Cowles' connection with the Iowa newspaper, the Cowles family made another move away from midwestern journalism. In November, it was announced that McClatchy Newspapers, Inc., was acquiring Cowles Media for approximately $1.4 billion; see *The Wall Street Journal,* November 14, 1997.

21. *Des Moines Register,* March 26, April 11, 1996; Gissler, "When Gannett Takes Over," 47; and Edwards, interview, June 25, 1998.

22. *Des Moines Register,* June 14, 1996.

23. Lisheron, "Retrenching Register," 30, 32.

24. Ibid., 34; Gissler, "When Gannett Takes Over," 43.

25. Although Larry Fruhling was born in Nebraska, he was with the R&T for more than 25 years and developed a thorough understanding of Iowa and its people. For Gartner's comments, see Gartner, interview; and transcript of Remarks of Michael Gartner, Joe Creason Lecture, University of Kentucky, April 14, 1997, 8.

26. Transcript of Remarks of Michael Gartner, 9,10.

27. Edwards, interview, June 25, 1998.

28. *Des Moines Register,* December 12, 1996; February 25, 1997.

29. *Daily Tribune* (Ames, Iowa), June 27, 1997.

30. Gissler, "When Gannett Takes Over," 45; Lisheron, "Retrenching Register," 33, 34.

31. On the use of reader advisory groups in general, see Leo Bogart, *Press and Public: Who Reads What, When, Where, and Why in American Newspapers* (Hillsdale, N.J.: Lawrence Erlbaum Associates, 1989), 354–55. For the R&T's use of such information and changes in the paper, see, for example, *Des Moines Register,* April 20, September 28, 1997, and May 3, 9, November 8, 1998.

32. See Lisheron, "Retrenching Register," 30.

33. On the renovation of the newsroom and the new computer system, see *Des Moines Register,* April 5, September 28, 1997. For the new production facility and presses, see *Des Moines Register,* April 20, 1997, and April 8, 1998.

34. *Des Moines Register,* April 20, 1997.

35. Henry is quoted in Lisheron, "Retrenching Register," 31. Ryerson is quoted in *Des Moines Register,* July 7, 1998.

36. Gilbert Cranberg, interview by author, Des Moines, Iowa, July 18, 1996.

37. Gartner, interview, June 11, 1997. Former R&T manager Richard Gilbert referred to the *Register* as a "bastion against smallness." See Richard Gilbert, interview by author, Des Moines, Iowa, September 14, 1992.

38. "The Ten Best U.S. Dailies," *Time,* April 30, 1984, 59. Geneva Overholser used the phrase "of and for Iowa" to describe the *Register.* See Lisheron, "Retrenching Register," 31.

INDEX